A Voting Rights Odyssey
Black Enfranchisement in Georgia

From slavery to the white backlash of the 1990s, *A Voting Rights Odyssey* is a riveting account of the crusade for equal voting rights in Georgia. Written by a veteran civil rights lawyer who has tried innumerable voting cases, the book draws upon expert reports and other court records, as well as trial testimony and interviews with the men and women who served as plaintiffs and witnesses in litigation that helped to forge a revolution in voting rights. The book explores, and repudiates, the myths of the Reconstruction era that blacks were incapable of voting and holding office. It also catalogues the extraordinary, and ultimately failed, attempts of the state leadership to maintain white supremacy after the abolition of the white primary, the demands of the civil rights movement, and passage of the historic Voting Rights Act of 1965. *A Voting Rights Odyssey* is essential reading for anyone interested in the way in which race has driven and distorted the political process in the South.

Laughlin McDonald has been director of the Southern Regional Office of the American Civil Liberties Union in Atlanta, Georgia, since 1972. He has represented minorities in numerous discrimination cases and specialized in the area of voting rights. He has testified frequently before Congress and written for scholarly and popular publications on civil liberties issues. His books include *The Rights of Racial Minorities* (1998) and *Racial Equality* (1977).

A Voting Rights Odyssey

Black Enfranchisement in Georgia

LAUGHLIN McDONALD

CAMBRIDGE
UNIVERSITY PRESS

PUBLISHED BY THE PRESS SYNDICATE OF THE UNIVERSITY OF CAMBRIDGE
The Pitt Building, Trumpington Street, Cambridge, United Kingdom

CAMBRIDGE UNIVERSITY PRESS
The Edinburgh Building, Cambridge CB2 2RU, UK
40 West 20th Street, New York, NY 10011-4211, USA
477 Williamstown Road, Port Melbourne, VIC 3207, Australia
Ruiz de Alarcón 13, 28014 Madrid, Spain
Dock House, The Waterfront, Cape Town 8001, South Africa

http://www.cambridge.org

First published 2003

Printed in the United Kingdom at the University Press, Cambridge

Typeface Sabon 10/12 pt.   *System* LATEX 2$_\varepsilon$ [TB]

A catalog record for this book is available from the British Library.

Library of Congress Cataloging in Publication data
McDonald, Laughlin.
A voting rights odyssey : black enfranchisement in Georgia / Laughlin McDonald.
   p.   cm.
Includes bibliographical references and index.
ISBN 0-521-81232-1 (hardback) – ISBN 0-521-01179-5 (pbk.)
1. African Americans – Suffrage – Georgia – History.   2. Election law – Georgia – History.
3. African Americans – Suffrage – History.   4. Election law – United States – History.
I. Title.
KFG420.85.S9 M39   2003
324.6'2'089960730758 – dc21   2002025749

ISBN 0 521 81232 1 hardback
ISBN 0 521 01179 5 paperback

Contents

Acknowledgments   *page* vii

Introduction   1

1 The Voting Rights Act of 1965: A Great Divide   8

2 After the Civil War: Recreating "the White Man's Georgia"   15

3 The Dawning of a New Day: Abolition of the White Primary   45

4 Passage of the Civil Rights Act of 1957: The White Response   60

5 One Person, One Vote: The End of the County Unit System
   and the Malapportioned Legislature and Congressional
   Delegation   80

6 The Election Code of 1964: Twilight of the Malapportioned
   Legislature   91

7 The Voting Rights Scene Outside the Golden Dome   103

8 The Voting Rights Act: How It Works   124

9 Increased Black Registration: The White Response   129

10 The 1970 Extension of the Voting Rights Act: More White
   Resistance   139

11 The 1975 Extension of the Voting Rights Act: The Private
   Enforcement Campaign   153

12 Redistricting in the 1980s   167

13 1982: Voting Rights in the Balance   174

14 Continued Enforcement of the Voting Rights Act   182

15 The Demise of Georgia's Nineteenth-Century Voter
   Registration System: Taking Stock of the Impact
   of the Voting Rights Act   191

16 Recreating the Past: The Challenge to the Majority-Vote
    Requirement   198
17 The White Backlash: Redistricting in the 1990s   211
18 Keysville, Georgia – A Voting Rights Crucible   238

    Index   246

Acknowledgments

I am deeply indebted to the lawyers who, on behalf of the black community, litigated the cases discussed in this book and to the expert witnesses who assisted them. Not only have they played a central role in advancing the cause of equal voting rights, but they compiled much of the material upon which I have drawn – transcripts, depositions, declarations, expert reports, articles from newspapers, archival material, minutes of city councils and county commissions, interview notes, and so on.

Some of the lawyers were on the staff of the American Civil Liberties Union's Voting Rights Project, which I have directed for nearly thirty years: Derek Alphran, Paula Bonds, Neil Bradley, Morris Brown, Emily Calhoun, Christopher Coates, Cristina Correia, Sarajane Love, Bryan Sells, Kathleen Wilde, Mary Wyckoff, and Maha Zaki. Others, too numerous to name, were in private practice, or worked for other civil rights organizations or the Department of Justice.

The expert witnesses, to whom I owe a special debt of gratitude, were Michael Binford, William Boone, Vernon Burton, Dan Carter, Selwyn Carter, Steven Cole, William Cooper, Richard Engstrom, Bob Holmes, Morgan Kousser, Steven Lawson, Allan Lichtman, Peyton McCrary, Larry Noble, and Alex Willingham.

I am also indebted to Charles Morgan, Jr., the first director of the Voting Rights Project, from whom I learned the central importance of equal voting rights, and to the executive and legal directors of the national ACLU with and for whom it has been my privilege and pleasure to work: Ira Glasser and Steve Shapiro, and before them Aryeh Neier, Bruce Ennis, Burt Neuborn, john powell, and Melvin Wolfe. Their support of the Voting Rights Project and the cause of racial equality has been unwavering and a constant source of encouragement.

Finally, I want to acknowledge the contribution of Donna Matern, the Voting Rights Project's office manager. Without her loyalty and long-term commitment to the work of the project, writing this book would have been a far more difficult task.

Any errors of fact or judgment that this book contains are, of course, of my own making.

Introduction

Universal suffrage is one of the cherished conceits of modern American democracy. But the historical reality was far different. When the nation was founded, almost the only people who could vote were free white male property owners over the age of twenty-one.[1]

Black men didn't get the right to vote as a matter of federal law until passage of the Fifteenth Amendment in 1870.[2] Women didn't get the comparable right to vote until 1920 with enactment of the Nineteenth Amendment. American Indians didn't get the general right to vote until passage of the Indian Citizenship Act of 1924.[3] Racially discriminatory grandfather clauses for voting endured until 1939.[4] Blacks were excluded from voting in Democratic Party primaries in the South until 1944.[5] Payment of a poll, or head, tax as a condition for voting was not abolished for federal elections until ratification of the Twenty-fourth Amendment in 1964. It took another two years for the Supreme Court to invalidate the use of the poll tax in state elections.[6] Eighteen- to twenty-year-olds didn't get the right to vote in state and local elections until ratification of the Twenty-sixth Amendment in 1971. Onerous durational residency requirements for voting were not struck down by the Supreme Court until 1972.[7] It was not until 1975 that

---

[1] See, e.g., Constitution of Georgia of 1777, Art. IX; 2 S.C. Stat. 249, No. 227 (1704), 3 S.C. Stat. 2, 3, No. 373 (1716). For a general discussion of the evolution of the franchise, see Chilton Williamson, *American Suffrage: From Property to Democracy, 1760–1860* (Princeton, N.J.: Princeton University Press, 1960).

[2] Throughout this book I have used "black," "person of color," "Negro," and "African American" more or less interchangeably, with some regard for the period of time in which the terms were current. I have also allowed people to speak in their own words, even when they used the pejorative "nigger."

[3] 8 U.S.C. §1401(a)(2).

[4] *Lane v. Wilson*, 307 U.S. 268 (1939).

[5] *Smith v. Allwright*, 321 U.S. 649 (1944).

[6] *Harper v. Virginia State Board of Elections*, 383 U.S. 145 (1966).

[7] *Dunn v. Blumstein*, 405 U.S. 330 (1972).

the Court finally ruled that ownership of property could not be required for voting in local elections.[8] The ban on literacy and other tests for voting was not made nationwide and permanent by Congress until amendments to the Voting Rights Act were passed in 1975.[9] Those convicted of felonies are still denied the right to vote in a majority of the states. For much of our national life, we have been an aristocracy, not a democracy, of voters.

Of all the clogs on the franchise, those which have distorted the American political process most have been those based upon race. That distortion is a reflection of the fundamental, irreconcilable contradiction upon which the nation was founded, that all people were equal but that enslavement of Africans was tolerable. The nation's belief in equality was contained in the Declaration of Independence of 1776, which said that one of the self-evident truths was that "all men are created equal." But its tolerance of slavery was embodied in the Constitution of 1787, which counted a slave as only three-fifths of a person for purposes of apportionment of the House of Representatives, prohibited Congress from abolishing the slave trade prior to the year 1808, and provided for the return of fugitive slaves to their owners.[10] The history of the United States as it relates to voting has been in large measure the story of its attempts to reconcile its stated belief in equality with its actual racial practices.

This book tells the story of racial discrimination in voting in Georgia, from the days of slavery to the present time. Georgia, of course, is not unique as far as discrimination in voting is concerned. Each of the southern states that seceded from the union in the middle of the nineteenth century has a similar history of slavery and of denying the franchise to blacks after the Civil War.[11] Despite having ratified the Fourteenth and Fifteenth Amendments guaranteeing equal rights of citizenship and voting to former slaves and other persons of color, the former Confederate states, in the words of the Supreme Court of Mississippi, "[w]ithin the field of permissible action under the limitations imposed by the federal constitution...swept the circle of expedients to obstruct the exercise of the franchise by the negro race."[12]

While Georgia was not an anomaly, no state was more systematic and thorough in its efforts to deny or limit voting and officeholding by African-Americans after the Civil War. It adopted virtually every one of the

---

[8] *Hill v. Stone*, 421 U.S. 289 (1975).

[9] 42 U.S.C. §1973aa.

[10] Constitution of the United States, Art. I, Sec. 2 and Sec. 9; Art. IV, Sec. 2.

[11] Those states, in order of their secession, were: South Carolina, Mississippi, Florida, Alabama, Georgia, Louisiana, Texas, Virginia, Arkansas, North Carolina, and Tennessee. White schoolchildren in South Carolina were still being taught 100 years later proudly to remember this progression of demi-sovereignties and the leading role their state had played in it, using the mnemonic that South Carolina – first in nullification and first in secession – had been followed out of the Union by "two gentlemen named M. F. Ag and L. T. Vant."

[12] *Ratliff v. Beale*, 74 Miss. 247, 20 So. 865, 868 (1896).

traditional "expedients" to obstruct the exercise of the franchise by blacks, including literacy and understanding tests, the poll tax, felony disfranchisement laws, onerous residency requirements, cumbersome registration procedures, voter challenges and purges, the abolition of elective offices, the use of discriminatory redistricting and apportionment schemes, the expulsion of elected blacks from office, and the adoption of primary elections in which only whites were allowed to vote. And where these technically legal measures failed to work or were thought insufficient, the state was more than willing to resort to fraud and violence in order to smother black political participation and safeguard white supremacy.

The southern states continued their opposition to equal voting rights into the twentieth century and after passage of the Voting Rights Act of 1965. When Congress strengthened and extended the act in 1982, it recited a litany of ongoing voting rights abuses in the South, including the maintenance of discriminatory election procedures, the adoption of new and more sophisticated devices that diluted minority voting strength, intimidation and harassment, discouragement of registration and voting, and widespread noncompliance with the special preclearance provision of the act requiring states with histories of discrimination in voting to get federal approval of any changes in their voting procedures. Congress concluded that "the schemes reported here are clearly the latest in a direct line of repeated efforts to perpetuate the results of past voting discrimination and to undermine the gains won under ... the Voting Rights Act."[13]

Georgia, once again, was in the forefront of the efforts to block the expansion of the franchise to blacks. It fought passage of the Civil Rights Acts of 1957, 1960, and 1964. Members of its congressional delegation and the staff of the state attorney general argued before Congress that the proposed Voting Rights Act of 1965 was unconstitutional. A former president of its state bar association denounced the act as a violation of states' rights. Its governor wrote directly to President Lyndon Johnson urging defeat of the voting rights bill.

When the Voting Rights Act was passed, Georgia immediately joined a lawsuit brought by South Carolina and asked the Supreme Court to declare it unconstitutional. And when the act was upheld, the state's flouting of the act's preclearance requirement, and its adoption of new measures blunting the increases in black voter registration, were the equal of any such efforts in the South.

The white leadership of Georgia also railed against and attempted to circumvent federal court decisions striking down the state's white primary, its discriminatory county unit system for nominating candidates for statewide office, and its malapportioned legislature. When it was finally forced to

---

[13] S. Rep. No. 417, 97th Cong., 2d Sess. 12 (1982), reprinted in 1982 U.S. Code Cong. & Adm. News 189.

reapportion in conformity with the principle of one person, one vote, the state's legislative and congressional plans were all rejected by the Department of Justice on the ground that they discriminated against black voters. In refusing to approve the state's 1982 congressional plan, a federal court in the District of Columbia held that the plan was the product of intentional discrimination and made the extraordinary finding that the plan's chief architect was "a racist."[14]

Georgia was also the battleground for some of the most important voting rights decisions of the last half of the twentieth century. The Supreme Court coined the phrase "one person, one vote" in 1963 in *Gray v. Sanders*,[15] which abolished the state's county unit system. The following year, in *Wesberry v. Sanders*, the Court invalidated Georgia's congressional apportionment under Article I, Section 2 of the Constitution and established the principle that "as nearly as is practicable one man's vote in a congressional election is to be worth as much as another's."[16] The one person, one vote principle established in these two decisions transformed the nation's electoral politics at every level of government.

In *Fortson v. Dorsey*, a challenge to Georgia's senate redistricting plan decided in 1965, the Supreme Court articulated for the first time the proposition that a legislative plan, even if it complied with one person, one vote, could still be unconstitutional if it "designedly or otherwise . . . operate[d] to minimize or cancel out the voting strength of racial or political elements of the voting population."[17] The concept of minimizing minority voting strength, or minority vote dilution, was subsequently used to strike down discriminatory at-large elections and other voting practices in Georgia, and in virtually every other state in the union, and was directly incorporated by Congress into the amendments to the Voting Rights Act passed in 1982. Other significant decisions of the Supreme Court involving Georgia were *City of Rome v. United States*,[18] which rejected a challenge to the 1975 extension of the critical preclearance requirement of the Voting Rights Act, and *Rogers v. Lodge*, the first decision of the Court invalidating the at-large method of electing a county-level government on the grounds that it diluted black voting strength.[19] Georgia ultimately acknowledged and accepted the

---

[14] *Busbee v. Smith*, 549 F. Supp. 494, 500 (D. D. C. 1982).

[15] 372 U.S. 368, 381 (1963).

[16] 376 U.S. 1, 7–8 (1964).

[17] 379 U.S. 433, 438–39 (1965).

[18] 446 U.S. 156 (1980).

[19] 458 U.S. 613, 618 (1982). The Supreme Court had previously affirmed a decision of a court of appeals finding that at-large elections for a parish school board in Louisiana diluted minority voting strength, but the affirmance had been for another, nonracial reason. See *East Carroll Parish School Board v. Marshall*, 424 U.S. 640, 638–39 (1976) ("[w]e . . . now affirm the judgment below, but without approval of the constitutional views expressed by the Court of Appeals").

principle of the equal right to vote, but only because it was forced to do so by court decisions, congressional acts, and a massive enforcement campaign by the minority and civil rights communities.

The Georgia experience underscores in an obvious and dramatic way the centrality of equal voting rights. Although the Supreme Court approved the disfranchisement of black voters during the Jim Crow years, in modern times it has acknowledged the transcendent place that the right to vote occupies in our constitutional scheme. The right to vote is "fundamental," the Court has said, because it is "preservative" of all rights.[20] Even the most basic civil rights "are illusory if the right to vote is undermined."[21] Georgia and the rest of the South, with their history of slavery and segregation, have surely taught us the truth of these pronouncements. The disfranchised are not simply denied the benefits of government, they inevitably become its victims.

One of the most striking, and perhaps one of the most reassuring, things about the black odyssey in pursuit of equal voting rights is that it demonstrates that racial attitudes are not immutable but are in a profound sense self-serving economic, political, legal, and social conventions. White Georgians had insisted throughout their history that they were incapable of racial change, in voting or in any other area of life, that the complete subordination of blacks was a "great physical, philosophical, and moral truth,"[22] that "people's inner feelings" and "customs cannot be successfully legislated upon,"[23] that any challenge to the racial status quo would "endanger . . . the very life of the nation,"[24] that attempts at integration would precipitate "violence,"[25] that segregation of the races "has been engrained forever in the hearts and minds of all Georgians,"[26] that political equality would cause the "adulteration" of the white race,[27] and that Georgians were prepared to shed their blood and lay down their lives to "preserve our Southern Way of Life."[28] Yet, within the lifetimes of some of these speakers, and even though racial prejudice had not been abrogated and attempts to restrict black political power had not entirely subsided, the Southern Way of Life had been

---

[20] *Reynolds v. Sims*, 377 U.S. 533, 562 (1964).

[21] *Wesberry v. Sanders*, 376 U.S. at 17.

[22] Statement of Alexander H. Stephens (1861), quoted in Kenneth Stampp, *The Causes of the Civil War* (New York: Touchstone, 1991), 153.

[23] Hearings before Subcommittee No. 5 of the Committee on the Judiciary, House of Representatives, Eighty-fifth Congress, First Session on Miscellaneous Bills Regarding the Civil Rights of Persons within the Jurisdiction of the United States, February 4, 5, 6, 7, 13, 14, 25 and 26, 1975, p. 113 (Rep. J. L. Pilcher).

[24] Charles J. Bloch, *States' Rights – The Law of the Land* (Atlanta: Harrison, 1958), 2.

[25] Hearings before Subcommittee No. 5, p. 817 (Atty. Gen. Eugene Cook).

[26] Ga. Laws 1960, p. 1137.

[27] Newell Edenfield, Address of the President, Report of the 77th Annual Session of the Georgia Bar Association (1960), 204.

[28] *Stewart-Webster Journal*, "To the Voters of the Southwestern Judicial Circuit," Sept. 8, 1960.

irrevocably changed. And it was changed in large measure because the racial barriers to political participation, which were the essential condition for maintaining the legal structure of segregation, had been thrown down.

While the white leadership of the state no longer calls for repeal of the Fourteenth Amendment or demands nullification of Supreme Court decisions applying the protections of the Constitution to blacks, equal voting rights are not entirely free of controversy. That was apparent from *Miller v. Johnson*,[29] in which a group of white voters, unhappy at being placed in Georgia's majority black eleventh congressional district, filed suit in 1994 charging that the district was unlawfully "segregated."[30] In concluding that the legislature had impermissibly subordinated traditional redistricting principles to race in drawing the district, the five-member majority of the U.S. Supreme Court took no notice whatsoever of the state's history of discrimination or of the continuing presence of racial bloc voting. Instead, it indulged the fiction of a color-blind political process which, in its view, the majority-black eleventh district offended. In *Miller v. Johnson* and other modern redistricting cases, the Court has also created special rules allowing white voters to challenge majority-minority districts and has applied dual standards in determining a district's constitutionality depending on whether the district was majority-white or majority-black or Hispanic. These decisions are not about – and indeed the plaintiffs have not alleged – individual harm or concrete injury to any group of voters, but can best be understood as an effort to restore the traditional white privilege of choosing elected officials.

A good deal has been written about discrimination in voting in the South during and after Reconstruction. Among the standard works discussing this history are *Southern Politics in State and Nation* by V. O. Key, Jr., *Origins of the New South* by C. Vann Woodward, *The Shaping of Southern Politics* by J. Morgan Kousser, and *Race, Class and Party* by Paul Lewinson. A number of books have also been written about the modern era of voting rights and the impact of the Voting Rights Act of 1965, including *Quiet Revolution in the South*, edited by Chandler Davidson and Bernard Grofman, *Black Votes Count* by Frank R. Parker, *The Transformation of Southern Politics* by Jack Bass and Walter De Vries, and Kousser's *Colorblind Injustice*. But no book has focused on Georgia, or any other single southern state, and told the story of the prodigious struggle for equal voting rights from beginning to end, from slavery to the present day. That is the task I set for myself in this volume.

Concentrating on one state, such as Georgia, rather than attempting a general synopsis of the southern region, offers distinct advantages. It allows one to see in a complete and detailed way how race has dominated and

---

[29] 515 U.S. 900 (1995).
[30] *Johnson v. Miller*, Civ. No. 194–008 (S. D. Ga.), Complaint for Declaratory and Injunctive Relief.

distorted the political process over time and at every moment of decision making. It also allows for a more focused, and hopefully a more dramatic, narrative. And given the limitations of space imposed by a single volume, it provides a better opportunity for the participants in the events to speak in their own voices.

The struggle for equal voting rights in Georgia was not waged simply by a small group of high-profile civil rights leaders in the glare of a national spotlight, but by hundreds of relatively obscure, courageous, and determined men and women in remote places such as Webster County and Keysville, and by the lawyers who represented them in numerous court battles. They have finally put to rest the Reconstruction-era myths that blacks could not be trusted with the ballot, that they had no concern for the general welfare, and that they were incapable of governing.

I

The Voting Rights Act of 1965: A Great Divide

On March 15, 1965, President Lyndon Johnson addressed the Congress and a prime time nationwide audience of 70 million people and demanded passage of a new voting rights act that would guarantee all Americans the equal right to vote.[1] In a voice that was passionate and full of resolve, he said:

There is no constitutional issue here. The command of the Constitution is plain. There is no moral issue. It is wrong – deadly wrong – to deny any of your fellow Americans the right to vote in this country. There is no issue of state's rights or national rights. There is only the struggle for human rights.... This time, on this issue, there must be no delay, no hesitation, and no compromise with our purpose.[2]

Johnson had announced his intention earlier that year to sponsor comprehensive voting rights legislation. However, the violent confrontation between civil rights demonstrators and state troopers on the Edmund Pettus Bridge in Selma, Alabama, on March 7, which came to be known as Bloody Sunday, was the catalyst for his nationwide address and his insistence that Congress act without further delay.[3]

At the Pettus Bridge, state troopers and sheriff's deputies had attacked some 525 people demonstrating for stronger federal voting laws. White spectators, waving Confederate flags, roared their approval as the troopers tear-gassed the marchers and beat them to the ground with clubs and whips. John Lewis, one of the leaders of the march, recalled more than thirty years later

---

[1] David J. Garrow, *Bearing the Cross: Martin Luther King, Jr. and the Southern Christian Leadership Conference* (New York: Vintage, 1988), 408–9.

[2] Lyndon B. Johnson, *The Vantage Point: Perspectives of the Presidency 1963–1969* (New York: Holt, Rinehart and Winston, 1971), 164.

[3] Garrow, *Bearing the Cross*, 396–97, 399; David J. Garrow, *Protest at Selma: Martin Luther King, Jr., and the Voting Rights Act of 1965* (New Haven, Conn.: Yale University Press, 1978), 31–77.

with disturbing clarity the shouts of a woman from the crowd. "Get 'em! *Get* the niggers!" she screamed.[4]

Two days later, a gang of whites attacked three Unitarian ministers as they left a black restaurant in Selma. One of the ministers, Rev. James Reeb of Boston, was knocked unconscious with a club and later died.[5]

Lyndon Johnson fully grasped the historic significance of these unfolding events. "At times history and fate meet at a single time in a single place to shape a turning point in man's unending search for freedom," he said. "So it was at Lexington and Concord. So it was a century ago at Appomattox. So it was last week in Selma, Alabama."[6]

When the House and Senate began hearings on the president's proposed voting rights bill a few days later, the white leadership of Georgia closed ranks to oppose it. Howard H. Callaway, a Republican from the third congressional district, while giving lip service to the concept of equal voting rights, told a House subcommittee that the provision authorizing the appointment of federal examiners and registrars by the attorney general would inevitably lead to partisan abuse. Democratic administrations would manipulate the law to register Democrats, and Republican administrations would do the same thing to register Republicans, he said.[7]

The "greatest injustice" in the proposed bill, Callaway asserted, was its abolition of literacy and other tests for voting, which had been adopted by the southern states in the aftermath of Reconstruction in order to disfranchise black voters.[8] To underscore his point, Callaway tendered to the subcommittee a letter from the chief registrar of majority-black Terrell County, J. W. Whitaker. Many voters, Whitaker wrote, lacked the intelligence and sophistication needed to cast a responsible ballot. "It seems absurd to us," he said, "that the literacy test be done away with as there are such things as constitutional amendments, bond issues and things of that nature, besides the election of public officials, to be voted on."[9] The literacy test was essential, he argued, in ensuring that only the well-educated could vote.

Callaway failed to tell the subcommittee that in 1960 a federal court had ruled that Terrell County registration officials "engaged in acts and practices which deprived Negro citizens" of the right to vote, and that there "are

---

[4] John Lewis, *Walking with the Wind: A Memoir of the Movement* (New York: Simon and Schuster, 1998), 326–27.

[5] *New York Times*, March 10, 1965; March 12, 1965.

[6] Johnson *The Vantage Point*, 165.

[7] Hearings before Subcommittee No. 5 of the Committee on the Judiciary, House of Representatives, Eighty-ninth Congress, First Session on H.R. 6400 and Other Proposals to Enforce the 15th Amendment to the Constitution of the United States, March 18, 19, 23, 24, 25, 29, 30, 31, and April 1, 1965, Serial No. 2, p. 542.

[8] Ibid., p. 543. The literacy test and other disfranchising measures adopted by Georgia are discussed in Chapter 2.

[9] Ibid., p. 548.

reasonable grounds to believe that the defendants will continue to engage in such acts and practices."[10] He also failed to tell the subcommittee that in 1962 the sheriff of Terrell County had arrested two civil rights workers engaged in voter registration on spurious charges of "vagrancy,"[11] and that only 2 percent of blacks in the county were actually registered to vote.[12] The white voting-age population, by contrast, and whether illiterate or not, was registered at the rate of 97 percent. Instead, Callaway told the subcommittee that the proposed voting rights bill was not only unconstitutional, but entirely unecessary.

Terrell County was not an exception in Georgia. In thirty-four counties, fewer than 10 percent of blacks were registered.[13] In the state's twenty-one counties with black voting-age majorities, an average of only 15 percent of blacks were registered, compared to 91 percent of whites.[14]

And while blacks were more than a quarter of the population,[15] there was only a tiny handful of black elected officials in the entire state. The first black elected to public office since shortly after the turn of the century was Dr. Rufus E. Clement, president of Atlanta University, to the Atlanta Board of Education in 1953.[16] The next blacks to be elected were Q. V. Williamson to the Atlanta City Council and Leroy Johnson to the state senate from Fulton County in 1962. In the elections of 1964, Horace T. Ward was also elected to the senate from Fulton County and B. L. Dent to the Augusta City Council.[17] On the eve of passage of the Voting Rights Act, this was the state's entire complement of black officeholders.

Paul Rodgers, Jr., an assistant attorney general, pleaded the state's case before the Senate Committee on the Judiciary on March 31, 1965. Testifying in the imposing New Senate Office Building, he said that the proposed bill "is

[10] *United States v. Raines*, 189 F. Supp. 121, 135 (M. D. Ga. 1960).

[11] Steven F. Lawson, *Black Ballots: Voting Rights in the South, 1944–1969* (New York: Columbia University Press, 1976), 270–72; "Federal Judge Refuses to Intervene in Terrell Case," *Dawson News*, August 16, 1962.

[12] U.S. Commission on Civil Rights, *Political Participation* (Washington, D.C.: Government Printing Office, 1968), 232–39.

[13] Ibid. The counties were Baker, Bleckley, Burke, Calhoun, Chattahoochee, Dawson, Early, Echols, Fayette, Forsyth, Glascock, Harris, Houston, Jeff Davis, Jefferson, Lee, Lincoln, McDuffie, Madison, Marion, Miller, Mitchell, Quitman, Seminole, Stewart, Sumter, Talbot, Terrell, Towns, Treutlen, Union, Warren, Webster, and Worth.

[14] Ibid. The counties were Baker, Burke, Calhoun, Clay, Crawford, Hancock, Lee, McIntosh, Macon, Marion, Peach, Quitman, Randolph, Stewart, Talbot, Taliaferro, Terrell, Twiggs, Warren, Washington, and Webster.

[15] Bureau of the Census, *1970 Census of Population, General Population Characteristics*, PC(1)-B12, Table 18 (showing blacks as 28.5 percent of the state's population).

[16] Clarence A. Bacote, "The Negro in Atlanta Politics," 16 Phylon 333, 349 (1955); Mary Louise Frick, "Influences on Negro Political Participation in Atlanta, Georgia" (M.A. thesis, Georgia State College, 1967), 21.

[17] U.S. Commission on Civil Rights, *Political Participation*, 216–17.

unconstitutional" and that "the elimination of the literacy test goes too far." Under the bill, the southern states "could not longer [sic] adopt legislation on their own." The bill was "a yoke of disgrace" that targeted the South, and its provisions were "very unjust."[18]

Another Georgian who testified against the bill was Charles J. Bloch, a Macon lawyer and former president of the Georgia Bar Association.[19] Bloch was one of the state's leading proponents of the doctrine of states' rights, a mixture of antifederalism and maintenance of the racial status quo. He was the author of a book, *States' Rights – The Law of the Land* (1958), that had been lavishly praised by Georgia politicians, including the state's two U.S. senators, Richard Russell and Herman Talmadge. "He who would sweep aside that doctrine [of states' rights]," Bloch had written, "is endangering the very life of the nation."[20] Bloch had also testified before Congress in opposition to civil rights bills in 1957 and 1960.[21] Echoing Rep. Callaway's comments in the House, Bloch said the voting rights measure wasn't needed and was unconstitutional.[22]

Carl Sanders, the Democratic governor, wrote directly to President Johnson on April 5, 1965, and added his voice to those urging defeat of the voting rights bill. In a nine-page letter, he argued that the states had exclusive power to prescribe voter qualifications, and that the abolition of literacy tests in the southern states and the federal registrar scheme was "an extreme measure . . . not even attempted during the vengeful days of the Reconstruction Period."[23]

---

[18] Hearings before the Committee on the Judiciary, United States Senate, Eighty-ninth Congress, First Session, on S. 1564 to Enforce the 15th Amendment to the Constitution of the United States, March 23, 24, 25, 29, 30, 31, and April 1, 2, 5, 1965, pp. 615–17, 621.

[19] Statement of Charles J. Bloch before the Judiciary Committee of the United States Senate, March 29, 1965, reprinted in 1965 U.S. Code Cong. & Adm. News, 89th Cong., 1st Sess., 2508–26.

[20] Charles J. Bloch, *States' Rights – The Law of the Land* (Atlanta: Harrison, 1958), 2.

[21] Hearings before the Committee on Rules and Administration, United States Senate, Eighty-sixth Congress, Second Session, on S. 2684, S. 2719, S. 2783, and S. 2814, Bills Providing under Certain Specified Circumstances for the Appointment of Temporary Federal Registrars to Register Qualified Voters for Federal Elections, S. 2722 and S. 2785, Bills Relating to the Preservation of Registration and Voting Records, S. 2535, A Bill to Establish a Permanent Congressional Elections Commission, January 18, 19, 21, 28, 29, and February 1, 2, 4, 5, 1960, p. 253.

Bloch had also represented the Democratic Party in an unsuccessful defense of the white primary system in 1946. *Chapman v. King*, 154 F. 2d 460 (5th Cir., 1946). During the 1950s, he fought off two challenges to the county unit system – *South v. Peters*, 339 U.S. 276 (1950), and *Hartsfield v. Sloan*, 357 U.S. 916 (1958) – before it was held unconstitutional in *Gray v. Sanders*, 372 U.S. 368 (1963). He represented Terrell County registration officials in *United States v. Raines*, 362 U.S. 17 (1960), in which he argued, unsuccessfully, that the Civil Rights Act of 1957, 42 U.S.C. §1971, was unconstitutional.

[22] Statement of Charles J. Bloch, 2508–26.

[23] LBJ Library, LE/HU 2–7, Box 70, p. 2.

The bill was also unnecessary, he claimed, because the state had enacted a "modern" election code in June 1964, "which provides sweeping safeguards for guaranteeing and inspiring exercise of the elective franchise."[24] Sanders failed to note that the new election code, besides retaining the discriminatory literacy test, included a new test for those who sought to register on the basis of "good character and understanding" that was even more difficult to pass than the preexisting one.[25] The new code also added new statewide majority-vote and numbered post requirements,[26] voting procedures widely acknowledged as having the potential for diluting minority voting strength.[27] Indeed, the chief sponsor of the majority-vote bill in the House, Representative Denmark Groover of Bibb County, who was a law partner of Charles Bloch, advised his colleagues that a majority-vote law was needed precisely because it would "thwart election control by Negroes and other minorities."[28]

Sanders closed his letter to President Johnson with a bombastic, states' rights flourish:

[I]f it is the will of the Congress that we march down the federal road, then I propose that we march under a national banner that affords nation-wide protection to Americans of all races and colors, irrespective of where they live – not under a banner cut into the grotesque and divisive shreds of provincial application . . . [and] not to the shrill discordant counterpoints of a war chant which seeks vengeance and is reminiscent of the harsh excesses of Reconstruction.[29]

The House approved the new voting rights bill on August 3 by a vote of 328 to 74.[30] The next day, the Senate followed suit by a vote of 79 to 18.[31] Georgia's two senators, Russell and Talmadge, voted against the act, as did eight of the state's ten House members – Howard Callaway, John Davis, John Flynt, Elliott Hagan, Phil Landrum, Maston O'Neal, Robert Stephens, and Russell Tuten. Two House members, James Mackay and Charles Weltner, voted for the bill. Mackay was to say later that his vote for the

---

[24] Ibid.

[25] Ga. Laws 1964, Ex. Sess., pp. 58–60. The grade necessary to pass the new test was raised from 67 percent to 75 percent correct answers. Cf. Ga. Laws 1949, pp. 1214–17.

[26] Ga. Laws 1964, Ex. Sess., pp. 89, 174–75, O. C. G. A., §§21-2-135 and 501.

[27] As the Court noted in *City of Rome, Georgia v. United States*, 446 U.S. 156, 183–84 (1980), a majority-vote requirement can "significantly" decrease the electoral opportunities of a racial minority. A numbered post provision disadvantages minorities because it "prevents a cohesive political group from concentrating on a single candidate." *Rogers v. Lodge*, 458 U.S. 613, 627 (1982).

[28] *Valdosta Daily Times*, February 21, 1963; *Atlanta Constitution*, March 1, 1963; J. Morgan Kousser, *Colorblind Injustice: Minority Voting Rights and the Undoing of the Second Reconstruction* (Chapel Hill: University of North Carolina Press, 1999), 200.

[29] LBJ Library, LE/HU 2–7, Box 70, p. 9.

[30] 89 Congressional Record H.19201, Aug. 3, 1965.

[31] 89 Congressional Record S.19378, Aug. 4, 1965.

James A. Mackay, one of only two members of Georgia's congressional delegation to vote in favor of the Voting Rights Act, campaigning in 1964 and surrounded by the Georgia Johnson Girls (photo from *Atlanta Journal-Constitution*).

Voting Rights Act "was the most satisfying moment emotionally in my life politically."[32]

President Johnson went to the rotunda of the Capitol on August 6, 1965, almost 100 years after ratification of the Thirteenth Amendment abolishing slavery, and signed the Voting Rights Act into law.[33] Gazing across the vaulted expanse at a statue of Abraham Lincoln, he called the act "one of the most monumental laws in the entire history of American freedom."[34]

The white leadership of Georgia could not have disagreed more. The state immediately joined a lawsuit brought by South Carolina challenging the constitutionality of the new voting rights law.[35] But in an opinion written by Chief Justice Earl Warren, the United States Supreme Court upheld the

---

[32] *Georgia v. Reno*, Civ. No. 90-2065 (D. D. C.), trial transcript, Oct. 12, 1994, p. 519.

[33] 42 U.S.C. §1973ff.

[34] Howard B. Furer, ed., *Lyndon B. Johnson 1908-* (Dobbs Ferry, N.Y.: Oceana Publications, 1971), 106; Vaughn Davis Bornet, *The Presidency of Lyndon B. Johnson* (Lawrence: University Press of Kansas, 1983).

[35] *South Carolina v. Katzenbach*, 383 U.S. 301, 307 n.2 (1966).

act as a valid exercise of congressional power in enforcing the equal voting rights provisions of the Fifteenth Amendment.[36]

The Voting Rights Act was to have the effect in Georgia that its opponents feared. It would break the white stranglehold on state and local politics, and do so in a way unlikely ever to be undone.

---

[36] The Fifteenth Amendment provides in relevant part that "[t]he right of citizens of the United States to vote shall not be denied or abridged by the United States or by any State on account of race, color, or previous condition of servitude."

2

After the Civil War: Recreating "the White Man's Georgia"

We are relieved from the body of this death, which has hung about our necks ever since the adoption of the Fourteenth and Fifteenth Amendments. This is the white man's Georgia from now on.

Atlanta Journal, October 8, 1908

I

The journey from slavery to passage of the Voting Rights Act was an arduous one for blacks in Georgia. Whether slave or free, blacks were disfranchised until after the Civil War. The state's first Constitution, adopted in 1777, limited the right to vote to "[a]ll male white inhabitants, of the age of twenty-one years."[1] The Constitution of 1789 simplified the statement of qualifications of electors by giving the right of suffrage to "citizens and inhabitants,"[2] but since neither slaves nor free Negroes were regarded as "citizens," blacks remained excluded from voting. The noncitizen status of free blacks was made explicit by statute, which provided that "[t]he free person of color is entitled to no right of citizenship, except such as are specially given by law. His status differs from that of the slave in this: No master having dominion over him he is entitled to the free use of his liberty, labor and property, except so far as he is restrained by law."[3]

The state supreme court provided the rationale for the noncitizen status of blacks in an 1853 decision holding that a free person of color lacked the capacity to dispose of slaves by deed of gift. All blacks, the court said, were "a race of Pagan slaves." Tracing the history of slavery from the ancient republics to modern times, the court concluded in a passage of torrid prose that "the social and civil degradation, resulting from the taint of blood adheres

[1] Constitution of Georgia of 1777, Art. IX.
[2] Constitution of Georgia of 1798, Art. IV.
[3] Ga. Code of 1861, §1612.

The home of Alexander H. Stephens, vice president of the Confederacy, in Taliaferro County. At a speech in Savannah on March 21, 1861, Stephens proclaimed that the foundation of the Confederate government rested upon the "great physical, philo-sophical, and moral truth" of white superiority over the Negro (photo by Patricia McDonald).

to the descendants of Ham in this country, like the poisoned tunic of Nessus; that nothing but an Act of the Assembly can purify, by the salt of its grace, the bitter fountain – the '*darkling sea*.'"[4]

The state court anticipated by some four years a similar conclusion reached by the U.S. Supreme Court in *Dred Scott v. Sandford*, which held that blacks, whether emancipated or not, were not "citizens" or "people" within the meaning of the Constitution and therefore had no federally protected rights. As the Court put it, when the Constitution was framed and adopted, blacks "had no rights which the white man was bound to respect."[5]

Alexander H. Stephens, a Georgian and vice president of the Confederacy, expressed his, and his newly formed government's, continuing view of the status of blacks in a speech he delivered in Savannah on March 21, 1861. The foundations of the Confederate government, he said,

are laid, its cornerstone rests, upon the great truth that the negro is not equal to the white man; that slavery, subordination to the superior race, is his natural and moral

[4] *Bryan v. Walton*, 14 Ga. 185, 198, 202 (1853).
[5] *Dred Scott v. Sandford*, 60 U.S. (19 How.) 393, 407 (1857).

condition. This, our new Government, is the first, in the history of the world, based upon this great physical, philosophical, and moral truth.[6]

The exclusion of blacks was again made explicit by the Constitution of 1861, adopted after Georgia seceded from the Union. It reintroduced the racial designation and limited voting to "free white male citizens."[7]

II

After the defeat of the Confederacy in the Civil War, state government in Georgia was reorganized under the administration of President Andrew Johnson. He appointed James Johnson, a unionist from Columbus, as provisional governor, but political power in the state remained in the hands of those who had been the leaders of the Confederate cause.[8]

The first postwar constitutional convention was held at the state capitol in Milledgeville in October 1865. The delegates were all white, and they proposed a constitution designed to maintain the old racial order. They repealed the state's secession ordinance, reluctantly "acquiesced" in the abolition of slavery,[9] and continued the exclusion of blacks from voting and officeholding.[10] Marriage between whites and persons of African descent was "forever prohibited."[11] As further evidence of its intention to relegate blacks to secondary, inferior status, the convention instructed the legislature "to provide by law for the government of free persons of color," including "the regulation of their transactions with citizens" and "the regulation or prohibition of their immigration into this State from other States of the Union, or elsewhere."[12] Statewide elections were held, and in December 1865 the legislature convened and ratified the Thirteenth Amendment.[13]

In November 1866, however, the state hewed to its pre-war policy of white supremacy and "decline[d]" to ratify the recently enacted Fourteenth Amendment,[14] which declared that "[a]ll persons born or naturalized in the United States... are citizens of the United States and of the State wherein they reside." The general assembly enacted laws continuing the exclusion

---

[6] Quoted in Kenneth Stampp, *The Causes of the Civil War* (New York: Touchstone, 1991), 153.

[7] Constitution of Georgia of 1861, Art. V, para. 1.

[8] Alan Conway, *The Reconstruction of Georgia* (Minneapolis: University of Minnesota Press, 1966), 42; Numan V. Bartley, *The Creation of Modern Georgia* (Athens: University of Georgia Press, 1983), 47.

[9] Journal of the Proceedings of the Constitutional Convention of 1865, pp. 17–18; Constitution of Georgia of 1865, Art. I, para. 20.

[10] Constitution of Georgia of 1865, Art. V, Sec. 1, para. 1.

[11] Constitution of Georgia of 1865, Art. V, Sec. 1, para. 9.

[12] Constitution of Georgia of 1865, Art. II, Sec. 5, para. 5.

[13] Ga. Laws 1865, p. 312.

[14] Georgia House Journal, November 13, 1866, pp. 67–8; Ga. Laws 1866, p. 216.

of blacks from juries,[15] defining "persons of color," that is, "all negroes, mulattoes, mestizoes, and their descendants, having one-eighth negro, or African blood, in their veins,"[16] prohibiting the performance of interracial marriage,[17] regulating family relationships "among persons of color,"[18] and restricting schools to "any white inhabitant" between the ages of six and twenty-one.[19]

Although blacks were nominally given "full and equal benefits of all laws,"[20] the law did not grant blacks the right to vote or to hold office. Alexander Stephens, elected in 1866 to the U.S. Senate from Georgia, explained to the Joint Committee on Reconstruction that, as regards the extension of political rights to Negroes, the "general opinion of the State is very much averse to it."[21]

The refusal of Georgia and other southern states to ratify the Fourteenth Amendment, their passage of the Black Codes regulating the conduct of newly emancipated slaves, and their general racial intransigence prompted Congress to pass several military reconstruction acts. The First Reconstruction Act of March 2, 1867,[22] placed Georgia in the third military district under the command of General John Pope, enfranchised blacks, disfranchised whites who had participated in the war, and provided for the election of delegates to a new state constitutional convention. Upon ratification of the new constitution by the voters, and upon approval by Congress, the state would be readmitted to the union.

The Second Reconstruction Act of March 23, 1867,[23] and its companion bill, the Third Reconstruction Act of July 19, 1867,[24] provided for the registration of voters under military supervision. General Pope divided the state into districts, in each of which he established a registration board consisting of a white man, a black man, and an agent of the military.[25] In Georgia, the registrars entered the names of approximately 200,000 new voters, nearly half of them black.[26]

---

[15] Ga. Laws 1866, p. 137.
[16] Ga. Laws 1866, p. 239.
[17] Ga. Laws 1866, p. 241.
[18] Ga. Laws 1866, p. 240.
[19] Ga. Laws 1866, p. 59.
[20] Ga. Laws 1866, p. 239.
[21] Quoted in Ralph Wardlaw, *Negro Suffrage in Georgia, 1867–1930* (Athens: University of Georgia Press, 1932), 17.
[22] 14 Stat. 428.
[23] 15 Stat. 2.
[24] 15 Stat. 14.
[25] Russell Duncan, *Freedom's Shore: Tunis Campbell and the Georgia Freedmen* (Athens: University of Georgia Press, 1986), 43; Wardlaw, *Negro Suffrage*, 22.
[26] Bartley, *Creation of Modern Georgia*, 48; C. Mildred Thompson, *Reconstruction in Georgia: Economic, Social, and Political, 1865–1877* (New York: Columbia University Press, 1915), 186.

"THE FIRST VOTE."—Drawn by A. R. Waud.—[See next page.]

Blacks first registered and voted in Georgia in 1867 under federal supervision during the Reconstruction period (illustration from *Harper's Weekly*).

A second constitutional convention to reorganize state government was held in Atlanta in December 1867. Although Milledgeville was still the state capital, the convention was moved because local hotel operators had announced that they would not rent rooms to black delegates.[27]

The convention was dominated by Republicans and included 37 blacks among its 165 delegates.[28] It adopted a constitution that guaranteed blacks citizenship,[29] protection of the law, and the right of male suffrage.[30] Confederate leaders were disfranchised until after 1870.[31] The proposed

[27] Bartley, *Creation of Modern Georgia*, 54–5; Conway, *Reconstruction of Georgia*, 149.

[28] Bartley, *Creation of Modern Georgia*, 54–5.

[29] Constitution of Georgia of 1868, Art. I, Sec. 2.

[30] Constitution of Georgia of 1868, Art. I, Sec. 2; Art. II, Sec. 2 (granting the franchise to "every male person" in the state who met age, residency, and other qualifications).

[31] Constitution of Georgia of 1868, §§684, 787–89; Journal of the Constitutional Convention of 1868, p. 501.

constitution also authorized the legislature to establish a system of free public education for children of both races,[32] and provided for elections in April 1868 to ratify the constitution and elect civil officers.

Prior to 1868, education had been provided to whites in an unsystematic way by private schools, publicly supported academies, allocations from the state's poor school fund, and various county and city systems.[33] As for blacks, far from making any provision for their education, state law made it a crime to teach "any slave, negro, or free person of color, to read or write" or to provide them books or writing material.[34]

As a revenue measure limited to supporting the new public schools, the convention authorized a poll, or head, tax of one dollar.[35] Henry M. Turner, a black delegate and former chaplain of a black military regiment, voted for the poll tax but later lamented, in light of its use to disfranchise black voters, that "I was inexperienced at the time. I made a great blunder."[36]

Democrats denounced the new constitution and derided the "nigger–New England" convention that had adopted it.[37] Wags of the day dubbed the assembly the "Unconstitutional Convention."[38] The *Augusta Daily Constitutionalist*, expressing the prevailing Democratic view, gave a scathing, color-obsessed description of the members of the black delegation.

They formed a motley and interesting gathering. From the light yellow mulatto to the coal black African, and from the obsequious barber to the sturdy cotton picker, there they were as large as life, and carrying themselves with a dignity and air of importance at once ludicrous and pitiful – a few out of the number are able to read and write; the majority are as innocent of all educational qualities as a babe of three weeks old. A single glance at this body of Negroes will tell you how utterly farcical must be a convention which contains such members.[39]

Despite the state's historic criminal prohibition on teaching blacks how to read and write, at least five of the Georgia-born Negro delegates to the convention were in fact literate.[40]

---

[32] Constitution of Georgia of 1868, Art. VI, Sec. 1.

[33] See, e.g., Ga. Laws 1849–50, pp. 21–36 (establishing private academies in various parts of the state). See also Charles E. Jones, *Education in Georgia* (Washington: Government Printing Office, 1889), 36; Adger M. Carter, "Public Education in Georgia from 1850 to 1887" (M.A. thesis, University of Georgia, 1939), 32–3.

[34] Code of Georgia of 1861, §§4496, 4500.

[35] Constitution of Georgia of 1868, Art. I, Sec. 29.

[36] Edmund L. Drago, *Black Politicians and Reconstruction in Georgia* (Baton Rouge: Louisiana State University Press, 1982), 45.

[37] Bartley, *Creation of Modern Georgia*, 59.

[38] Ethel Kime Ware, *A Constitutional History of Georgia* (New York: Columbia University Press, 1947), 141.

[39] December 20, 1867, quoted in Ware, ibid., 138.

[40] Drago, *Black Politicians*, Appendix: Black Delegates and Convention Delegates, 1867–1872.

Because of the intense opposition of white Democrats, including some white Republicans, the convention did not expressly guarantee the right of blacks to hold office. A proposed clause conferring that right was defeated, with blacks themselves voting with the majority. They had been assured by the white leadership of the Republican Party that blacks were eligible to hold office and that a special provision was unnecessary. The black delegates, to their subsequent regret, took the representations at face value.[41] Henry Turner later said that he "foolishly" voted against the black officeholder provision.[42]

The elections held in April 1868 were accompanied by an extremely high level of violence. L. N. Trammell, who was later elected president of the senate when the Democrats gained control in 1871,[43] advised a friend in March 1868 that "the negroes should as far as possible be *kept from the polls*. I think that the organization of the KKK might effect this more than anything else."[44] Democrat John C. Reed, who was defeated in his run for the constitutional convention in 1868, was equally blunt about the party's strategy: "We resolved that the whites should win every election possible."[45]

The Ku Klux Klan was organized in Georgia in 1868, following a visit to Atlanta that year by the former Confederate general Nathan B. Forrest. During its early years, the Klan functioned essentially as the terrorist wing of the Democratic Party, with its main purpose being to drive the Republicans from political power by every means possible.[46]

Republicans, with blacks voting for the first time in the state's history, elected Rufus B. Bullock, a Republican and unionist from Columbus, as governor and captured majorities in both houses of the general assembly.[47] Twenty-five blacks were elected to the house and three to the senate. The voters also ratified the proposed new state constitution.

Congress passed a law in June 1868 readmitting Georgia into the union, provided that it ratified the Fourteenth Amendment.[48] The state did so on July 21, 1868.[49]

The Democrats promptly launched a counteroffensive to exclude the blacks who had been elected to the general assembly and replace them with

---

[41] Thompson, *Reconstruction in Georgia*, 196; Elizabeth S. Nathans, *Losing the Peace: Georgia Republicans and Reconstruction, 1865–1871* (Baton Rouge: Louisiana State University Press, 1968), 67; Bartley, *Creation of Modern Georgia*, 57.

[42] Speech delivered in Savannah, Aug. 21, 1874, quoted in Drago *Black Politicians*, 44.

[43] Georgia Senate Journal, November 1, 1871, p. 4.

[44] L. N. Trammell to Alex [Irwin?], March 30, 1868, quoted in Drago, *Black Politicians*, 152 (emphasis in original).

[45] Ibid., p. 154.

[46] Conway, *Reconstruction of Georgia*, 171; Bartley, *Creation of Modern Georgia*, 59.

[47] Bartley, *Creation of Modern Georgia*, 59.

[48] 15 Stat. 73.

[49] Georgia House Journal, July 21, 1868, pp. 49–50.

Statue behind the state capitol in Atlanta commemorating the twenty-eight blacks expelled from the legislature in 1868 on the ground that Negroes were ineligible under state law to hold office. Four mulattoes escaped expulsion because their light skin color made it impossible to prove that they contained the requisite quantum of one-eight Negro or African blood (photo by Patricia McDonald).

their losing Democratic opponents. By September 1868 the Democrats, although a minority in both houses, had secured enough white Republican allies that they were able to pass resolutions excluding all black members from both the house and senate on the grounds that they were "ineligible" to serve under the state Constitution.[50] The speaker of the house, a Republican, ensured passage of the resolution in the lower chamber by ruling that the black legislators could not vote on the issue of their own expulsion.[51] Four mulattoes had also been elected to the house and were originally targeted for expulsion. According to John Hope Franklin, the four held onto their seats

[50] Georgia House Journal, Aug. 26, 1868, p. 222; Sept. 3, 1868, pp. 242–43; Georgia Senate Journal, Sept. 7, 1868, pp. 243–44; Sept. 11, 1868, pp. 272–73; Sept. 12, 1868, pp. 277–78.
[51] Georgia House Journal, Aug. 26, 1868, p. 224; Drago, *Black Politicians*, 49.

"because their fair complexion made it impossible to prove that they were African American."[52]

Tunis Campbell, a justice of the peace from majority-black McIntosh County, and George Wallace from Baldwin County were both expelled from the senate. They recorded, to no avail, their "solemn protest against the illegal, unconstitutional, unjust, and oppressive action of this body . . . declaring us ineligible on account of color."[53]

As a result of the purge of black elected officials, the Democrats gained control of the house, although Republicans retained control of the senate. Many of the Republicans, however, sided with the Democrats on issues of race.[54]

In the November 1868 general election, the Democrats, running on a platform of white supremacy and home rule, perfected and intensified the tactics of intimidation and violence they had employed in the preceding April election.[55] The Freedmen's Bureau reported that in August, September, and October of 1868, there were thirty-one murders, forty-eight attempted murders, and sixty-three beatings inflicted upon blacks.[56] Much of the violence in the state, not to mention economic and social coercion, went unreported.

In the town of Camilla in Mitchell County an undetermined number of blacks were killed and thirty to forty wounded by whites who turned a black political rally into a race riot.[57] A local history of the county, sponsored by the Rotary Club of Camilla, reported that "[t]here were eleven negroes buried in the Camilla cemetery after that battle, and many dead reported found in the sloughs and in Rock Lake; no white men were killed or seriously injured."[58] From the white perspective, the Camilla riot had a chastening effect on black political participation. The local history noted with obvious satisfaction that:

After the excitement of the riot had abated, there seemed to be no ill-feeling between the whites and the negroes of Mitchell County. The few local negroes, incited by the carpetbaggers, realized they were unequipped by training and by inheritance for any governmental offices or positions, and upon the departure of these offenders from the county, became the citizens they should be. They settled upon small farms, or

---

52 John Hope Franklin, *Reconstruction after the Civil War* (Chicago: University of Chicago Press, 1994), 130. See also Drago, *Black Politicians*, 69.

53 Georgia Senate Journal, Sept. 12, 1868, pp. 278–79.

54 Bartley, *Creation of Modern Georgia*, 62; Drago, *Black Politicians*, 49.

55 Bartley, *Creation of Modern Georgia*, 62.

56 Ibid.; Allen W. Trelease, *White Terror: The Ku Klux Klan Conspiracy and Southern Reconstruction* (New York: Harper and Row, 1971), 117.

57 Nathans, *Losing the Peace*, 139; Bartley, *Creation of Modern Georgia*, 62–3; Lee W. Formwalt, "The Camilla Massacre of 1868: Racial Violence as Political Propaganda," 71 Ga. Hist. Q. 399 (1987).

58 Margaret Spence and Anna M. Fleming, *History of Mitchell County, 1857–1976* (Thomasville, Ga.: Camilla Rotary Club, 1976), 2.

became the paid servants of their former masters and lived much as they did 'before the war.'[59]

On election day there were open confrontations between blacks and whites in various parts of the state, including Elberton, Augusta, and Savannah.[60] The situation in Savannah was described as bordering "on civil war."[61] In many Georgia counties, the Klan kept blacks from the polls at gunpoint.[62] According to Allen Trelease:

Election day saw companies of armed whites assembling around the polls, confiscating Republican ballots before they could be distributed and threatening violence to Negroes who insisted on the right to cast them.[63]

The expulsion of blacks from the general assembly, along with continuing racial violence and terrorism across the state, prompted Congress to place Georgia once again under military supervision. Congress refused to seat the representatives from Georgia and passed a bill providing that the exclusion of any person from the state legislature on the basis of race "would be illegal and revolutionary and is hereby prohibited."[64] The expelled black state legislators were ordered restored to their seats, and the state was directed to ratify the Fifteenth Amendment, which prohibited denial of the right to vote "on account of race, color, or previous condition of servitude."

The Georgia legislature met again on January 10, 1870. General Alfred Terry, the new military commander of the state, returned the expelled blacks to the general assembly and disqualified under the Fourteenth Amendment twenty-two Democrats who had held public office before the war and then served as military officers or officeholders under the Confederacy.[65] Control of the house returned to the Republicans, strengthening the position of the more radical members of the party.[66] The general assembly again ratified the Fourteenth Amendment, and for the first time ratified the Fifteenth Amendment.[67] On July 15, 1870, the state was readmitted to the union for the second time.[68]

[59] Ibid.
[60] Drago *Black Politicians*, 150.
[61] Bartley *Creation of Modern Georgia*, 63.
[62] Ibid., p. 139.
[63] Trelease *White Terror*, 118.
[64] 16 Stat. 59.
[65] Bartley *Creation of Modern Georgia*, 68. Section 3 of the Fourteenth Amendment provided that no person could hold state office who, having previously taken an oath to support the Constitution of the United States, "shall have engaged in insurrection or rebellion against the same, or given aid or comfort to the enemies thereof."
[66] James E. Sefton, *The United States Army and Reconstruction, 1865–1877* (Baton Rouge: Louisiana State University Press, 1967), 198–205.
[67] Ga. Laws 1870, Resolutions 1 and 2, pp. 491, 493.
[68] 16 Stat. 363–64.

The Republican-controlled majority passed a "like and equal accommodations" law in 1870 applicable to common carriers,[69] and established ward elections for Macon and Atlanta.[70] The ward election plan in Atlanta was denounced by Democrats because it "threatens to put negroes on our City Council."[71] At the election held in December 1870, two blacks were in fact elected to the council in Atlanta, and a black was elected alderman in Macon.[72] An Atlanta resident wrote in his diary that the election "resulted in getting two *niggers* in as aldermen!"[73] The *Atlanta Constitution* noted that "[t]he election of Radical Aldermen is due to the change in the law.... The necessity of changing back is therefore apparent."[74] In Macon, the *American Union* described the election of a black alderman as "a most complete revolution in our city government. Heretofore the negro has not even been allowed to vote for any office, much less be voted for."[75]

Despite these successes, blacks never achieved significant officeholding at the local level during the Reconstruction period. In the November 1868 elections, for example, only seventeen blacks were elected to county offices, of whom nine were elected to the relatively insignificant position of coroner.[76]

In an effort to protect voters from intimidation, the Republican legislature enacted a law in 1870, known as the Akerman Law, prohibiting any person from challenging or hindering voters at the polls.[77] It also abolished the poll tax, because it found that "certain bodies politic, incorporations and local authorities of this State are in the habit of violating ... [the] Constitution by assessing and collecting capitation taxes as registration fees."[78]

The general assembly enacted legislation in 1870 intended to implement the public education provisions of the 1868 Constitution.[79] The bill was introduced by James Porter, a black Republican from Savannah.[80] It

---

[69] Ga. Laws 1870, p. 398.

[70] Ga. Laws 1870, pp. 208, 486.

[71] *Atlanta Constitution*, Nov. 16, 1870.

[72] Howard Rabinowitz, *Race Relations in the Urban South, 1865–1890* (New York: Oxford University Press, 1978), 268; Drago, *Black Politicians*, 81.

[73] S. P. Richard diary, Dec. 10, 1879, quoted in Drago, *Black Politicians*, 81 (emphasis in original).

[74] Rabinowitz, *Race Relations*, 269; *Atlanta Constitution*, Dec. 9, 1870.

[75] Dec. 15, 1870, quoted in Drago, *Black Politicians*, 81.

[76] Ibid., p. 79.

[77] Ga. Laws 1870, p. 63.

[78] Ga. Laws 1870, p. 432. An exception was created for collection of the "street tax, and that only after opportunity to work the streets."

[79] Ga. Laws 1870, p. 49.

[80] Drago, *Black Politicians*, 97–8. The public school law was largely the work of the Georgia Teachers Association, an organization composed primarily of white Democratic educators, under the leadership of Gustavus J. Orr. Orr's plan was contained in a "Report on a System of Public Schools for the State of Georgia" submitted to the legislature, which provided that

established a board of education in each county, to consist of "one person from each militia district, and one person from each ward in any city in the county, and one from each incorporated town, who shall be elected by the legal voters of said district, ward or incorporated town."[81] The school law also provided for the election of three trustees from each school district within the county. The trustees were required to maintain the schools in their subdistricts on a racially segregated basis, but to "provide the same facilities for each [race], both as regards schoolhouses and fixtures, and the attainments and abilities of teachers, length of term-time, etc."[82]

The state's Democrats never reconciled themselves to sharing political power with blacks. On the contrary, the principal thing that held the Democratic Party together was its desire to maintain white supremacy and to eliminate, either totally or as nearly so as possible, black political participation in state politics, particularly officeholding.[83]

In the legislative elections scheduled for December 1870, in an effort to recoup their losses the Democrats resorted to their earlier tactics of fraud and intimidation. Klansmen and assorted posses and paramilitary units controlled the countryside and the polling places,[84] while Democratic election officials selectively required blacks to produce proof of payment of poll taxes as a condition for voting, despite the fact that the tax had been repealed.[85] General Terry allowed the intimidation in the 1870 election to prevail and refused to take more than halfway measures to check it.[86] As a result, the Democrats won control of a substantial majority in the general assembly that was scheduled to convene in the fall of 1871.

Elections for members of the newly created boards of education and for district trustees were set for January 1871. Newspapers in the state, reflecting the intense white opposition to black officeholding, called attention to the elections and warned against the dangers of electing blacks. According to the *Augusta Chronicle and Sentinel*:

It is very important that the persons elected be honest, faithful and competent. We know that the whole people rarely take interest in these merely local elections, and

---

county school boards should be elected "by the people." Oscar H. Joiner, *A History of Public Education in Georgia, 1734–1976* (Columbia, S.C.: R. L. Bryan Co., 1979), 71; Dorothy Orr, *A History of Education in Georgia* (Chapel Hill: University of North Carolina Press, 1950), 196. A section requiring ward elections was added by the bill's Republican sponsors in the legislature. *Atlanta Constitution*, Aug. 24, 1870; *Atlanta Daily New Era*, Aug. 24, 1870.

[81] Ga. Laws 1870, p. 52, sec. 16.

[82] Ga. Laws 1870, p. 57, sec. 32.

[83] *Vereen v. Ben Hill County*, Civ. No. 88-4-ALB-AMER (DF) (M. D. Ga. 1988), deposition of Dan T. Carter, July 24, 1989, p. 42.

[84] Bartley, *Creation of Modern Georgia*, 70.

[85] Trelease, *White Terror*, 240–41; Nathans, *Losing the Peace*, 205.

[86] Trelease, *White Terror*, 241.

"COLORED RULE IN A RECONSTRUCTED (?) STATE," the prevailing view of the white South (illustration from *Harper's Weekly*).

for that reason we urge them to be sure and control this one. We may rest assured that if we fail to present and vote for good men the scalawags and negroes will take possession of this most important matter.[87]

A week later the paper underscored the "importance of having experienced, prudent, intelligent and *honest* men to fill" the various school posts. Leaving little doubt as to who these men were, the paper carried a companion story reporting the "glorious victory of the Democratic party in Jefferson county," noting the problems of the "Rads" in getting "a white man in the county to run on the nigger ticket."[88]

The elections were held, and some blacks, although the number is unknown, were elected in various places around the state, including Savannah

[87] *Augusta Chronicle and Sentinel,* Dec. 24, 1870.
[88] *Augusta Chronicle and Sentinel,* Dec. 30, 1870.

and Milledgeville.[89] Newspapers in the state noted the racial significance of
the elections and reported with satisfaction the defeat of black candidates.
The *Columbus Daily Sun*, in an article entitled "The Election Yesterday – The
Whites Win," observed that:

The election for a County Board of Education and Trustees excited little comment
yesterday until it was reported the negroes were endeavoring to elect colored men in
the First and Ninth wards. The following shows the result, which is another white
man's triumph. A negro has not yet been elected to an office in Muscogee County
since bayonets were removed.[90]

The *Augusta Chronicle and Sentinel* reported "Another Democratic
Victory" and noted that "[i]n only one ward – the fourth – did the negroes have a ticket."[91] The *Savannah Republican* observed that in the first
district "only one ticket was run, the Radical ticket," which included black
Republicans for three of the four school board seats. In the second district,
however, "[t]he Democrats had it all to themselves and elected, without
opposition...good men."[92]

The overall results of the 1871 school board elections were mixed. In
thirty-seven of the counties in the state all the offices had been elected;
in eighty a majority had been elected; in sixteen a minority had been
elected; and in three no elections had been held.[93] In his first report to the
legislature on the state of the public schools, State Superintendent John
R. Lewis reported that "[i]n most instances the result has been most satis-
factory, and in very few counties could better men be selected for this most
responsible duty." The problems encountered in filling all the offices resulted
"principally from want of confidence in the permanency of the system.
The splendid results accomplished in many of the counties show what
could have been done in most of them by the same united and intelligent
action."[94]

Control of school board elections was critical from the white point of
view, not only to maintain segregation but also to determine the curriculum
and to dictate what was taught about the war and the South. Members of the
legislature, for example, charged that Superintendent Lewis had deliberately
secured the adoption of textbooks from northern publishing houses,

---

[89] *Savannah Republican*, Jan. 8, 1871; *Savannah Morning News*, Jan. 9, 1871; *Milledgeville Federal
Union*, Jan. 10, 1871.

[90] *Columbus Daily Sun*, Jan. 8, 1871.

[91] *Augusta Chronicle and Sentinel*, Jan. 8, 1871.

[92] *Savannah Republican*, Jan. 8, 1871.

[93] Orr, *History of Education*, 198.

[94] J. R. Lewis, "School Commissioner's Report" (Atlanta, Ga.: Department of Education,
1871), 5–7.

"which contain matter offensive to the taste and feelings of the Southern people."[95]

Representative Garnett McMillan was particularly critical of one of the texts, which gave accounts of "Sherman's masterly Atlanta campaign" and "the inhuman massacre of the garrison of Fort Pillow, in which special mention is made of the 'colored troops' as among the sufferers." McMillan charged that Lewis was trying to "execrate" the memory of the Confederate dead.[96] The press asked rhetorically, "Can we permit our children to be taught that their fathers were 'rebels' and 'traitors'? The question answers itself."[97]

Klan violence, intimidation, bribery, and undue influence remained so pervasive that in 1871 Congress ordered an investigation. Hearings were held in Washington and Atlanta that documented numerous abuses against blacks and the manipulation of the black vote by members of both parties.[98]

Rufus Bullock remained governor, but he was certain to be impeached by the Democratic majority when the legislature convened in November 1871. Rather than face a legislative trial, he resigned.[99]

Upon Bullock's departure, the legislature adopted a resolution that he had "left the State under circumstances creating grave suspicion that he is guilty of high crimes and misdemeanors," and it appointed a joint committee to inventory "all the house and kitchen furniture, silverware and all other articles and implements, etc. connected with the Executive Mansion."[100] Bullock was arrested in 1876 in his hometown of Albion, New York, and brought back to Georgia for trial on various charges of corruption. He was acquitted and, in yet another dramatic reversal of fortune, went on to become a successful businessman and president of the Atlanta Chamber of Commerce.[101]

In the ensuing special gubernatorial election in 1871, the Democratic candidate, James M. Smith, ran unopposed. With Smith's election, the Democrats had finally recaptured full control of the executive and legislative branches of government.[102] Blacks were no longer a significant element in state politics, and the way was paved for the complete restoration of white supremacy and the redemption of the few pockets of local government still under black influence.[103]

---

95 *Atlanta Constitution*, Dec. 9, 1871.
96 Ibid.
97 *Atlanta Constitution*, Aug. 25, 1870.
98 Report of testimony taken by the Georgia Sub-Committee on Ku Klux Conspiracy in 1871–2, 42 Cong., 2d Sess., reports number 41, part 6, and number 22, part 7.
99 Drago, *Black Politicians*, 65; Bartley, *Creation of Modern Georgia*, 70–1.
100 Ga. Laws 1871, pp. 263–64.
101 Conway, *Reconstruction of Georgia*, 201–2, 214; Bartley, *Creation of Modern Georgia*, 73.
102 Wardlaw, *Negro Suffrage*, 30–1.
103 Thompson, *Reconstruction in Georgia*, 272, 275.

III

The Democratic legislature proceeded to nullify black suffrage within the limits imposed by the Fourteenth and Fifteenth Amendments. It repealed the 1870 Akerman voter challenge law.[104] It reinstituted the poll tax.[105] It eliminated elections in McIntosh County, the political base of Tunis Campbell, and substituted a system of county government appointed by the governor.[106] It also abolished ward elections for the city of Atlanta.[107] At the next Atlanta city election, white Democrats won a sweep of council seats.[108]

A bill to abolish local school board elections in favor of grand jury appointments was introduced in the house on December 4, 1871.[109] The bill's chief sponsor was Representative Isaac Russell, an ardent Democrat and a white supremacist. According to Russell, "the old law often resulted in the election of ignorant men, and as the grand jury is most generally composed of the most intelligent men in the county, selections thus made would be good." The bill was opposed by three white Republicans – J. R. Griffin, H. L. Hillyer, and F. F. Putney. They argued that the selection of the trustees or board members "should be left to the people."[110] The Georgia Teachers

---

[104] Ga. Laws 1871, p. 28, repealing Ga. Laws 1870, p. 62.

[105] Ga. Laws 1871, p. 74, repealing Ga. Laws 1870, pp. 431–32. Every one of the ex-Confederate states eventually adopted a poll tax – Virginia in 1875, Florida in 1889, Mississippi and Tennessee in 1890, Arkansas in 1892, South Carolina in 1895, Louisiana in 1898, North Carolina in 1900, Alabama in 1901, and Texas in 1902. V. O. Key, Jr., *Southern Politics in State and Nation* (Knoxville: University of Tennessee Press, 1984), 578–79; J. Morgan Kousser, *The Shaping of Southern Politics* (New Haven, Conn.: Yale University Press, 1974), 63, 239. The Mississippi Supreme Court described the tax in that state not as a legitimate revenue measure but as a "clog upon the franchise" and one of the "expedients to obstruct the exercise of the franchise by the negro race." *Ratliff v. Beale*, 74 Miss. 247, 20 So. 865, 868–69 (1896).

[106] Ga. Laws 1871, p. 265. Abolishing elective offices to preempt black office holding was resorted to by other southern states as well. During his second term as governor of South Carolina, Benjamin R. ("Pitchfork Ben") Tillman was instrumental in securing passage of legislation abolishing local elected government in favor of county and township commissioners appointed by the governor upon the recommendation of the county's legislative delegation. 1894 S.C. Acts 481, 483, No. 320; 1899 S.C. Acts 1, 2, No. 1; 1899 S.C. Acts 113, 113–14, No. 86. Since, as Tillman was fond of noting, whites had "absolute control" of state government, the legislation put it beyond possibility that blacks, even if they were in an overwhelming majority, would have a voice in choosing their local officials. Laughlin McDonald, "An Aristocracy of Voters: The Disfranchisement of Blacks in South Carolina," 37 S. C. L. Rev. 557, 570 (1986). See also *Vander Linden v. Hodges*, 193 F. 3d 268, 270 (4th Cir. 1999) ("the legislative delegation system, which developed in place of locally elected county government [in South Carolina], was similarly created out of fear of African-American voting power").

[107] Ga. Laws 1871, p. 87.

[108] Drago, *Black Politicians*, 81–2; Eric Foner, *Reconstruction: America's Unfinished Revolution* (New York: Harper and Row, 1988), 423.

[109] Georgia House Journal, Dec. 4, 1871, p. 345.

[110] *Atlanta Daily Sun*, Dec. 5, 1871.

Association, in a memorial presented to the legislature in November 1871, had similarly urged that the existing system of education and elections "by the people" be retained.[111] The arguments and recommendations of the supporters of elected school boards were to no avail.

The general assembly repealed the method of electing county boards of education the following year and provided instead that the grand jury of each county "shall...select from the citizens of their respective counties five freeholders, who shall constitute the county board of education."[112] The freeholder requirement, standing alone, disqualified a disproportionate number of blacks, because they were far less likely than whites to own real property.

While appointed school boards are not uncommon, Georgia is apparently the only state that has put the appointment power in the hands of county grand juries.[113] The effect of the entire grand jury scheme, aside from the freeholder requirement for board membership, was to insure that blacks would be excluded from the process of selecting members of school boards.

The grand jury in Georgia was by tradition and law an all-white institution.[114] While the state was under congressional reconstruction in 1867, General Pope published an order giving blacks the right to serve on juries for the first time. Judge Augustus Reese of the Superior Court for the Ocmulgee Circuit refused to obey the order on the grounds that it was inconsistent with state law. General Pope ordered Judge Reese removed from office.[115]

When three freedmen were chosen to sit on the grand jury in Whitfield County, the *Milledgeville Federal Union* questioned "the expediency, the practicability or utility of this innovation on the time honored custom of selecting the grand jury from the best men of the county – men of intelligence and moral worth." According to the paper, local officials had apparently misapprehended the "intentions of the Order [of General Pope], relative to the Grand Jury box," while "the freedman himself can[not] so misunderstand his true position to fill any such position of honor and trust."[116]

The Constitution of 1868 removed the racial restriction on jury service, but the right of blacks to serve on juries was left ambiguous, or at least

---

[111] Orr, *History of Education*, 201–2.

[112] Ga. Laws 1872, p. 279.

[113] U.S. Department of Commerce, Bureau of the Census, *1987 Census of Government, Vol. 1, No. 2: Government Organization; Popularly Elected Officials*, Appendix A [GC 87 (1) -2] (January 1990) (identifying only Georgia as providing for grand jury appointment of boards of education).

[114] See Ga. Code of 1867, §3841 (requiring grand jurors to be "free white male citizens").

[115] Thompson, *Reconstruction in Georgia*, 177–78; Conway, *Reconstruction of Georgia*, 147–48.

[116] *Milledgeville Federal Union*, Oct. 15, 1867.

subject to local discretion, by the requirement that jurors be "upright and intelligent persons."[117] The Republican leader Amos T. Akerman said that the phrase would "enable the Constitution to be differently interpreted upon that subject in different parts of the state."[118]

The legislature of 1869 (the same legislature that had expelled the black members from the house and senate) then passed a statute that made it even more unlikely that blacks would be chosen for jury service.[119] It continued the requirement that the commissioners select "upright and intelligent persons" to serve as jurors, and placed the selection process in the hands of the county ordinary, the clerk of the superior court, and three commissioners appointed by the judge of the superior court. These county officials were invariably white. According to Mildred Thompson, "[s]ince county officers were mostly Democrats . . . they did not put the names of negroes in the jury box, not classing them as 'upright and intelligent persons.'"[120]

The act also required that the names of jurors be drawn from tax returns, rather than from voter registration lists as previously provided for in General Pope's order. Blacks were underrepresented on property tax lists to a much greater extent than on registration lists.

Few, if any, blacks actually served on county grand juries.[121] In June 1870, General Terry wrote to General William T. Sherman that "[t]here is no distinction of color authorized by law, but in practice until now the name of no negro had been put in the box." As a result, in cases between blacks and whites "Sambo generally goes to the wall."[122] Governor Smith expressed the prevailing view of white Democrats on the place of blacks on juries in a May 8, 1872, letter to Colonel John Rutherford of Macon. "When I shall have acted in that matter [of judgeships in your circuit]," he said, "*the white folks will have no cause of complaint against me. I do not fancy 'nigger juries'.*"[123]

The 1872 education act was amended in August of the same year.[124] The amendments carried forward the grand jury method of selecting freeholders to serve on school boards and continued to require the operation of racially segregated schools. However, whereas both the 1870 and the January 1872 education acts had provided that school officials "shall provide the same

---

[117] Art. V, Sec. 13, para. 2.
[118] Drago, *Black Politicians*, 40–1.
[119] Ga. Laws 1869, p. 139.
[120] Thompson, *Reconstruction in Georgia*, 354.
[121] Ibid.
[122] Alfred H. Terry to William T. Sherman, June 20, 1870, quoted in Drago, *Black Politicians*, 95–6.
[123] Papers of Governor James M. Smith, Georgia Department of Archives and History, Atlanta (emphasis in original).
[124] Ga. Laws 1872, p. 64.

facilities for each [race]," the August act provided only that separate but equal facilities be provided "as far as practicable."[125]

Despite the various disfranchising measures undertaken by the legislature and the effectiveness of intimidation and violence in restoring Democratic control, Reconstruction was vivid in the memory of whites, and they continued to feel deeply threatened by the possibility of resurgent black political power, particularly black officeholding. H. M. Branch of Savannah wrote to Governor Smith in July 1872 requesting that the officers of the Savannah Cadets be given their commissions as soon as possible so that they could act as an official arm of the state "in case of trouble with the blacks" at the ensuing elections scheduled for October. William Stevens wrote to the governor at the same time requesting assistance in the formation of a troop in Liberty County because of an attempt "by the colored population to organize . . . giving them a preponderance in strength over the white population." In a similar vein, W. T. Cannon of Wilkinson County wrote to the governor inquiring about the organization of a white militia unit in the county and warned that "ignorant blacks" were "organizing . . . for an electioneering scheme."[126]

The elections in 1872 were characterized by widespread fraud and violence. According to one contemporaneous account, in Macon "the colored men were driven away from the polls by pistol-shots and brickbats, two of their number being murdered outright, and others severely wounded." In Dougherty County more than 1,000 Republican votes were "polled," but only 300 were "returned" by the Democratic poll managers. Burke County, which had a Republican majority of 1,500, had "been Ku-Kluxed into showing a Democratic majority of 800." The roads were patrolled by Democratic "sabre clubs" in order to intimidate blacks, and the poll tax was rigorously and selectively enforced by Democratic election officials.[127]

Only four blacks were elected to the house, and none to the senate, in 1872.[128] Tunis Campbell polled the highest number of votes for the second district senate seat. However, Liberty County election officials, in a transparent subterfuge, voided the returns from two precincts because in one the polls had remained open past the six o'clock closing time, and in the other the election managers had signed themselves as "JP" and "FH," rather than Justice of the Peace and Freeholder. Throwing out these two precincts gave the election to Campbell's white opponent, H. W. Mattox. Campbell filed an election protest, but the senate rejected it by a vote of 37 to 2.[129] Although Campbell had filed his protest promptly after the

---

[125] Ga. Laws 1870, p. 57; Ga. Laws 1872, p. 281; Ga. Laws 1872, p. 69.

[126] Papers of Governor James M. Smith.

[127] *Harpers Weekly*, October 19, 1872.

[128] Wardlaw, *Negro Suffrage*, 33.

[129] Georgia Senate Journal, Jan. 22, 1874, p. 67.

H. G. "LET US CLASP HANDS OVER THE BLOODY CHASM."—[SEE PAGE 805.]
"A Great Victory has been won in Georgia..... The verdict in Georgia is certainly conclusive."—*New York Tribune*, October 2, 1872.

By 1872, the legislative and executive branches of state government in Georgia were once again firmly in the control of white Democrats, who resorted to a variety of tactics, including fraud, intimidation, and violence, to take away the vote from blacks, despite ratification of the Fifteenth Amendment in 1870 guaranteeing the right to vote without regard to "race, color, or previous condition of servitude" (illustration from *Harper's Weekly*).

election, the senate dismissed it "on the ground that no legal notice of contest was given by said Campbell to said Mattox of his intention to contest the election."[130]

In 1873, the general assembly increased the residency requirement for voters in the state from six months to one year, and in the county from thirty days to six months, in order to take advantage of the supposed itinerant habits of blacks and deprive them of the vote.[131] Aside from these ostensibly "legal" methods of limiting the black vote, when the need arose political operatives resorted to the old stratagems of intimidation, violence, vote buying, stealing ballot boxes, fraud, and the use of "tissue ballots," which facilitated stuffing ballot boxes and altering the results of elections.[132]

In the 1874 elections, only three blacks were elected to the house and none to the senate.[133] Tunis Campbell, no doubt fearing a repeat of election fraud in Liberty County, ran for a house seat in McIntosh County in the 1874

---

[130] Ibid.; Duncan, *Freedom's Shore*, 95–6.
[131] Ga. Laws 1873, p. 25; Wardlaw, *Negro Suffrage*, 25.
[132] Wardlaw, *Negro Suffrage*, 46.
[133] Ibid., p. 38.

election and won a majority of the votes in a three-way contest. One of his white opponents, A. S. Barnwell, contested the election, and the house duly set it aside, declaring Barnwell the winner.[134] The house held that one of the election managers in the Darien precinct was not a freeholder as required by law, and that as a result all the votes cast in that precinct were invalid. Throwing out the Darien votes gave the election and the house seat to Barnwell.[135] The ruses used to deny Campbell a seat in the house, and earlier in the senate, were hardly plausible, but the white majority felt under no obligation to deal fairly with Campbell or any other black elected official.

Exclusion from the legislature was not the last or least of Campbell's troubles. In 1875, he was indicted on charges of malpractice in office as a justice of the peace for imprisoning a white man named Isaac Rafe for contempt of court. Campbell was convicted, removed from office, and sentenced to a year at hard labor in the penitentiary.[136] He served nearly a year in jail pending various appeals, and then, at the age of sixty-three, was leased for a year as a convict laborer under the state's convict-lease law. After the expiration of his lease in January 1877, Campbell left the state for Washington, D.C. "Georgia," he fumed later, was "the Empire State of Rascality." "[T]he colored people of Georgia," he said, "were . . . in the hands of their enemies, to do with them as they choose . . . they have no protection whatever."[137]

Campbell's experience in Georgia was not unique. From 1867 to 1872, at least a quarter of the state's black legislators were jailed, threatened, bribed, beaten, or killed.[138]

The state adopted a new Constitution in 1877. The leader of the constitutional convention was Robert Toombs, a native of Wilkes County, who had served as secretary of state of the Confederacy and later as a general in the Army of Northern Virginia. After the Civil War, Toombs refused to swear allegiance to the United States government and never regained his United States citizenship. He derided the Constitution of 1868 as the product of "negroes and thieves"[139] and pledged: "Give us a convention,

---

[134] Georgia House Journal, Feb. 9–10, 1875, pp. 291–92, 318.

[135] Bartley, *Creation of Modern Georgia*, 70; Duncan, *Freedom's Shore*, 103.

[136] Drago, *Black Politicians*, 100–1. Campbell had previously been convicted in 1872 of imprisoning another white man, John M. Fisher, but the conviction was overturned by the state supreme court on the grounds that the trial judge had improperly charged the jury that malice was presumed if the defendant acted illegally, and that the jury had been improperly selected. The judge had dismissed "eight colored men and two white men, who could not read and write according to the views of the court," and their replacements had been improperly selected by the sheriff, rather than by the jury commissioners. *Campbell v. State of Georgia*, 48 Ga. 354, 356 (1873).

[137] Duncan, *Freedom's Shore*, 109.

[138] Drago, *Black Politicians*, 146, Appendix.

[139] Speech to the legislature, January 1876, quoted in Ware, *Constitutional History of Georgia*, 159.

Portrait of Robert Toombs, a native of Wilkes County, secretary of state of the Confederacy and later a general in the army of Northern Virginia. After the Civil War, Toombs refused to swear allegiance to the United States government and denounced Georgia's Reconstruction-era Constitution of 1868 as the product of "negroes and thieves." "Give us a convention," he pledged, "and I will fix it so that the people shall rule and the Negro shall never be heard from." Toombs was a leader of the constitutional convention of 1877, which adopted a cumulative poll tax for voting, one of the most effective measures for disfranchising poor blacks (photo courtesy of the Atlanta History Center).

and I will fix it so that the people shall rule and the Negro shall never be heard from."[140]

The convention incorporated the new statutory residency requirements and added larceny to the list of disfranchising offenses that blacks were thought more likely to commit than whites.[141] It also adopted a requirement

---

[140] *Atlanta Constitution*, Jan. 26, 1876, quoted in Kousser, *Shaping of Southern Politics*, 209.

[141] Constitution of Georgia of 1877, Art. II, Sec. 2, para. 1; Wardlaw, *Negro Suffrage*, 45 (1932). Disfranchisement for conviction of offenses was used in other southern states to deny blacks the vote. Typically, theft and various domestic offenses that blacks were thought likely to commit were included, while crimes of violence that whites were thought more likely to commit were excluded. In *Hunter v. Underwood*, 471 U.S. 222 (1985), the Court held that Alabama's petty crimes disfranchising statute was unconstitutional because the offenses had been chosen in an effort to disfranchise blacks. David D. Wallace, a leading South Carolina historian who had attended that state's 1895 convention at which a disfranchising

that all taxes incurred since the adoption of the Constitution be paid as a condition for voting.[142] Since the taxes could accumulate indefinitely, the requirement was an extremely effective bar to Negro suffrage.[143]

IV

While the state moved to secure white supremacy, a countervailing tendency was the Populist revolt of the early 1890s, led in Georgia by the firebrand Tom Watson. Watson, from rural McDuffie County, was elected to the Georgia house in 1882 and to Congress in 1890 as a Democrat, but left the party to run for Congress as a Populist in 1892. The Populists were composed of the agrarian masses, including small and large landowners, tenant farmers, and an emerging blue-collar proletariat. They called for a united front of black and white farmers to oppose the oppressive forces of capitalist finance and industrialism.[144] The Populists were never advocates of social equality between the races, but their platform repudiated race hatred and lynch law and promoted a program of mutual self-interest that would be "immensely beneficial to both races and injurious to neither." Watson spoke before integrated audiences and shared platforms with blacks, some of whom were active in his campaign. One of them, Rev. W. H. Doyle, reportedly gave sixty-three speeches on Watson's behalf.[145]

The reaction of white Democrats to the Populist insurgence was predictable. They accused the Populists of plotting a return to Negro rule and proclaimed the absolute necessity of maintaining white dominion. The *Atlanta Constitution* warned that "[t]he old issue of sectionalism is confronting the South" and that white supremacy was more important than "all the financial reform in the world."[146] In the 1892 election, the Democrats resorted to the time-honored techniques of multiple voting, fraud, and intimidation and brought about Watson's defeat.[147]

Watson ran for Congress as a Populist in 1894 and was defeated once again. With the defeat of the Populist candidate for president, William

statute had been adopted, similarly acknowledged the "black squint" of the disfranchising law. David D. Wallace, *South Carolina Constitution of 1895* (Columbia: University of South Carolina Press, 1927), 35.

[142] Constitution of Georgia of 1877, Art. II, Sec. 1, para. 2.

[143] Alfred Holt Stone, *Studies in the American Race Problem* (New York: Doubleday, Page, 1908), 355; Kousser, *Shaping of Southern Politics*, 210.

[144] Bartley, *Creation of Modern Georgia*, 90–1; Kousser, *Shaping of Southern Politics*, 216.

[145] Gerald H. Gaither, *Blacks and the Populist Revolt: Ballots and Bigotry in the "New South"* (University, Ala.: University of Alabama Press, 1977), 96.

[146] *Atlanta Constitution*, July 15, 1892, quoted in C. Vann Woodward, *Tom Watson: Agrarian Rebel* (Savannah, Ga.: Beehive Press, 1973), 192.

[147] Woodward, *Tom Watson*, 208; John D. Dittmer, *Black Georgia in the Progressive Era 1900–1920* (Urbana: University of Illinois Press, 1977), 6.

Jennings Bryan, in 1896, the fortunes of the party rapidly declined in Georgia as well as nationally.

Populism failed in Georgia because whites became convinced that white supremacy was the paramount goal, and that the achievement of that goal depended upon the unity of whites within the Democratic Party. The glimmer of racial accommodation in the Populists' plea for economic fairness and their repudiation of lynch law was snuffed out by the demagogic and destructive use of the race issue by state and local politicians.[148]

Although relatively few blacks registered to vote, they were still a very substantial proportion of the population of Georgia (47 percent) in 1890.[149] In that year, in an effort to remove the temptation to appeal to the potential black vote, the legislature passed a law giving party officials the exclusive power to regulate and conduct primary elections.[150] This allowed parties to enact formal rules excluding blacks, which local Democratic Parties in cities with large concentrations of black population proceeded to do: Atlanta in 1892, Augusta in 1900, Macon in 1901, and Savannah in 1904.[151] The state Democratic Party also adopted rules in 1900 limiting voting in all state primaries to whites.[152] Since victory in the Democratic primary was tantamount to election, exclusion from the primary effectively eliminated blacks from meaningful participation in Georgia politics.

Aside from securing white supremacy, disfranchisement was frequently justified as benefitting the Negro. A Sumter County historian writing in 1894 concluded that as a consequence of their removal from politics, "a more orderly, law-abiding, peaceful, contented and happy race than the Georgia negroes has never been seen on earth."[153]

In an ongoing effort to draw racial distinctions with ever-increasing rigidity, the legislature passed laws in 1891 requiring all railroads doing business in the state to provide Jim Crow, or segregated, cars for white and colored passengers. Violations were a misdemeanor. Streetcar conductors were also

---

[148] Sheldon Hackney, Introduction to Gaither, *Blacks and the Populist Revolt*, xvi; Dittmer, *Black Georgia*, 6.

[149] Department of Commerce, Bureau of the Census, *Thirteenth Census of the United States Taken in the Year 1910*, Population–Georgia, Table 1, p. 367.

[150] Ga. Laws 1890, p. 210.

[151] Dittmer, *Black Georgia*, 94.

[152] Lynwood Holland, *The Direct Primary in Georgia* (Urbana: University of Illinois Press, 1949), 50, 54; Dewey W. Grantham, Jr., "Georgia Politics and the Disfranchisement of the Negro," 32 Ga. Historical Quarterly 1–21 (1948). For a discussion of the adoption of the white primary system in other southern states, see Paul Lewinson, *Race, Class and Party* (New York: Russell and Russell, 1963), Appendix 3; Key, *Southern Politics*, 620; Kousser, *Shaping of Southern Politics*, 73–80.

[153] "The New South: Southwestern Georgia, Americus, Sumter County" (Americus: Times-Recorder, 1894), 18.

required to separate white and colored passengers "as much as practicable," and were given police power to enforce segregation.[154]

In 1894, the legislature passed yet additional disfranchising measures, including a law that required registration by race and proof of payment of "taxes due."[155] Given the climate of the times, this law merely facilitated fraud and discrimination against blacks.[156]

The decade of the 1890s saw an extraordinary number of lynchings (132) in Georgia, the justifications for which were frequently cast in the most explicit and odious of racial terms. Lynching was seen, even by those who were opposed to it, as an outgrowth of "a natural race antipathy," the causes for which were evident:

The color of the negro's skin, his kinky hair, and his general physiognomy, especially his flat nose and protruding lips with receding (actual or apparent) forehead, – all are widely diverse from the white man's standard of beauty and symmetry. Measured by the Caucasian ideal the features of the negro are coarse and animal-like.

There was also the issue of the supposed smell of black people. "To most white persons . . . the odor arising from an assemblage of negroes is extremely disagreeable." Given the innate differences between blacks and whites, "it is most natural and indeed almost inevitable that prejudice should arise between them."[157]

Lynching was most frequently defended on the grounds that it was necessary to punish and deter the crime of rape by black men against white women. There was in the South, according to one commentator, a "thoroughly lewd and vicious" population of blacks. "Among the Southern people," he said, "the conviction is general that terror is the only restraining influence that can be brought to bear upon vicious negroes."[158]

Tom Watson himself eventually turned to virulent racism and anti-Semitism and became a strong supporter of lynch law. "In the South," he said, "we have to lynch him [the Negro] occasionally, and flog him, now and then, to keep him from blaspheming the Almighty, by his conduct, on account of his smell and color. . . . *Lynch law is a good sign: it shows that a sense of justice yet lives among the people.*"[159] When he ran for president on the Populist ticket in 1904, Watson's platform included "White Supremacy and the principle of Home Rule."[160] Six years later, Watson declared that "[t]he hour has struck for the south to say that the fifteenth amendment is not

---

[154] Ga. Laws 1891, p. 157.
[155] Ga. Laws 1894, pp. 115, 117.
[156] Wardlaw, *Negro Suffrage*, 52.
[157] James Elbert Cutler, *Lynch-Law: An Investigation into the History of Lynching in the United States* (Montclair, N.J.: Patterson Smith, 1969), 200, 202.
[158] Ibid., p. 274.
[159] Quoted in Woodward, *Tom Watson*, 374 (emphasis in original).
[160] Bartley, *Creation of Modern Georgia*, 152.

law, and will no longer be respected." He admonished the state legislature to "propose an amendment to our state constitution restricting suffrage to the whites."[161] A local McDuffie County historian explained that "Watson, like virtually every other liberal and reformer in the South, had by this time concluded that the only hope for reform candidates being elected was to eliminate the Negro from politics, enabling the white majority to have elections without the old abuses of Negro intimidation, vote buying, and repeat voting."[162]

As effective as the prior disfranchising measures had been, the centerpiece of Georgia's efforts to deny the vote to blacks was enacted in 1908. Few blacks were still registered at that time, but the large black presence and the memory of the Populist revolt underscored the need, from the white Democratic perspective, to more thoroughly remove blacks from the political process.[163] Thomas W. Hardwick, a state legislator and a longtime supporter of literacy tests for voter registration, explained that a new law was needed to ensure "that the Negro shall not be left around the corner, awaiting the awakening hand of the corruptionist whenever division shall again break the white ranks and discord lift its threatening hand."[164]

Hoke Smith, in his successful campaign for governor in 1905–6, made the total elimination of blacks from state government a major issue in his campaign.[165] He supported the use of educational qualifications for voting because, he said, "[t]he negro is inferior mentally to the white man. He cannot, as a rule, fit himself by education for the tests put upon him."[166] The *Atlanta Journal*, which was a strong supporter of Smith, ridiculed his opponent, Clark Howell, because he "appears to be unable to understand why it is that we wish the legal disfranchisement of the 223,000 male negroes of voting age in Georgia....Because we are the superior race and do not intend to be ruled by our semi-barbaric inferiors."[167]

Smith made open appeals to the sexual phobias of the state's whites by claiming that disfranchisement was essential to prevent "intermingling" of

---

[161] *Atlanta Constitution*, Sept. 3, 1910.

[162] Tom Watson Brown, "Thomas E. Watson," in Pearl Baker, ed., *A Handbook of History: McDuffie County, Georgia, 1870–1970* (Progress-News Publishing, n.d. [1971?]), 202.

[163] In 1900, blacks were still 47 percent of the population. By 1910, the proportion had dropped only slightly to 45 percent. *Thirteenth Census of the United States Taken in the Year 1910*, Table 1, p. 367.

[164] *Atlanta Constitution*, Sept. 5, 1906, quoted in Kousser, *Shaping of Southern Politics*, 221. An earlier attempt by Hardwick to enact a disfranchisement law in 1899 had been defeated, in large measure because most whites felt the law was unnecessary. Dittmer, *Black Georgia*, 96.

[165] A. J. McKelway, "The Suffrage in Georgia," 87 The Outlook 63, 64 (1907); Grantham, "Georgia Politics," 7.

[166] *Atlanta Journal*, Jan. 10, 1906.

[167] Quoted in Gary M. Pomerantz, *Where Peachtree Meets Sweet Auburn* (New York: Scribner, 1996), 73.

the races. "Already," he told a spellbound crowd in Cherokee County, "some of the alleged prominent negroes were advocating a new race by the mixing of the whites and blacks." The best way to stamp out such notions, he said, was to take the ballot out of the hands of the black man.[168]

The racial atmosphere in Georgia was so poisoned at the time that one of the bloodiest race riots in the state's history broke out in Atlanta in September 1906, a month after Smith won the Democratic primary. Several whites and some two dozen blacks were killed, with hundreds more injured.[169]

Following his election, and as he had promised, Smith led the effort to pass a new disfranchising law. Without disguising his motives or purposes, in his message to the legislature he labeled the proposed bill the "Disfranchising Act."[170]

The new law provided for registration by any male who was sane, had no criminal record, had paid all taxes since 1877, had met the existing residency requirements, and had satisfied one of the following additional requirements: (1) had served honorably in wars of the United States or in the forces of the Confederate States, (2) had descended from persons who had such service records, (3) was of "good character" and could understand the duties of citizenship, (4) could read and write in English any paragraph of the state and federal constitutions or could understand and give a reasonable interpretation of any paragraph of such constitutions, or (5) owned at least forty acres of land or property assessed for taxation at a value of $500.[171]

Few blacks could meet any of these requirements. They had not fought in wars in significant numbers, and neither had their ancestors. The good character, literacy, and understanding tests, aside from the fact that they were designed to exclude uneducated blacks, were administered by white Democrats who made sure that blacks did in fact fail. The qualification through the ownership of property, given the disadvantaged economic position of blacks in the South, was for them an illusion. In *South Carolina v. Katzenbach*, the Supreme Court acknowledged that the 1908 Georgia scheme was "specifically designed to prevent Negroes from voting."[172]

William H. Rogers, from McIntosh County, was the sole black left in the general assembly by 1908. He opposed the Disfranchising Act and, after it was passed, resigned from office.[173] No black would serve in the legislature

---

[168] *Atlanta Journal*, Aug. 20, 1905.
[169] Pomerantz, *Peachtree*, 75.
[170] Georgia House Journal, June 24, 1908, p. 11.
[171] Ga. Laws 1908, p. 27. Georgia was actually the last of the southern states to adopt a literacy test for voting. Mississippi had been the first in 1890, followed by South Carolina in 1895, Louisiana in 1898, North Carolina in 1900, Alabama in 1901, and Virginia in 1902. Kousser, *Shaping of Southern Politics*, 57, 239; Key, *Southern Politics*, 557–58.
[172] 383 U.S. 301, 310–11 (1966).
[173] Bartley, *Creation of Modern Georgia*, 149.

until Leroy Johnson was elected to the senate from Fulton County almost a half-century later.

Once the new constitutional provisions were approved by the voters, Thomas Hardwick, by then a member of Congress, noted with great gratification that

Georgia has taken out a splendid insurance policy for the future by eliminating, as far as possible under federal limitations, the negro vote as the balance or power, or even a possible factor in the political battles of the future. Whatever divisions are yet to come, whatever issues are yet to be met, we will be able to meet them and settle them on a white basis.[174]

The *Atlanta Journal* crowed that "Georgia takes her place among the enlightened and progressive states which have announced that the white man is to rule. She has declared in clear and specific terms for Anglo-Saxon supremacy and for the integrity of the ballot."[175] Three days later, still relishing the white triumph, the paper expressed a deep sense of relief that "[w]e are relieved from the body of this death, which has hung about our necks ever since the adoption of the Fourteenth and Fifteenth Amendments. This is the white man's Georgia from now on."[176]

Five years after the act, disfranchisement was intensified by a system of permanent registration requiring all voters to submit to examination by a board of registrars.[177] Since the boards were composed of whites who were hostile to black voting, many blacks were denied registration or were discouraged from even attempting it.[178]

V

Although Georgia was the principal architect of black disfranchisement in the state, Congress and the U.S. Supreme Court were its willing partners. In a series of acts and decisions, they seriously weakened civil rights enforcement and created a legal environment in which discrimination could flourish.

In *The Slaughter-House Cases* (1873),[179] the Court interpreted the Fourteenth Amendment for the first time and gave it an exceedingly narrow construction. The case involved, not blacks, but butchers who claimed that the grant of a monopoly by the Louisiana legislature to a New Orleans slaughterhouse denied them property rights protected by the "privileges or immunities of citizens" clause of the Fourteenth Amendment. In ruling against the butchers, the Court held that the "privileges and immunities"

---

[174] *Atlanta Journal*, Oct. 8, 1908.
[175] Ibid.
[176] *Atlanta Journal*, Oct. 11, 1908.
[177] Ga. Laws 1913, p. 115.
[178] Wardlaw, *Negro Suffrage*, 67–8.
[179] 83 U.S. (16 Wall.) 36 (1873).

clause protected federal, not state, rights of citizenship, and that federal rights of citizenship included only such things as travel upon the high seas, governmental protection in a foreign country, and the availability of the writ of habeas corpus. Virtually all other rights, that is, "nearly every civil right for the establishment and protection of which organized government is instituted," including the property rights of the butchers, were incident to state citizenship and therefore were not protected by the Fourteenth Amendment.[180] The definition and protection of civil rights were left to the states, which had little or no interest in defining and protecting the rights of blacks.

Two years later, in *United States v. Cruikshank*[181] and *United States v. Reese*,[182] the Court restricted the scope of, or held unconstitutional, federal statutes designed to prevent discrimination in voting on account of race and expressly held that the right to vote was a state-created, not a federal, right. According to the Court, the "right of suffrage is not a necessary attribute of national citizenship" protected by the Constitution or the postwar amendments.[183] The effect of the decisions was to leave black voting rights essentially at the mercy of the white majority.

Reconstruction effectively ended with the Hayes-Tilden Compromise of 1877. Southern Democrats agreed to support the Republican, Rutherford B. Hayes, in the contested 1876 presidential election by awarding him the disputed votes of three southern states, with the understanding that thereafter federal troops would be withdrawn from the South.[184] The compromise was a clear indication that the nation had grown weary of sectional strife, and that it had determined to let southern whites resolve the vexing issue of race as they saw fit.

The low point in Supreme Court decision making in the area of minority voting rights was plumbed in *Williams v. Mississippi*[185] and *Giles v. Harris*,[186] in which the Court upheld the constitutionality of literacy tests and poll taxes,

[180] 83 U.S. at 76.
[181] 92 U.S. 542 (1875).
[182] 92 U.S. 214 (1875).
[183] 92 U.S. at 555. In other decisions, the Court held unconstitutional several laws enacted by Congress to enforce the Fourteenth and Fifteenth Amendments, for example, *James v. Bowman*, 190 U.S. 127 (1903) (invalidating section 5 of the First Enforcement Act of May 31, 1879, prohibiting bribery to prevent persons from voting); *United States v. Harris*, 106 U.S. 629 (1883) (invalidating section 2 of the Third Enforcement Act of April 20, 1871, prohibiting conspiracies to deprive citizens of equal protection of the law). There were, however, a few exceptions, such as *Ex parte Yarbrough*, 100 U.S. 651 (1884), which held constitutional a federal law prohibiting conspiracies to deny blacks the right to vote through the use of force and violence.
[184] See generally C. Vann Woodward, *Reunion and Reaction: The Compromise of 1877 and the End of Reconstruction* (Boston: Little, Brown, 1966).
[185] 170 U.S. 213 (1898).
[186] 189 U.S. 475 (1903).

as well as the outright refusal of state officials to register black voters. In *Williams v. Mississippi*, the Court, despite acknowledging that the purpose of the laws was "to disfranchise citizens of the colored race," held that the poll tax and literacy test merely took advantage of "the alleged characteristics of the negro race" and were therefore not unconstitutional.[187] Five years later, in *Giles v. Harris*, the Court dismissed a petition that alleged that 5,000 blacks in Montgomery County, Alabama, had been denied registration solely because of their race in violation of the Fourteenth Amendment. The author of the opinion, Justice Oliver Wendell Holmes, wrote:

Unless we are prepared to supervise the voting in that state by officers of the court, it seems to us that all the plaintiff could get from equity would be an empty form. Apart from damages to the individual, relief from a great political wrong, if done, as alleged, by the people of a state and the state itself, must be given by them or by the legislative and political department of the United States.[188]

Giles v. Harris revealed the extent to which the Court had simply abandoned the cause of equal voting rights for blacks.

Civil rights enforcement was further blunted by Congress in 1894, when it repealed all but seven of the forty-nine sections of the enforcement acts at a single stroke.[189] Civil rights and suffrage laws were weakened even further when the federal criminal code was adopted in 1909.

The *Nation* reported in 1908 that Georgia had "closed the door of political hope in the faces of one million of its citizens."[190] A commentator writing more than twenty years later noted that following passage of the Disfranchisement Act, there was "almost absolute exclusion of the Negro voice in state and federal elections."[191]

Two local historians from McDuffie County, writing under the sponsorship of the Ida Evans Eve Chapter of the United Daughters of Confederacy, expressed the prevailing white view that "[t]he negro gained nothing by his adventure in politics; he did not have the stability nor reasoning power to really give to politics any thing worth while and was only the tool in the hands of others. Finally by constitutional amendments the negro vote was reduced until it ceased to be a menace."[192]

---

[187] 170 U.S. at 222.
[188] 189 U.S. at 488.
[189] 28 Stat. 36 (1894).
[190] "The Georgia Disfranchisement," *Nation*, August 8, 1908, 113–14.
[191] Wardlaw, *Negro Suffrage*, 69.
[192] Mrs. W. C. McCommons and Miss Clara Stovall, *History of McDuffie County, Georgia (1870–1933)* (Tignall, Ga.: Boyd Publishing, 1933), 239.

3

The Dawning of a New Day: Abolition
of the White Primary

I

The state's restrictive registration procedures continued to exclude most blacks from voting well into the twentieth century. Some blacks, of course, were able to meet one or more of the requirements for registration. Some owned property. Some had served in the armed forces. Many could read and write. Despite that, black registration in the rural areas remained negligible, and even in the cities of Atlanta, Augusta, Macon, and Savannah, which had substantial black populations, during the years from 1920 to 1930 the combined total black vote never exceeded 2,700. [1]

Most blacks who were active politically in Georgia remained faithful to the Republican Party, the party of Lincoln and the party of reform during the Reconstruction years. They were frequent delegates to Republican national conventions, and some held important federal patronage positions, most notably John H. Deveaux, who was appointed collector of customs in Savannah; Henry L. Rucker, who served as collector of internal revenue in Atlanta; and Judson Lyons, who became register of the United States Treasury. All three eventually fell from power within the first decade of the new century. Lyons was not reappointed to his post as register. Deveaux died in 1909, and Rucker was replaced in the following year by a white man.[2]

The votes of blacks in the Republican primaries and in the general elections were in any event essentially meaningless. Since victory in the white

---

[1] Paul Lewinson, *Race, Class and Party: A History of Negro Suffrage and White Politics in the South* (New York: Russell and Russell, 1963), 218. Morgan Kousser notes that in Bibb County, of which Macon is the county seat, "[i]n 1920, 30.5 percent of the registered voters ... were black, ... though this number had dwindled to 9.3 percent in 1944." J. Morgan Kousser, *Colorblind Injustice: Minority Voting Rights and the Undoing of the Second Reconstruction* (Chapel Hill: University of North Carolina Press, 1999), 213.

[2] John Dittmer, *Black Georgia in the Progressive Era 1900–1920*, (Urbana: University of Illinois Press, 1977), 91, 94.

Democratic primary was tantamount to election in Georgia, the votes cast
by blacks were mainly symbolic.

The state's registration laws, even when administered as they were written,
were designed to have, and had, the effect of depressing black voter registration. But the laws were not always administered as they were written, and
in some cases they were not administered to blacks at all.

John Cross, the owner of a small taxicab company in Moultrie, and several
other blacks first tried to register to vote in Colquitt County in the early
1940s, but were simply turned away. On one occasion, Cross said, "they told
three of us that it was too late in the day. You know, it was about four o'clock
and they just closed the window." On another occasion, "they told us...we
had to pay poll tax....I was unable to pay."[3] In tiny Webster County, a
remote rural county south of Columbus, blacks who tried to register were
turned away by courthouse officials who told them bluntly that "it wasn't
time" for black people to vote.[4]

In Terrell County, registration was segregated, with white applicants filling
out white forms and black applicants filling out green forms. Local officials
accepted registration applications from blacks but generally refused to process them. As a federal district court later concluded, "this distinction in
processing applications of whites and Negroes was based upon the race and
color of the respective applicants."[5]

When the applications of blacks *were* processed in Terrell County, the literacy test was administered in a racially selective manner, and blacks were held
to a higher standard of literacy than whites. One black applicant, Eddie G.
Lowe, was perfectly capable of reading and writing the Constitution, but the
registrar dictated at such speed that it was impossible for Lowe to write down
what was being said. As the district court found, Lowe was denied registration not because he couldn't read and write, "but actually upon his race and
color." Blacks were also tested individually; whites, if they were tested at all,
were tested in a group. Several black schoolteachers were denied registration
as being illiterate. No white was ever denied registration by reason of failure
to pass the literacy test. Although Terrell County was 64 percent black, only
48 blacks – compared to 2,810 whites – were registered to vote in 1958.[6] As
late as 1964, only 2.4 percent of age-eligible blacks were registered.[7]

Baker County was majority-black, but no blacks were allowed to register
or vote there. According to one local official, if anyone had suggested that

---

[3] *Cross v. Baxter*, Civ. No. 76-20 (M. D. Ga.), trial transcript, pp. 30, 59 (testimony of John
Cross).

[4] Author's interview with Rev. George Neely, June 18, 1999 (interview notes on file with
author).

[5] *United States v. Raines*, 189 F. Supp. 125, 126 (M. D. Ga. 1960).

[6] Ibid., pp. 125, 127, 129–30, 132.

[7] U.S. Commission on Civil Rights, *Political Participation* (Washington, D.C.: Government Printing Office, 1968), 236.

blacks should be allowed to vote, "why people here would have laughed in your face."[8]

When the need arose, whites also resorted to the old tactics of intimidation and threats of violence to discourage the black vote. Willie Simpson, a longtime black resident of Harris County, recalled that blacks first attempted to vote after Franklin Roosevelt was elected president in 1933. Roosevelt had a retreat in the county at Pine Mountain, and a few blacks, encouraged by this federal presence, went to the polls to vote. Just prior to the next two elections, said Simpson, "they dug some graves there by the courthouse ... some short graves and burned some crosses at the crossroads."[9] Though blacks were about half the population in Harris County, as of 1964 only 8.5 percent of blacks were registered.[10]

Between 1889 and 1930, there were more than 450 lynchings reported in Georgia, an average of nearly one every month.[11] Lynchings were a cathartic release for the racial fears and anger of whites, but they were also intended to terrorize the larger black community.

John Cross vividly recalled the lynching of a black man named John Henry Williams in Colquitt County in 1921 for the alleged murder of a white girl. He "was tied to a tree about three feet off the ground and a fire built under him," Cross said. "They castrated him and put his genitals in his mouth, and then showed a picture of the charred corpse in the black community as a warning."[12]

A year later, another black in Colquitt County was charged with an attempted criminal attack on a white woman. He was seized by a mob, handcuffed, shot, and dragged behind an automobile. A grand jury was convened the next day to investigate the lynching, but adjourned after a few hours without issuing any indictments. The *Moultrie Observer* reported that the lynching was a small affair, presumably because the corpse had not been mutilated:

It was pointed out that he was not swung from a tree and that he was shot less than twenty-five times, most of the bullets penetrating the chest and head. It was hardly believed that this would have been the way the body would have been found if the crowd that participated had been of the proportion mobs usually assume on such occasions.[13]

The graves and burned crosses reported by Willie Simpson when blacks attempted to vote in Harris County in 1933 were far from a bluff or a

[8] *Atlanta Constitution*, July 30, 1963.
[9] *Brown v. Reames*, Civ. No. 75-80-COL (M. D. Ga.), trial transcript, pp. 115, 118 (testimony of Willie Simpson).
[10] U.S. Commission on Civil Rights, *Political Participation*, 234.
[11] Numan V. Bartley, *The Creation of Modern Georgia* (Athens: University of Georgia Press, 1983), 139.
[12] Author's interview with John Cross, 1975.
[13] *Moultrie Observer*, July 28, 1922.

harmless comedy designed to frighten a credulous black community. They were clear, unmistakable signals for blacks to stay away from the polls.

II

The first substantial legal challenge to white Democratic control after the redemption period came in 1944, when the Supreme Court held in *Smith v. Allwright* that the exclusion of blacks from voting in the Democratic primary in Texas was unconstitutional.[14] Litigation involving the white primary had a long and complicated history beginning in the 1920s, and reflected the Court's ambivalence about whether the white primary was state action subject to regulation by the Fourteenth and Fifteenth Amendments, or purely private activity beyond their reach.

In a case decided in 1927, the Court held unconstitutional a Texas statute excluding blacks from voting in Democratic party primary elections.[15] In an effort to circumvent the decision, the Texas legislature passed a new statute delegating to the Democratic Party the right to fix qualifications for voting in party elections. A challenge was brought to the statute and to the continued exclusion of blacks from voting in primary elections, and the Court held the scheme unconstitutional on the ground that "[d]elegates of the state's power have discharged their official function in such a way as to discriminate invidiously between white citizens and blacks."[16] In response to this second judicial setback, the Democratic Party in Texas, unaided by the legislature, passed a resolution limiting membership and voting to "all white citizens of the State." And this time, the party's perserverance paid off. The Court held that the action of the party in limiting membership and voting in the primaries to whites was an aspect of private associational rights protected by the constitution.[17]

In *Smith v. Allwright*, however, the Court reversed itself and said that the conduct of primary elections was a "state function" that made the private acts of the party the actions of the state for purposes of the Fourteenth and Fifteenth Amendments.[18] Since Georgia's white Democratic

---

[14] 321 U.S. 649, 666 (1944).

[15] *Nixon v. Herndon*, 273 U.S. 536 (1927).

[16] *Nixon v. Condon*, 286 U.S. 73, 89 (1932).

[17] *Grovey v. Townsend*, 295 U.S. 45, 52 (1935).

[18] 321 U.S. at 660. The white primary was not finally laid to rest in Texas until the decision in *Terry v. Adams*, 345 U.S. 461 (1953). In Fort Bend County, Texas, the Jaybird Association, a private organization whose membership was composed of white Democrats, held an initial primary that was followed by the Democratic Party's primary, upon whose ballot the nominees of the Jaybird Party appeared. With but few exceptions, the Jaybird's candidates won the primary and general elections. The Court held that the Fort Bend scheme was state, not private, action and that it violated the Fifteenth Amendment. Ibid., pp. 469–70: "[T]he effect of the whole procedure, Jaybird primary plus Democratic primary plus general election, is to do precisely that which the Fifteenth Amendment forbids – strip Negroes of every vestige

primary was similar to the primary in Texas, the state's system was plainly vulnerable.

One of the blacks who was registered to vote in Georgia at that time was Primus King, a barber and a minister from Muscogee County. Relying upon *Smith*, King sued the county Democratic executive committee for denying him the right to vote in the party's primary. The county executive committee, with no irony intended or apparently recognized, had held the racially exclusive election on July 4, the date on which the American colonists had declared their independence from Great Britain in 1776, in large measure because the crown had denied them the right to vote on matters that affected their interests. One of the principal grievances against the king was his "absolute Tyranny" in "imposing taxes on us without our Consent."[19] The federal district court, applying *Smith*, took a far more generous view of minority rights than the Muscogee County executive committee and ruled that the Democratic Party had violated Primus King's equal right to vote as protected by the Fourteenth and Fifteenth Amendments. It invalidated the white primary and ordered the defendants to pay King $100 in damages.[20]

The abolition of the white primary set in motion two opposing forces in the state, mobilization in the black community and countermobilization in the white community. In 1940, the estimated black registration in Georgia was just 20,000.[21] After the abolition of the white primary, black voter registration organizations sprang up across the state, including the All-Citizens Registration Committee of Atlanta (ACRC), which has claimed the distinction of being "the oldest continuous political education and registration organization of its kind in the South."[22] It was through the efforts of ACRC and other groups that 125,000 blacks, 18.8 percent of the eligible population, were registered by late 1947.[23]

Two other factors had an impact upon voter registration in the 1940s – lowering the voting age from twenty-one to eighteen in 1943,[24] and abolition of the poll tax in 1945.[25] By the middle of the decade there were simply more people, black and white, eligible to register and vote in the state.

of influence in selecting the officials who control the local county matters that intimately touch the daily lives of citizens."

[19] Declaration of Independence, July 4, 1776.

[20] *King v. Chapman*, 62 F. Supp. 639, 650 (M. D. Ga. 1945), *aff'd sub nom. Chapman v. King*, 154 F. 2d 460 (5th Cir. 1946).

[21] Southern Regional Council, "Forty Years since the End of the White Primary" (Atlanta, 1984); Alexander Heard, *A Two-Party South?* (Chapel Hill: University of North Carolina Press, 1952), 302.

[22] Mary Louise Frick, "Influences on Negro Political Participation in Atlanta, Georgia" (M.A. thesis, Georgia State College, 1967), 44–55.

[23] Southern Regional Council, "Forty Years"; Joseph Bernd and Lynwood Holland, "Recent Restrictions upon Negro Suffrage: The Case of Georgia," 21 J. of Politics 487, 488 (1959).

[24] Ga. Laws 1943, p. 39.

[25] Ga. Laws 1945, p. 129.

The eighteen-year-old voter law was passed at the height of World War II. Supporters of the provision argued that it was only fair to grant the vote to "youth who are driving tanks and manning machine guns on the battlefield."[26] But no matter how strong the purely "good government" arguments were for lowering the voting age, any proposed change in the state's election laws was inevitably scrutinized under, and distorted by, the microscope of race.

Opponents of the bill, such as J. Robert Elliott of Muscogee County, who was later appointed to the federal district court, made open racial appeals in calling for its defeat and linked the proposal to the Communist Party. The "Communist Party and Mrs. Roosevelt are 100 percent behind this proposal," he said, and its passage would "throw open the ballot box to everybody – 18, 19 or 20 – regardless of their color or whether they had paid their poll tax." M. K. Hicks of Rome warned that giving the vote to the young would make Georgia a "hotbed for every subversive influence under the heavens."[27]

Georgia Assistant Attorney General Paul Rodgers, in his testimony to the senate subcommittee in 1965, dismissed the idea that lowering the voting age might be part of a "Communist conspiracy to seize the Black Belt." He did, however, volunteer that the provision had been passed during the administration of Governor Ellis Arnall, and that Arnall "was quite liberal and . . . wanted to inject into the electorate a younger age group in the hope that it would help him politically."[28]

The Georgia poll tax, which had withstood a constitutional challenge in 1937,[29] was also repealed during Arnall's administration.[30] Arnall had initially proposed the formation of a committee to study the continued use of the tax, and had pledged to base his decision about its future of

---

[26] *Atlanta Journal*, March 2, 1943. Proponents of the bill adopted the slogan, "Fight at 18, Vote at 18." V. O. Key, Jr., *Southern Politics in State and Nation* (Knoxville: University of Tennessee Press, 1984), 559 n.5.

[27] *Atlanta Journal*, March 2, 1943.

[28] Hearings before the Committee on the Judiciary, United States Senate, Eight–ninth Congress, First Session, on S. 1564 to enforce the 15th Amendment to the Constitution of the United States, March 23, 24, 25, 29, 30, 31, and April 1, 2, 5, 1965, p. 621.

[29] *Breedlove v. Suttles*, 302 U.S. 277 (1937). The Court displayed its traditional tolerance for southern regulation of the franchise by concluding that "[t]he payment of poll tax as a prerequisite to voting is a familiar and reasonable regulation long enforced in many states and for more than a century in Georgia." Ibid., pp. 283–84. Congress subsequently made numerous attempts to abolish the poll tax. See Janice E. Christensen, "The Constitutionality of National Anti-Poll Tax Bills," 33 Minn. L. Rev. 217 (1949). Not until 1964, however, with ratification of the Twenty-fourth Amendment, did Congress ban the tax in federal elections. Two years later in a case from Virginia, the Supreme Court, reversing its earlier decision, declared use of the poll tax in state elections unconstitutional because "the affluence of the voter or payment of any fee" was not a proper "electoral standard." *Harper v. Virginia State Board of Elections*, 383 U.S. 663, 666 (1966).

[30] Ga. Laws 1945, p. 129.

the committee's findings. However, Eugene Talmadge, a former governor and perennial candidate for office, one whose credentials as a Negrophobe were impeccable, unexpectedly came out in support of abolition. This forced Arnall's hand and prompted him to call for immediate repeal.[31]

One contemporary pundit surmised that Talmadge's support for repeal of the poll tax was pure self-interest politics.

Ole Gene, meanwhile, has come out against the poll tax... but with a political wisdom that is going to pay dividends. It won't be hard for him to make his followers see that the poll tax has nothing to do with Negro voting. Neither should it be hard to make them see that, with Gene among the 'outs' now, a broadening of the franchise is indicated.[32]

Leaders of the general assembly, such as speaker Roy Harris, had indeed assured their colleagues that repeal would increase white voter participation but would not affect the state's white primary.[33] Primus King, of course, proved them wrong.

The poll tax had in any case been selectively applied in Georgia because of its impact upon whites. In Ware County, for example, the board of registrars ruled in 1940 that anyone who paid five dollars could vote, no matter how much tax they owed. As the chair of the board explained, "so many people got behind during the depression – good people... and they couldn't pay up." In another county, local officials simply suspended the tax for white voters.[34]

Despite abolition of the poll tax, the city of Fort Valley continued to enforce a provision of its charter conditioning the right to vote upon payment of "all taxes legally imposed." In April 1970, a week before a scheduled election for city council in which a black, Claybon Edwards, had announced his candidacy, the city purged 192 people from the voters list for failure to pay city ad valorem taxes. Of those purged, 150 were black. Edwards and six of the purged electors immediately filed suit in state court, which issued an injunction allowing the 192 electors to vote on a special machine. Thirty-four votes were cast on the special machine, thirty-one of which were for Edwards, which gave him the margin of victory. The state court then entered an order upholding the provisions of the city charter under which the electors had been purged, and as a result Edwards lost the election for city council by five votes.[35]

Some counties had better records of registering blacks than others. Jacob Henderson, one of the founders of ACRC, said that by the time the

---

[31] Frederick D. Ogden, *The Poll Tax in the South* (University, Ala.: University of Alabama Press, 1958), 186; Key, *Southern Politics*, 116 n.9.

[32] John Temple Graves in the *Birmingham Age-Herald*, January 18, 1945, as quoted in Ogden, *Poll Tax*, 107.

[33] *Atlanta Constitution*, February 1, 1945.

[34] Quoted in Ogden, *Poll Tax*, 107.

[35] *Edwards v. Sammons*, 437 F. 2d 1240, 1241 (5th Cir. 1971).

white primary was abolished, "Fulton County had already more or less come around with not too many obstacles in letting the blacks register."[36] In Fulton County, some 19,000 blacks were added to the voter rolls as a result of the registration drives. In other counties, abolition of the white primary, repeal of the poll tax, and lowering the voting age had little, if any, impact on black registration.

Walter Daniel, a lifelong resident of Putnam County, the home of Joel Chandler Harris and the Uncle Remus Museum, first tried to register to vote in 1946 after he was honorably discharged from the army. "I went to the courthouse to register my discharge and to register to vote in that August primary coming up in 1946," he recalls, but the clerk of court said "they wasn't registering blacks." After that, Daniel gave up on the idea of registering, frankly admitting that "I was afraid to try again." As he explained, "At that time blacks didn't have nothing. We were sharecropping, we lived on halves on plantations. Anything like that come up, if we were told not to do something and did it they would put you out. You would have nowhere to go. So you had to do what they said."[37]

Two years later, showing the arbitrariness of the registration system, Daniel was given permission by a politically influential white dentist in Eatonton to register and was allowed to become a voter. "I was having some dental work at the tooth dentist down there," he recalled,

and I think he was the mayor along at that time, and he charged me $200 to do the work and when I got through I gave him a check and he asked me was I registered to vote and I told him I wasn't. He said any man who could write a $200 check could register to vote. He wrote me a note to carry to the courthouse and I taken it up there and they signed me up.[38]

Eugene Talmadge, a candidate for governor in 1946, responded to the abolition of the white primary by orchestrating challenges to black voters for allegedly being improperly registered and thus ineligible to vote in the primaries. Blacks were challenged en masse in more than 30 counties, and an estimated 15,000 to 25,000 were purged.[39] In Putnam County, for example, approximately 250 blacks were registered. The Talmadge forces challenged every one of them, and a compliant board of registrars issued subpoenas for their appearance.[40]

The applicable state statute required the challengers to "specify the grounds of the challenge."[41] But far from being specific, the

---

[36] Interview with Jacob Henderson, June 8, 1989, p. 12 (Georgia State University Archives).
[37] *Bailey v. Vining*, Civ. No. 76-199 (M. D. Ga.), evidentiary hearing, pp. 184–86 (testimony of Walter Daniel).
[38] Ibid., p. 185.
[39] Key, *Southern Politics*, 570; Bernd and Holland, "Recent Restrictions," 488–89.
[40] *Eatonton Messenger*, July 11, 1946.
[41] Ga. Code of 1933, §34-605.

challenges – forms with blank spaces for the name of the voter and county of residence – alleged a laundry list of disqualifications: that the voter was not a resident, was not eighteen, was not a person of good character, could not read the English language, and so forth.[42] There was no way the Talmadge people could have known the qualifications of the thousands of voters whom they challenged, but that was irrelevant. What they did know was that they were black, and that was enough.

Some of the challenges collapsed under their own weight. John Cross of Moultrie, who finally registered to vote in 1946, said that the Talmadge people challenged every black on the county voter rolls. "I think we had about, at that time … approximately 500 people registered and I would say 90% of them came to the courthouse in response to the challenge notice." There were so many challenged voters, in fact, that it proved impossible to process all of them on election day, and as a result the blacks were allowed to vote.[43]

In majority-black Greene County, the local paper warned that if blacks voted in any appreciable numbers in the primary, "some hooded and secret order such as the Ku Klux Klan will ride again, and all power acquired by the ballot will be lost by terrorism." The paper reasoned that "[i]f California has the right to have a law keeping a Japanese from owning property it seems to us that Georgia can have a white primary."[44]

Cross remembers that black voters were often cajoled or intimidated by white politicians. During a 1950 campaign he was told to go to the headquarters of a white candidate named Fred Alverson.

I walked in to the front and he was sitting in the front and he told me to come in the back and I went on in the back and sat down, and he said … the words he used, "most of the niggers is on our side. We want you to join with us." And I told him no. After that he told me "don't be down there on the polls come election time because if you do, the Ku Klux Klan will visit your house."[45]

In Bleckley County, Representative James M. Dykes publicly announced that forms had been prepared to challenge black voters and "safeguard our Democratic White Primary."[46] County residents, however, were more than willing to resort to extrajudicial measures to ensure that blacks would not vote.

Lewis Carswell, a black World War II veteran, and several other blacks attempted to vote in the 1946 election in Bleckley County at the segregated Thompson Street school but discovered that there were no ballots at the

---

[42] *Bowdry v. Hawes*, Civ. No. 176-128 (S. D. Ga.), Pl. Ex. 76 (challenge to registration of Aline Lee, McDuffie County, July 5, 1946).

[43] *Cross v. Baxter*, Civ. No. 76-20 (M. D. Ga.), trial transcript, pp. 31–2 (testimony of John Cross).

[44] *Harris County Journal*, June 28, 1946 (reprinted from *Greensboro Herald Journal*).

[45] *Cross v. Baxter*, trial transcript, pp. 34–5 (testimony of John Cross).

[46] *Hall v. Holder*, Civ. No. 85-242-2-MAC (M. D. Ga.), Pl. Ex. 33.

precinct. The sheriff told them, "Y'all niggers go around to the back of the Courthouse. We're going to let y'all vote around there." Carswell and the others did as directed but were confronted by a group of twenty to thirty armed whites, who prevented them from entering the polls. The blacks left without voting. Carswell did not try to vote again until the Johnson–Goldwater presidential election in 1964, because he felt "it would've been impossible."[47]

Two years after Carswell attempted to vote, the *Cochran Journal*, in a report on the 1948 election in Bleckley County, said that "[i]t is interesting to not [sic] that there were no Negro votes cast in the entire county. No Negroes appeared to vote and little if any interest was shown by them in the election."[48] The paper did not speculate on the cause of the black voters' supposed lack of interest.

Another response to the invalidation of the white primary was the "slowdown." In Savannah during the 1946 election, several thousand blacks were unable to vote before the polls closed because of the delaying tactics of poll officials and were simply turned away.[49] Similar tactics, with similar results, were used in Augusta during the 1948 elections.[50]

In Spalding County, 558 blacks were purged from the voter lists on the eve of the September 1948 primary election.[51] An upsurge of Klan activity and violence directed at black voters was also reported in both the 1946 and 1948 elections.[52]

Talmadge won the July 1946 election, an event joyfully reported in the *Harris County Journal* as "[c]ompletely vindicating the issue of white supremacy."[53] Talmadge died prior to the inauguration, however, and following conflicting claims to the governorship by Lt. Governor M. E. Thompson and Talmadge's son Herman, who had received several hundred write-in votes, the state supreme court awarded Thompson succession until a special election could be held to fill the vacancy in 1948.[54]

Despite the decision in Primus King's case, the legislature made a last-ditch effort in 1947 to salvage the white primary and evade federal judicial oversight by repealing all the statutes linking the primary to any action by the state.[55] The effect of the bill would have been to allow the Democratic Party

---

[47] *Hall v. Holder*, trial transcript, pp. 255, 257 (testimony of Lewis Carswell).

[48] *Hall v. Holder*, Pl. Ex. 5.

[49] Bernd and Holland, "Recent Restrictions," 501; *Savannah Morning News*, July 18, 1946.

[50] Ibid.; *Augusta Herald*, September 8, 1948.

[51] *Atlanta Journal*, Sept. 8, 1948.

[52] Bernd and Holland, "Recent Restrictions," 502.

[53] *Harris County Journal*, July 19, 1946.

[54] *Thompson v. Talmadge*, 201 Ga. 867 (1947). For the younger Talmadge's version of the events, see Herman E. Talmadge, *Talmadge: A Political Legacy, A Politician's Life* (Atlanta: Peachtree, 1987), 84–95.

[55] Ga. Laws 1947, p. 23.

to operate entirely without state supervision. One of those who supported the measure was Willis Smith, a representative from Carroll County. He said that "Georgia is in trouble with the Negroes unless this bill is passed. This is white man's country and we must keep it that way."[56]

The city of Eatonton, in a similar attempt to blunt the impact of the King decision, had its charter amended by the legislature in 1947, abolishing municipal primary elections.[57] There were no black registered voters in the city at that time.

The statewide white primary bill was vetoed, however, by Governor Thompson. Thompson was not opposed to the white primary, but he questioned the legality of the bill and said it was an invitation to fraud.[58] He proposed that the black vote be contained by more restrictive education requirements, and that the voting process be segregated.[59]

III

When Eugene Talmadge's son Herman was elected governor at the special election held in 1948, the outright exclusion of blacks from the primaries was no longer an option. J. Robert Elliott of Muscogee County was nonetheless confident that "Herman will think up something new to keep the niggers away from the polls, and when the Supreme Court rules that unconstitutional, he'll think of something else, and when the Court rules that out, he'll think of something else again."[60]

To curb the black vote, the legislature resorted to the old strategy of making the registration process more difficult. In 1949, it enacted a registration and purge law.[61] Voters who failed to vote in at least one election during a two-year period were automatically dropped from the rolls, unless they requested a renewal of their registration.

One distinctive feature of the new law was a requirement that all who sought reregistration on the basis of good character and understanding the duties of citizenship take a formal test and successfully answer ten out of thirty questions.[62] Prior to 1949, the determination of whether a registrant had good character and understood the duties of citizenship had been left to the discretion of local registration officials. Under the new test, some, but not all, of the questions were answered in the statute. Even the correct answers to those that were answered necessarily changed over time and thus

---

[56] *Carrollton Branch of NAACP v. Stallings*, 829 F. 2d 1547, 1551 (11th Cir. 1987).

[57] *Bailey v. Vining*, 514 F. Supp, 452, 455 (M. D. Ga. 1981).

[58] *Atlanta Constitution*, March 21, 1947.

[59] Key, *Southern Politics*, 636.

[60] Quoted in Calvin Kytle and James A. Mackay, *Who Runs Georgia?* (Athens: University of Georgia Press, 1998), 62.

[61] Ga. Laws 1949, p. 1204.

[62] Ga. Laws 1949, pp. 1214–17.

became the wrong answers, for example, "Who is Chief Judge of the Court of Appeals of Georgia?" The new test was widely acknowledged by Talmadge and others as designed to curb the Negro vote.[63] The following year, to ease the potential burden the new voter test might place on whites, the Talmadge administration secured passage of a bill allowing those registered under the preexisting statutes to remain on the voter rolls.[64]

As a practical matter, whites were unwilling to submit to literacy examinations or to take understanding tests and were registered as a matter of course. V. O. Key, Jr., was of the view that "if any test of understanding were applied at all to any substantial number of citizens of status, the registrars would be hanged to the nearest lamp post and no grand jury could be found that would return a true bill."[65]

Blacks continued to organize voter registration drives. William Randall and a number of others formed a Voters League in Macon in the early 1950s and launched an aggressive campaign to register black voters. "We would load up buses and cars, and we just flooded the courthouse," said Randall. Because of "the pressure that we exerted, they were not near as hard – they began to relent in Bibb County, and they even dropped the Constitution thing and began to sign up people."[66]

It was a far different story in Bleckley County. Wilson C. Roberson, a black minister, moved to Bleckley County in 1955 to take a teaching job in the segregated public schools in Cochran. He went to the courthouse to register but was immediately hustled outside by the chief of police, who told him that "[n]o niggers register in this courthouse." Roberson complained about the incident to his school superintendent, but the superintendent told him, "Just don't push the issue." The following year someone burned a cross in Roberson's yard. Roberson did not try to register again until 1964. At the time the Voting Rights Act was passed, only forty-five blacks (3 percent of the black voting-age population) were registered to vote in Bleckley County. Even after passage of the act some blacks, according to Roberson, were fearful of registering at the courthouse. Black voter registration did not increase significantly in Bleckley County until 1984, when satellite registration was first allowed.[67]

In majority-black Randolph County, blacks were only 17 percent of registered voters in 1952. Prior to the 1954 elections, the local registrars challenged approximately 525 blacks as being unqualified. Of the 225 who

---

[63] Ogden, *Poll Tax*, 131; *Atlanta Constitution*, June 21, 1957 ("[w]hen the registration act was passed in 1949, it was generally recognized that the voter test was aimed at large-scale registration by Negroes").

[64] Ga. Laws 1950, p. 126.

[65] Key, *Southern Politics*, 576–77.

[66] Interview of William P. Randall, Feb. 4, 1989, p. 13 (Georgia State University Archives).

[67] *Hall v. Holder*, trial transcript, pp. 55, 57, 73, 110, 279–80, 335–36, 338 (testimony of Wilson Roberson).

responded to the challenges, 175 were purged because of their alleged failure to read and interpret the Constitution of the United States. Ben T. Shorter, the chair of the Randolph County Voters League, said that the purged blacks tried to get a local attorney to represent them to contest the purges, but "[t]he local attorneys said it would simply ruin their reputation to be involved in a case where we had lost our voting rights, and...it would cost too much of their usual business."[68] The purged voters passed the hat and were able to raise $2,000, enough to hire a lawyer, who filed suit in federal district court. The court, after finding that their removal "constituted an illegal discrimination against them on account of their race and color," ordered that the purged voters be restored to the voter rolls and that they collect damages from the registrars in the amount of twenty dollars per person.[69] Despite the court order, black voter registration in Randolph County actually declined, from approximately 750 in 1952 to 423 in 1964.[70]

A similar strategy was used in Peach County, where scores of blacks were purged because of their failure to pass the new voter test or to read and interpret the Constitution.[71] Although Peach County was majority-black, in 1954 only 18 percent of its registered voters were black. Several hundred blacks were also purged in Pierce County in 1956, but the district court refused to take any action.[72]

In Burke County, the chief registrar, D. L. Stone, said that blacks were not turned away in any significant numbers, but "we have not put a premium on them registering."[73] Although blacks were a substantial majority of the population, in 1958 only 425 blacks, compared to 4,000 whites, were registered. By the time the Voting Rights Act was enacted, the number of blacks on the voter rolls in Burke County was 427, a net gain of only two voters.[74]

---

[68] Hearings before the Subcommittee on Constitutional Rights of the Committee on the Judiciary, United States Senate, Eighty-fifth Congress, First Session, on S. 83, an amendment to S. 83, S. 427, S. 428, S. 429, S. 468, S. 500, S. 501, S. 502, S. 504, S. 505, S. 508, S. 509, S. 510, S. Con. Res. 5, Proposals to Secure, Protect, and Strengthen Civil Rights of Persons under the Constitution and Laws of the United States, February 14, 15, 16, 18, 19, 20, 21, 26, 27, 28, and March 1, 4, 5, 1957, statement of Ben T. Shorter, pp. 574–75.

[69] *Thornton v. Martin*, 1 R. R. L. Rptr. 213, 215 (M. D. Ga. 1956).

[70] Ibid.; U.S. Commission on Civil Rights, *Political Participation*, 236.

[71] Brailsford R. Brazeal, "Studies of Negro Voting in Eight Georgia Counties and One of South Carolina" (unpublished study for the Southern Regional Council, Atlanta, Ga., June 6, 1960), 44–6, as cited in Lawrence J. Hanks, *The Struggle for Black Political Empowerment in Three Georgia Counties* (Knoxville: University of Tennessee Press, 1987), 94–5.

[72] *Harris v. Echols*, 146 F. Supp. 607 (S. D. Ga. 1956).

[73] D. L. Stone to Election Law Study Committee, December 15, 1958 (Georgia Department of Archives and History, Atlanta, Election Law Study Committee Papers).

[74] U.S. Commission on Civil Rights, *Political Participation*, 232.

IV

Despite the intransigence of local officials in places such as Randolph, Peach, and Burke Counties, nationwide the forces of racial change were gathering irresistible momentum. Before and during the First World War, a substantial number of southern blacks had migrated north, and many had voted for the first time. More than 350,000 blacks served in the armed forces, albeit in Jim Crow units, and when they returned home they began to demand a fuller role in the democracy they had fought to preserve. The federal government, in response to increased pressure from the minority community, appointed a number of blacks to key positions in the New Deal administration and in 1939 created a new Civil Rights Section in the Department of Justice.

American intervention in World War II had further, profound implications for race relations in the United States. It was difficult, indeed impossible, to make war against Nazi racism in Europe and defend white supremacy at home.

The inconsistency between American foreign and domestic policies was evident from the Charter of the United Nations, to which the United States was a signatory, drafted in San Francisco in 1945. It reaffirmed "faith in fundamental human rights, in the dignity of the human person, [and] in the equal rights of men and women." Article 1 declared that a main purpose of the UN was to "achieve international cooperation... in promoting and encouraging a respect for human rights and fundamental freedoms for all without distinction as to race, sex, or religion."[75] If the charter was to have any meaning at all, and if the country's participation in the UN was to be more than an act of hypocrisy, it was clear that the United States had to reassess, and change, its domestic racial policies.

The basic premise of racial discrimination – the belief that blacks were naturally inferior – was further undermined by the publication in 1944 of *An American Dilemma: The Negro Problem and Modern Democracy*, written by the Swedish economist Gunnar Myrdal. In his influential study of race relations in the United States, Myrdal concluded that the status of blacks was the result not of inherent qualities but of segregation itself. Negroes were trapped, according to Myrdal, by a self-fulfilling prophecy, a circle of "cumulative causation" in which the status of blacks, caused by discrimination, was in turn the cause for perpetuating discrimination.[76]

Nowhere was the operation of the self-fulfilling prophecy more apparent and inequitable than in education. In his book published in 1930, *Financing Schools*, Fred McCuiston reported that Georgia spent $35.42 on each white student enrolled in school but only $6.38 on each Negro student, a

---

[75] Charter of the United Nations, Article 1.
[76] Gunnar Myrdal, *An American Dilemma: The Negro Problem and Modern Democracy* (New York: Harper, 1944), 76.

differential of 453.6 percent. And even these figures are misleading, for local school boards often diverted to the white schools funds appropriated to the black schools. In Georgia, according to the Georgia Department of Education, the total amount diverted from black to white schools in 1933 was a million and a half dollars.[77] There is little wonder that the academic performance of whites, given the disproportionate financial support they received, generally eclipsed that of blacks.

In recognition of the injustices of the Jim Crow system, President Truman created the President's Committee on Civil Rights in 1946 to determine ways to strengthen and improve the protection of civil rights. The following year, the committee issued a report, *To Secure These Rights*, and recommended the expansion of the Civil Rights Section of the Department of Justice, the establishment of a permanent Commission on Civil Rights, the enactment of federal legislation to end discrimination in voting and the administration of justice, and the end of racial desegregation in public education.

On July 26, 1948, Truman integrated the armed forces by executive order.[78] Despite dire predictions of bloodshed and race riots, the desegregation proceeded without serious incident.

The Supreme Court also began to show a greater willingness to scrutinize efforts to circumvent the guarantees of the Fourteenth Amendment. It breached as a formal matter the doctrine of separate but equal when it declared unconstitutional a city ordinance that was designed to maintain segregation in residential areas.[79] The Court later struck down as unenforceable private agreements or covenants in deeds preventing the sale of property to "colored persons."[80] As a practical matter, these decisions had little, if any, impact on residential segregation, but they did breathe new life into the moribund Fourteenth Amendment.

In other cases, the Court held that racial segregation on buses and in railway dining cars was an impermissible burden on interstate commerce.[81] And in 1954, the Court handed down its epochal decision in *Brown v. Board of Education*[82] invalidating racial segregation in public schools.

Brown and the larger national movement for equal rights would lead to passage in 1957 of the first federal civil rights law since Reconstruction – a law that the white leadership of Georgia would bitterly oppose.

[77] Franz Boas and Edward M. David, "Race: America's Social Barrier" (New York: Public Affairs Committee, Inc., 1940), 14.

[78] Executive Order 9981.

[79] *Buchanan v. Warley*, 245 U.S. 60 (1917).

[80] *Shelley v. Kraemer*, 334 U.S. 1 (1948).

[81] *Morgan v. Commonwealth of Virginia*, 328 U.S. 373 (1946); *Henderson v. United States*, 339 U.S. 816 (1950).

[82] 347 U.S. 483 (1954).

4

Passage of the Civil Rights Act of 1957:
The White Response

> In the name of decency, in the name of democracy, in the name of world
> leadership, in the name of God, let us pass strong civil rights legislation.
>
> Rev. William H. Borders (Atlanta, Georgia, February 28, 1957)

I

Building on the momentum of *Brown v. Board of Education*, Congress began
considering a variety of civil rights acts in 1956, including a law prohibiting
discrimination in voting and authorizing the attorney general to bring suit
against jurisdictions that denied registration to blacks.[1] But despite *Brown*
and the mounting civil rights activity in Congress and the rest of the nation,
the reality in Georgia during the mid-1950s was complete, rigid segregation.

In an effort to draw the distinction between the races as sharply as possible, the state in 1927 repealed its one-eighth blood quantum definition of
"persons of color" in favor of an even stricter standard. The new test defined
persons of color as "[a]ll Negroes, mulattoes, mestizos, and their descendants, having *any ascertainable trace* of either Negro or African, West Indian,
or Asiatic Indian blood in their veins."[2] To be admitted to the charmed circle
of "white persons," one had to be free not only of all "colored" blood, but
of Mongolian, Japanese, and Chinese blood as well.[3]

---

[1] Hearings before the Committee on the Judiciary, United States Senate, Eighty-fourth
Congress, Second Session, on S. 900 (Anti-lynching); S. 902 (Civil Rights Division); S. 903
(Political Participation); H.R. 5205 (Armed Forces); S. J. Res. 29 (Qualification of Electors);
S. Con. Res. 8 (Joint Congressional Committee); S. 904 (Labor-Peonage); S. 905 (Supplement
Existing Statutes); S. 906 (Civil Rights Commission); S. 907 (Omnibus Bill); S. 1089 (Armed
Forces); S. 3604 (Additional Assistant Attorney General); S. 3605 (Bipartisan Commission);
S. 3415 (Federal Commission); S. 3717 (Strengthen Statutes); S. 3718 (Right To Vote), April
24, May 16, 25, June 1, 12, 25, 26, 27, and July 6, 13, 1956.
[2] Ga. Laws 1927, p. 272 (emphasis added).
[3] Ga. Laws 1927, p. 278.

To maintain the purity of the white blood line, the general assembly attempted to legislate miscegenation out of existence. A half-dozen statutes imposed fines and imprisonment upon those who, under a variety of circumstances, performed or participated in interracial marriage.[4] It was a felony "for a white person to marry any save a white person."[5] To ensure that the laws were effectively enforced, state law required all residents to register with the state board of health and to designate their race. Applications for marriage licenses had to be cross-checked with the registration data to ferret out any would-be offenders. The board of health was obligated to report the birth of any mixed-race child to the state attorney general, whose duty it was "to institute criminal proceedings against the parents of such child." Even to suggest that a white female had had sexual intercourse with a person of color was "slanderous without proof of special damage."[6]

State law required segregation of the races in nearly every area of public life – schools,[7] hospitals,[8] the bookmobile,[9] prisons,[10] training schools,[11] public transportation (an exception was made for "colored nurses or servants" attending their employers),[12] courthouses,[13] public housing,[14] and tax records.[15] Segregation in public accommodations – theaters,[16] restaurants, hotels, clubs, billiard rooms,[17] civic and community organizations, the American Legion,[18] golf courses, swimming pools,[19] libraries,[20] and so forth – was the prevailing norm.

---

[4] Ga. Code of 1933, §§53-9902–9908.

[5] Ga. Laws 1927, p. 277.

[6] Ga. Code of 1933, §53-314 and §105-707.

[7] Constitution of 1945, Art. VIII, Sec. 1, Para. 1. State law restricted property tax exemptions and endowments to segregated colleges and institutions. Constitution of 1945, Art. VII, Sec. 1, Para. 4.

[8] Ga. Code of 1933, §35-225.

[9] *Hall v. Holder*, Civ. No. 85-242 (M. D. Ga.), Pl. Ex. 56.

[10] Ga. Code of 1933, §77-9904; Ga. Laws 1956, pp. 161, 173.

[11] Ga. Code of 1933, §77-613.

[12] Ga. Code of 1933, §§18-206 and 209.

[13] The *Dawson News* reported on Dec. 15, 1966, that blacks in Terrell County "shattered another tradition by sitting freely in the courtroom heretofore occupied only by white persons."

[14] See e.g., *Bailey v. Vinning*, 514 F. Supp. 452, 456 (M. D. Ga. 1981).

[15] Ga. Code of 1933, §92-6307.

[16] See e.g., *Atlanta Journal*, Sept. 30, 1963, for an account of the first attempt to desegregate movie theaters in Americus in 1963.

[17] Ga. Laws 1925, p. 286.

[18] State Constitution of the American Legion, Georgia Division, Art. I, para. 3, extended membership only to "white persons." *Harris County Journal*, Oct. 10, 1919.

[19] *Bailey v. Vining*, 514 F. Supp. at 454, 457.

[20] Rome, Georgia, maintained two public libraries segregated on the basis of race. *Askew v. City of Rome, Georgia*, Civ. No. 4:93-CV-0028 (N. D. Ga.), Pl. Ex. 23.

Membership in the state bar association, which traditionally supplied much of the political leadership of the state, was reserved for whites only. Blacks had a separate organization, the Gate City Bar. But since none of the state's public or private law schools would admit blacks, there were very few black lawyers – fewer than two dozen, most of whom practiced in the Atlanta metropolitan area.[21]

The judiciary, whose duty it was to defend the state's bill of rights and protect the citizenry against the excesses of the legislative and executive branches of government, was a reflection and extension of the segregated, virtually all-white bar. According to Donald Hollowell, one of the state's few black attorneys:

[A]ll the judges were white. Without exception, all the district attorneys were white, and virtually all the assistant district attorneys and prosecutors were white. All the clerks of court were white. All the bailiffs were white, and most of the juries who heard serious cases were white. You might find a black janitor, but there were no black citizens in any position of responsibility or authority.[22]

The police were also segregated. The city of Atlanta hired its first black police officers in 1948, but they served in a segregated unit and patrolled at night. "We were called the '6 p.m. watch,'" says Billy McKinney, a former city policeman and a member of the Georgia house of representatives. "We could only go in the black neighborhoods and under no circumstances were we to approach or arrest a white person. If we saw a white breaking the law, we were supposed to call a white officer. And that was the norm everywhere in the state." After being on the police force for four years, McKinney arrested a white man and was promptly suspended.[23]

The only instrumentality of justice in the state that was thoroughly desegregated was the electric chair. As of 1983, a total of 412 people had been executed in Georgia, 82 percent of whom were black.[24]

J. B. Fuqua, a senator from Augusta and president of the state Democratic Party, summed up the reality of segregation in the state when he said that back in the fifties he was one of "only three white people who would shake hands with a black man on Broad Street in Augusta, Georgia." The other two were Carl Sanders, who later became governor, and a man whose name Fuqua could no longer remember.[25]

John Cross's experience when he took over a black cab company in Moultrie during the 1960s was typical. He said that the owner of the town's

---

[21] *Georgia v. Thornburg*, Civ. No. 90-2065 (D. D. C.), declaration of Donald L. Hollowell. See also *Holmes v. Danner*, 191 F. Supp. 394 (M. D. Ga. 1961), describing the first attempts to desegregate the University of Georgia.

[22] Ibid.

[23] Author's interview with Billy McKinney, Sept. 8, 2001.

[24] *Atlanta Constitution*, December 15, 1983.

[25] *Brooks v. Miller*, No. 1:90-CV-1001-RCF (N. D. Ga.), trial transcript, May 15, 1966, p. 407.

rival white cab company approached him and said that "we have an understanding that we don't haul colored peoples and ya'll don't haul white folks." Cross's response was that "the understanding went out the window because I would haul whoever called the cab company. Whoever had the fare."[26] In reality, Cross had few white fares.

Even cemeteries, whose residents were surely beyond caring any longer about race, were segregated. An ordinance of the city of Rochell in Wilcox County, for example, provided that "[a]ll interment of whites within the corporate limits of the city shall be in Pine View [Morningside], and all interments of colored citizens shall be in Oak Grove, and any person or persons violating this ordinance shall be punished as prescribed in section 95 of this Code."[27] In Butts County, a cyclone fence ran down the middle of the Jackson municipal cemetery, with whites buried on one side and blacks on the other.[28] In Barnesville, in Lamar County, only whites were buried in Greenwood Cemetery; the O'Neal Cemetery was reserved for blacks. Greenwood Cemetery was finally desegregated in 1987, when C. R. Jones, the town's first black council member, was interred there.[29]

Any breach in the wall of segregation, no matter how minor, could set off a howl of white protest and reaction. When Koinonia Farm, a small religious commune in Sumter County, announced in 1956 its plan to hold a nonsegregated summer camp for boys and girls, the county immediately got an injunction from the local superior court closing the camp down.[30] Koinonia also became the target of night riders, who dynamited the farm's roadside produce stand, and the object of a near-complete economic boycott by area merchants and suppliers.[31]

A delegation of more than 100 members of the Ku Klux Klan visited Koinonia in February 1957 with an offer to buy the farm out. As Clarence Jordan, the farm's founder, recalled, "they made a pilgrimage to Koinonia to ask us to sell out and move away. They kindly offered their assistance. It seems they wanted to buy our farm but not our farm products, such as white eggs, laid by white hens who live in white buildings, but alas, whose yokes are colored."[32]

An incident alleged to have been masterminded by Koinonia involving the supposed integration of a bag of popcorn set local whites abuzz and even more firmly against the farm. George Hooks, the manager of a store in Americus, charged that "[t]hey're trying to change our customs, that's

[26] *Cross v. Baxter*, Civ. No. 76-20 (M. D. Ga.), trial transcript, p. 121 (testimony of John Cross).

[27] Ordinances of the City of Rochell, Georgia, Section 5.

[28] *Atlanta Constitution*, June 8, 1984.

[29] *Strickland v. Lamar County Board of Commissioners*, Civ. No. 86-167-2-Mac (M. D. Ga.), hearing on preliminary injunction, pp. 81–2 (testimony of Theodore R. Bush).

[30] *Sumter County v. Koinonia Farm, Inc.* (Sup. Ct. Sumter County, Ga., June 9, 1956).

[31] *Atlanta Journal*, Nov. 15, 1964.

[32] *Atlanta Journal*, April 15, 1957.

all. They put a white girl and a Negro boy together up town. They paraded around town, eating popcorn out of the same bag. No sir, I don't approve of it."[33] Florence Jordan, Clarence's wife, denied that Koinonia was behind the popcorn incident. "The farm people would always respect the customs of the community," she said. "We believe all people are equal, and we never practiced segregation, but we never made a point of being integrated when we went into town."[34]

A black dentist from Albany, E. D. Hamilton, who also maintained an office in Americus, said that he was "sure" the girl in the popcorn incident was actually a black patient of his from Montezuma, who happened to be "very light." But such explanations didn't mollify local whites. A reporter for an Atlanta paper concluded that "ninety-nine and ninety-nine one-hundredths per cent of Sumter County citizens do not like Koinonia, and wish its occupants would go away."[35]

In April of 1957 the Sumter County grand jury investigated Koinonia and in its formal report to the court reached the startling conclusion that the residents of Koinonia had *themselves* dynamited their roadside stand, burned down one of their houses, and committed other acts of violence for purposes of "propaganda" and "pecuniary gain." The grand jury, reciting the southern mantra that integration and Communism went hand in hand, also reported that while "the evidence is insufficient to convict of Communism in a Court of Law . . . there exists extremely close kinship between the Communist Party and Koinonia."[36] Officials at Koinonia denied the charge.[37]

Koinonia, which remained in Sumter County but refused to embrace the prevailing view of segregation, was visited by a second delegation of whites in 1964. This time the delegation included, not the Klan fringe, but the leading citizens of the county – the chair of the county commission, the president of the chamber of commerce, the editor of the local newspaper, and their spokesperson, Charles F. Crisp, an Americus banker. "See if you don't think you'll be serving the best interests of the community and certainly the best interests of your Lord," Crisp told Jordan, "to move and leave us in peace."[38] Again, Koinonia declined to move.

No detail of life in the state was too small to be regulated on the basis of race. News in the black community was reported, if at all, in a special "colored" section of the local newspaper.[39] The *Moultrie Observer*

33 *Atlanta Journal,* April 19, 1957.
34 Author's interview with Florence Jordan, 1978 (interview notes on file with author).
35 *Atlanta Journal,* April 19, 1957.
36 Sumter County Grand Jury presentments, 2 Race Rel. L. Rep. 682, 684, 686-87 (Ga. 1957).
37 *Atlanta Journal,* April 14, 1957.
38 *Americus Times-Recorder,* Aug. 8, 1964, quoted in William Bailey Williford, *Americus through the years* (Atlanta: Cherokee, 1975), 338.
39 *Eatonton Messenger,* March 5, 1964.

in Colquitt County reported news of the black community in a separate section, called the "black sheet," that was not circulated in the white community.[40] A Heart Fund Campaign in Eatonton had two chairs, one for the white community and another for the black community.[41] Jobs were regularly advertised and sought in the private and public sectors on a racial basis. The LaRue Company advertised in the *Harris County Journal* in 1945 that "WE WANT WHITE LABOR!" in a Pine Mountain canning plant.[42] The McDuffie County Board of Commissioners wrote to the American Brake Shoe Company in February 1957 urging it to locate a plant in the county as a way of increasing "white male employment."[43]

White racial phobia extended even to segregating the streets. In 1956, the Sumter County Board of Education tried to halt construction of a new black elementary school, not because segregation had been held unconstitutional in *Brown* two years earlier, but because local white citizens had complained that the school would be "too close" to an existing white school. According to the white parents, "the children, both colored and white, would have to travel the same streets and roads in order to reach their respective schools."[44] One member of the board, a former naval officer named Jimmy Carter who had returned to Sumter County to take up peanut farming and politics, made a motion to request the state board of education to hold up construction of the "Elementary Negro School" until a new site could be selected. The state board turned down the request because of "the staggering cost" involved in delaying construction, but Carter and the other members of the local board assured the white parents that the board "would do everything in its power to minimize simultaneous traffic between white and colored students in route to and from school."[45]

Immediately after the *Brown* decision, the legislature passed a flurry of laws and resolutions designed to maintain segregation and beat back the federal assault on what white southerners reverentially called "the Southern Way of Life." In 1955, it provided that no money could be appropriated or spent for public schools unless they were racially segregated.[46] Violation of the law was made a felony. The legislature "memorialized" Congress to

---

[40] *Cross v. Baxter*, trial transcript pp. 116–17 (testimony of Rice).

[41] *Eatonton Messenger*, February 2, 1978.

[42] *Harris County Journal*, November 8, 1945.

[43] *Bowdry v. Hawes*, Civ. No. 176-128 (S. D. Ga.), Pl. Ex. 56.

[44] Minutes of the Sumter County Board of Education, Sept. 24, 1956.

[45] Minutes of the Sumter County Board of Education, Oct. 5, 1956. Carter, who later became, in his words, "quite liberal on such issues as civil rights," has acknowledged that "I was not directly involved in the early struggles to end racial discrimination." Jimmy Carter, *Keeping Faith* (New York: Bantam Books, 1982), 74, 141–42. It would be more accurate to say that at that point in his political career, he supported segregation as did other whites in Sumter County.

[46] Ga. Laws 1955, p. 174.

adopt an amendment to the Constitution giving the state exclusive authority over schools so that they could be operated in perpetuity on a segregated basis.[47] It also asked Congress to amend the Constitution to provide that no person could be required to serve in the armed forces with members of another race.[48] It commended a Georgia congressman, E. L. Forrester, for sponsoring legislation restricting the jurisdiction of federal courts in cases involving the operation of the public schools. Among several miscellaneous resolutions, the legislature proposed an alternative method of allowing the states to amend the Constitution without the intervention of Congress,[49] and protested the confirmation of John Marshall Harlan as a member of the Supreme Court.[50]

Harlan was the grandson of a former justice of the Supreme Court of the same name who had dissented in *Plessy v. Ferguson*, in which the majority had upheld a Louisiana law requiring segregation in railway cars and thus sanctioned the entire Jim Crow system.[51] The first Justice Harlan had written, to no avail, that "[o]ur constitution is color-blind, and neither knows nor tolerates classes among citizens.[52] The second Justice Harlan was presumed to be equally liberal on the issue of race, but his name alone was calculated to give deep offense to the South's white supremacists. Although he did support desegregation, on other issues Harlan proved to be one of the most conservative members of the Court.[53]

At the invitation of Governor Marvin Griffin, a State's Rights Council of Georgia was organized in Atlanta in September 1955. The organizational meeting, according to press accounts, "was attended by 200 of the State's most prominent government officials and political, business and civic leaders representing all political factions in the state." At the meeting, the council dedicated itself to "preservation of the traditional establishment of segregation in both public and private areas."[54] State's Rights Councils were soon established in other parts of the state.[55]

The state's former governor, Herman Talmadge, lent his support to the state's rights movement by confidently announcing that no less an authority than "God advocates segregation." Drawing upon the popular, and discredited, race mythology of the late nineteenth century, Talmadge claimed that God created "five different races: white, black, yellow, brown and red.... He did not intend them to be mixed or He would not have

[47] Ga. Laws 1955, pp. 4, 9.
[48] Ga. Laws 1955, p. 185.
[49] Ga. Laws 1955, p. 327.
[50] Georgia House Journal, Feb. 8, 1955, p. 514.
[51] 163 U.S. 537 (1896).
[52] Ibid., p. 559 (Justice Harlan dissenting).
[53] Richard Kluger, *Simple Justice* (New York: Knopf, 1976), 715.
[54] *Stewart-Webster Journal*, Jan. 12, 1956.
[55] E.g., Mitchell County. See the *Camilla Enterprise*, April 13, 1956.

segregated them."[56] Modern scholars, while acknowledging the persistence of racial beliefs and prejudices of the kind held by Talmadge, have concluded that the concept of "race" has no biological meaning or basis in scientific fact.[57]

In 1956, the legislature made appropriations to public schools on a racially segregated basis,[58] authorized the governor to close the schools rather than desegregate them, provided for tuition grants for private education, and gave local school boards the authority to lease public school property for use as private schools.[59] It authorized state and local officials to sell or lease parks, playgrounds, golf courses, swimming pools, and other public property to private citizens or associations as an alternative to operating them on a desegregated basis,[60] and made it a crime to trespass on public property that had been closed to the public.[61] It required segregated waiting rooms for intrastate passengers, including "separate toilets and separate facilities for drinking water."[62] It gave state law enforcement officials the right to enter any county or municipality to make arrests and enforce the laws requiring segregation or separation of the races.[63]

With only one dissenting vote, that of Hamilton Lokey of Fulton County, the legislature adopted an "Interposition Resolution" in 1956 declaring the *Brown* decision "null, void and of no force or effect."[64] The legislature said that the Court had acted beyond its powers, and pledged "to take all appropriate measures honorably and constitutionally available to the State, to avoid this illegal encroachment upon the rights of her people."[65] It "vigorously" opposed federal aid to public education because it feared

---

[56] Herman E. Talmadge, *You and Segregation* (Birmingham, Ala.: Vulcan Press, 1955), 44.

[57] See the monograph by Franz Boas and Edward M. David, "Race: America's Social Barrier" (New York: Public Affairs Committee, Inc., 1940), 7 ("the belief in 'racial purity' and 'racial superiority' is without scientific foundation"); Joseph L. Graves, *The Emperor's New Clothes: Biological Theories of Race at the Millennium* (New Brunswick, N. J.: Rutgers University Press, 2001); E. Nathaniel Gates, *The concept of 'Race' in Natural and Social Science* (New York: Garland, 1997), ix ("[t]he incremental advance of genetic science demonstrated definitively that 'race' as conceived and defined by men of science from the late nineteenth century onward, had no scientifically verifiable referents"). Dr. J. Craig Venter, whose company, Celera Genomics, mapped the human genome, has concluded that "there is no basis in the genetic code for race." "Skin Deep; Shouldn't a Pill Be Colorblind?," *New York Times*, May 13, 2001, sec. 4, p. 1.

[58] Ga. Laws 1956, pp. 753, 756.

[59] Ga. Laws 1956, pp. 6, 10, 11.

[60] Ga. Laws 1956, p. 22.

[61] Ga. Laws 1956, p. 9.

[62] Ga. Laws 1956, pp. 673, 685.

[63] Ga. Laws 1956, p. 605.

[64] Ga. Laws 1956, p. 642; Georgia House Journal, Feb. 8, 1956, pp. 782–83; Georgia Senate Journal, Feb. 13, 1956, p. 629.

[65] Ga. Laws 1956, p. 647.

the money could be used to coerce desegregation.[66] It commended Georgia Congressman Carl Vinson for introducing a constitutional amendment preserving states' rights,[67] and censured U.S. Attorney General Herbert Brownell for conducting an "unwarranted investigation" of jury discrimination in Cobb County.[68] The investigation had been triggered by a Supreme Court decision that had reversed the conviction of a black man based upon "a strong showing of systematic exclusion" of blacks from the county grand jury.[69]

Expressing its disdain for federal desegregation decisions, the legislature defiantly adopted a new state flag incorporating the design of the battle flag of the Confederacy.[70] Denmark Groover, the administration's floor leader, said the adoption of the new flag will "leave no doubt in anyone's mind that Georgia will not forget the teachings of Lee and Stonewall Jackson," and "will show that we in Georgia intend to uphold what we stood for, will stand for and will fight for."[71]

In an attempt to demonstrate that *Brown* was misguided, and to head off attempts to pass federal civil rights legislation, state Attorney General Eugene Cook compiled the state's constitutional and statutory provisions "relating to segregation of the races." Surveying his handiwork, he proudly pronounced:

A perusal of the many segregation laws included herein, affecting as they do almost every phase of human endeavor to which the authority of government traditionally extends, convincingly demonstrates the predominant influence that racial segregation has exerted in the sociological development of the two races in this state.

"Nothing could illustrate more vividly," Cook said, "the wisdom of *Stare Decisis*" and the necessity of maintaining the existing racial "status." He expressed the hope that "a Supreme Court of tomorrow, dedicated to a different theory of sociology, may well find the 14th Amendment itself to be longer tenable."[72]

The segregation laws compiled by Cook also vividly illustrated, from the black point of view, the evil that lay at the root of black disfranchisement. Since blacks were neither voters in any appreciable numbers, nor office holders, whites controlled the ballot box and elective office and were therefore free to pass whatever laws they wished. Laws institutionalizing

---

[66] Ga. Laws 1956, p. 397.

[67] Ga. Laws 1956, p. 2718.

[68] Ga. Laws 1956, p. 126.

[69] *Reece v. State of Georgia*, 350 U.S. 85, 88 (1955).

[70] Ga. Laws 1956, p. 38.

[71] *Atlanta Journal*, Feb. 10, 1956.

[72] State Law Department, "Compilation of Georgia Laws and Opinions of the Attorney General Relating to Segregation of the Races" (April 1956), pp. 2–3.

racial segregation and white supremacy were the inevitable consequence. Any change in the existing status presupposed the meaningful extension of the franchise to blacks.

II

Cook carried the message of states' rights and unlawful federal encroachment to Washington on July 13, 1956, when he testified before a Senate committee in opposition to the pending civil rights bills. They would destroy the "association of sovereign states.... conceived by the founding fathers to preserve our liberties," he said. He charged that the National Association for the Advancement of Colored People (NAACP), which he linked with the Communist Party in its support of civil rights, was conducting "a conspiracy against the white man" and was "urging the colored people to revolt and take up arms against their white brothers."[73]

The next year, Cook, joined by members of the U.S. House and Senate from Georgia, renewed the attack on the proposed civil rights bills with the usual litany of southern arguments for maintaining the racial status quo – the proposed federal laws were unconstitutional; law couldn't change custom; whites would never accept desegregation; blacks were incapable of exercising equal rights because they were uneducated and had no culture; the civil rights movement was antiwhite and a communist or left-wing plot; blacks preferred segregation, and so on. Cook said that the South had done "a noble job" in dealing with "the terrific ... race problem" and in trying to civilize a people who "were uneducated, with no cultural background, and only 150 years removed, some of them – the descendants, rather – from cannibalism." "[T]the white people ... love the Negro," he said, adding the usual caveat, but "in his right place." Cook also delivered a stern warning to the committee. "I want to make this clear to you," he said – the choice in Georgia is the existing order or "violence."[74]

J. L. Pilcher, the representative from the second congressional district, expressing what was clearly the white point of view, said that federal legislation was futile because "people's inner feelings cannot be legislated upon, customs cannot be successfully legislated upon, nor can pride and morals be legislated upon." James C. Davis, a representative from Stone Mountain, said that the proposed bills were "unconstitutional," "absurd," "ridiculous," and

---

[73] Hearings before the Committee on the Judiciary, United States Senate, July 13, 1956, statement of Eugene Cook, pp. 322–23.

[74] Hearings before Subcommittee No. 5 of the Committee on the Judiciary, House of Representatives, Eighty-fifth Congress, First Session on Miscellaneous Bills Regarding the Civil Rights of Persons within the Jurisdiction of the United States, February 4, 5, 6, 7, 13, 14, 25, and 26, 1957, pp. 813, 817.

"unnecessary."[75] Herman Talmadge, now a united states senator, expressed similar views.[76]

One of those who spoke in favor of the legislation was the Atlanta attorney A. T. Walden, an early civil rights leader in the state and an icon in the black community. Not all whites were opposed to Negro registration, he said, citing several examples of white officials refusing to cooperate with discriminatory challenges to black voters. In Ware County, for example, two women resigned as registrars rather than be parties to illegal racial purges. Federal legislation was needed, however, for "the implementation of our democratic ideals and making our constitutional concept of equal justice under law a living reality."[77]

Referring to Cook's testimony, Walden said that he was "a little better spokesman for Negroes" than those who claimed that "Negroes do not desire integration" and who professed to love "Negroes in their place." "[M]ost of those who profess to love us while denying to us our constitutional rights, reserve unto themselves the exclusive prerogative of pointing out, designating, and circumscribing what 'their (our) places' are," he said.[78]

The most eloquent testimony in support of the legislation was given by William H. Borders, the pastor of the Wheat Street Baptist Church in Atlanta, one of the largest black churches in the South. Remedying the harm of racial discrimination "is the urgent business of democracy," he told the committee. "In the name of decency, in the name of democracy, in the name of world leadership, in the name of God, let us pass strong civil rights legislation," he declared.[79]

The following month, the Georgia legislature adopted a resolution calling for the impeachment of Chief Justice Earl Warren and several other justices of the Supreme Court on the grounds that they had commited high crimes and misdemeanors by rendering decisions, such as *Brown v. Board of Education*, that gave aid and comfort to "Godless communism." Decisions of the court invalidating segregation in intrastate bus transportation were condemned as being part of a "procommunist racial integration policy." In a cascade of frenzied prose, the resolution accused Justice Felix Frankfurter, who had served as a member of the legal committee of the NAACP, of assisting "that organization in making plans for and in the realization of its objectives as a communist front organization to advocate, propagandize and litigate to

---

[75] Ibid., pp. 113, 1196.
[76] Hearings before the Subcommittee on Constitutional Rights of the Commitee on the Judiciary, United States Senate, Eighty-fifth Congress, First Session, on S. 83, and Amendment to S. 83, S. 427, S. 428, S. 429, S. 468, S. 500, S. 501, S. 502, S. 504, S. 505, S. 508, S. 509, S. 510, S. Con. Res., February 14, 15, 16, 18, 19, 20, 21, 26, 27, 28, March 1, 4 and 5, 1957, pp. 252–53.
[77] Ibid., p. 566.
[78] Ibid., p. 569.
[79] Ibid., p. 529.

bring racial strife to secure racial integration from which his own race is immune upon religious grounds, as a part of the communist objective in the United States."[80]

During the same session, the general assembly adopted a resolution by unanimous vote in both houses calling for repeal of the Fourteenth and Fifteenth Amendments to the Constitution because they "were malignant acts of arbitrary power" and "are null and void and of no effect."[81] It also enacted a so-called anti-barratry statute aimed at civil rights lawyers and civil rights lawsuits, making it a crime to "engage in exciting and stirring up" litigation.[82] The Supreme Court subsequently invalidated a similar statute enacted in Virginia, after noting that "[w]e cannot close our eyes to the fact that the militant Negro civil rights movement has engendered the intense resentment and opposition of the politically dominant white community.... In such circumstances, a statute broadly curtailing group activity leading to litigation may easily become a weapon of oppression."[83]

Governor Marvin Griffin took the unprecedented step of intruding himself in local Atlanta politics in order to forestall the election of a black man, T. M. Alexander, to the city's board of aldermen. Alexander had won about a third of the votes in the 1957 primary in a three-way contest with two whites, and had forced a runoff. Griffin, distraught at the prospect of a black being elected, called upon "all friends of segregation to support" Alexander's opponent, Jack Summers. It was not readily apparent that Alexander, a prominent insurance company executive, was less qualified to serve as an alderman than Summers, a barber supply salesman. But qualifications were not the issue. Griffin, sounding a common white theme, insisted that "it is no time" to elect a Negro "at this critical period in our affairs." "We are on the verge of developments in Atlanta and the rest of Georgia relative to segregation in our schools and other concomitant fields," the governor said, "which makes it a paramount necessity for the voters of Atlanta to elect a white man in this race."[84] Alexander was defeated, but the political editor of the *Atlanta Constitution* noted that "the election has caused much concern in some state political quarters."[85]

On September 9, 1957, Congress passed the first civil rights act since Reconstruction. The act established the federal Commission on Civil Rights and contained several modest provisions designed to protect the right to vote. It prohibited interference with voting in federal elections, and gave

[80] Ga. Laws 1957, pp. 553, 561–62.
[81] Ga. Laws 1957, p. 348; Georgia Senate Journal, Feb. 8, 1957, p. 257; Georgia House Journal, Feb. 13, 1957, p. 661.
[82] Ga. Laws 1957, p. 658.
[83] *N.A.A.C.P. v. Button*, 371 U.S. 415, 435-36 (1963).
[84] *Atlanta Constitution*, May 18, 1957.
[85] *Atlanta Constitution*, June 7, 1957.

Marvin Griffin being inaugurated as governor of Georgia on January 11, 1955. In the wake of the decision of the Supreme Court invalidating racial segregation in public schools and increased civil rights activity in the state, Griffin warned that "the majority race in Georgia is under siege" and urged "a Solid White Vote" in all elections "until sanity, and with it safety, returns" (photo from *Atlanta Journal-Constitution*).

the Attorney General power to enforce the new law.[86] Every member of Congress from Georgia voted against the bill, with the exception of Prince H. Preston from Statesboro, who didn't vote.[87] The 1957 act, which depended upon litigation for enforcement, would prove to be too time-consuming and cumbersome to adequately remedy the problems of discrimination in voting, but it set the stage for passage of additional voting rights legislation in the 1960s.

III

With a watchful eye to the deliberations of Congress, the Georgia legislature established an Election Laws Study Committee (ELSC) in 1957 to rewrite the state's election laws.[88] Racial concerns played a key role in the committee's deliberations. The ELSC proposed to revamp the existing good character and citizenship test by making the questions more difficult and raising the passing score from ten correct answers to twenty correct answers.[89] Committee

---

[86] 71 Stat. 634; 42 U.S.C. §§1971(b) and (c).
[87] 85 Congressional Record S.13900, Aug. 7, 1957; 85 Congressional Record H.6127, Aug. 29, 1957.
[88] Ga. Laws 1957, pp. 257–60.
[89] *United States v. Raines*, 189 F. Supp. at 124.

member Peter Zack Geer, who supported the revision, said that "the white voters of Georgia will be willing to put up with some inconvenience to see that illiterate black voters don't get on the registration lists."[90] He advised the Georgia attorney general, however, that the law should not be made retroactive, because "I can foresee that upon prospective negro voters being disqualified under the new law, that they might then challenge on masse the registered and qualified voters on the list, and attempt to subject the old voters to the new examination." Such a result, he said, would "be catastrophic."[91] In Miller County, where Geer lived, there were only six black registered voters. More than 100 percent of age-eligible whites, some 3,220, were on the voter rolls.[92]

Senator James S. Peters, also a member of the ELSC, said that he supported party registration as a way of keeping blacks out of the Democratic primaries.[93] Since most blacks at that time were Republicans, a party registration requirement would, as a practical matter, segregate the elections. Another proposal of the ELSC was to disfranchise persons convicted of certain crimes, including adultery, bigamy, fornication, and child abandonment. According to Geer, "90 percent of the Negroes in my section could be convicted of adultery or bigamy."[94] The press reported that committee members "had made it clear they desired to discourage Negro registrations."[95] Geer was particularly outspoken about his desire to bar "illiterate Negro bloc voters" from the ballot.[96] A third major recommendation of the ELSC aimed at deterring black voter registration was a requirement that new voter applicants appear in person before the local board of registrars in order to qualify.[97]

None of the ELSC proposals were written explicitly in racial terms. Some state officials, including Attorney General Cook,[98] out of obvious concern that direct statements of racial purpose would render the proposals vulnerable to federal challenge, denied the existence of any intent to discriminate. But members of the committee had already made it abundantly clear that their chief objective was to minimize the black vote.[99] Even Cook acknowledged that some members of the ELSC "feel that perhaps there should be a

[90] *Atlanta Constitution*, November 22, 1957.
[91] Peter Zack Geer to Frank Edwards, November 29, 1957 (Georgia Department of Archives and History, Atlanta, Election Law Study Committee Papers).
[92] U.S. Commission on Civil Rights, *Political Participation* (Washington, D.C.: United States Printing Office, 1968), 236.
[93] *Atlanta Constitution* , July 19, 1957.
[94] *Atlanta Constitution*, November 22, 1957.
[95] *Atlanta Journal*, December 13, 1957.
[96] *Atlanta Constitution*, December 13, 1957; *Atlanta Journal*, December 13, 1957.
[97] *Atlanta Constitution*, November 22, 1957.
[98] *Atlanta Journal*, December 13, 1957.
[99] *Atlanta Constitution*, November 22, 1957; *Atlanta Constitution*, November 23, 1957; *Atlanta Journal*, December 13, 1957.

retaliatory position that could meet that unwholesome situation on the part of the NAACP." The unwholesome situation he was referring to was the NAACP's "efforts to increase the vote power of the Negroes to bloc vote to the point that they will be able to control some elections."[100]

The legislature adopted the new, more stringent voter test in 1958, and Governor Griffin signed it into law.[101] Unlike the 1949 law, the 1958 statute provided no answers to any of the test questions.

The thirty questions were difficult for even the best-educated person to answer. They were an insurmountable barrier to illiterate blacks, particularly since the tests were administered by unsympathetic whites.[102] Among the questions were: What is a republican form of government? How does the Constitution of the United States provide that it may be amended? What does the Constitution of the United States provide regarding the suspension of the privilege of the writ of habeas corpus? How does the Constitution of Georgia provide that a county site may be changed? How may a new state be admitted to the union?

One question, with no irony apparently intended, was: What does the Constitution of the United States provide regarding the right of citizens to vote? Robert Flanagan, for many years the field director of the Georgia NAACP, said that there was actually only one correct answer to each question, and that was "white folks ain't going to let black folks vote."[103]

After it was enacted, twenty-two white women who were members of the elite Atlanta Voters Guild took the new voter test "[j]ust for fun." Only seven passed. All agreed that it would take "a remarkable illiterate" to pass the test. "What hope does a genuine illiterate have?" one of them asked.[104]

A survey by the *Atlanta Journal-Constitution* in 1958 reported that "[f]ew, if any illiterates have qualified as voters by taking and passing the 30-question test on government. Most registrars don't expect many to try."[105] It was the difficulty of the test, in fact, that provoked rumbles from whites. According to the *Atlanta Journal*, "[o]bservant people over the state are going to realize that a law touted as a means of keeping down the registration of the new Negro voters is, in actual fact, keeping down the registration of a great many new white voters, too."[106]

Still, from the white perspective the "problem" of black registration was getting worse, not better. The NAACP announced a southern voter registration campaign, which was reported in the press as being "a clear

---

[100] Election Law Study Committee Papers, minutes, December 12, 1957.
[101] Ga. Laws 1958, p. 269.
[102] Joseph Bernd and Lynwood Holland, "Recent Restrictions upon Negro Suffrage: The Case of Georgia," 21 J. of Politics 487 (1959).
[103] Author's interview with Robert Flanagan, April 30, 1990.
[104] *Atlanta Journal*, April 17, 1958.
[105] *Atlanta Journal-Constitution*, April 27, 1958.
[106] *Atlanta Journal*, April 27, 1958.

challenge to white voters."[107] Martin Luther King, Jr., a charismatic and eloquent young minister from Atlanta, founded the Southern Christian Leadership Conference (SCLC) in 1957 and promised a "crusade for citizenship," which included encouraging Negro voter registration.[108] By 1958, the number of black registered voters in the state had grown to 158, 051.[109]

IV

The Georgia legislature continued its fight against the new federal laws and court decisions. In 1958, it repealed the compulsory school attendance law in districts where operation of the public schools had been discontinued.[110] It censured President Eisenhower for sending "storm troopers" to integrate the schools in Little Rock, Arkansas, and, ringing a cherished theme, said that the president had "sacrificed the honesty and integrity of our highest executive office on an altar of political expediency to appease the NAACP and other radical, communist-sympathizing organizations."[111] The following year, it authorized the governor to close the public schools in order to maintain "the good order, peace and dignity of the State,"[112] and again petitioned Congress to adopt an amendment to the Constitution giving states the exclusive authority to operate their own school systems.[113]

In 1960, the general assembly created a committee, known as the Sibley Committee after its chairman, John A. Sibley, to study the feasibility of closing the public schools in favor of a system of direct tuition grants for use in private schools.[114] According to the legislature, "there has been ingrained forever in the hearts and minds of all Georgians the custom of segregation of the races in the schools of the state." It pledged "to maintain segregated schools at all costs."[115] The Sibley Committee held a series of public hearings around the state and concluded in its final report that an "overwhelming majority of people in Georgia" favored segregation.[116] The committee recommended amending the state Constitution to provide that no child could be compelled to attend a public school "with a child of the opposite race," and proposed the enactment of legislation establishing

[107] *Atlanta Journal,* November 18, 1957.
[108] Pat Waters and Reese Cleghorn, *Climbing Jacob's Ladder* (New York: Harcourt, Brace and World, 1967), 49.
[109] Southern Regional Council, "The Negro Voter in the South" (Atlanta, 1958), 3.
[110] Ga. Laws 1958, p. 231.
[111] Ga. Laws 1958, p. 13.
[112] Ga. Laws 1959, p. 15.
[113] Ga. Laws 1959, p. 383.
[114] Ga. Laws 1960, p. 1187.
[115] Ibid., pp. 1137, 1190.
[116] General Assembly Committee on Schools, Majority Report, April 28, 1960, p. 3.

a system of private tuition grants as an alternative to integrated public schools.

Others counseled a different approach. Newell Edenfield, who was president of the all-white Georgia Bar Association and was later appointed to the federal bench, suggested in an address to association members in 1960 that the best course for the state might be simply to "repeal all of our segregation laws and do so at once." He assured his colleagues that "[w]hen our segregation laws were passed I was as much in favor of them as everyone else." But, he reasoned, "[w]here a fixed policy of enforced segregation appears, either by statute or otherwise, the negroes consistently have won their case. Where no such policy appears they have consistently lost." He expressed the hope that by effort and forethought the state could achieve "a plateau on which again we can live in dignity and in harmony, both with the Constitution and our way of life."[117]

In a further effort to deter civil rights lawsuits, the legislature increased the penalty for barratry from a misdemeanor to a felony punishable by a fine and imprisonment for up to three years.[118] It also passed a law designed to prevent blacks from desegregating restaurants and lunch counters by making it a crime to refuse to leave the premises of an establishment after being requested to do so by the owner.[119] Both measures were described in the press as being "reinforcements to the state's anti-integration armor."[120]

In its continuing, and vain, attempt to block school desegregation, the legislature followed the Sibley Committee's recommendation and adopted a constitutional amendment in 1961 providing that "[f]reedom from compulsory association at all levels of public education shall be preserved inviolate."[121] Although proponents of the measure conceded that it did not override the U.S. Constitution, they nonetheless resisted subsequent efforts, spearheaded by Sen. Leroy Johnson, to repeal it, insisting that it had "some," presumably symbolic, meaning.[122]

The legislature was not the only institution of government in the state alarmed over integration and the threat posed by the rising "bloc vote." In 1960, Judge Oscar Long and two other superior court judges asked the grand jury in Bibb County to investigate "Negro bloc voting." In his charge to the jury, Long said that candidates were rumored to have paid influential members of the black community to deliver the black

---

[117] Address of the President, Report of the 77th Annual Session of the Georgia Bar Association (1960), 194, 197-98, 205.
[118] Ga. Laws 1960, p. 1135
[119] Ga. Laws 1960, p. 142.
[120] *Atlanta Constitution*, February 19, 1960.
[121] Ga. Laws 1961, p. 595.
[122] *Macon Telegraph*, June 16, 1964.

vote, and that the practice, "if it is true, strikes at the very foundation of our government, and will ultimately destroy it." According to Long, the "money is supposedly accepted for expenses of newspapers advertisements, radio announcements, letters, workers, etc. in the solicitation of the Negro vote."[123] He told the grand jurors that state law made it a crime to hire workers "for the purpose of canvassing for or influencing votes in behalf of any candidate" and charged them to ferret out the guilty parties.[124]

The Bibb County sheriff, James Wood, who had been elected in 1956 with black support, and who decided not to seek reelection, condemned Long's investigation as "a crude attempt at judicial intimidation of Negro voters and leaders." He pointed out that white candidates regularly hired people to solicit and get out the vote. "If we seriously wish to enforce the old law against hiring workers for canvassing or influencing voters," he said, "then let us start by indicting our U.S. senators, congressmen, and governors and almost all elected state officials." The grand jury investigation targeting blacks was "the type of political-legal action which brings down ridicule and demands for civil rights legislation against the South," Wood said.[125]

Wood also wrote a tongue-in-cheek open letter to the grand jury in which he called their attention "to that gigantic 'bloc vote' which is controlled by a handful of men known as The Bibb County Democratic Executive Committee." "The situation in this county has so deteriorated," he said, "that almost no one can obtain any local office without first securing the sanction and approval of this handful of people." There were accusations, he continued, that the committee "openly and notoriously violates the law of this State by soliciting the voters of this community on behalf of the nominees securing their approval."[126]

The Macon Bar Association, failing to see either wit or wisdom in the sheriff's comments, issued a statement that Wood's criticism of the grand jury investigation was "deplorable."[127] The next month, the superior court cited Wood for contempt and then proceeded to convict him.[128] The Georgia Court of Appeals affirmed,[129] but the U.S. Supreme Court reversed the conviction on the grounds that the sheriff's statements did not present a danger to the administration of justice and that the conviction denied his freedom to express his opinions.[130]

---

[123] *Macon News*, June 6, 1960.
[124] Georgia Code of 1933, §34-9907.
[125] *Macon News*, June 7, 1960.
[126] *Wood v. Georgia*, 103 Ga. App. 305, 310 (1961).
[127] *Macon News*, June 7, 1960.
[128] *Macon News*, July 8, 1960.
[129] *Wood v. Georgia*, 103 Ga. App. at 324 ("we can only conclude that the sheriff's intemperate actions constituted contempt and the convictions...were proper").
[130] *Wood v. Georgia*, 370 U.S. 375, 395 (1962).

Atlanta University students picketing against segregation at the Georgia state capitol, February 1, 1962 (photo from *Atlanta Journal-Constitution*).

The Bibb County grand jury completed its deliberations but returned no indictments. It did, however, say that "[w]e abhor the insulting and unfounded statements issued" by Sheriff Wood. As for the superior court judges, the jurors commended them for "their devotion to duty, courage and fearlessness in speaking out against an evil that could, if not corrected, destroy our democratic form of government."[131] The legislature eventually repealed the old, and surely unconstitutional, law making it a crime to "influence votes" on behalf of a candidate,[132] providing in retrospect some vindication for the outspoken Bibb County sheriff.

Despite the best efforts of the legislature and the white leadership of the state, time was running out on the Jim Crow system in Georgia and the

---

[131] *Macon Telegraph*, July 2, 1960.
[132] Georgia Laws 1964, Ex. Sess., p. 197.

containment of black political power. The decade of the 1960s would see an intensified level of registration and political activity in the black community, while the state would be rocked by new federal court decisions striking down three of its most vaunted supports of segregation – the county unit system and the malapportioned, all-white state legislature and congressional delegation.

5

One Person, One Vote: The End of the County Unit System and the Malapportioned Legislature and Congressional Delegation

I

In 1962, in the aftermath of *Baker v. Carr*,[1] the federal courts invalidated Georgia's county unit system, its malapportioned house and senate, and its plan for electing members of Congress. *Baker v. Carr* was not a racial discrimination case, but its concept that voting districts must be composed of substantially equal populations was to prove one of the keys that opened the door to minority officeholding in Georgia.

Prior to *Baker v. Carr*, the Supreme Court had treated claims of unfairness in apportionment or districting as "political questions" that could not be considered by the federal courts. The traditional view was expressed in a 1946 opinion by Felix Frankfurter, who said that "[i]t is hostile to a democratic system to involve the judiciary in the politics of the people." In *Baker v. Carr*, the Court held that the political question doctrine properly understood involved "the relationship between the judiciary and the coordinate branches of the Federal Government, and not the federal judiciary's relationship to the States."[3] The doctrine was thus no bar to a court's remedying the gross inequities in voting power produced by state voting practices such as the county unit system and severely malapportioned legislatures and congressional delegations.

II

The county unit system was adopted in statutory form by the Neill Primary Act of 1917 and provided the method for nominating candidates for

---

[1] 369 U.S. 186 (1962).
[2] *Colegrove v. Green*, 328 U.S. 549, 553–54 (1946).
[3] 369 U.S. at 210.

statewide office in primary elections.[4] Primary elections, of course, were the only elections that really mattered in Georgia. As late as 1950, the Democratic nominee had won every statewide general election since 1872.[5]

V. O. Key, Jr., in his classic work, *Southern Politics in State and Nation*, slyly pilloried the unit system as the "Rule of the Rustics."[6] Under the unit system, counties were assigned twice as many unit votes as they had representatives in the state house. The eight most populous counties each had three representatives and six unit votes; the next thirty in size had two representatives each and four unit votes; and the remaining 121 had one representative each and two unit votes. The 121 counties containing a minority of the population controlled nearly 60 percent of the unit votes.[7]

The system was inherently nonmajoritarian. The candidate for nomination who received the most popular votes in a county was entitled to all of the county's unit votes. Candidates for governor and U.S. senator were nominated by a majority of the unit votes; candidates for secretary of state, attorney general, and appellate court judges were nominated by a plurality of unit votes; and candidates for Congress were nominated, whether by county unit or not, at the option of the local county political parties.[8] In no instance was a majority of the popular vote necessary for nomination.

Candidates were often nominated by a simple plurality – Nathaniel E. Harris for governor in 1914, Eugene Talmadge for governor in 1932, and Walter F. George for U.S. senator in 1938.[9] In 1954, Marvin Griffin captured a majority of unit votes but only 35 percent of the popular vote.[10] It was even possible for a candidate to lose the nomination with a majority of the popular vote. James V. Carmichael won a majority of the popular vote for governor in 1946, but was defeated by Eugene Talmadge, who got a majority of the unit votes.[11]

The votes of residents of the urban counties were systematically degraded under the unit system. Each vote outside Fulton County, for example, which

---

4 Ga. Laws 1917, p. 183. Political parties in Georgia traditionally nominated candidates for statewide office in state conventions, with each county having twice as many votes in the convention as it had representatives in the state house. The parties began to hold statewide primaries in 1898, after the decline of the Populist movement, and in 1917 the unit system was enacted in statutory form. *South v. Peters*, 89 F. Supp. 672, 677 (N. D. Ga. 1950).

5 *South v. Peters*, 89 F. Supp. at 677.

6 V. O. Key, Jr., *Southern Politics in State and Nation* (Knoxville: University of Tennessee Press, 1984), 106.

7 *Gray v. Sanders*, 372 U.S. 368, 371 (1963).

8 Ibid., p. 371; Georgia Democratic Party, Rules and Regulations, 1946–60; Georgia Democratic Party, Rules and Regulations, 1962; "Majority of Unit Votes Needed in Third District," *Macon Telegraph*, April 27, 1962.

9 Albert B. Saye, "Georgia's County Unit System of Election," 12 J. of Politics 93, 103 (1950).

10 *Brooks v. Miller*, Civ. No. 1:90-CV-1001-RCF (N. D. Ga.), Pl. Ex. 300, declaration of Steven F. Lawson, September 25, 1995, p. 15.

11 Saye, "Georgia's County Unit System," 103.

had the largest population of any county in the state, had on average eleven times the weight of a vote in Fulton County. In forty-five counties a vote had twenty times the weight of a vote in Fulton County. In one county a vote had over 120 times the weight of a vote in Fulton County.[12]

Whatever its historic justification, the county unit system in modern times served two fundamental purposes. One was to ensure control of statewide offices by the rural counties with a minority of the state's population. The other, which had become more critical since the abolition of the white primary, was to contain the black vote in the urban areas of the state.[13] James C. Bonner, a professor at the Women's College of Georgia in Milledgeville, identified, as did Key, rural antagonism against urban centers and the desire to disfranchise Negroes as the modern rationale for the unit system.[14]

Eugene Talmadge, an unabashed white supremacist, railed against critics of the unit system as "liberals, white primary antagonists, integrationists, and political idealists."[15] Supporters of the system argued openly that it protected the state from "sinister and subversive elements in the form of Negroes, Yankee influence, labor unions, agents of the Soviet Union, etc."[16] Peter Zack Geer of rural Colquit County, who was elected lieutenant governor in 1962, said that without the unit system candidates would campaign only in five or six cities in the state. He urged voters to support only those candidates who believed in the unit system.[17] Abolish the county unit system, he warned, and government would be "turned over to left-wing radicals and Pinks." "If we lose the county unit system," he continued, "there won't be enough votes in the whole of the Second Congressional District to match the bloc Negro vote in Atlanta."[18]

Even more moderate politicians such as Carl Sanders strongly supported the county unit system. In a speech at the annual convention of the Georgia County Officers Association in Atlanta in 1960, Sanders declared that "abolition of the county unit system would abandon control of state government to 'pressure groups or bloc votes.'" He described the unit system as

---

[12] *South v. Peters*, 339 U.S. 321, 278 (1950) (Justice Douglas dissenting).

[13] Key, *Southern Politics*, 122; Joseph Bernd and Lynwood Holland, "Recent Restrictions upon Negro Suffrage: The Case of Georgia," 21 J. of Politics 487, 508 (1959).

[14] Quoted in the *Macon Telegraph*, April 27, 1962. Justice William O. Douglas similarly noted in his dissenting opinion in *South v. Peters*, 339 U.S. at 278, that "the County Unit System heavily disenfranchises . . . [the] urban Negro population" and constituted "the 'last loophole' around our decisions holding that there must be no discrimination because of race in primary as well as in general elections."

[15] *Brooks v. Miller*, declaration of Steven F. Lawson, p. 13, citing Louis T. Rigdon II, *Georgia's County Unit System* (Decatur, Ga.: Selective Books, 1961), 48.

[16] Joseph L. Bernd, *Grass Roots Politics in Georgia* (Atlanta: Emory University Research Committee, 1960), 16.

[17] *Macon Telegraph*, June 10, 1960.

[18] *Camilla Enterprise*, April 5, 1962.

"Georgia's greatest protection for keeping representative government, maintaining conservative government and keeping liberals and radicals from taking over." The county unit system, he said, "is our protection for states' rights, and, thus, the foundation stone in preserving constitutional government."[19]

Opposition to the unit system came, not surprisingly, from metropolitan areas such as Atlanta. William B. Hartsfield, who served as mayor of Atlanta for twenty-four years, said that candidates had declared openly that "they didn't care to campaign in any area that had streetcars." The unit system, he said, makes it "profitable for ambitious candidates to create false and prejudicial issues dividing city from county, race from race, and labor from capital."[20]

Following the decision in *Baker v. Carr*, the general assembly, recognizing that the county unit system was vulnerable to a constitutional challenge, passed legislation intended to remedy some of the scheme's worst inequities in voting power by giving more unit votes to the most populous counties. But under the amended system, the vote of each citizen still counted for progressively less as the population of the county increased. The vote of a resident of Webster County, for example, which contained 3,247 people, was worth 8 times that of a resident of Fulton County, the largest county in the state. The vote of a resident of Echols County, which contained only 1,876 people, was worth 14 times that of a voter in Fulton County.[21]

The county unit system had survived five constitutional challenges during the 1940s and 1950s, one of which had been brought by Mayor Hartsfield.[22] But little over a month after the decision in *Baker v. Carr*, and the day after the general assembly had attempted to shore up the state's protection against "bloc votes" and "liberals and radicals," the modified unit system was struck down by a three-judge federal court in *Sanders v. Gray*.[23] The decision was affirmed the following year as *Gray v. Sanders*, in which the Supreme Court first used the phrase "one person, one vote." The Court held the county unit system unconstitutional because it denied "equality of voting power."[24] The outgoing governor, Ernest Vandiver, mourned the

[19] *Macon Telegraph*, June 10, 1960.
[20] *Macon Telegraph*, April 27, 1962.
[21] *Sanders v. Gray*, 203 F. Supp. 158, 170 n.10 (N. D. Ga. 1962).
[22] *Cook v. Fortson*, 329 U.S. 675 (1946); *Turman v. Duckworth*, 329 U.S. 675 (1946); *South v. Peters*, 339 U.S. 276 (1950); *Cox v. Peters*, 342 U.S. 936 (1951); *Hartsfield v. Sloan*, 357 U.S. 916 (1958). In *South v. Peters*, 339 U.S. at 277, citing *Colegrove v. Green*, the Court held that "[f]ederal courts consistently refuse to exercise their equity powers in cases posing political issues arising from a state's geographical distribution of electoral strength among its political subdivisions."
[23] 203 F. Supp. at 170.
[24] *Gray v. Sanders*, 372 U.S. at 381.

passing of the unit system "as a bulwark against . . . big city and minority bloc control."[25]

III

Immediately following *Sanders v. Gray*, the district court in *Toombs v. Fortson*[26] struck down the state's legislative apportionment on similar grounds of unequal voting power. The legislative scheme had the same basic defect as the county unit system, in that the least populist counties had disproportionate representation in the house and senate. The representatives from the 103 smallest counties, which had only about 22 percent of the population of the state, were a majority of the members of the house. The senators from the twenty-eight smallest districts, which had only about 21 percent of the population of the state, were a majority of the members of the senate.[27] As a remedy, the court directed the state to apportion at least one of its legislative houses on the basis of equal population among districts.

In areas of the state with high concentrations of black population, drawing districts of equal size would inevitably mean creating at least some districts that were majority-black. And majority-black districts, given the increases in black voter registration, would have the potential to elect black officeholders, even if whites voted as a solid bloc. The prospect of black elected officials sent tremors of fear and foreboding through the traditional white leadership of the state.

The transcendent importance of race in state politics was evident in the 1962 gubernatorial campaign involving Marvin Griffin and Carl Sanders. Griffin, an avowed racist, made open and inflammatory racial appeals. "Make no mistake," he warned, repeating his familiar admonition, "the majority race in Georgia is under siege" from the "colored race." "[W]e, frankly, ask and urge . . . a Solid White Vote in this election, in other elections to come, until sanity, and with it safety, returns." Griffin also rebuked "the candidate," meaning Sanders, who was seeking "the self-serving bloc vote of the colored race."[28] Griffin's campaign strategy was widely reported as "bear[ing] down hard on the race issue, and stress[ing] his claim that Martin Luther King is one of Sanders' chief supporters."[29] Under Griffin's racial calculus, self-interest voting by blacks was condemnable, while self-interest voting by whites was the highest civic duty.

Sanders was more restrained in his rhetoric than Griffin, but he was still a staunch supporter of racial segregation. His platform for governor contained

[25] *Macon Telegraph*, April 29, 1962.
[26] 205 F. Supp. 248 (N. D. Ga. 1962).
[27] Ibid., p. 251.
[28] *Macon Telegraph*, September 11, 1962.
[29] *Dawson News*, Aug. 2, 1962.

a formal "Segregation" plank in which he pledged "a continued legal fight to maintain segregation and resistance of federal court litigation in the race relations field."[30] As Sanders explained:

My record in support of legislation over the years to maintain segregation is long, continuing, and well-known. It is not one of empty oratory, but concrete results. . . . As your governor, every legal means and every lawful recourse available will be utilized to the fullest to strengthen and to maintain Georgia's traditional separation, sponsored by the responsible leadership of the state, and passed almost unanimously by the General Assembly. Legal attacks against Georgia's institutions in the federal courts will be resisted with every available defense.[31]

Every modern Georgia governor, through the election of Lester Maddox in 1966, was in fact a vocal supporter of the Jim Crow system.[32] Even Ellis Arnall, who enjoyed a reputation for being relatively liberal on matters of race, was a staunch defender of segregation. "Hell," he said years later, "if I had defied Southern [racial] orthodoxy, I wouldn't have been elected door keeper."[33]

Candidates for ostensibly nonpolitical offices, such as judges and solicitors, often ran campaigns that made open appeals to race. Donald Hollowell recalls that W. I. Geer, who served as superior court judge of the Pataula judicial circuit until the mid-1970s, campaigned for office openly advising the electorate that he did not want any "nigger votes."[34] In Stewart County, "Friends of Eugene Horne" ran an ad in the local newspaper urging people to vote for Horne for solicitor because he "will not tolerate any infringement on the Southern Way of Life." Indeed, he would "not hesitate to sacrifice his blood to protect our Southern life." Charles Burgamy, the former solicitor and a candidate for superior court, assured the voters in his campaign ad that "I shall always do all within my power to help preserve our Southern Way of Life and the separation of the races."[35] Potential black litigants in the superior court could not have been reassured by these declarations of prosecutorial and judicial bias.

Griffin's charge that Sanders was seeking the black vote was so potentially damaging to Sanders's standing with white voters that he publicly denied that he had the backing of black organizations or black leaders. Speaking from Jekyll Island, where he was attending the convention of the Georgia

---

30 *Macon Telegraph*, October 18, 1962.
31 *Atlanta Journal and Constitution*, July 1, 1962.
32 Marilyn Davis and Alex Willingham, "Politics and Race in the Cracker State: Our First Look at Andrew Young and the Georgia Governor's Election in 1990," paper presented at the annual meeting of the National Conference of Black Political Scientists, Atlanta, Georgia, March 1990, p. 10.
33 Arnall interview, Feb. 2, 1986, quoted in Harold Paulk Henderson, *The Politics of Change in Georgia: A Political Biography of Ellis Arnall* (Athens: University of Georgia Press, 1991), 138.
34 *Georgia v. Thornburg*, Civ. No. 90-2065 (D. D. C.), declaration of Donald L. Hollowell.
35 *Stewart-Webster Journal*, Sept. 8, 1960.

Municipal Association, Sanders assured white voters that "I do not have the support of the NAACP or Martin Luther King."[36]

There was nothing unusual about race baiting in the Georgia politics of the day. Fred Hasty of Bibb County, who was running for the state legislature, accused his opponent, William Laite, of meeting "with Negro leaders" and seeking their support. Laite vehemently denied the charges, accused Hasty of "dragging this campaign in the political mud," and, expressing great sorrow, said that he "never dreamed, when I entered this race, that my opponent, in his desperation, would resort to such disgraceful levels of behavior."[37] Such a mea non culpa was obligatory in discrediting the suggestion that a reliable white candidate would actually seek the support of black voters.

In the fall of 1962, the legislature set about reapportioning the senate in response to the decision in *Toombs v. Fortson.* The solons were deeply preoccupied with race. Eugene Patterson, a former editor and political columnist for the *Atlanta Journal and Constitution,* noted that during the early 1960s the Georgia "legislature was in the hands still of the county segregationists," and the "political wheels that turned in the state capitol... were all driven by race.... The whole politics of the state turned on that issue."[38]

A principal concern in the redistricting was how to elect senators from urban counties, such as Fulton, which had substantial black populations and were entitled to more than one senator. Although the state Constitution required senators to be elected from single-member districts, Sanders, who had won the Democratic gubernatorial nomination in September 1962 but was still president pro tem of the senate, recommended countywide elections in counties with more than one senator.[39]

It was generally understood at the time that Leroy Johnson, a young black attorney from Atlanta, was planning to run for one of the seven senate seats in Fulton County.[40] If he ran in a majority-black single-member district, his chances for election would be very good.

Sanders's floor leader, Rep. Guy Rutland of DeKalb, was reported as saying that the reason Sanders favored countywide elections was "to avoid the possible countywide election of a Negro from Fulton."[41] The press

---

[36] *Macon Telegraph,* June 12, 1962.

[37] *Macon Telegraph,* September 7, 1962.

[38] *Brooks v. Miller,* Joint Ex. 1, transcript of interview of Mr. Eugene Patterson by Dr. Steven F. Lawson, June 13, 1991, pp. 4–9.

[39] *Macon Telegraph,* September 19, 1962; *Cordele Dispatch,* October 5, 1962.

[40] *Brooks v. Miller,* declaration of Steven F. Lawson, p. 19.

[41] *Cordele Dispatch,* October 4, 1962. Newspaper coverage must always be approached with care. Patterson, however, believed that the newspapers did a good job of accurately reporting the facts in their coverage of the general assembly during the 1960s. Particularly when the newspapers quoted a member of the general assembly, "[t]he quotation would be accurate." *Brooks v. Miller,* trial transcript, May 15, 1996, p. 452. Milton Carlton, a member of the

reported that "Gov. Nominee Carl Sanders has been quoted as favoring countywide elections to reduce the chances of Negroes being elected to the Senate."[42] Other supporters of the countywide provision argued, publicly and privately, "that it would rule out the election of Negro senators from Fulton County."[43] And as the president of the Georgia League of Women Voters noted, "the argument was frankly used that countywide electing would be less likely to produce Negro senators than letting citizens of only a specific district do the voting."[44]

Rep. Frank Twitty, who led the fight for Sanders's reapportionment bill on the house floor, promised that he was "not going to vote for anything that would put a member of a minority group in the state Senate."[45] He warned that "unless candidates in multi-district counties were required to run countywide, then 'a member of the minority race' would be elected in Fulton County."[46] According to Eugene Patterson, the "racially motivated segregationist resisters to elections of blacks" were saying, in effect, "we don't want Leroy Johnson from Atlanta sitting in the next chair from us. So this is the most blatant racist approach to this issue. But these people made the majority of votes in that legislature."[47]

Even those who opposed countywide voting for the senate did so for racial reasons, that is, because they felt it gave too much power to black voters. Rep. George Bagby of Paulding County complained that countywide voting "will give the Negro (on Hunter Street) in Atlanta seven votes and the cotton picker in Paulding one vote."[48] Rep. Brooks Culpepper of Talbot County proposed an unsuccessful amendment to strike the countywide election provision from the bill. He charged that "the provision was a 'scheme' to aid the 'bloc vote' because it would permit a Negro voter in Fulton County to vote for seven senators, whereas a white voter in a multi-county district could vote for only one."[49] The general assembly adopted the Sanders redistricting plan, with a majority-vote requirement, for state senators.[50]

---

general assembly during the 1960s, agreed that the newspaper accounts of the time "were generally accurate." *Brooks v. Miller*, preliminary injunction transcript, July 13, 1990, vol. 5, p. 14.

42 *Atlanta Daily World*, October 6, 1962.

43 *Macon Telegraph*, October 4, 1962.

44 Quoted in Peyton McCrary and Steven F. Lawson, "Race and Reapportionment, 1962: The Case of Georgia Senate Redistricting," 12 J. Policy Hist. 293, 304 (2000).

45 *Macon Telegraph*, October 5, 1962; *Atlanta Daily World*, October 6, 1962. Twitty opposed any plan "that would automatically put a member of a minority race in the Senate."

46 *Macon Telegraph*, October 9, 1962. See also *Atlanta Constitution*, October 8, 1962; *Atlanta Constitution*, October 2, 1963.

47 *Brooks v. Miller*, transcript of interview of Mr. Eugene Patterson, pp. 13–14.

48 *Cordele Dispatch*, October 5, 1962.

49 *Macon Telegraph*, October 5, 1962.

50 Ga. Laws 1962, Ex. Sess., p. 30.

In an effort to head off the charge that the redistricting bill violated the state Constitution, Sanders also pushed through with nearly unanimous support a resolution to amend the Constitution to permit countywide voting in counties such as Fulton.[51] The Achilles' heel of this tactic was that the constitutional amendment could not be presented to the voters for approval until the November general election – one month *after* the scheduled October 16 primary. And what could go wrong, did go wrong. An Atlanta attorney, George Finch, challenged the at-large voting requirement for Fulton County in the federal and state courts. The federal court abstained, but Judge Durwood T. Pye of the Fulton County Superior Court, an ardent segregationist who enjoyed a reputation for handing down punitive sentences to civil rights demonstrators,[52] issued an order less than seven hours before the polls were to open on election day that the at-large measure violated the state Constitution.[53]

Under the new plan, Johnson ran for the senate against three white opponents and got a majority of the votes in the predominantly black district in which he lived, district 38. He got only a plurality countywide, and in a runoff against a white opponent, Ed Barfield, the odds are that he would have lost.[54] The *Atlanta Constitution* predicted that in the expected countywide runoff for district 38 "most white voters in Fulton County would support the candidacy of Mr. Barfield and that he would win because the vote would be polarized along racial lines."[55]

Johnson believed that the newspaper's prediction was sound:

[F]ew white voters in Fulton County in those years were willing to vote for a black candidate. In other words, the Constitution's editorial reflected the general understanding in Georgia in those years that a runoff election allows white voters to unite behind a single white candidate in any head-to-head contest against a black candidate.[56]

Eugene Patterson agreed that it probably would have been impossible for a black to be elected at that time running countywide in Fulton County.[57]

Johnson was declared the nominee from his district[58] and went on to win the general election against a black Republican. Despite the legislature's best

[51] Ga. Laws 1962, Ex. Sess., p. 51; *Cordele Dispatch*, October 5, 1962; *Macon Telegraph*, October 9, 1962.

[52] See J. Morgan Kousser, *Colorblind Injustice: Minority Voting Rights and the Undoing of the Second Reconstruction* (Chapel Hill: University of North Carolina Press, 1999), 209–10, 226.

[53] *Finch v. Gray*, No. A96441 (Fulton Cty. Sup. Ct. 1962). For a discussion of the state court decision, see *Fortson v. Dorsey*, 379 U.S. 433, 434 n.1 (1965).

[54] *Macon Telegraph*, October 20, 1962.

[55] *Atlanta Constitution*, October 17, 1962.

[56] *Brooks v. Miller*, Pl. Ex. 306, p. 5 (testimony of Leroy R. Johnson).

[57] *Brooks v. Miller*, trial transcript, May 15, 1996, pp. 453–54.

[58] *Macon Telegraph*, October 21, 1962; *Macon Telegraph*, October 22, 1962.

efforts to exclude him through countywide voting, Johnson became the first black elected to the Georgia legislature since Reconstruction.[59] And more would follow. When the Supreme Court later ruled in *Reynolds v. Sims* that *both* chambers of a state's legislature must comply with one person, one vote,[60] the stage was set for the creation of majority-black districts in the house as well.

The controversial countywide voting requirement was ratified by the voters in the 1962 general election, although too late to deny Leroy Johnson his seat. Voters in Fulton and DeKalb Counties challenged the new provision on the one person, one vote theory that as residents of multimember senatorial districts their voting strength was denied equal weight with that of residents of single-member districts. The Supreme Court disagreed. In *Fortson v. Dorsey*, it held that multimember districts were not per se unconstitutional, and that there was no evidence that the vote of a resident of Fulton County was not "approximately equal in weight to that of any other citizen in the State."[61]

The plaintiffs also alleged that the countywide method of elections had been adopted in order to minimize the strength of racial and political minorities in the populous urban counties. But they presented no evidence to support the allegation, and the Supreme Court accordingly refused to consider it. The Court did, however, articulate for the first time the proposition that a legislative plan could be unconstitutional if it "designedly or otherwise . . . operate[d] to minimize or cancel out the voting strength of racial or political elements of the voting population."[62] This concept of minimizing or diluting minority voting strength, as opposed to denying it outright, was subsequently used by the courts to invalidate districting plans even when they fully complied with one person, one vote.[63]

IV

The state's congressional redistricting was struck down by the Supreme Court in 1964 in *Wesberry v. Sanders*,[64] a suit brought by registered voters of Fulton County. The challenged plan dated back to 1931 and, like the county unit system and the malapportioned legislature, seriously undervalued the votes of residents of the most populous counties. The fifth district, which contained

---

[59] *Brooks v. Miller*, Pl. Ex. 307, p. 631 (testimony of Leroy R. Johnson).

[60] 377 U.S. 533 (1964).

[61] *Fortson v. Dorsey*, 379 U.S. at 438 (quoting *Reynolds v. Sims*, 377 U.S. at 579).

[62] Ibid., p. 439.

[63] See, e.g., *White v. Regester*, 412 U.S. 755, 766 (1973) (invalidating multimember legislative districts in Texas on the grounds that blacks and Mexican-Americans "had less opportunity than did other residents in the district to participate in the political processes and to elect legislators of their choice").

[64] 376 U.S. 1 (1964).

Fulton, DeKalb, and Rockdale Counties, was on average twice as large as the state's other nine congressional districts. One district, the ninth, had less than a third of the population of the fifth.

The Supreme Court invalidated the state's plan under Article I, Section 2 of the Constitution, which requires representatives to be chosen "by the People of the several States," and established a rule that "as nearly as is practicable one man's vote in a congressional election is to be worth as much as another's."[65] The one person, one vote principle of *Gray v. Sanders*, applicable to state and local redistricting, and the "as nearly as practicable" standard of *Wesberry v. Sanders*, applicable to congressional redistricting, shifted redistricting permanently from a geographical to a population-based concept. And coupled with the minority-vote dilution principle articulated in *Fortson v. Dorsey*, the two standards would transform electoral politics, not just in Georgia, but in the nation as a whole and at every level of government.

[65] Ibid., pp. 7–8.

6

The Election Code of 1964: Twilight of the Malapportioned Legislature

> It behooves all of us to remember we will never have the opportunity as a
> rural-dominated House to pass another election code.
>
> Rep. Johnnie Caldwell (Upson County, June 22, 1964)

I

When it met in 1963, the legislature appointed another Election Laws Study Committee to revise the state's election laws.[1] The membership of the new ELSC, like its predecessors, was all-white,[2] consisting of five members of the general assembly, four members from the state at large appointed by the governor, and the secretary of state and attorney general.

The ELSC was directed to consider a broad revision of the state's election laws, but Freeman Leverett, an assistant attorney general, advised Secretary of State Ben Fortson that one of the most critical issues to be taken up by the ELSC was "replacing the invalid county unit law with provisions governing primary elections, run offs, plurality or majority vote."[3] Willis J. Richardson, Jr., another member of the ELSC, agreed that the committee would have to "decide two basic questions which will greatly affect our entire work" – whether to have open or closed primaries and "whether or not the vote is to be on a majority or plurality basis."[4]

---

[1] Ga. Laws 1963, p. 492. A second ELSC had been established in 1961 (Ga. Laws 1961, p. 276), but it was dissolved without taking any action because of the uncertainty in the law created after the county unit system and state legislative apportionment were declared unconstitutional. Georgia House Journal, January 15, 1963, pp. 116–17.

[2] *Brooks v. Miller*, Civ. No. 1: 90-cv-1001-RCF (N. D. Ga.), preliminary injunction transcript, July 13, 1990, vol. 5, p. 142 (testimony of Melba Williams).

[3] Freeman Leverett to Ben W. Fortson, June 13, 1963 (Georgia Department of Archives and History, Atlanta, Election Law Study Committee Papers).

[4] Willis J. Richardson to Ben W. Fortson, Jr., August 28, 1963, Election Law Study Committee Papers.

The senate had been reapportioned during the preceding year, but the members of the house had been elected under the old malapportioned system. As a consequence, the rural legislators dominated the lower chamber and would play a decisive role in shaping the new election code.

At the beginning of the 1963 legislative session, Rep. Denmark Groover of Bibb County introduced a statewide majority vote requirement for local, state, and federal elections.[5] He argued that a comprehensive majority-vote requirement was essential to restoring the "protection" that had been lost with the county unit system. The measure was needed, he said, "to prevent special pressure groups from controlling elections" and to thwart election control by Negroes and other minorities.[6] He repeatedly justified his bill as a way of preventing "bloc groups" from electing candidates to office.[7]

The "bloc vote" was a euphemism or code word for the black vote. "That was just the general term that was used in polite society," says Eugene Patterson, a former editor of the *Atlanta Constitution*. "Everybody knew what it meant – the negro vote."[8]

A majority-vote rule ensures that a politically cohesive numerical majority will always be able to elect the candidates of its choice. Even if the majority splits its vote among several candidates in the primary so that a minority candidate wins a plurality, the majority can simply regroup and elect the candidate of its choice in the runoff between the two highest vote-getters. As the Supreme Court has observed, where a white majority votes as a bloc, a majority-vote requirement "would permanently foreclose a black candidate from being elected."[9]

Groover has described himself as "a segregationist. I was a county unit man.... And I was raised in a country county and I had many prejudices, and I don't mind admitting it.... If you want to establish that some of my political activity was racially motivated, it was."[10] Groover's hostility to the black "bloc vote" can be traced, not simply to his general racial attitudes, but to his defeat in 1958 in an election for the general assembly. As his loss became clear, he launched an attack on "Negro 'bloc voting,'" and called for a recount of the ballots in the black precincts. Groover said he was "unwilling" to allow the votes of whites to be "destroyed without a proper recount and recheck

[5] Georgia House Journal, Jan. 25, 1963, p. 301.
[6] *Valdosta Daily Times*, February 21, 1963.
[7] *Valdosta Daily Times*, February 20, 1963; *Macon Telegraph*, February 21, 1963.
[8] *Brooks v. Miller*, transcript of cross-examination of Eugene C. Patterson, May 5, 1996, p. 15. See also Peyton McCrary and Steven F. Lawson, "Race and Reapportionment, 1962: The Case of Georgia Senate Redistricting," 12 J. Policy Hist. 297 (2000) ("[t]he term 'bloc vote' was used by politicians of that era as a racial code word to designate black voters").
[9] *City of Port Arthur v. United States*, 459 U.S. 159, 167 (1982).
[10] J. Morgan Kousser, *Colorblind Injustice: Minority Voting Rights and the Undoing of the Second Reconstruction* (Chapel Hill: University of North Carolina Press, 1999), 214.

of the block voting."[11] Given his racial attitudes, the fact that Groover got few votes in the black precincts should not have surprised him.

Georgia's traditions, as its long use of the county unit system demonstrates, were hardly rooted in the concept of majority vote or rule. At the county level, whether to use a majority-vote or a simple plurality-vote requirement was optional. Most counties used a plurality-vote system, that is, the candidate who got the most votes – or who was "first past the post" – was declared the winner.[12] Democratic party officials estimated that as many as 100 of Georgia's 159 counties nominated candidates by plurality vote.[13]

There were a few exceptions to the local-option rule. In Fulton County, candidates for the general assembly and judges of the superior court were required by state law to be nominated by "receiving a plurality of the votes cast."[14] This local law was to assume critical importance when two whites and one black ran for a Fulton County judgeship in 1964.

The first statewide majority-vote provision had been enacted in 1962 as part of the senate plan designed to prevent blacks from being elected in Fulton and other urban counties. That same year, the Democratic Party also adopted a majority-vote requirement for statewide primaries.[15]

Groover's majority-vote bill passed in the house by a vote of 133 to 41 and was sent to the senate.[16] Not everyone who voted for it did so for reasons of race. James Mackay voted for the bill because he thought plurality voting would perpetuate rural control. Mackay was convinced, however, that "[r]ace was a dominant factor in the thinking and decision-making of the white members of the General Assembly during my service there and I do not think that the statewide majority vote requirement would have passed had these members not been convinced of the racially discriminatory potential of the runoff system."[17]

An analysis by Morgan Kousser of the February 1963 roll call vote in the house strongly suggests that other legislators supported the majority-vote bill for the same reasons as Groover. The greater the difference in registration between blacks and whites, and the smaller the proportion of blacks

---

[11] *Macon Telegraph*, September 11, 1958.

[12] The phrase was used by the Supreme Court in *Timmons v. Twin Cities Area New Party*, 520 U.S. 351, 362 (1997), which described plurality vote as one of the "features of our political system."

[13] *Savannah Evening Press*, April 1, 1964; *Macon News*, April 1, 1964.

[14] Ga. Laws 1925, p. 205. Another exception was counties having a population of no fewer than 18,524 and no more than 18,540 inhabitants based on the 1940 census. They (in reality only one) were required to nominate for all county offices, including the general assembly, by majority vote. Ga. Laws 1945, p. 1087.

[15] *Macon Telegraph*, June 28, 1962.

[16] Georgia House Journal, Feb. 20, 1963, pp. 645–48.

[17] *Brooks v. Miller*, Pl. Ex. 308, pp. 3–4 (direct testimony of James A. Mackay).

registered – both of which are indicators of discrimination in registration – the more likely the legislators from that county were to vote for the majority-vote requirement.[18]

The senate rules committee, when it considered the majority-vote bill from the house, initially voted a "do not pass" resolution. In an effort to revive the bill, Groover appeared before the committee and again made open racial appeals in urging its passage. He warned the committee that the federal government "intercedes to increase the registration of Negro voters," and that a majority-vote rule would prevent the election by plurality vote of a candidate supported only by a local courthouse ring or by a bloc vote group.[19]

Lt. Governor Geer, the chair of the senate committee, said "a majority vote requirement suits me" but that the senate should deal with Groover's proposal.[20] The senate committee withdrew its resolution and assigned the bill to a three-member subcommittee for further study. The majority-vote bill did not come to the floor of the senate during the remaining two weeks of the legislative session.[21] Committee members expected that the ELSC would consider Groover's proposal as part of its overall deliberations during the coming year.[22]

II

As the ELSC began its deliberations, the state was experiencing the most dramatic increase in black registration since Reconstruction. Although the estimates varied, the number of black registered voters in 1963 was put as high as 225,000. There was no dispute, in the words of Hal Gulliver, a political reporter for the *Atlanta Constitution*, that "Negro voting in Georgia is more significant now than at any time in this century."[23]

The deliberations of the ELSC, and public reaction to it, reflected a deep, pervasive preoccupation with race and a concerted effort to contain the emerging black political power. One of the ELSC's initial proposals was to repeal the state's literacy and understanding tests for registration and replace them with a prohibition on all assistance to voters, except for those who were physically disabled.[24] The white leadership believed that the federal government was poised to challenge the state's existing registration laws and viewed the voter assistance provision as an alternative, more secure disfranchisement mechanism.

[18] Kousser, *Colorblind Injustice*, 236.
[19] *Atlanta Constitution*, March 1, 1963.
[20] Ibid.
[21] *Brooks v. Miller*, declaration of Steven F. Lawson, pp. 29–30.
[22] Ibid., pp. 30–1; Kousser, *Colorblind Injustice*, 218.
[23] *Atlanta Constitution*, May 2, 1963.
[24] Election Law Study Committee Papers, minutes, October 15–16, 1963.

J. B. Fuqua, a senator from Augusta and a member of the ELSC, wrote to Fortson in November 1963:

I can tell you very confidentially that I happen to know that the Justice Department is sitting on some cases in Georgia, waiting the final outcome of the recommendations of the Election Laws Study Committee in regard to changes in the registration laws. I think we should handle our own problems and not bring on Federal interference because of our failure to face up to the realities of the times.[25]

As Fortson explained in a letter to the judge of the court of ordinary of Burke County, the ELSC's goal was to preempt a federal court challenge to the literacy test and to "attempt to try to set up something that would help us protect ourselves [and] . . . prevent block-voting."[26]

There was quick and widespread opposition by whites to the proposal to repeal the state's voter tests. More than a 103 residents of Columbus submitted a petition to the ELSC "protest[ing] the proposed Constitutional revision eliminating the literacy requirement for voting in the State of Georgia." The chair of the Muscogee County Democratic Party executive committee "was against the abolition of literacy tests as has been proposed," as was the chief registrar. A state representative from the county said that "the people with whom he has been in contact do not favor the abolition of literacy tests."[27] The former registrar of Talbot County and the chief registrar of Upson County were also adamantly "against abolition of literacy tests."[28]

At the public hearing held by the ELSC in Savannah on November 14, 1963, a number of people spoke against repeal of the literacy test.[29] Others wrote to the ELSC expressing their concerns about black voter registration and the dreaded "bloc vote." Ed Barfield, who had lost the senate race the year before to a black lawyer, Leroy Johnson of Atlanta, predicted that "within a short period of 5 years . . . the negro, through *Block Vote* will elect a negro sheriff, mayors, senators, etc." He pleaded with Fortson to "[s]ee what you can do that will awaken the white people to register & vote."[30]

The mayor of Montezuma wrote to Fortson that he was "really dumbfounded at the proposals." "I have watched their voting pattern for many

---

[25] J. B. Fuqua to Ben W. Fortson, Jr., November 25, 1963, Election Law Study Committee Papers. Fuqua, one of the more progressive members of the committee, condemned the gross registration irregularities that had been practiced in some counties, but he doubted that "we could get it [repeal of literacy requirements] through the General Assembly – however, we should make the requirements just as liberal as it is possible to get through the Legislature." Ibid.

[26] Secretary of state to John J. Jones, October 25, 1963, Election Law Study Committee Papers.

[27] Election Law Study Committee Papers, minutes of public hearing, November 7, 1963.

[28] Ibid.

[29] Election Law Study Committee Papers, minutes of public hearing, November 14, 1963.

[30] Ed Barfield to Ben Fortson, June 13, 1963, Election Law Study Committee Papers.

years and I don't believe I have ever seen them go to the polls on any issue of consequence when they did not vote en masse or block," he said. "Lord knows what would happen if we turned the general rabble of their race loose at the polls. I have one very strong belief and that is they would takeover Macon County and run it according to their own beliefs and consciences."[31]

A member of the Macon County Democratic Party executive committee was "appalled" at the ELSC's recommendation. "Have we reached the stage in Georgia," he wanted to know, "that for the sake of creating a national image you and your fellow committeemen are willing to destroy Macon County and others that have a colored population exceeding the white?" He said it was "ridiculous to invite our masses of illiterate negros [sic] to our polling places and hope to be able to throw their votes out because they can not mark the ballot. What is to prevent the NAACP to furnish them mock ballots which they would merely have to copy?"[32] Fortson wrote back: "I can assure you that I would be opposed to anything that did not give protection to the people of my state."[33]

Ely Horne, the clerk of court of Sumter County, complained that "if we have people in this state who are willing to open the polls to everyone then we are in perfect accord with the scalawag element of this nation which is led by Kennedy and his Harvard advisers."[34] Henry Crisp, a law student at the University of Georgia, wrote to Fortson expressing his disdain for "this extremely left-wing proposal" that "would allow any uninformed and illiterate citizen to be a voter." Invoking patriotism and the generations – presumably white – still to come, he gushed that he looked forward "with relish upon the day when an aroused citizenry will see through this and similar schemes and fill our State and National offices with patriots who are aware of their duty to preserve our Republic for people yet unborn."[35]

Station WDAK in Columbus, known as Big Johnny Reb, called the plan to abolish literacy tests "nauseating" and said it was "a deliberate attempt to give suffrage to people who don't know how to vote." The station president, Allen M. Woodall, confided to Fortson: "Honestly, Ben, I haven't talked to a single person who isn't dead set against changing our registration regulations."[36] Officials of the Swift Manufacturing Company in Columbus said

---

[31] C. P. Savage, Sr., to Ben W. Fortson, October 17, 1963, Election Law Study Committee Papers.

[32] Lewis H. McKenzie to Ben W. Fortson, October 22, 1963, Election Law Study Committee Papers.

[33] Ben Fortson to Lewis H. McKenzie, October 25, 1963, Election Law Study Committee Papers.

[34] Ely Horne to Ben Fortson, October 18, 1963, Election Law Study Committee Papers.

[35] Henry L. Crisp to Ben Fortson, November 12, 1963, Election Law Study Committee Papers.

[36] "A Big Johnny Reb Special Editorial," October 22, 1963, Election Law Study Committee Papers.

that "I.Q. tests and literacy tests should, in our opinion, be a minimum requirement to qualify as a voter in the State of Georgia." They added that "[t]he prospects of an uninformed electorate are frightening."[37]

Calvin F. Craig, the Ku Klux Klan Grand Dragon of the Realm of Georgia, denounced the ELSC proposal as a scheme by state officials to get "tens of thousands of illiterate negroes registered to vote" so that the state could be thrown to John Kennedy in 1964. "The Public's confidence in the present State Administration is slipping badly throughout Georgia," he said.[38]

G. R. McCrimmon, a Lincoln County commissioner, wrote to Fortson: "I'm sure you would find 95% of the white voters of Georgia against your proposal for voter qualification."[39] In responding to McCrimmon, Fortson assured him that "I have never and never will support anything that I think will hurt the people of my section or of the State."[40]

Two organizations that communicated to the ELSC their support for abolishing the voter tests were the Southern Christian Leadership Conference (SCLC)[41] and the Citizens Democratic Club of Georgia.[42] Both were predominantly black.

Attorney General Cook, another member of the ELSC, was an initial supporter of the effort to recast the literacy test into a more legally acceptable form. He changed his mind, however, because "[i]t was our thought originally that this gesture would insulate us against federal court suits.... Upon further study, however, I perceive that it takes no great degree of sophistication to discern that this is a mere play on words." He proposed retention of a literacy requirement that would test "not only ability to read and write, but also comprehension."[43]

Opie Shelton, the vice president of the Atlanta Chamber of Commerce, added his voice to those who were alarmed over the prospect of increased black voting power. In an address to the Northside Kiwanis Club, he predicted that Atlanta would become majority-black by 1975 and, citing the inevitable decline of other cities that had become majority-black, said that Atlanta was "on the threshold of a major catastrophe unless we develop

[37] Garland Embry, Jr., to Ben W. Fortson, Jr., October 23, 1963, Election Law Study Committee Papers.

[38] Calvin F. Craig to Ben W. Fortson, Jr., October 18, 1963, Election Law Study Committee Papers.

[39] G. R. McCrimmon to Ben Fortson, October 23, 1963, Election Law Study Committee Papers.

[40] Secretary of state to G. R. McCrimmon, October 25, 1963, Election Law Study Committee Papers. See also secretary of state to Ely Horne, October 25, 1963, Election Law Study Committee Papers; secretary of state to Henry L. Crisp, November 15, 1963, Election Law Study Committee Papers.

[41] Septima P. Clark to Ben W. Fortson, Jr., October 18, 1963, Election Law Study Committee Papers.

[42] Leroy Wilson to Ben Fortson, December 13, 1963, Election Law Study Committee Papers.

[43] Eugene Cook to Ben W. Fortson, November 20, 1963, Election Law Study Committee Papers.

the political capacity to prevent it." He proposed more "realistic" annexation and zoning laws to ensure that Atlanta remained majority-white and
prosperous.[44]

The ELSC bowed to the overwhelming white opposition. In its final proposal it recommended that the literacy requirement and an understanding
test be retained, but that the thirty questions be replaced with ten questions
to be devised by the commissioner of elections.[45]

The ELSC also recommended adoption of a majority-vote requirement.
The provision had been drafted for the committee by Assistant Attorney
General Paul Rogers, Jr., and was identical to the one proposed earlier by
Groover.[46] Rogers, a determined foe of equal voting fights, would later testify
before Congress in support of literacy tests and in opposition to passage of
the Voting Rights Act, calling the proposed bill "unconstitutional" and a
"yoke of disgrace."[47]

Some members of the ELSC expressed strong good-government reasons
for not adopting a majority-vote rule. In September 1963, Fugua wrote to
Ben Fortson that "as a practical matter, the present practice of plurality rather
than majority vote has not resulted in widespread inequities or dissatisfac-
tion." Fuqua "would prefer to see us stay on the plurality basis, or, as an alternative, require a run-off only provided no candidate received more than, say,
35% of the vote cast in a primary."[48] His reason for preferring the plurality
vote in local primaries was the expense involved in conducting runoff elections. Because counties financed their own primaries, "changing to the majority vote might make things even worse in some of the smaller counties."[49]

William J. Schloth, another member of the ELSC, also favored a plurality-
vote requirement. He considered the runoff system "costly and without merit
sufficient to justify the requirement of a majority vote."[50]

Fuqua, in another letter to Fortson, reiterated his concern that a majority-
vote requirement for local primaries would prove impractical and expensive.
"As long as we had the plurality rule, the fees collected from statehouse candidates and local candidates were usually adequate to pay for the September
primaries," he said.[51] Fuqua backpedalled on his opposition to the

---

[44] *Atlanta Journal*, December 13, 1963.

[45] Georgia House Journal, February 21, 1964, p. 2360; *Brooks v. Miller*, declaration of Stephen
F. Lawson, p. 40.

[46] Election Law Study Committee Papers, Minutes of subcommittee meetings, August 27, 1963.

[47] Hearings before the Committee on the Judiciary, United States Senate, Eighty-ninth
Congress, First Session, on S. 1564 to Enforce the 15th Amendment to the Constitution
of the United States, March 23, 24, 25, 29, 30, 31, and April 1, 2, 5, 1965, pp. 615–17, 621.

[48] J. B. Fugua to Ben W. Fortson, Jr., September 7, 1963, Election Law Study Committee Papers.

[49] *Brooks v. Miller*, trial transcript, May 15, 1996, p. 5.

[50] William J. Schloth to Ben W. Fortson, Jr., September 3, 1963, Election Law Study Committee
Papers.

[51] J. B. Fugua to Ben Fortson, October 14, 1963, Election Law Study Committee Papers.

majority-vote requirement, however, once Sanders's support for it became clear. On October 15, 1963, with only Schloth dissenting, Fuqua and the other members of the ELSC recommended passage of the majority-vote provision.[52]

At the beginning of the 1964 session, the legislature paused from its consideration of election law reform long enough to adopt a resolution condemning the proposed federal Civil Rights Act of 1964. Sparing no invective, it called the provisions of the bill prohibiting segregation in public accommodations "a grossly unfair, unjust, and diabolical attempt to usurp from the citizens of the United States their God-given and Constitutional freedom to conduct their business and lives in any manner they deem proper."[53]

Richard B. Russell, known as "Mr. South" in the U.S. Senate and one of Georgia's most influential elected officials, continued to lead the fight by southern whites in Congress to block passage of civil rights laws. In March 1964 he resurrected a proposal he had first made in 1949 to redistribute the black population. He proposed creating a Racial Relocation Commission, which would move blacks from the South voluntarily and distribute them so that each state would have a population that was 10.5 percent black, the national average. Doing this, he reasoned, would dampen the enthusiasm of legislators from states that had few black residents, such as Mike Mansfield of Montana and Hubert Humphrey of Minnesota, from trying to change the existing "social order." Once they experienced the "problems" associated with having large concentrations of Negros in their states, they would, he believed, back off from their support of civil rights laws.[54] Congress passed the civil rights bill in July of that year over Russell's opposition and the Georgia legislature's protests.[55]

III

The ELSC presented its proposal to the general assembly on February 21, 1964.[56] It contained an impressive array of discriminatory voting practices – a literacy requirement, a voter understanding test, a comprehensive majority-vote requirement, and a provision prohibiting assistance in voting except in case of physical disability. It also contained a numbered-post requirement that candidates for multiseat bodies run for specific seats.[57] A numbered-post

52 *Brooks v. Miller*, declaration of Steven F. Lawson p. 36; Kousser, *Colorblind Injustice*, 213–32.
53 Georgia House Journal, Feb. 5, 1964, p. 680; Feb. 10, 1964, p. 896.
54 *Dawson News*, March 19, 1964; *Atlanta Journal*, March 16, 1964.
55 Pub. L. 88-352.
56 Georgia House Journal, February 21, 1964, p. 2360.
57 Election Laws Study Committee, proposed election code, §§34-617, 618, 1102, 1317, 1514; Freeman Leverett, "Summary of Basic Changes in Proposed Election Code" (Dec. 1963).

requirement forces candidates to run head to head and thus prevents a cohesive minority from concentrating its votes on a single candidate in a multiseat race.[58]

When the proposed new election code was taken up by the senate, it adopted the proposals of the ELSC but exempted county commissions composed of two or more members from the numbered-post and majority-vote requirements.[59] Since only a few counties used a form of government consisting of only one member,[60] the senate exception essentially removed counties from the majority-vote provision.

Senator Dan MacIntyre, a Fulton County Republican, also proposed a delay in implementation of the majority-vote requirement until 1965, because three candidates – Paul Webb, Jr., a racial moderate; Judge Durwood Pye, an avowed segregationist; and Donald Hollowell, a black civil rights lawyer – had entered the race for superior court judge in Fulton County.[61] Hollowell hoped to get a plurality, the method of nomination provided for under existing state law, on the assumption that Webb and Pye would split the white vote.[62] Under a majority-vote rule, Hollowell's chances would be greatly reduced.[63] MacIntyre's proposed amendment was defeated in the senate by a vote of 32 to 8.[64]

Senator Leroy Johnson, appealing to the senate's sense of fair play, moved to delay implementation of the majority-vote requirement in Fulton County *only*. His appeal was also rejected.[65] On another motion by Senator Johnson, however, the senate voted to revise the "good character and understanding" test by reducing the existing thirty questions to six.[66]

The senate also passed an anti–facsimile ballot provision, prohibiting voters from taking sample ballots or lists of candidates into the polling booths. Senator Julian Webb, Sanders's assistant floor leader in the senate, explained that "the intent of the provision 'is to discourage bloc voting' by preventing

---

[58] City of Rome v. United States, 446 U.S. 156, 185 (1980); Rogers v. Lodge, 458 U.S. 613, 627 (1982).

[59] Georgia Senate Journal, Ex. Sess., May 18, 1964, pp. 96, 153–54; Atlanta Constitution, "Majority Vote Wins – One Exception," May 23, 1964; Macon Telegraph, May 27, 1964.

[60] Holder v. Hall, 512 U.S. 874, 877 (1994). Georgia is the only state in the union that authorizes a sole commissioner form of county government.

[61] Atlanta Constitution, May 28, 1964; Atlanta Journal, May 18, 1964.

[62] Atlanta Daily World, May 7, 1964; Atlanta Constitution, May 15, 1964; Georgia v. Reno, Civ. No. 90-2005. (D. D. C.), Pl. Ex. 307, p. 651 ("Hollowell qualified believing that he could get a plurality vote and thereby . . . would have been the first black judge" – Leroy Johnson).

[63] Atlanta Daily World, May 13, 1964; Atlanta Journal, May 18, 1964.

[64] Georgia Senate Journal, Ex. Sess., May 27, 1964, p. 277.

[65] Atlanta Constitution, May 28, 1964; Atlanta Journal, May 28, 1964; Atlanta Journal, May 28, 1964.

[66] Georgia Senate Journal, May 20, 1964, pp. 200–1; Brooks v. Miller, declaration of Steven F. Lawson, p. 48.

someone from filling out a facsimile ballot for someone else to use."[67] Other proponents of the provision said more plainly that it was designed to curb "bloc voting by Negroes."[68]

The house had voted on May 19, 1964, by a vote of 178–10, to maintain its existing apportionment, or more correctly malapportionment, "based on geography."[69] But on June 15, 1964, the Supreme Court ruled in *Reynolds v. Sims*[70] that both houses of a state's bicameral legislature had to comply with one person, one vote.

In response to the decision in *Reynolds v. Sims*, the house adopted a resolution requesting that the state's two U.S. senators introduce legislation depriving the federal courts of power to hear reapportionment cases. *Reynolds v. Sims*, according to the resolution, represented "the saddest day in American history." Expressing their abiding concern for the rights of the state's rural *white* minority, house members said that "as a result of such decision the minority will thus be stripped of all protection, checks and balances against the unrestrained power and will of the majority."[71] Before the month was out, the district court had invalidated Georgia's house apportionment, shortened the terms of house members, and provided for special elections to be held in 1965.[72]

The members from the 121 smallest counties had banded together and formed a "Committee of 121," which had the power to block legislation and constitutional amendments, but the days of dominance of the rural legislators were numbered.[73] Rep. Johnnie Caldwell of Upson County, acknowledging that fact, called upon his colleagues to act quickly on the new election code: "It behooves all of us to remember we will never have the opportunity as a rural-dominated House to pass another election code."[74]

The malapportioned house, flexing its political muscle for the last time, rejected several of the proposals passed by the senate. It refused to adopt the anti–facsimile ballot provision because it would require election officials to search those who came in to vote.[75] Groover was one of those who opposed the measure, not because it was designed to dilute the black vote, but because it would require poll officials to "ask a little old lady to open up her pocket

67 *Atlanta Constitution*, May 15, 1964; *Atlanta Journal*, May 18, 1964; *Atlanta Constitution*, May 21, 1964 ("everyone knew the intent of the section was to prevent an 'organized bloc vote'").
68 *Macon Telegraph*, June 11, 1964.
69 Georgia House Journal, Ex. Sess., May 19, 1964, p. 189.
70 377 U.S. 533 (1964).
71 Georgia House Journal, Ex. Sess., June 16, 1964, p. 876.
72 *Tombs v. Fortson*, 275 F. Supp. 128, 130 (N. D. Ga. 1966).
73 *Macon Telegraph*, May 14, 1964.
74 *Atlanta Journal*, June 23, 1964.
75 Georgia House Journal, Ex. Sess., June 10, 1964, p. 781; *Macon Telegraph*, June 11, 1964.

book to see if she had some memoranda in there."[76] The house also removed the exemption of county commissions with two or more members from the majority-vote and numbered-post requirements.[77] It voted to adopt a voter understanding test containing twenty questions, and raised the grade necessary to pass from 67 percent to 75 percent correct answers.[78]

The bill finally enacted by the general assembly included a majority-vote requirement, which was identical in substance to Groover's bill that had been approved by the house,[79] and a numbered-post provision.[80] It contained a literacy requirement for voter registration[81] and the more stringent and discriminatory house version of the character and understanding test.[82]

The legislature postponed until the following year the application of the majority-vote requirement to the election of county governments, but required its immediate implementation for other elections, including the controversial election for superior court judge of Fulton County.[83] In the Fulton County election, the white vote was indeed split, but Hollowell, the black candidate, came in third. In the runoff, Pye triumphed. The *Atlanta Times*, underscoring the racial significance of the election and Hollowell's failed strategy of trying to take advantage of a split white vote, headlined: "Judge Pye defeats black vote in victory for judicial integrity."[84]

In an election that same year for sheriff of Chatham County, the majority-vote requirement worked exactly as Groover and other supporters had envisioned that it would. Sam Williams, a black Savannah businessman, won a plurality against four whites in the primary, outdistancing his nearest opponent by some 400 votes. In the ensuing runoff, the white voters regrouped and defeated Williams two to one.[85]

Not every member of the legislature in 1964 acted out of bias or prejudice, and not every decision the general assembly made was based upon race. Many of the provisions of the new code were positive, progressive measures, such as the creation of a state election board to oversee the conduct of elections and the establishment of a single date for all primary elections. But it is impossible to survey the laws affecting voting that the legislature enacted in 1964 without concluding that race, and the desire to curb black political power, was a powerful motivating factor in the decision-making process.

---

[76] Ibid.
[77] *Atlanta Journal*, June 4, 1964; *Atlanta Constitution*, June 16, 1964.
[78] Georgia House Journal, June 4, 1964, pp. 616–18; *Brooks v. Miller*, declaration of Steven F. Lawson, p. 48 (1995).
[79] Ga. Laws 1964, Ex. Sess., pp. 174–75.
[80] Ga. Laws 1964, Ex. Sess., p. 89.
[81] Ga. Laws 1964, Ex. Sess., pp. 57.
[82] Ga. Laws 1964, Ex. Sess., pp. 58–60.
[83] Ga. Laws 1964, Ex. Sess., p. 174.
[84] *Atlanta Times*, September 22, 1964.
[85] *Savannah Morning News*, September 24, 1964.

7

The Voting Rights Scene Outside the Golden Dome

> Look there. There is a good gas station nigger. He's got no complaints and
> makes a good week's pay.
>
> White gas station owner (Dawson, Georgia, July 21, 1962)

I

As the legislature was maneuvering under the golden dome of the state
capitol in Atlanta to stave off the one person, one vote revolution and
blunt the rising "bloc vote" through enactment of a new election code,
blacks were intensifying their voter registration efforts around the state.
The founding of the Voter Education Project (VEP) by the biracial Southern
Regional Council in Atlanta in 1963 gave an added impetus to the
registration campaign. VEP, working with scores of local organizations
and national groups such as the NAACP, SCLC, the Student Nonviolent
Coordinating Committee (SNCC), and the Congress of Racial Equality
(CORE), financed voter registration drives in Georgia and other southern
states.[1]

Black voter registration efforts met the stiffest, and frequently the most
openly violent, resistance in counties with substantial black populations
where black political power, from the white point of view, was most threatening. One of them was Terrell County in southwest Georgia, north of Albany,
dubbed "Terrible Terrell" by civil rights activists.

In the summer of 1962, Ralph Allen, a young white man, was a rising
junior at Trinity College in Connecticut. He was majoring in English, had
been a member of the swimming team, and expected to be commissioned
as a lieutenant in the Marine Corps upon graduation. He came south to
Terrell County in July to work with SNCC and to encourage black voter

[1] Pat Waters and Reese Cleghorn, *Climbing Jacob's Ladder* (New York: Harcourt, Brace and
World, 1967), 46.

Headquarters of the Dougherty County Crusade for Voters, 1964 (courtesy of the Southern Regional Council).

registration. He was motivated, he says, by "a moral conviction about the democratic standards of our nation."[2]

Almost as soon as he began canvassing in black neighborhoods in Dawson, Allen was arrested by the chief of police, who said he was holding him for "investigation." The chief released Allen after several hours, but warned him about "walking around in 'nigger town'" and told him to leave the county. Allen, however, resumed his canvassing, and five days later was arrested again, this time for driving without a headlight and not having a valid license. After spending more than a week in jail, he was tried and convicted on the headlight charge and fined twelve dollars.[3]

Allen returned once again to voter registration, but within a few days he was nearly run down on the street in Dawson by a truck driven by a white man who owned a local gas station. Allen retreated toward the relative safety of some nearby railroad tracks, but the driver got out of the truck and followed him.

"What business do you have in Dawson?" he demanded.

[2] *United States v. Zeke T. Mathews*, Civ. No. 516 (M. D. Ga.), affidavit of Ralph W. Allen, August 10, 1962.
[3] Ibid.

"Working in a voter registration project with SNCC," Allen replied.

"You should get out of town" he said. "Do you understand?" He then pointed to a black man who was sitting in the cab of his truck. "Look there," he said, "there is a good gas station nigger. He's got no complaints and makes a good week's pay." The black man said nothing.

Two other white men soon joined them, and the three attacked Allen. One knocked him to the ground, put his foot on his neck, and drew out a knife. The other two kicked him. "Should we kill him right here or give him a chance to get out of town?" one of them asked.

"No," said another, "we've broken his ribs already. Let him go."

Allen was seriously bruised by the beating, but he had no broken bones.[4]

Lucious Holloway, a Dawson native who had served as a platoon sergeant in Korea in the 1950s, was one of the leaders of the voting rights movement in Terrell County. He had tried to register a number of times after his discharge from the army in 1955, but did not succeed until 1961. After that, he and other blacks in the county formed an organization to encourage black registration. On a steamy night in July 1962 the group met in the small wood-frame Mount Olive Baptist Church at Sasser to discuss their ongoing voter registration efforts. Zeke Mathews, the Terrell County sheriff, accompanied by several deputies, the sheriff from neighboring Sumter County, and an entourage of local whites, paid the group an unannounced visit. Their purpose was to put a stop to voter registration in the black community. Whites, after all, had succeeded in excluding blacks from the political process for nearly a century. There was no reason, some whites thought, that they couldn't continue to do so indefinitely.

The scene Holloway described at the Mount Olive church was distinctly intimidating. "Before they came into the church," he recalled, "I could hear the white people calling out the license plate numbers. Someone would shout, 'have you got that one,' and another person would answer, 'yes.'" The whites then trooped into the church, the officers armed with pistols, where they "milled around, shining their flashlights among the Negroes and speaking to some of them. An assistant deputy spoke up and said he wanted everybody's name and address who were in the church."[5]

Sheriff Mathews then addressed the group and told them that whites were "getting disturbed by these secret meetings." He explained what, in his view, was wrong with black voter registration. "We are a little fed up with this registering business," he said. "Negras down here have been happy for a hundred years, and now this has started. We want our colored people to live like they've been living. There was never any trouble before all this started. It's caused great dislike between colored and white."[6]

---

4 Ibid.
5 *United States v. Zeke T. Mathews*, affidavit of Lucious Holloway, August 8, 1962.
6 Waters and Cleghorn, *Climbing Jacob's Ladder*, 166.

A man sitting in one of the pews spoke up. "We want to vote," he said. A deputy quickly wheeled around. "Vote for *what?*" he retorted.[7]

The law enforcement officers were particularly annoyed that whites were at the meeting. Sheriff Mathews, who spotted Ralph Allen, warned him to leave Terrell County. "'I can't protect you from all of the people,' he said."[8] The delegation of whites then trooped to the back of the church and took up positions near the door.

Holloway called for reports on the progress of voter registration in several neighboring counties. After the reports were given, the blacks filed out of the church between the armed whites standing guard at the door. Outside, "the white people stood around with their flashlights on," recalled Holloway. "They would shine them into the cars as they drove out of the church yard. They shined a light into the car ahead of me, into mine, and the one behind me."[9]

Holloway predicted that the show of force by whites would make it harder to get blacks in the county to register. "Most of the Negroes are afraid. They say that they aren't going up there to register and fool around because they will be fired or get in trouble. I know the trouble we had at our meeting will just help to discourage them more."[10]

Sheriff Mathews proved to be a prophet when he told Ralph Allen that he couldn't protect him if he remained in Terrell County. But it was Mathews himself, and the Dawson chief of police, who several weeks later locked up Allen and Charles Sherrod, the field secretary for SNCC and a divinity school graduate, on trumped-up charges of vagrancy.[11] The federal court, in a suit brought by the Department of Justice, later enjoined Mathews and other county officials from intimidating or prosecuting persons to prevent them from registering or voting.[12]

Carolyn Daniels, a black beautician in Dawson, was also active in the registration campaign in Terrell County and put up several SNCC workers in her home. One evening in August 1962, as the group was preparing a midnight snack after returning from a trip to Albany, several shotgun blasts ripped through the house. John Chatfield, a twenty-year-old white college student from Vermont, was struck twice.[13] Several months later, Daniels's home was bombed, causing extensive damage. The home of a neighbor, Willie Westin, was sprayed with more than fifty rounds of submachine gun fire.[14]

[7] *United States v. Zeke T. Mathews*, affidavit of Lucious Holloway, August 8, 1962.

[8] *United States v. Zeke T. Mathews*, affidavit of Ralph W. Allen, August 10, 1962.

[9] *United States v. Zeke T. Mathews*, affidavit of Lucious Holloway, August 8, 1962.

[10] Ibid.

[11] *United States v. Zeke T. Mathews*, affidavit of Ralph W. Allen, August 10, 1962; *Dawson News*, August 16, 1962.

[12] *United States v. Zeke T. Mathews*, 9 R. R. L. Reptr. 225 (M. D. Ga. 1964).

[13] *Dawson News*, August 16, 1962; *Atlanta Constitution*, April 29, 1963.

[14] *Dawson News*, Dec. 12, 1963.

Voter registration meetings had also been held in nearby Lee County at the Shady Grove Baptist Church. Agnew James, a forty-three-year-old black man living in Leesburg who had first registered in March 1962, was one of the leaders of the local registration movement. One evening in July, he drove over to the church with his wife and sixteen-year-old daughter to attend a voters' meeting, but found the entrance to the churchyard blocked by policemen. "A man who seemed to be wearing state patrol clothes waved his flashlight at me," recalled James, "and I stopped. He throwed his light right in my face, so I turned my head away; I seen three white men standing in the back of my car. One of them called out the number of my license plate."[15]

The man in the patrol clothes then began questioning James. "Nigger, you know what kind of meeting they're having? Whose plantation do you live on?" When James told him that he lived on land owned by a black, "that is when he got to cursing," says James's wife, Odethia, who was sitting in the seat beside him. "I guess every other word he said after that was cursing. He said, 'Nigger you can go in that church and we will beat damn hell out of you or you can turn around and go back the way you came from.'"[16]

Agnew James looked at his wife and daughter, briefly considered his options, and concluded that it would be too dangerous to go into the church. "My wife kept pulling at my sleeve," he recalls, "saying 'let's go.' I never did cut my motor off. I backed out and went down the road."[17]

The next month, arsonists burned the Shady Grove church to the ground.[18] Two more black churches were burned several weeks later, the Mount Olive Church at Sasser and the Mount Mary Church at Chickasawhatchee in Terrell County.[19]

The Dawson paper speculated that blacks themselves had burned the churches and shot into the Daniels's home. After all, the paper asked, "[w]ho had the most to profit – to gain – from the shooting into the negro house and the burning of the churches. Certainly it was not the good white people of Terrell County."[20]

As it turned out, the white people of Terrell County did have a hand in the church burnings. Three local white men eventually confessed to burning one of the churches.[21] In October 1962, two white men from Lee County were charged with burning the Shady Grove Baptist Church.[22]

---

[15] *United States v. Zeke T. Mathews*, affidavit of Agnew James, August 8, 1962.
[16] *United States v. Zeke T. Mathews*, affidavit of Odethia James, August 8, 1962.
[17] *United States v. Zeke T. Mathews*, affidavit of Agnew James, August 8, 1962.
[18] *Dawson News*, August 16, 1962.
[19] *Dawson News*, Sept. 13, 1962. Another black church, the High Hope Baptist Church near Dawson, had been torched the preceding year. *Macon Telegraph*, Oct. 5, 1962.
[20] *Dawson News*, Sept. 13, 1962.
[21] *Dawson News*, Sept. 20, 1962.
[22] *Dawson News*, Oct. 11, 1962.

There was widespread violence in Albany, where civil rights groups had been waging a two-year campaign, known as the Albany Movement, against segregation. Hundreds of men, women, and children who participated in a series of massive civil rights demonstrations were arrested.[23] Four homes where voter registration organizers were staying were riddled with bullets in the summer of 1962. Days later, someone fired three shotgun blasts into the home where Charles Sherrod was sleeping.[24]

White opposition to black enfranchisement was also fierce in Webster County. Though the county was majority-black, not a single black was on the registration lists. Florrie McKinnon, the clerk of court, explained that there were not a dozen Negroes in the entire county who were, in her judgment, even "qualified" to vote.[25]

It wasn't simply that whites in Webster County made the registration process cumbersome and difficult. They also made it extremely dangerous. Rev. George W. Neely, a man of great dignity and courage, who at various times had worked as a school bus driver and as a process server for a local magistrate, gives the following gritty account of his first attempt to register at the Webster County Courthouse in June 1963.

I had known several blacks who went to the courthouse to register, but they always told them it wasn't time for black people to register. Just turned them away. Well, John Hawkins and his nephew Ollis Hawkins and I decided that we would go and try to register. We went to the courthouse and they handed each of us a piece of paper and said 'sign your name,' which we did. We left and I went on to Columbus where I was working at the time. Later that afternoon I got a call from my wife, saying that John Hawkins wanted me to stop by his house on my way home. I did and John said he had gotten a call from Jim Deckle, who was the city administrator at that time – he has passed since then – and he told John that he and Ollis needed to come back to the courthouse and get their names, that they might lose their jobs if they didn't. They knew they couldn't touch me because I worked in Columbus. And John said to Deckle, 'why don't you just throw it away if that's what you want?' and Deckle said 'no, you have to go get it.' You see, he wanted them to be the ones responsible for removing their names. Then John asked me, 'what should we do?' I knew they had families and they could lose their jobs, so I said that it wasn't my place to tell them what to do, and John said 'I've made up my mind not to go back. I intend to die with my name up there.' And then Ollis said, 'well I'm happy to hear you say that 'cause I'm going to die with my name up there too.'[26]

[23] John Lewis, *Walking with the Wind: A Memoir of the* Movement (New York: Simon and Schuster, 1998), 186.

[24] Lewis, *Walking with the Wind*, 191; *United States v. Zeke T. Mathews*, affidavit of Charles Melvin Sherrod, August 10, 1962.

[25] *Atlanta Constitution*, May 10, 1960; *Columbus Enquirer*, May 11, 1960.

[26] *Neely v. Webster County*, Civ. No. 88-203 (M. D. Ga.), author's interview with Rev. George Neely, June 18, 1999.

The Webster County Courthouse, where blacks attempting to register in the 1960s were turned away and told that "it wasn't time" for black people to vote (courtesy of the Atlanta History Center).

That was not, however, the end of the matter. Rev. Neely continues his narrative:

A few days later, I got a letter from the registrar saying that my registration had been turned down. Didn't give a reason, just said my application had been denied. And then the letter said, 'lastly, don't come back here.'

After that they poured gasoline in the yard in front of Ollis's house. They poured it all around and lit it and there was a big blaze.

I was coming home one evening about that time, and I saw five cars parked on the bridge that crossed the creek up from my house, two cars at each end and one in the middle. There was a crowd of white men standing on the bridge and they were shooting their guns into the creek. I took out a pistol I had and put it on the seat beside me, and I said to myself, like John and Ollis Hawkins, if it comes to it I'm going to die on that bridge. I drove on up and said to one of the men, 'let me pass,' and after a few moments one of 'em said, 'let him through,' and they moved the car and I drove on home. It wasn't long, though, before those five cars drove by my house, driving real slow, slower than you would in a funeral procession. They were giving me a message. Now that was Webster County.[27]

Undeterred by the white resistance and show of force, Neely contacted the U.S. Department of Justice about the problem blacks were having in

[27] Ibid.

registering, and the department threatened Webster County with a lawsuit. The registrar finally relented and allowed a few blacks to register. But prior to enactment of the Voting Rights Act, there was still a total of only nine black registered voters in Webster County.[28]

The intimidation of blacks and their fear of reprisals were so widespread in places like Webster and Terrell Counties during the early 1960s that, despite the efforts of civil rights workers, very few blacks actually registered, and those who did were mainly eighteen-year-old high school students and the elderly. According to Carolyn Daniels, the others were "afraid they'll lose their jobs if they register."[29] And many of those who registered did not vote. "They were scared, scared they'd be hanged," says Emma Kate Holloway, the wife of Lucious Holloway. "They were working for the white man and scared he'd take their job and they couldn't provide."[30]

Luther Wilson, a black school principal in McDuffie County, said that "fear of economic, physical, and psychological harm" kept many blacks from registering.[31] Adell Page and Martha Tillman, both residents of Terrell County, experienced that harm firsthand.

Page, a fifty-three-year-old black woman with ten children, had attended the meeting at the Mount Olive church. As fate would have it, one of the white men who accompanied Sheriff Mathews was Clyde Hayes, whose baby she took care of and for whom she did housework. Hayes was not slow in showing his displeasure over the political activism building in the local black community.

"Mr. Hayes came by early the next morning," Page remembers. "I usually walk to his house, but that day he drove up and blew his horn."

"Well, Adell," he said, handing her a check. "We won't need you anymore."

"I said, 'thank you,' and took my check and went on in the house."[32]

Martha Tillman, who worked as a cook in the Hayes household, had also attended the meeting at the church. She had been warned earlier by Hayes's mother not to go to civil rights meetings, but she went anyway because, in her words, "I would like to vote." When she went to work the next morning, Tillman confessed to Ms. Hayes that she had attended the voters' meeting the night before, expecting that she would be fired. But Hayes told her to go to the kitchen and cook breakfast. Moments later, Clyde Hayes came into the kitchen and dismissed her on the spot. "He pointed at me and said, 'get

---

[28] U.S. Commission on Civil Rights, *Political Participation* (Washington, D.C.: Government Printing Office, 1968), 238.
[29] *Atlanta Constitution*, April 29, 1963.
[30] *Atlanta Journal*, Nov. 25, 1979.
[31] *Bowdry v. Hawes*, Civ. No. 176-128 (S. D. Ga.), Luther Wilson interview.
[32] *United States v. Zeke T. Mathews*, affidavit of Adell Page, August 10, 1962.

The Burke County Courthouse, an imposing structure and a source of pride to local whites, but described by Herman Lodge, one of the first blacks elected to the county commission after litigation in the 1980s, as "a stigma. Everything about it was segregated, courtroom seating, juries, employment, drinking fountains. They even had two outhouses for blacks" (photo courtesy of the Atlanta History Center).

out of here,' " Tillman recalled. "He told me not to give him any back talk. He was mean."[33]

The fact that registration was conducted at the courthouse, which was quite literally the citadel of white supremacy and racial suppression, was another major obstacle for many blacks. "The courthouse was a stigma," explains Herman Lodge, one of the first blacks elected to the county commission of Burke County. "People were reluctant to go there. Everything about it was segregated – courtroom seating, juries, employment, drinking fountains. They even had two outhouses for blacks. When they finally desegregated the drinking fountains they went to using paper cups so whites wouldn't have to drink after blacks."[34] They also installed a device, known locally as a "nigger-hook," to make sure that blacks couldn't put their mouths on the orifice of the fountain.[35] Judge Anthony Alaimo, writing about Burke County in 1978, commented upon the effects of past discrimination that "still haunt the

---

[33] *United States v. Zeke T. Mathews*, affidavit of Martha Tillman, August 9, 1962.
[34] *Lodge v. Buxton*, Civ. No. 176-55 (S. D. Ga.), Herman Lodge interview.
[35] *Lodge v. Buxton*, Oct. 26, 1978, slip op. at p. 12.

county courthouse," including "the toilet signs for 'Coloreds' and 'Whites' [that] still appear through faded paint."[36]

Even when blacks were allowed to register, they were often met with icy hostility from local officials. As a prominent white resident of Dawson explained, "Nobody stops them [blacks from registering], and nobody molests them. Of course, they look on them like you would a rattlesnake."[37]

A middle-aged black woman from Sumter County who registered at the courthouse in 1963 confessed that "I went down to register and my knees were shaking and I could hardly sign my name. But it was all right, and maybe now I can get up the nerve to vote."[38]

II

To visit Americus in the spring of the year in the days when it languished in the iron grip of segregation was to see a south Georgia county seat in all its charm and contradictions. The ornate red-brick courthouse, with its old clock tower, still dominated the downtown. Across the way the Windsor Hotel, a victorian jewel fallen into disrepair, maintained a silent, dignified vigil. And south from the center of town stretched the impressive historic district of white homes, many of them built before the Civil War in the classical style and laid out along broad, oak-lined avenues ablaze with azaleas and flowering dogwood.

But cross the town square north onto Cotton Avenue and into the black quarter, and there the streets were narrow and mostly unpaved. The houses were two- and three-room shacks, and many were without indoor plumbing. Vacant lots were rat-infested and choked with weeds. Lillie Mae Bownes, who lived in the black quarter with her husband, recalled years later that "we was living in the sunshine and rain. That old house wasn't good for nothing else but to tear down."[39] When the civil rights movement finally came to Americus and Sumter County the effect was explosive, like a wildfire racing through a pine forest in the blistering heat of a long and dry summer.

There were large-scale demonstrations against segregation in Americus in the summer of 1963, as well as equally large-scale arrests of civil rights demonstrators. Some 250 people were taken into custody and held in various jails in Americus and neighboring counties.[40] Some of the demonstrators were locked up in an abandoned brick building behind the Americus post

---

[36] Ibid.
[37] *Atlanta Constitution*, April 29, 1963.
[38] Waters and Cleghorn, *Climbing Jacob's Ladder*, 146.
[39] Laughlin McDonald, "Building on Fellowship," 29 Foundation News 38, 41 (1988), Lillie Mae Bownes interview.
[40] *Atlanta Journal*, Oct. 3, 1963.

office. "The building was boarded up. It had one toilet," recalls Warren Fortson, a young white lawyer living in Americus at the time. "It was like Germany."[41]

The Americus city council, seeking to control the media as well as the protestors, tried to impose press censorship. It directed all news media "not to print or broadcast news of racial disturbances without the council's prior approval."[42]

Local officials took law and order to new and extraordinary heights on August 8, 1963, when Sheriff Fred Chappell arrested four civil rights workers – John Perdew, Don Harris and Ralph Allen of SNCC, and Zev Aeloney of CORE – who had been encouraging people to register and vote. Allen was the student from Trinity College. Perdue, a white man, was from Denver and a student at Harvard. Harris, who was black, was a Rutgers graduate. Aelony, also white, was from Minneapolis.[43] While most of the earlier arrests had been for relatively minor offenses such as parading without a permit and disturbing the peace, these four were charged with "insurrection," which carried the death penalty, despite the fact that the insurrection law had been declared unconstitutional by the U.S. Supreme Court twenty-five years earlier.[44]

The evidence of insurrection, according to prosecutor Stephen Pace, Jr., consisted of material circulated by Aelony appealing to parents to keep their children out of segregated schools. Since Georgia had a compulsory attendance law, Pace reasoned that the appeal to parents was in defiance of the law and thus insurrectionary.[45] By such logic, virtually any violation of the law, no matter how minor, could be elevated to a capital offense. A federal court eventually ruled once again that the insurrection statute was unconstitutional, ordered the four defendants admitted to bail, and enjoined their prosecution. [46]

Pace later explained that "the basic reason for bringing these [insurrection] charges was to deny the defendants ... bond ... and convince them that this type of activity ... is not the way to go about it."[47] Indeed, the insurrection charges, together with the other arrests in Sumter County, had the effect the white leadership sought, and that was squelching the demonstrations. John Barnum, an Americus resident and one of the leaders of the civil

[41] *Wilkerson v. Ferguson*, Civ. No. 77-30 (M. D. Ga.), Warren Fortson interview.

[42] *Atlanta Journal*, August 11, 1963.

[43] *Atlanta Journal*, Oct. 12, 1963; *Atlanta Journal*, Nov. 1, 1963.

[44] *Herndon v. Lowry*, 301 U.S. 242 (1937). Arrests and threatened prosecutions under the statute were recurring events in Georgia, at least where SNCC workers or civil rights activities were involved. See *Wells v. Hand*, 238 F. Supp. 779 (M. D. Ga. 1965), aff'd *Wells v. Reynolds*, 382 U.S. 39 (1965); *Carmichael v. Allen*, 267 F. Supp. 985 (N. D. Ga. 1967).

[45] *Atlanta Journal*, Nov. 1, 1963.

[46] *Harris v. Chappell*, 8 R. R. L. Rptr. 1355 (M. D. Ga. 1963).

[47] William Bailey Williford, *Americus through the Years* (Atlanta: Cherokee, 1975), 357.

rights movement in Sumter County, admitted that a decision had been made to call off the street demonstrations. "I see very little point in loading these jails back up," he said. "There's too much suffering."[48]

Pace sought the Democratic nomination from the third congressional district the following year and bragged to white campaign audiences that he had put civil rights activists in jail, where "[t]hey stayed locked up and they stayed locked up and they stayed locked up."[49] Not to be outdone in making racial appeals, a rival candidate, Ed Wohlwender, Jr., a Columbus lawyer and businessman, denounced the civil rights movement as "a black menace" led by "goatee wearing pinks and punks."[50] Howard Callaway, a Republican, won the disputed seat running on a pledge to seek repeal of federal civil rights laws.[51]

III

Although the white primary had been invalidated a decade and a half earlier, voter registration and voting by blacks, where it was allowed, continued to be conducted on a racially segregated basis in many areas of the state into the mid-1960s. In Moultrie, for example, voter registration lists were maintained on a segregated basis, and whites voted at city hall and blacks at the fire station.[52] Voting in Lamar County was segregated, with whites voting downstairs and blacks upstairs in the courthouse.[53] Separate booths were set up for black and white voters in Thomson in McDuffie County.[54] In Peach County, blacks and whites voted in the courtroom of the county courthouse, but blacks entered through the back door and voted in booths located on the east side of the courtroom, while whites entered through the front door and voted in booths on the west side of the courtroom.[55]

In Albany and Dougherty County, separate lists were maintained for black and white voters. Blacks voted in the city auditorium and whites at the county courthouse. A group of black voters, represented by Donald Hollowell and C. B. King, two of the state's leading black civil rights lawyers, filed suit challenging the segregation. The district court, in an order issued on January 8, 1962, held that segregated voting violated both the Fifteenth Amendment

---

[48] *Atlanta Journal*, October 3, 1963.

[49] *Atlanta Journal*, July 31, 1964.

[50] Ibid.

[51] Williford, *Americus through the Years*, 359–60.

[52] *Cross v. Baxter*, Civ. No. 76-20 (M. D. Ga.), trial transcript, testimony of John Cross, pp. 139–40.

[53] *Strickland v. Lamar County Board of Commissioners*, Civ. No. 86-167-2-Mac (M. D. Ga.), hearing on preliminary injunction, testimony of Theodore R. Bush, p. 74.

[54] *Bowdry v. Hawes*, Civ. No. 176-128 (S. D. Ga.), Pl. Ex. 62, minutes of meeting of mayor and council, Nov. 8, 1956.

[55] Statement of Bernard A. Young, ordinary, Peach County, April 19, 1960.

and the Civil Rights Act of 1957. The court declined to issue an injunction, however, because it found that the white defendants were "all honorable people" and would comply with the law once it was judicially determined.[56]

In June 1962, the U.S. Department of Justice identified forty-eight counties and seventeen municipalities in Georgia that were still segregating voting and vote counting. Assistant Attorney General Burke Marshall wrote letters to the various jurisdictions advising them that such segregation was unlawful and asking them voluntarily to end it.[57] Most did, but lawsuits were required to stop segregated voting in Bibb County in 1962,[58] in Jones County in 1963,[59] and in Johnson County in 1967.[60]

In Bibb County, the Democratic Party executive committee had refused voluntarily to desegregate voting, despite the prior ruling in Dougherty County, and predicted that desegregation of the polls would cause "utter chaos." Lawton Miller, the committee chair, said that he "deeply resent[ed] federal interference in our local affairs" and that the federal courts and the U.S. Department of Justice would have to assume full responsibility for the consequences of their actions.[61] After the court entered its order desegregating the polling places, Miller vowed to appeal and charged that the federal government was destroying "every vestige of local self-government."[62]

One of the remarkable things about Miller's appeal to local self-government, like so many similar appeals by whites at the time to states, rights and self-determination, was that it treated blacks as if they did not exist. There was no conceivable role for them in the governance of the communities in which they lived.

The reaction of white officials in Jones County was similar. James Balkcom, the chair of the Democratic Party executive committee, declared that the Kennedy administration was a "dictatorship"[63] and that "therefore, I refuse to capitulate to [Attorney General] Bobby Kennedy.... If there's any trouble stirred up in Jones County, it'll be by the Justice Department and not by us."[64] Sumter County also refused to desegregate its voting, a decision that would ignite a racial conflagration more severe than the one that had engulfed the county in the summer of 1963.

[56] *Anderson v. Courson*, 203 F. Supp. 806, 810, 814 (M. D. Ga. 1962).

[57] *Atlanta Constitution*, June 13, 1962.

[58] *United States v. Bibb County Democratic Executive Committee*, 222 F. Supp. 493 (M. D. Ga. 1962).

[59] *United States v. Jones County Democratic Executive Committee*, 8 R. R. L. Reptr. 1091 (M. D. Ga. 1963).

[60] *United States v. Attaway*, Civ. No. 962 (S. D. Ga. 1967); *United States v. Brantley*, Civ. No. 694 (S. D. Ga. 1967).

[61] *Macon Telegraph*, April 21, 1962.

[62] *Albany Herald*, May 17, 1962.

[63] *Macon Telegraph*, June 14, 1963.

[64] *Macon News*, June 14, 1963.

When blacks tried to vote at the white polling place in Americus in a July 20, 1965, special election for justice of the peace, four black women were arrested, including Mary Kate Bell, who was one of the candidates.[65] Election officials also allowed a large crowd of whites to gather near the polls and intimidate blacks who were attempting to vote.

One of Bell's poll watchers was Collins McGee, a twenty-year-old black man from Americus who had been active in the Sumter County movement. When he complained that a deputy sheriff was trying to steer a black woman into voting for a particular candidate, the deputy threatened to throw him out. According to McGee, "the deputy said, 'If you don't get your black ass out of this goddamned building I'll kick it out.' " McGee left the polling place and got in a car driven by a friend, Sammy Mahone. The deputy, however, followed McGee out of the building and came over to the car. "At this point," says McGee, "he reached in the window of the car and hit me on the head with his fist. I got out of the car and yelled to the police officers standing around, but they didn't do anything. Didn't even look at us. I got back into the car and we left."[66]

Mary Kate Bell's husband, Charles, was in the army at the time, assigned to a military police unit in Stuttgart, Germany. He had just come home on leave, and he drove his wife and three other women to the polls on election day. He watched as all four were arrested for refusing to enter the polling place through the back entrance reserved for Negroes. Charles Bell returned to duty in Stuttgart the next month to defend American freedom from the cold war threat of the Soviet Union, with his wife's fate in racially segregated Sumter County still unresolved.[67]

The arrests in Sumter County triggered another series of massive demonstrations in Americus. As Warren Fortson put it, "all hell broke loose."[68] Hosea Williams, director of voter projects for SCLC, and John Lewis, national chair of SNCC, announced at a joint press conference in Atlanta that "we have united our forces to do whatever is necessary to bring about justice here and now." They pledged "an all out effort" to insure that "Negroes be allowed to participate in free and open elections."[69]

In the days that followed, hundreds of blacks marched to the county courthouse and conducted prayer vigils. They also presented the county with a list of demands, which included the release of the four women who had been arrested, setting aside the special election, increased police protection, appointment of a black registrar or clerk, and the creation of a biracial committee.[70]

---

[65] *Atlanta Constitution*, July 27, 1965.
[66] *United States v. Zeke T. Mathews*, statement of Collins McGee.
[67] *United States v. Zeke T. Mathews*, affidavit of Charles L. Bell, July 27, 1965.
[68] *Wilkerson v. Ferguson*, author's interview with Warren Fortson.
[69] *Atlanta Journal*, July 27, 1965.
[70] Ibid.; *Atlanta Constitution*, July 28, 1965.

A young white man, Andrew Whatley, Jr., was shot and killed in Americus on the night of July 29, 1965, after he stopped near the courthouse on his way home from work to watch the demonstration. Two black men were later arrested and charged with the slaying, but black leaders denied that the two had any connection with the civil rights movement.[71] In response to the shooting, Governor Sanders dispatched 100 state troopers to Americus, called for an end to the demonstrations, and urged the parties to settle their grievances peacefully. Reconciliation, however, was a scarce commodity in Sumter County in the summer of 1965.

Two days later, at 6:30 in the evening, a group of some twenty-five black and white civil rights volunteers set out walking from the Friendship Baptist Church in Americus to the Sumter County Courthouse to protest the recent election and the hiring practices of the local Kwik Chek Supermarket. They were soon set upon by a gang of whites armed with pistols, leather straps, chains, and clubs. Members of the Georgia State Patrol and the Americus Police Department stood by as the whites clubbed several of the volunteers to the ground.

Jesse Hill, Jr., a seventeen-year-old black SNCC volunteer from Georgia, said that he was hit on the arm and side by one of the whites, who used a nightstick that had been given to him by an Americus policeman. As he was making his escape, Hill remembers being taunted by a state patrolman, who warned that "the next time they get you it will be worse. If you want to take the law into your hands buy you a pistol."[72]

A state patrolman did, however, intercede when a white man pointed a pistol directly at one of the demonstrators. "He came over and ordered the white man to put the pistol back in his pocket," recalls Sammy Mahone, one of those who had been attacked, "but he made no effort to take the pistol from the white man nor to arrest him."[73]

Several days later another volunteer, twenty-three-year-old William Rau of Evanston, Illinois, reported that he had been attacked and chased by three carloads of whites in Plains, eight miles southeast of Americus.[74] He had been soliciting blacks to register when the white men drove by and hit him with a brick. He was treated for a two-inch gash on his chin at the hospital in Albany.

Whites launched counterdemonstrations. Lester Maddox, who was soon to be governor of Georgia, told a cheering white crowd gathered at the Sumter County Courthouse in early August that President Lyndon Johnson had "gone mad" and that "what we need is George Wallace in Washington."

[71] *Atlanta Constitution*, July 30, 1965.
[72] *United States v. Zeke T. Matthews*, statement of Jessie Hill, Jr., August 3, 1965.
[73] *United States v. Zeke T. Matthews*, statement of Sammy Mahone, August 2, 1965.
[74] *Atlanta Journal*, August 5, 1965.

The next day some 600 members of the Ku Klux Klan marched silently through town.[75]

The demonstrations in Sumter County eventually subsided, but it took a federal court order to secure the release of Mary Kate Bell and the other women who had been jailed and to block their prosecution in state court.[76] The federal court subsequently went to the extraordinary length of setting aside the results of the election on the ground that it had been conducted "[i]n the face of gross, unsophisticated, significant, and obvious racial discrimination."[77]

In some counties, elections were run by private white clubs. In Mitchell County, the precincts at Camilla, Pelham, and Baconton were staffed by members of the Rotary, Pilot, and Lions Clubs respectively, none of which had any black members.[78] Elections in Moultrie were run by the all-white Lions Club.[79] In Bleckley County, the only polling place for the entire county was in Cochran at the Jaycee Barn, owned and operated by the white Jaycees.[80] Elections in the city of Kingsland in Camden County were held in the Kingsland Woman's Club, a club for white members only.[81]

IV

During the summer of 1965, when Congress was considering passage of the Voting Rights Act, a flurry of confrontations between civil rights demonstrators and whites took place throughout the state. A Taliaferro County man was charged in May 1965 with beating a white civil rights demonstrator. The defendant, along with another white man, was later indicted by a Greene County grand jury and charged with attempted murder for shooting at five blacks.[82] The two whites were allowed to plead guilty to greatly reduced charges of assault and battery, conditioned only upon payment of a fine of $300 and replacing the windows of the car the blacks had been driving at the time of the attack, which had been shattered by the gunfire.[83]

In majority-black Baker County, whites were overregistered at the astonishing, and impossible, rate of 143 percent of age-eligible voters. By contrast,

---

[75] *Atlanta Journal*, August 8, 1965; *Atlanta Journal*, August 9, 1965; Williford, *Americus through the Years*, 365.

[76] *United States v. Chappell*, 10 R. R. L. Reptr. 1247 (M. D. Ga. 1965); *Bell v. Southwell*, 376 F. 2d 659, 661 (5th Cir. 1967).

[77] *Bell v. Southwell*, 376 F. 2d at 664.

[78] *Cochran v. Autry*, Civ. No. 79-59-ALB (M. D. Ga.), deposition of Janice B. Williams, pp. 11–13.

[79] *Cross v. Baxter*, trial transcript, pp. 139–40 (testimony of John Cross).

[80] *Hall v. Holder*, 955 F. 2d 1563, 1566 and n.3 (11th Cir. 1992).

[81] Letter to John J. Ossick, Jr., from William Bradford Reynolds, assistant attorney general, January 3, 1983.

[82] *Atlanta Constitution*, July 27, 1965.

[83] *Atlanta Journal*, July 28, 1965.

less than 2 percent of age-eligible blacks were registered. One problem facing blacks was that registration was permitted only at the county courthouse and only on one day each month. Two SNCC workers, Jack Holt and Charles Sherrod, began demonstrating at the courthouse in July 1965 for increased opportunities for voter registration, and were set upon by a group of whites.[84] Someone struck Holt on the head with a pistol, inflicting relatively minor damage. Sherrod was more seriously injured and was taken to nearby Albany for treatment. The next day SNCC continued its demonstrations, but found the courthouse surrounded by a group of approximately sixty white men, some armed with guns and clubs.[85] The demonstrators, in something of an understatement, described the situation as "very tense," but there was no repeat of violence.

Someone threw a molotov cocktail onto the porch of a black home in Ocilla where two young civil rights workers were staying.[86] Flames shot thirty feet in the air before the blaze was put out. Demonstrators picketing a restaurant in Cordele that refused to serve blacks were attacked by whites on two separate occasions in July 1965.[87] Thirty-one blacks were arrested for civil rights picketing in Crawfordville that same month.[88] Fifteen civil rights demonstrators were arrested in Columbus for picketing Buck's Barbecue, which refused to serve blacks.[89] In Newton, four civil rights workers conducting a voter registration campaign were jailed, one on the flimsy charge of driving with a defective taillight.[90]

V

White opposition to equal rights and to giving the franchise to blacks had, of course, a great deal to do with simply holding onto political power and maintaining the white privilege in all its forms. But it was also driven by a deep, underlying fear of race mixing, or what was called "racial amalgamation" or "racial adulteration." With black political equality, many whites feared, would come social equality, and inevitably intermarriage and the "mongrelization" of the white race.

Former governor Herman Talmadge, in a book he wrote in 1955 entitled *Segregation and You*, espoused a prevailing white view that "history shows that nation's composed of a mongrel race lose their strength and become weak, lazy and indifferent. They become easy preys to outside nations."

---

[84] U.S. Commission on Civil Rights, *Political Participation*, 232; *Atlanta Constitution*, July 22, 1965.
[85] *Atlanta Constitution*, July 23, 1965.
[86] *Atlanta Journal*, July 22, 1965.
[87] *Atlanta Constitution*, July 12, 1965.
[88] *Atlanta Journal and Constitution*, July 18, 1965.
[89] *Atlanta Constitution*, July 23, 1965.
[90] *Atlanta Journal and Constitution*, July 18, 1965.

According to Talmadge, "[t]he decline and fall of the Roman Empire came after years of intermarriage with other races. Spain was toppled as a world power as a result of the amalgamation of the races."[91]

Newell Edenfield, the president of the state bar association in 1960, rejected the more extreme tenets of white supremacy, but he argued that the black race was "socially immature and culturally different" from the white race, and that to mix the "superior with the inferior" would be a catastrophic form of "adulteration."[92] Charles F. Crisp, a Sumter County banker, expressed similar views and predicted that the civil right movement, if unchecked, would lead to an "amalgamation of the people like they have in Cuba."[93]

The marriage of Charlayne Hunter, the first black to graduate from the University of Georgia, to a white man in 1963 and the revelation that she was pregnant brought forth condemnation and outrage from some of the state's most prominent officials. The president of the University of Georgia, O. C. Aderhold, issued a statement that neither Hunter nor her husband would ever be allowed to reenter the university. "Interracial marriage is prohibited by Georgia law," he pointed out, "and secret marriages are contrary to University of Georgia regulations."[94]

Governor Carl Sanders denigrated the marriage as "a disgrace" and "a shame." Attorney General Eugene Cook pronounced the marriage "illegal" and said he was investigating the matter for a possible violation of the criminal code.[95] State laws prohibiting interracial marriage were not held unconstitutional by the Supreme Court until four years later.[96]

The *Dawson News*, always outspoken on racial matters, reported that Georgians were "shocked" by Hunter's behavior. "In this marriage," the paper said, "the couple has demonstrated a contempt for society as well as University rules and are entitled to no consideration."[97]

Local newspapers in places such as Terrell and Sumter Counties were both fascinated and repelled by the fact that the civil rights movement was, at least to some extent, biracial and that whites and blacks were actually living together. A headline of the *Dawson News* reported in August 1962: "Young White Girl, Negroes In Meet At Sasser Church."[98] The following week, the paper ran a picture of the woman in question, a smiling, demure eighteen-year-old named Penelope Patch, a resident of Englewood,

---

[91] Herman E. Talmadge, *You and Segregation* (Birmingham, Ala.: Vulcan Press, 1955), 44–5.
[92] Newell Edenfield, Address of the President, Report of the 77th Annual Session of the Georgia Bar Association (1960), 204.
[93] *Atlanta Journal*, Oct. 3, 1963.
[94] *Atlanta Journal*, Sept. 3, 1963.
[95] *Atlanta Constitution*, Sept. 6, 1963.
[96] *Loving v. Virginia*, 388 U.S. 1 (1967).
[97] *Dawson News*, Sept. 5, 1963.
[98] *Dawson News*, August 2, 1962.

New Jersey, and a student at Swarthmore. "The young white girl," the paper said pointedly, "has been living and working among negroes in this section for some weeks."[99]

In another story reporting on a voter education meeting at the Shady Grove church in Lee County, the paper, unable to shake its preoccupation with Patch, went out of its way to note that she was *not* present. "The face of Penelope Patch, the 18-year old white girl of Englewood, New Jersey, who has been living and working with negroes in Lee County, was missing," the paper said.[100]

The paper expressed great consternation that

[a]t this very moment in the City of Dawson ... three young white boys are living with negroes. They have moved in bag and baggage. They eat and sleep in their houses. They associate only with negroes. They walk the streets and ride the highways with them. They go to meetings together. They embrace publicly and unashamedly – male and female.... Of course, this is disturbing to the good white people of our county and section.

As one Terrell County man put it, "there's bound to be resentment when people see a young white boy and a Negro girl walking down the street together in Dawson."[101]

In Webster County, Rev. Neely allowed several people from SCLC, whites among them, to stay at his house while they conducted voter registration drives. "I'd let them use my car to carry people to the courthouse, and so forth," he explained. "One day I was sent word 'to get the white people out of the house,' saying they were just 'white trash.'" Rev. Neely didn't respond to the demand or to the racial slur. "I didn't pay it no mind," he said. [102]

The notion that desegregation would "adulterate" the white race and destroy civilization continued as a recurring theme in public debate. The *Dawson News*, expressing its admiration for the "power" of Germany and England, editorialized in 1976 that "a study of history shows that of the world's peoples only those who originated in the area around the North Sea have made democracy work successfully for any period of time." "Are we," the paper asked rhetorically, "to ignore history which shows that homogeneous nations have exhibited great progress, power and unity in the past?"[103] Answering the question some months later, the paper confidently opined that "[t]he Anglo-Saxon heritage is the basis and reason for our success in self-government, and in the ideals, beliefs, freedoms and restraints of that heritage."[104]

[99] *Dawson News*, Aug. 9, 1962.
[100] Ibid.
[101] *Dawson News*, Sept. 13, 1962.
[102] Author's interview with Rev. George Neely, June 18, 1999.
[103] *Dawson News*, May 20, 1976.
[104] *Dawson News*, Sept. 23, 1976.

Returning a year later to the subject of Anglo-Saxon dominance, the *Dawson News* said that it was "a reckless gamble...to change the racial majority in this country....[O]nly peoples derived from Europe have shown a talent for...governmental art."[105]

VI

One of the sharpest ironies of the voter registration movement was that SNCC itself was finally able to accomplish what many whites before it had been unable to do, and that was to get white SNCC workers such as Ralph Allen and Penelope Patch out of the black community.

Since its formation in 1960, SNCC had been gradually moving away from a commitment to nonviolence – the "N" in the acronym stood for Nonviolent – and embracing a philosophy of Black Power. Black Power was a combustible combination of aggressive militancy and black nationalism. It was rooted in a number of convictions – that whites would never submit to a truly biracial society, that the strategy of nonviolence had largely failed, and that the civil rights movement, properly understood, was an indigenous black liberation movement in which there was no role for whites.[106]

Black Power was also an expression of rage over the indignities blacks had suffered at the hands of white society. As James Forman, executive secretary of SNCC, bluntly put it, "[i]f we can't sit at the table of democracy, we'll knock the fucking legs off."[107]

Led by Stokely Carmichael, and later by H. "Rap" Brown, the Black Power advocates succeeded in 1966 in ousting the more moderate John Lewis as chair and adopting a resolution that white SNCC volunteers could no longer work in the black community. According to Carmichael, the "need for psychological equality" required the expulsion of the whites: "Only black people can convey the revolutionary idea that black people are able to do things themselves. Only they can help create in the community an aroused and continuing black consciousness that will provide the basis for political strength."[108] SNCC eventually purged whites from the organization entirely.[109] In a position paper on Black Power published in the *New York Times*, SNCC declared that "[i]f we are to proceed toward true liberation, we

---

[105] *Dawson News*, March 17, 1977.
[106] Lewis, *Walking with the Wind*, 189–90, 340–41, 348–50, 370–72.
[107] Ibid., 340.
[108] Stokely Carmichael, "What We Want," *New York Review of Books*, September 22, 1966, as quoted in Maning Marable and Leith Mullins, eds, *Let Nobody Turn Us Around: Voices of Resistance, Reform, and Renewal* (Lanham, Md.: Rowman and Littlefield, 2000), 447.
[109] Lewis, *Walking with the Wind*, 365.

must cut ourselves off from white people.... [O]ur organization (S.N.C.C.) should be black-staffed, black-controlled and black-financed."[110]

VII

Congress had strengthened voting rights protection twice since passage of the Civil Rights Act of 1957. The Civil Rights Act of 1960 gave federal officials power to investigate discrimination in voting and to register qualified voters.[111] The Civil Rights Act of 1964, which prohibited discrimination in public accommodations, employment, and federally assisted programs, also provided that black registration be based upon the same standards as had traditionally been applied to whites, and that completion of the sixth grade carried a presumption of literacy.[112] Still, as places such as Baker, Lee, Webster, Sumter, and Terrell Counties demonstrated, existing federal laws were slow and ineffective in remedying discrimination in voting. That was true primarily because they depended upon time-consuming litigation for enforcement, which gave the advantages of inertia and delay to those who were practicing the discrimination.

The Department of Justice brought one of its first suits under the Civil Rights Act of 1957 against Terrell County in 1959, seeking an injunction against its discriminatory registration practices.[113] Although the department eventually won an injunction, by 1960 only five blacks had been added to the county voter rolls. The attorney general of the United States testified before Congress in 1965 that registration under the existing laws was measured "not in terms of months, but in terms of years."[114] Even after the federal court issued its order in Terrell County, the sheriff locked up two civil rights workers engaged in voter registration.

The states could also evade the federal civil rights laws simply by enacting new, and discriminatory, laws of their own. Georgia had done exactly that when it enacted its thirty-question test for voter registration in response to the Civil Rights Act of 1957.

Clearly, if the problems of discrimination in voting were to be effectively redressed, some method other than the time-consuming, expensive, case-by-case litigation method would have to be devised. That method would be the Voting Rights Act of 1965, without doubt the toughest civil rights law ever enacted by Congress.

---

[110] SNCC, "Position Paper on Black Power," *New York Times*, August 5, 1966, quoted in Marable and Mullins, eds., *Let Nobody Turn us Around*, 450.

[111] Pub. L. No. 86-449; 42 U.S.C. §1971 (d) and (e).

[112] Pub. L. No. 88-352; 42 U.S.C. §1971.

[113] *United States v. Raines*, 172 F. Supp. 552 (M. D. Ga. 1959), rev'd, 362 U.S. 17 (1960).

[114] *South Carolina v. Katzenbach*, 383 U.S. 301, 314-15 (1966).

8

The Voting Rights Act: How It Works

> Hopefully, millions of non-white Americans will now be able to participate for the first time on an equal basis in the government under which they live.
>
> Chief Justice Earl Warren, March 7, 1966

I

The Voting Rights Act of 1965 was a complex, interlocking set of permanent provisions that applied nationwide along with special five-year provisions that applied only in jurisdictions that had used a "test or device" for voting and in which registration and voting were depressed. One of the most important permanent provisions, Section 2, prohibited the use of voting practices or procedures that denied or abridged the right to vote "on account of race or color."[1] Other permanent provisions authorized civil and criminal sanctions against interference with the right to vote, facilitated challenges to the imposition of poll taxes for state and local elections, and exempted citizens educated in American schools conducted in a foreign language from required English-language literacy tests.[2]

The special provisions, described by the Supreme Court as the "heart of the Act," were aimed at states or places, known as "covered" jurisdictions, where discrimination in voting had been most persistent and flagrant.[3] Coverage was determined by the attorney general and the director of the census based upon registration and turnout in the 1964 presidential election.[4] There was no appeal from a coverage decision, but jurisdictions could

---

[1] 9 Stat. 437, 42 U.S.C. §1973.
[2] 42 U.S.C. §§1973b(e), (h), (j).
[3] *South Carolina v. Katzenbach*, 383 U.S. 301, 315 (1966).
[4] 42 U.S.C. §1973(b). A court could also subject a noncovered jurisdiction to Section 5 if it found a violation of voting rights protected by the Fourteenth or Fifteenth Amendment. See, e.g., *McMillan v. Escambia County*, 638 F. 2d 1539 (5th Cir. 1981).

"bail out" from this provision – Section 5 of the act – by showing that they had not used a discriminatory test or device within the preceding five years.[5] The covered jurisdictions were Georgia, Alabama, Louisiana, Mississippi, South Carolina, Virginia, forty counties in North Carolina, Alaska, and a handful of counties in Arizona, Hawaii, and Idaho.[6]

The special provisions did two things. First, they suspended the use in the covered jurisdictions of tests, such as literacy and good character and understanding tests, that had been used to deny minorities the right to vote.[7] Second, under Section 5, they required the covered jurisdictions to get federal approval, or preclearance, of their new voting laws or practices before they could be implemented.[8] Other special provisions authorized the attorney general to appoint federal examiners to register qualified voters and poll watchers to observe the conduct of elections.[9]

Section 5 was designed to prohibit states from replacing their registration tests with other, equally discriminatory voting practices. The courts have interpreted Section 5 broadly to cover practices that alter the election laws of a covered jurisdiction in even a minor way.[10] Covered changes have run the gamut from redistricting plans,[11] to annexations,[12] to setting the date for a special election,[13] to moving a polling place.[14]

Section 5 contained two unique features that have been essential to its operation. Preclearance can only be granted by the Federal District Court for the District of Columbia in a lawsuit, or by the U.S. attorney general in an administrative submission. Local federal courts have the power, and duty, to enjoin the use of unprecleared voting practices, but they have no jurisdiction to determine whether a change should be approved.[15] That decision is reserved exclusively for the District of Columbia court or the attorney general. Section 5 also placed the burden of proof on the jurisdiction to show that a proposed voting change does not have a discriminatory purpose

---

[5] 42 U.S.C. §1973b(a).

[6] S. Rep. No. 295, 94th Cong., 2d Sess. 12 (1975), reprinted in 1975 U.S. Code Cong. & Admin. News 774. Several jurisdictions successfully bailed out from Section 5: the state of Alaska (*Alaska v. United States*, No. 101-66, D. D. C. August 17, 1966); Wake County, North Carolina (*Wake County v. United States*, No. 1198-66, D. D. C. January 23, 1967); Elmore County, Idaho (*Elmore County v. United States*, No. 320-66, D. D. C. Sept. 22, 1966); and Apache, Navaho, and Coconino Counties, Arizona (*Apache County v. United States*, 256 F. Supp. 903, D. D. C. 1966).

[7] 42 U.S.C. §§1973b, 1973aa.

[8] 42 U.S.C. §1973c.

[9] 42 U.S.C. §1973 d and f.

[10] *Allen v. State Board of Elections*, 393 U.S. 544, 566–67 (1969).

[11] *Beer v. United States*, 425 U.S. 130 (1976).

[12] *City of Richmond v. United States*, 422 U.S. 358 (1975).

[13] *Henderson v. Harris*, 804 F. Supp. 288 (M. D. Ala. 1992).

[14] *Perkins v. Matthews*, 400 U.S. 379, 387–90 (1971).

[15] *Allen v. State Board of Elections*, 393 U.S. at 555–56 n.19.

or effect.[16] The statute was designed "to shift the advantage of time and inertia from the perpetrators of the evil [of discrimination in voting] to its victims."[17] Congress placed the initial burden of "voluntary" compliance with the statute on the covered jurisdictions,[18] but it also authorized the attorney general and private citizens to bring suit in local federal courts to block the use of uncleared voting practices,[19] and made it a crime to fail to comply with the act.[20]

The preclearance requirement was undoubtedly the most controversial feature of the Voting Rights Act. Justice Hugo Black, an Alabamian, expressed the resentment of many white southerners over Section 5 in a bitter dissenting opinion in *South Carolina v. Katzenbach*, the 1966 Supreme Court decision that held the basic provisions of the act constitutional. He characterized Section 5 as "a radical degradation of state power" and said that forcing "any one of the States to entreat federal authorities in far-away places for approval of local laws before they can become effective is to create the impression that the State or States treated in this way are little more than conquered provinces."[21] Returning to the subject in a later case, he complained that preclearance was "reminiscent of old Reconstruction days when soldiers controlled the South and when those States were compelled to make reports to military commanders of what they did."[22] The majority of the Court acknowledged that Section 5 was an uncommon exercise of congressional power, but found that it was justified by the "insidious and pervasive evil which had been perpetuated in certain parts of our country through unremitting and ingenious defiance of the Constitution."[23]

Congress defended the requirement that covered jurisdictions seek judicial preclearance in the District of Columbia, rather than in local federal courts, as necessary to provide a uniform interpretation and application of Section 5 standards.[24] But there is little doubt that Congress also acted out of distrust of some federal judges in the South, fearing that they would not enforce Section 5 effectively or would be swayed by the hostile, anti–civil rights sentiment that pervaded the region. After all, a federal judge in Georgia had ruled that the voting rights provisions of the Civil Rights Act of 1957 were

---

[16] A voting change has a discriminatory effect under Section 5 if it leads to a "retrogression" in minority voting rights, i.e., makes minorities worse off. *Beer v. United States*, 425 U.S. at 141.

[17] *South Carolina v. Katzenbach*, 383 U.S. at 328.

[18] *Perkins v. Matthews*, 400 U.S. at 396.

[19] 42 U.S.C. §§1973j (d) and (f).

[20] 42 U.S.C. §1973j (a).

[21] 383 U.S. at 359–60.

[22] *Allen v. State Board of Elections*, 393 U.S. at 595.

[23] *South Carolina v. Katzenbach*, 383 U.S. at 309.

[24] H.R. Rep. No. 227, 97th Cong., 1st Sess. 36 (1981); *McDaniel v. Sanchez*, 452 U.S. 130, 151 (1981) ("centralized review enhances the likelihood that recurring problems will be resolved in a consistent and expeditious way").

unconstitutional and unenforceable,[25] and the condemnation of new civil rights laws by state officials was strident and unrelenting. In the euphemism of the Senate report that accompanied subsequent amendments of the act, placing venue in the District of Columbia over actions involving Section 5 would "ensure judicial decision making free from local pressures."[26]

II

Congress assumed, or at least hoped, that once the formal barriers to registration were thrown down in states such as Georgia, and once they were prohibited from enacting new discriminatory voting laws, blacks would participate in politics on a basis of equality with whites. Congress also thought, in retrospect naively, that the five-year "cooling-off" period prescribed by Section 5 was sufficient "to permit dissipation of the long-established political atmosphere and tradition of discrimination in voting because of color" that existed in the covered jurisdictions.[27] Chief Justice Earl Warren expressed a similar optimistic view in *South Carolina v. Katzenbach*. "After enduring nearly a century of widespread resistance to the Fifteenth Amendment," he wrote, "Congress has marshaled an array of potent weapons against the evil [of discrimination in voting].... Hopefully, millions of non-white Americans will now be able to participate for the first time on an equal basis in the government under which they live."[28] The reality, however, proved to be far different.

In its second decision in *Brown v. Board of Education*, known as *Brown II*, the Supreme Court ordered school desegregation to proceed under the supervision of the districts courts "with all deliberate speed."[29] Implicit in the directive was the belief, as in *South Carolina v. Katzenbach*, that once the law was made plain, responsible whites in the South would proceed in good faith to implement it. But most did not. Instead, they waged a campaign of massive resistance to *Brown* that delayed meaningful desegregation of schools in Georgia and other southern states for nearly fifteen years.[30] Desegregation was achieved only after the Court finally rejected "all deliberate speed" and held school districts to the duty of abolishing their segregated school systems "*now.*"[31]

---

[25] *United States v. Raines*, 172 F. Supp. 552, 561 (M. D. Ga. 1959).
[26] S. Rep. No. 417, 97th Cong., 2d Sess. 58 (1982), reprinted in 1982 U.S. Code Cong. & Admin. News 236.
[27] H. Rept. 439, 89th Cong., 1st Sess. 15 (1965), reprinted in 1965 U.S. Code Cong. & Adm. News 2446.
[28] *South Carolina v. Katzenbach*, 383 U.S. at 337.
[29] 349 U.S. 294, 301 (1955).
[30] Richard Kluger, *Simple Justice* (New York: Knopf, 1976), 752–53; Laughlin McDonald, *Racial Equality* (Skokie, Ill.: National Textbook Co., 1977), 57–63.
[31] *Green v. County School Board of New Kent County*, 391 U.S. 430, 439 (1968).

The experience in *Brown*, as well as the state's entire history of opposition to minority voting rights – from slavery, to the overthrow of the Reconstruction experiment, to the Disfranchising Act of 1908, to the opposition to new civil rights laws, to the efforts to stymie black voter registration – strongly suggested that there would be a similar campaign of resistance to implementation of the Voting Rights Act in Georgia. And that is exactly what took place.

9

Increased Black Registration: The White Response

They can keep on electing him till Gabriel blows his trumpet, but they ain't ever gonna get him in here.

State Representative Denmark Groover, 1966

I

After passage of the Voting Rights Act, with its suspension of literacy and other tests for voting, blacks made important gains in voter registration. The U.S. Commission on Civil Rights estimated that the number of blacks registered to vote in Georgia in 1963 was 167, 663, or 27 percent of the eligible population.[1] By the summer of 1968, an estimated 56 percent of the black voting-age population was registered.[2]

Some of the increases in registration can be traced to the efforts of federal examiners appointed under the Voting Rights Act. In 1967, they registered 1,465 blacks in Terrell County, 475 in Lee County, and 1,448 in Screven County.[3] But the main work of voter registration continued to be done by national and regional civil rights organizations, such as VEP, SCLC, NAACP, SNCC, CORE, and scores of local black clubs and civic leagues from around the state.[4]

The state's cumbersome registration process, however, minus the discriminatory tests, still remained in place. Faithful to their white redeemer roots, Georgia's procedures were needlessly complex. They placed the burden of

---

[1] U.S. Commission on Civil Rights, *Political Participation* (Washington, D.C.: United States Printing Office, 1968), 238.

[2] H. Rept. 397, 91st Cong., 2d Sess. (1970), reprinted in 1970 U.S. Code. Cong. & Adm. News 3281.

[3] U.S. Commission on Civil Rights, *The Voting Rights Act: Unfulfilled Goals* (Washington, D.C.: United States Printing Office, 1981), 103.

[4] Pat Waters and Reese Cleghorn, *Climbing Jacob's Ladder* (New York: Harcourt, Brace and World, 1967), 143.

John Lewis, former chair of the Student Nonviolent Coordinating Committee and
director of the Voter Education Project, registering voters in downtown Atlanta in
the late 1960s (courtesy of the Southern Regional Council).

registration on the voter and vested enormous discretion in local officials.
Registration, for example, could be conducted only at fixed sites designated
by local registrars and had to be advertised in advance.[5] The entire system
continued to depress the level of black voter registration. Three years after
passage of the Voting Rights Act, less than half of age-eligible blacks were
registered in sixty-eight of Georgia's counties; in twenty-seven, the rate was
less than 35 percent.[6]

II

Georgia also systematically ignored the special preclearance provisions of
Section 5. Although the state enacted or implemented hundreds of new voting
practices, during the first three years of operation of the Voting Rights Act
it submitted only *one* for preclearance.[7] And many of the new enactments
had the effect of diminishing the effectiveness of the increasing black vote.

---

[5] O.C.G.A. §§21-2-218 and 21-3-123.
[6] 1970 U.S. Code. Cong. & Adm. News at 3280.
[7] U.S. Department of Justice, "Number of Changes Submitted under Section 5 and Reviewed
   by the Department of Justice, by State and Year, 1965–December 31, 1980"; S. Rep. No. 295,
   94th Cong., 1st Sess. 16 (1975), reprinted in 1975 U.S. Code Cong. & Adm. News 782.

A favorite voting change was from district to at-large elections. The vast majority of the state's counties elected their county governments at large, but some used single-member districts. In a scenario reminiscent of the attempt by the legislature in 1962 to prevent the election to the senate of a black from a single-member district in Fulton County, a substantial number of the single-member district counties switched to at-large voting. And most of them did so without complying with Section 5.

The Supreme Court has noted the potential for discrimination inherent in at-large voting and why its adoption is subject to scrutiny under Section 5:

Voters who are members of a racial minority might well be in the majority in one district, but in a decided minority in the county as a whole. This type of change could therefore nullify their ability to elect the candidate of their choice just as would prohibiting some of them from voting.[8]

And aside from the theoretical impact of at-large voting, as of 1970 there were only three black county commissioners in Georgia. Two were elected from majority-black Hancock County and the third from a majority-black district in Chatham County.[9] In majority-white counties, given the persistence of white bloc voting, at-large elections meant that most, if not all, county elected officials would be white.

Two of the single-member district counties, Bacon[10] and Crisp,[11] adopted at-large elections shortly before the Voting Rights Act was passed, but with implementation of the changes to take place after November 1, 1964, which became the effective date for compliance with Section 5.[12] Other single-member district counties that had significant black populations, and that almost certainly would have had one or more majority-black districts under a fair apportionment plan, followed suit and switched to at-large voting: Calhoun, Clay, Dooly, and Miller in 1967;[13] Early, Henry, and Tattnall in 1968;[14] and Meriwether and Walton in 1970.[15] The only county that complied with Section 5 was Meriwether.[16]

Fourteen counties also adopted at-large elections for their boards of education immediately before or shortly after passage of the Voting Rights

---

[8] *Allen v. State Board of Elections*, 393 U.S. 544, 569 (1969).

[9] *National Roster of Black Elected Officials* (Washington: Metropolitan Applied Research Center, 1970), 26.

[10] Ga. Laws 1963, p. 2665.

[11] Ga. Laws 1964, p. 2253.

[12] Coffee County also adopted at-large elections in 1960, but escaped preclearance by providing for implementation of its new system in 1964. Ga. Laws 1960, p. 2147.

[13] Ga. Laws 1967, pp. 3068, 3489, 2586, 2387.

[14] Ga. Laws 1968, pp. 2110, 3378, 2080.

[15] Ga. Laws 1970, pp. 2842, 2475.

[16] U.S. Department of Justice, "Number of Changes Submitted under Section 5."

Act: Greene and Screven in 1964;[17] Terrell and Marion in 1965;[18] Henry
in 1966;[19] Cook and Dooly in 1967;[20] Miller, Coffee, Wayne, and Jenkins
in 1968;[21] Walton in 1969;[22] and Bulloch and Mitchell in 1970.[23] As with
county commissions, at-large elections for school boards were a proven
way to minimize black influence in the political process. All of the school
boards implemented the changes without seeking Section 5 review.

The Johnson administration (1963–69) contributed to the problem of
nonsubmission by lax enforcement of the statute, the Nixon administration
(1969–74) by active opposition to it. The major emphasis during the Johnson
years was on voter registration. The Department of Justice has estimated
that its forty lawyers in the Civil Rights Division spent 90 percent of their
time enforcing the ban on literacy and other tests and 10 percent on all
other provisions of the act, including Section 5.[24] The Nixon administration
advocated the outright repeal of Section 5 in 1970, and excluded annexations
and redistricting from review,[25] although both voting practices are covered
by the statute. Meriwether, the only county to make a Section 5 submission
of its switch to at-large elections, was rewarded for its efforts by the Nixon
administration with a "no objection" letter.[26]

Although proof of a discriminatory purpose is not required for an objection under Section 5, a shift to a more dilutive system of elections in the face
of the Voting Rights Act and increasing black registration cannot reasonably
be interpreted as anything other than continuing white resistance to black
political participation. Unless one makes the assumption that white officials
were indifferent to retaining political power and staying in office, or were
simply ignorant of how election systems actually worked, there can be little
doubt that they knew at-large voting would make it more difficult for blacks
to win office and adopted it for that reason.

III

In many of the counties that switched to at-large elections, the board of education had previously been appointed by the grand jury. A change to elected

[17] Ga. Laws 1964, pp. 969, 835.
[18] Ga. Laws 1965, pp. 746, 742.
[19] Ga. Laws 1966, p. 919.
[20] Ga. Laws 1967, pp. 2507, 2922.
[21] Ga. Laws 1968, pp. 2529, 2177, 3361, 2965.
[22] Ga. Laws 1969, p. 2054.
[23] Ga. Laws 1970, pp. 2790, 2239.
[24] Howard Ball, Dale Krane, and Thomas Lauth, *Compromised Compliance: Implementation of the 1965 Voting Rights Act* (Westport, Conn.: Greenwood Press, 1982), 57.
[25] David Hunter, *Federal Review of Voting Changes* (Washington, D.C.: Joint Center for Political Studies, 1974), 6; Ball, Krane, and Lauth, *Compromised Compliance*, 67–71.
[26] U.S. Department of Justice, "Number of Changes Submitted under Section 5."

boards expands the franchise, but in some instances it could actually make it more difficult for blacks to become school board members – where, for example, blacks served on the grand jury, and thus had access to the power to make appointments, and the new elections were at-large. In addition, the changes came at a time when the exclusion of blacks from juries was being systematically challenged in the courts, strongly suggesting that the grand jury system was abandoned not in order to expand the franchise, but simply to forestall the appointment of blacks to school boards by integrated grand juries.

Litigation challenging jury discrimination was widespread in Georgia in the 1960s and 1970s. Challenges were brought in most of the judicial circuits in the state by blacks who had been denied the right to serve on juries, as well as by defendants who had been indicted and convicted by racially exclusive juries.[27]

Well into the twentieth century, the grand jury in Georgia, faithful to its nineteenth-century roots, remained an elite, white institution. Its members were still selected from a county's racially segregated tax digests and were required by state law to be "the most experienced, intelligent, and upright citizens."[28] In many counties the requirement was interpreted and applied by local jury commissioners simply to mean "white" citizens, despite the fact that the exclusion of black from juries had long been held to violate the Fourteenth Amendment.[29]

Johnson County did not allow blacks to serve on juries until the mid-1960s, and then only within the limits of tokenism and Jim Crow. John Folsom, who worked for a local ice house before it was put out of business by the electric refrigerator, was the first black to serve on a county grand jury, but he was made to sit upstairs in the balcony reserved for "colored" spectators. "I just sat up there," Folsom recalls. "I was just a figurehead."[30]

In Mitchell County, where blacks were 45 percent of the population, the federal court of appeals set aside the conviction of a Negro defendant in 1964 after finding that "[n]o Negro has ever served on a grand jury or on a petit

---

[27] For example, Alcovy (*Jones v. Brooks*, Civ. No. 75-52 [M. D. Ga. 1976]); Atlanta (*Jones v. Smith*, 420 F. 2d 774 [5th Cir. 1969]); Atlantic (*Grovner v. Poppell*, Civ. No. 275-71 [S. D. Ga. 1977]); Augusta (*Sapp v. Rowland*, Civ. No. 176-94 [S. D. Ga. 1977]); Chattahoochee (*Robinson v. Kimbrough*, 652 F. 2d 458 [5th Cir. 1981]); Coweta (*State v. Gould*, 232 Ga. 844 [1974]); Dougherty (*Thompson v. Sheppard*, 490 F. 2d 830 [5th Cir. 1974]); Flint (*Sullivan v. Georgia*, 390 U.S. 410 [1967]); Macon (*Berry v. Cooper*, 577 F. 2d 322 [5th Cir. 1978]); Middle (*Birt v. Montgomery*, 709 F. 2d 690 [11th Cir. 1983]); Northern (*Barrow v. State*, 239 Ga. 162 [1977]); Ogeechee (*Mann v. Cox*, 487 F. Supp. 147 [S. D. Ga. 1979]); Ocmulgee (*Amadeo v. Zant*, 486 U.S. 214 [1988]); Pataula (*Foster v. Sparks*, 506 F. 2d 805 [5th Cir. 1975]); South Georgia (*Broadway v. Culpepper*, 439 F. 2d 1253 [5th Cir. 1971]); Southwestern (*Allen v. State*, 110 Ga. App. 56 [1964]); Toombs (*Turner v. Fouche*, 396 U.S. 346 [1970]); Waycross (*Sims v. Georgia*, 389 U.S. 404 [1967]).

[28] Ga. Code Ann. §59-106.

[29] See, e.g., *Strauder v. West Virginia*, 100 U.S. 303 (1880); *Reece v. Georgia*, 350 U.S. 85 (1955).

[30] *Atlanta Constitution*, Dec. 30, 1984.

jury in Mitchell County." The court ordered the defendant to be reindicted and retried by juries "from which Negroes have not been systematically excluded."[31] Not surprisingly, no blacks were ever appointed by the segregated Mitchell County grand jury to serve on the school board.[32]

In a later opinion in the same case, the Supreme Court called into question the constitutionality of the state's entire "segregated system" of jury selection.[33] The general assembly, in recognition of the fact that the state could not secure constitutional convictions from racially exclusive juries, enacted legislation in 1967 requiring juries to be selected from the list of registered voters, and providing that if jury lists were not fairly representative of "any significantly identifiable group in the county," they should be supplemented.[34] Mitchell County soon abolished its system of grand jury appointments and, ignoring Section 5, adopted at-large elections for the county board of education in 1970.[35]

Terrell County had a similar history of all-white juries and all-white school boards. Prior to September 1966 no black had ever served on a jury, although blacks were 55.5 percent of the county's population. The jury commissioners claimed that they had read the tax digests "from A to Z," but "could never find a single qualified Negro." A federal court later commented that "[t]he kindest words that can be said for this explanation is that it is incredible."[36]

Terrell County adopted at-large elections for its board of education in 1965,[37] shortly before black residents filed a lawsuit requesting the court to order the jury commissioners to reconstitute the jury lists to include a representative cross section of the entire community.[38] The county failed to submit the change under Section 5 and held illegal at-large elections over the next decade. No blacks were ever elected to the school board under the at-large scheme.[39]

In Harris County, blacks were 57 percent of the population, but in 1955 there were no blacks on the grand jury list and only seven (2.3 percent) blacks on the trial jury list.[40] No blacks were ever appointed by the grand jury to serve on the school board.[41]

---

[31] *Whitus v. Balkcom*, 333 F. 2d 496, 510 (5th Cir. 1964).
[32] Laughlin McDonald, *Voting Rights in the South: Ten Years of Litigation Challenging Continuing Discrimination against Minorities* (New York: American Civil Liberties Union, 1982), 50.
[33] *Whitus v. Georgia*, 385 U.S. 643, 548 (1967).
[34] Ga. Laws 1967, p. 251.
[35] Ga. Laws 1970, p. 2239.
[36] *Pullum v. Greene*, 396 F. 2d 251, 254 (5th Cir. 1968).
[37] Ga. Laws 1965, p. 746.
[38] *Pullum v. Greene.*
[39] McDonald, *Voting Rights*, 50.
[40] *Gamble v. Grimes*, 11 R. R. L. Rptr. 2028 (N. D. Ga. May 20, 1966).
[41] *Brown v. Reames*, Civ. No. 75-80-COL (M. D. Ga.), trial records, pp. 113, 172; trial transcript, pp. 59–60, 88–9.

IV

Another voting change widely adopted by cities in Georgia after passage of the Voting Rights Act was a majority-vote requirement. The general assembly extended the requirement to municipalities in 1968,[42] but exempted from coverage those whose charters provided for a plurality vote. Some twenty-three Georgia cities with plurality-vote provisions in their charters promptly repealed them in favor of majority-vote provisions, and most of them ignored Section 5 preclearance.[43] These changes were adopted not only at a time when black political participation was increasing, but often under overtly racial circumstances – for example, after the near-win of a black candidate by a plurality vote, or after the resignation of a long-term white incumbent, or after a black entered a contest against several white candidates who would likely split the white vote.

Douglas adopted a majority-vote requirement by municipal decree in 1967, and later by statute in 1968,[44] after it became generally known that a black, Frederick Richardson, would run for a seat on the city council.[45] Neither change was submitted for preclearance. Richardson came in second in a field of four, but in the runoff was buried in a landslide by his white opponent.[46]

The first blacks to run for city office in Moultrie were Frank Burke for the city council and Edward Starkey for the school board in 1964. At that time, a plurality rule was in effect for city elections. Both blacks lost, but Burke came in fourth in a field of six candidates.[47] The next year, the city adopted a majority-vote requirement but did not submit it for Section 5 preclearance.[48]

John Cross later ran for a seat on the Moultrie City Council in 1973 and received a plurality of the votes. Since the majority-vote requirement had not been precleared and was therefore invalid, he should have been declared the winner. Instead, he was forced into an illegal runoff election and was defeated by his white opponent.[49]

[42] Ga. Laws 1968, p. 977.

[43] The cities included Alma, Americus, Bainbridge, Blackshear, Brunswick, Buford, Conyers, Covington, Douglas, Fort Valley, Gainesville, Gordon, Hawkinsville, Manchester, McRae, Monroe, Moultrie, Norcross, Ocilla, Perry, Quitman, Rome, and St. Marys. See *Election Law Changes in Cities and Counties in Georgia* (Atlanta: Voter Education Project, 1976); Department of Justice, Civil Rights Division, "Complete Listing of Objections Pursuant to Section 5 of the Voting Rights Act of 1965" (Sept. 30, 1988).

[44] Ga. Laws 1968, p. 2085.

[45] Thomas Affleck and Michael P. Froman, Georgia Legal Services Programs, to J. Stanley Pottinger, May 22, 1975 (copy on file with author).

[46] *Douglas Enterprise*, July 6, 1967.

[47] *Cross v. Baxter*, Civ. No. 76-20-THOM (M. D. Ga.), trial record, 133–34.

[48] Ibid., Pl. Ex. 13.

[49] Ibid., trial transcript, pp. 39–40.

Americus adopted a majority-vote requirement in 1968, but never submitted it for preclearance. It used the invalid law to exclude plurality-winning blacks from office on two occasions – Willie Pascal in 1972 and Raymond Green in 1977.[50]

V

Legislative redistricting following passage of the Voting Rights Act, particularly the efforts of the house of representatives to deny Julian Bond the seat to which he had been elected, reflected the continuing significance of race in the state's political processes. After the Supreme Court held that the one person, one vote principle required a state to apportion both houses of its legislature on the basis of population, the district court ordered further reapportionment in Georgia. This litigation created a series of interim plans and special elections, and culminated in the adoption of single-member and multimember districts for the house.[51]

Julian Bond, the communications director of SNCC, was one of a handful of blacks elected to the house in a special election held in 1965. The son of a college president, Bond was sophisticated, extremely articulate, and self-assured to the point of being cocky. And he made no effort to disguise his abiding contempt for segregation and the white privilege. He proved to be a natural lightning rod for the pent-up anger of many whites, who felt that they had been condescended to and bullied by the civil rights movement.

Bond won a landslide victory in district 136, where 92 percent of the voters were black. Before Bond took office, he and SNCC issued a statement strongly criticizing continued racial discrimination in the United States and the Vietnam War. "We know that for the most part, elections in this country, in the North as well as the South, are not free," the statement said. "We have seen that the 1965 Voting Rights Act and the 1964 Civil Rights Act have not yet been implemented with full federal power and sincerity." The statement went on to say that "[w]e are in sympathy with and support the men in this country who are unwilling to respond to a military draft which would compel them to contribute their lives to United States aggression in Viet Nam in the name of 'freedom' we find so false in this country."[52]

The statement by SNCC had been triggered by the death of Samuel Young, a Tuskegee Institute student and navy veteran, who had been killed while trying to use the segregated bathroom of a local service station. According to Bond, SNCC refused to allow "the irony of Young losing the life he had

---

[50] *Wilkerson v. Ferguson*, Civ. No. 77-30-AMER (M. D. Ga.), consolidated pretrial order, p. 8.
[51] *Toombs v. Fortson*, 241 F. Supp. 65, 67 (N. D. Ga. 1965); 277 F. Supp. 821 (N. D. Ga. 1967).
[52] *Bond v. Floyd*, 385 U.S. 116, 120 (1966).

offered his country over a segregated toilet" to go unnoticed and without public comment.[53]

Before the house convened on January 10, 1966, to swear in its newly elected members, seventy-five representatives petitioned to have Bond excluded on the ground that he could not validly take the oath of office to support the Constitutions of the United States and Georgia because of his opposition to the war and the draft. By ten o'clock on the appointed day the gallery was packed, and the atmosphere in the house chamber was electric. Shortly after Bond arrived, the speaker gaveled the house to order.

"All members take their seats," he intoned. "All reporters take their seats in the press box. Door keeper close the door."

The chaplain for the day came to the well of the house and solemnly read the beatitudes from the Gospel according to St. Matthew. "Blessed are the poor in spirit, for theirs is the kingdom of heaven. Blessed are the peacemakers, for they shall be called the children of God. Pray for the men called upon to fight this war in Viet Nam," he continued, "and Lord, may thy favor rest on every member of the House."[54]

The speaker then asked the representatives-elect to stand and raise their right hands to take the oath of office. But turning to Bond, he told him to step aside, noting that several challenges to his right to be seated had been filed. After the swearing-in of the other representatives, Bond was allowed to make a statement. "The hostility from white legislators," he recalled later, "was nearly absolute."[55] He thanked the speaker for allowing him to appear, and read a brief statement in which he refused to recant any of his prior statements. "I must say that I sincerely feel that I have done no wrong," he said, "and therefore, no further explanation is required of me."[56]

The house referred the petition to a special committee, which met that afternoon and recommended that Bond not be seated. The same day the house, in an action eerily reminiscent of the expulsion of blacks from the state legislature a hundred years earlier, adopted the recommendation of the committee. By a vote of 184 to 12, it passed a resolution that "Bond shall not be allowed to take the oath of office...and...shall not be seated as a member of the House of Representatives."[57]

Undaunted, Bond challenged his expulsion in federal court, arguing that it violated his right of free speech protected by the First Amendment and that it was the product of racial prejudice. The governor, in the meantime,

---

53 Julian Bond, "A Participant's Commentary," paper presented to the New England Historical Association, Boston, April 21, 1990.
54 Notes of Charles Morgan, Jr., January 10, 1966 (copy on file with author).
55 Bond, "A Participant's Commentary."
56 Statement by Julian Bond, representative-elect, Georgia House of Representatives, January 10, 1966.
57 *Bond v. Floyd*, 385 U.S. at 125.

called a special election to fill the vacant seat. Bond entered the race and won overwhelmingly. He again refused to recant his antiwar statements and once again was denied the oath of office. Bond ran a third time in the regular 1966 election and won yet again with a decisive majority.[58] Denmark Groover, the principal author of the state's majority-vote requirement, reportedly laughed that "[t]hey can keep on electing him till Gabriel blows his trumpet, but they ain't ever gonna get him in here."[59]

The lawsuit, which had been making its way through the courts, was argued in the U.S. Supreme Court by Bond's brother-in-law, Howard Moore, two days after the November 1966 election. The next month, the Court ruled that the house had denied Bond his freedom of expression and had unlawfully excluded him from the legislature. The Court found it unnecessary to address the issue of whether Bond had also been denied his seat because of his race. Bond was finally allowed to take the oath of office, but the hostility toward him continued to simmer and periodically boiled to the surface during the two decades he would serve in the general assembly.

[58] Ibid., p. 128.
[59] John Lewis, *Walking with the Wind: A Memoir of the Movement* (New York: Simon & Schuster, 1998), 361.

10

The 1970 Extension of the Voting Rights Act: More White Resistance

> The Voting Rights Act is illegal, unconstitutional and ungodly and un-
> American and wrong against the good people in this country.... And phooey
> on anything that says otherwise.
>
> Governor Lester Maddox, July 1969

I

Congress began considering legislation in 1969 to extend the special provisions of the Voting Rights Act for an additional five years. Georgia's governor, Lester Maddox, and its attorney general, Arthur Bolton, led the fight against the proposed legislation.

Maddox was a longtime foe of civil rights. An unsuccessful candidate for mayor of Atlanta in 1957 and 1961, and for lieutenant governor in 1962, he came to national attention when he refused to serve blacks at his restaurant in Atlanta, The Pickrick, after passage of the public accommodations provisions of the Civil Rights Act of 1964.[1] Maddox was a caricature of the shrill, provincial southern segregationist. Under the watchful and frequently incredulous gaze of the media, he paraded in front of his restaurant, brandishing an axe handle, turning blacks away at gunpoint, and denouncing a host of what he regarded as modern devils – socialists, atheists, "communist inspired racial agitators," "enemies" of private property, President Lyndon Johnson, and the "Great Black Father," meaning Martin Luther King, Jr.[2]

The Pickrick was eventually ordered to desegregate after a lawsuit was brought by three blacks who had been refused service.[3] But rather than cater to blacks and hated "integrationists," Maddox shut down The Pickrick and turned once again to politics. To the delight of many, and the embarrassment

[1] Bruce Galphin, *The Riddle of Lester Maddox* (Atlanta: Camelot Press, 1968), 32, 38.
[2] *Atlanta Journal*, July 4, 1964; *Atlanta Constitution*, July 18, 1964.
[3] *Willis v. The Pickrick*, 10 R. Rel. L. Reptr. 353 (N. D. Ga. 1965).

of some, he was elected governor in 1966 by the Georgia general assembly after no candidate in the three-way general election received a majority of the votes. Howard Callaway, running as a Republican, got 47.07 percent of the vote. Maddox, the Democratic nominee, was close behind with 46.88 percent. Former governor Ellis Arnall, a spoiler who had been defeated by Maddox in the primary but was running as a write-in candidate under the banner "Write In Georgia," got 6.05 percent.[4]

The state's constitution provided that in the event no candidate received a majority, the Georgia general assembly would decide between the two top vote-getters.[5] The largely Democratic legislature predictably elected Maddox, giving him 182 votes to Callaway's 66.[6] The state's unique gubernatorial election scheme survived a constitutional challenge in 1966,[7] but was amended by the legislature two years later to provide for a runoff election in the event no candidate for governor received a majority of the popular vote.[8]

In testimony before the U.S. Senate, Maddox blasted the Voting Rights Act as an "outrageous piece of legislation."[9] Taking full advantage of a national platform, he said the act was "illegal, unconstitutional and ungodly and un-American and wrong against the good people in this country.... And phooey on anything that says otherwise."[10]

Arthur Bolton, the state official with primary responsibility for ensuring compliance with Section 5, was more restrained than Maddox in his rhetoric but was equally opposed to the preclearance requirement. In a letter to Senator Sam Ervin, Jr., and the Senate subcommittee, he advised them that "it will come as no great shock to you to discover that my office is not overly fond of Section 5 of the Voting Rights Act of 1965."[11]

Fletcher Thompson, a congressman from East Point, complained bitterly about the "unequal treatment" that Section 5 imposed on the covered jurisdictions. He told the House committee that "[i]t would be unjust in the extreme to punish my state and those others now affected by this law for another five years."[12]

---

[4] *Fortson v. Morris*, 385 U.S. 231, 236 (1966).

[5] Ga. Code Ann. §2-3004.

[6] Lester Maddox, *Speaking Out: The Autobiography of Lester Garfield Maddox* (Garden City, N.Y.: Doubleday, 1975), 92.

[7] *Fortson v. Morris*.

[8] Ga. Laws 1968, p. 1562.

[9] Hearings before the Subcommittee on Constitutional Rights of the Committee on the Judiciary, United States Senate, Ninety-first Congress, First and Second Sessions, on S. 818, S. 2456, S. 2507, and Title IV of S. 2029, Bills to Amend the Voting Rights Act of 1965, July 9, 10, 11, and 30, 1969, February 18, 19, 24, 25, and 26, 1970, p. 342.

[10] Ibid., p. 351.

[11] Ibid., p. 669.

[12] Voting Rights Act Extension, Hearings before Subcommittee No. 5 of the Committee on the Judiciary, House of Representatives, Ninety-first Congress, First Session, on H.R. 4249, H.R. 5538, and Similar Proposals, to Extend the Voting Rights Act of 1965 with Respect to

Not all Georgians were opposed to Section 5. One of those who testified in 1970 in favor of extending the statute was Vernon Jordan, director of VEP in Atlanta. He warned that without the preclearance requirement, Georgia and other southern states "that were the most efficient, determined, and malicious in their efforts to keep black people off the registration rolls can be expected to be the most efficient, determined, and malicious in their efforts to cancel out the growing black vote." Particularly in rural areas, he said, "hundreds of... southern communities stand poised and ready to eliminate the burgeoning black vote."[13]

Congress, citing the continued depressed levels of black voter registration and the significant noncompliance with Section 5 by the covered jurisdictions, voted to extend the special coverage provisions of the act for another five years. It concluded that extension "is essential... in order to safeguard the gains in Negro voter registration thus far achieved, and to prevent future infringements of voting rights based on race or color."[14] Congress also made the suspension of tests or devices for voting effective nationwide, and revised the coverage formula to include the 1968 presidential election. As a result of the revision, several counties in New York (Kings, New York, and Bronx), Arizona, California, and Wyoming, and several towns in Connecticut, New Hampshire, Maine, and Massachusetts were brought under the coverage of Section 5.[15]

The submission of voting changes by Georgia and other covered jurisdictions gradually increased after the attorney general issued regulations for the administration of Section 5 in 1971,[16] and after several decisions of the Supreme Court clarified the scope and reach of the statute.[17] But many changes remained unsubmitted, and jurisdictions continued to enact new voting practices without seeking federal review.

II

Counties in Georgia with single-member district elections continued to switch to at-large voting after extension of the Voting Rights Act in 1970.

the Discriminatory Use of Tests and Devices, May 14, 15, June 19, 26, and July 1, 1969, p. 85.

[13] Hearings before the Subcommittee on Constitutional Rights of the Committee on the Judiciary, United States Senate, Ninety-first Congress, First and Second Sessions, on S. 818, S. 2456, S. 2507, and Title IV of S. 2029, July 9, 10, 11, and 30, 1969, February 18, 19, 24, 25, and 26, 1970, p. 449.

[14] H. Rep. No. 397, 91st Cong., 2d Sess. (1970), reprinted in 1970 U.S. Code Cong. & Adm. News 3281.

[15] S. Rep. No. 295, 94th Cong., 1st Sess., 13 n.5 (1975), reprinted in 1975 U.S. Code Cong. & Adm. News 779 n.5.

[16] 28 C.F.R. §51.

[17] For example, *Allen v. State Board of Elections*, 393 U.S. 544, 566-67 (1969); *Perkins v. Matthews*, 400 U.S. 379 (1971).

Morgan, Newton, and Twiggs Counties abandoned their district systems in 1971.[18] Wilkes and McDuffie followed suit in 1972.[19] McDuffie made a submission of its change, which was precleared in 1972.[20] That same year, however, the attorney general "reluctantly" objected to the change submitted by Twiggs because "the voting strength of the Negro community would be minimized and effectively cancelled out" by countywide voting.[21] Newton finally made a submission in 1975 and also drew an objection.[22]

One county with district elections before passage of the Voting Rights Act that did *not* change to at-large voting was Seminole County (35 percent black). Its districts were grossly malapportioned and already discriminated against minority voters. The county's plan had been enacted in 1933,[23] and over the course of the decades the district encompassing the county seat of Donalsonville, which contained 40 percent of the county's population and its largest concentration of blacks, had grown to over 2,200 voters. By contrast, the Rock Pond district, which also elected one member of the county government, had only 170 registered voters. Through a combination of "packing" blacks in one district and "stacking" them against a concentration of whites, the county's apportionment effectively minimized the impact of black voters in county elections.

Seventeen counties also adopted at-large elections for their boards of education after the 1970 extension of the act: Newton and Bibb in 1971;[24] Baldwin, Treutlen, McDuffie, Camden, Putnam, Pike, Spalding, and Wilkes in 1972;[25] Toombs, Sumter, and Clarke in 1973;[26] Harris, Charlton, and Taylor in 1975;[27] and Long in 1976.[28] Thirteen of the counties – Bibb, Treutlen, Charlton, Pike, Sumter, Clarke, Long, Newton, Taylor, Baldwin, Spalding, Wilkes, and Harris – eventually submitted their plans for Section 5 review; only the submission from Treutlen was precleared.[29]

The timing of the adoption of at-large elections in Pike County strongly suggested that race was a factor in the decision. The county abolished its

---

[18] Ga. Laws 1971, pp. 2638, 3022, 3564.

[19] Ga. Laws 1972, pp. 3337, 2536.

[20] U.S. Department of Justice, "Number of Changes Submitted under Section 5 and Reviewed by the Department of Justice, by State and Year, 1965–December 31, 1980."

[21] David L. Norman to Rabun Faulk, Aug. 7, 1972.

[22] Department of Justice, Civil Rights Division, "Complete Listing of Objections Pursuant to Section 5 of the Voting Rights Act of 1965" (Sept. 30, 1988).

[23] Ga. Laws 1933, p. 656.

[24] Ga. Laws 1971, pp. 2881, 3926.

[25] Ga. Laws 1972, pp. 3325, 2345, 2538, 3717, 2678, 3003, 2418, 1518.

[26] Ga. Laws 1973, pp. 3022, 2127, 3374.

[27] Ga. Laws 1965, pp. 2960, 3952, 3486.

[28] Ga. Laws 1976, p. 3536.

[29] U.S. Department of Justice, "Number of Changes Submitted Under Section 5"; J. Stanley Pottinger to J. Shaw, July 16, 1976; J. Stanley Pottinger to John P. Howell, Nov. 3, 1975; J. Stanley Pottinger to William Solomon, May 30, 1974.

grand jury appointment system in 1967, but replaced it with a school board elected from single-member districts.[30] Two blacks ran for the board in 1970, marking the first time in history that blacks had run for a county office. The two were defeated, but both ran strong races, and one, Rev. Robert Curtis, made it into a runoff.[31] Before the next election, and without seeking preclearance, the county switched to at-large voting.

In Harris County, the grand jury had traditionally appointed the members of the school board. The grand jury was finally desegregated by court order in 1974,[32] and proceeded to appoint two blacks to the board of education, Willie James Brown and Henry Lewis Walker.[33] The next year, county officials secured passage of the law requiring the board of education to be elected at-large.

In objecting to the county's submission of the new voting procedure, the attorney general concluded:

[M]inority candidates have not been able to become elected to any county-wide office in Harris County because of the county's system of at-large elections. The use of an at-large system under these circumstances has the discriminatory effect of diluting the ability of minority candidates to participate as members of the Board of Education.[34]

The county asked for reconsideration of its at-large plan, representing that the two black members of the board of education "were in favor of the bill."[35] In fact, they were not. Reconsideration was denied.

In objecting to the submission from Bibb County, the attorney generally noted similarly that "prior to the change, two of the school board members were black. Under the at-large feature of the change such representation may be a practical impossibility."[36]

III

Cities also continued to adopt majority-vote requirements after the 1970 extension of Section 5, including Augusta, Alapaha, Ashburn, Athens, Butler, Cairo, Camilla, Cochran, Crawfordville, East Dublin, Hartwell, Hinesville, Hogansville (including the board of education), Homerville, Jesup, Jonesboro, Lakeland, Louisville, Lumber City, Madison, Nashville, Newnan,

---

[30] Ga. Laws 1967, p. 3152.

[31] *Atlanta Constitution*, Dec. 10, 1980; Laughlin McDonald, *Voting Rights in the South: Ten Years of Litigation Challenging Continuing Discrimination against Minorities* (New York: American Civil Liberties Union, 1982), 49, 59.

[32] *Robinson v. Kimbrough*, Civ. No. 74-12-COL (M. D. Ga.).

[33] *Brown v. Reames*, Civ. No. 75-80-COL (M. D. Ga.), trial record, pp. 113, 172; trial transcript, pp. 59–60, 88–9.

[34] J. Stanley Pottinger to Ken Askew, Aug. 18, 1975.

[35] *Brown v. Reames*, trial transcript, pp. 250, 264–65, 267.

[36] David L. Norman to E. S. Sell, Jr., Aug. 24, 1971.

Palmetto, Sandersville, Sylvester, Thomasville (school board), Thomson, Wadley, Waynesboro, and Wrens. The attorney general eventually objected to twenty-six of the changes under Section 5.[37]

Jonesboro adopted its majority-vote requirement after the first black was elected to the city council in 1969 under a plurality-vote system. At the next election, with the majority-vote requirement in place, the black incumbent was defeated.[38] Athens, Hogansville, and Wadley also adopted majority-vote requirements after blacks were first elected to their city councils under a plurality system. They submitted their changes for preclearance, and preclearance was denied.[39]

Events surrounding the adoption of a majority-vote requirement in Thomson, the county seat of McDuffie County, not only showed that local officials were keenly aware that the requirement was a way of neutralizing the black vote, but also demonstrated the remarkable ability of a group of influential whites to manipulate the election procedures in order to maintain their control.

The charter for the city of Thomson in existence before passage of the Voting Rights Act provided for a mayor and a four-member council elected by a simple plurality vote, with no post or staggered-term provisions. Staggered terms limit the number of seats to be filled at any given election and, like numbered posts, have the effect of forcing head-to-head contests that deprive cohesive minorities of the ability to concentrate their votes effectively.[40] In 1973, the city adopted a new charter providing for a mayor and a five-member council elected to staggered terms and from designated posts, with a majority-vote requirement for election of the mayor.[41] The Thomson city attorney submitted the changes for preclearance and assured the Department of Justice in his Section 5 submission letter that "[t]here is no way that the change in said voting procedures herein outlined could affect the voting rights of any minority race."[42] The timing of the changes, coming as they did after the first political stirings in the black community, raised more than a suspicion that they were in fact adopted with an eye to "affecting" minority voting rights.

---

[37] *Election Law Changes in Cities and Counties in Georgia* (Atlanta: Voter Education Project, 1976); Department of Justice, Civil Rights Division, "Complete Listing of Objections Pursuant to Section 5"; William Bradford Reynolds to J. J. Rayburn, Oct. 20, 1986; William Bradford Reynolds to Ken W. Smith, July 8, 1988; John R. Dunne to William L. Tribble, April 26, 1991; John R. Dunne to Knox Bell, July 3, 1991; James P. Turner to Alex Davis, June 25, 1993.

[38] David L. Norman to Lee Hutcheson, Feb. 4, 1972.

[39] J. Stanley Pottinger to Joseph J. Gaines, Oct. 23, 1975; J. Stanley Pottinger to James T. Hunnicutt, Aug. 2, 1973; J. Stanley Pottinger to Sidney Shephard, Oct. 30, 1974.

[40] *City of Rome v. United States*, 446 U.S. 156, 185 (1980).

[41] Ga. Laws 1973, p. 2132.

[42] Jack D. Evans to Department of Justice, July 1, 1974.

The first black to run for public office in McDuffie County in modern times was Ephriam Pettit, a candidate for the board of education in 1964. Pettit taught bricklaying and masonry at a nearby federal military installation, Fort Gordon, and had been recruited to run for the school board by the predominantly black Thomson Progressive Civic Club. Pettit was a likely candidate because he was employed outside the county by the federal government and was not subject to retaliation by the loss of his job. Still, after he qualified a group of whites visited him and tried to persuade him to get out of the race. "They told me," Pettit recalls, "that 'the time is not right for a black to run,' and that I would hurt President Johnson's race. I laughed. I told them they should tell Mr. Johnson to withdraw."[43] Pettit stayed in the election but was defeated.[44]

Pettit's experience in running for office was not unique. Walter Daniel of Putnam County declared his candidacy for the local board of education in 1974. Shortly after that, when Daniel was in the Farmers and Merchants Bank in Eatonton, Milton Vining, a member of one of the county's most influential white families, approached him and asked him point blank to get out of the race.

He came up to me and asked was I the one, you know, running for that post in the race and I told him I was. He asked me to get out. I asked him why. He said that we black folks wanted to tear Putnam County up and that he had helped build it up and we were just trying to get in there to tear it down. He told me if I didn't get out that he had some connections and he could see to me not getting elected.[45]

Vining also warned Daniel not to campaign on the "north side of town," where whites lived. Daniel concluded that it was futile to try to get the white vote. He concentrated his campaign in the black community and was defeated.

In McDuffie County, another black, Rev. J. H. West, ran for the school board in 1968. He made a slightly better showing than Pettit but was also defeated.[46]

The first black to run for the Thompson City Council was Joseph Greene in 1970. Greene, an agent for the Pilgrim Insurance Company, came in sixth in a field of nine candidates. Whether or not the presence of a black candidate was the cause, the turnout was described by the local paper as "the largest voter turn-out within recent history."[47] While only about 500 people had voted in the 1968 town election involving only white candidates,

[43] Author's interview with Ephriam Pettit.

[44] *McDuffie Progress*, Nov. 12, 1964.

[45] *Bailey v. Vining*, Civ. No. 76-199 (M. D. Ga.), trial Transcript, p. 191 (testimony of Walter Daniel).

[46] *McDuffie Progress*, Nov. 14, 1968.

[47] *McDuffie Progress*, Dec. 3, 1970.

1,436 people – 77 percent of the eligible voters – cast ballots in the 1970 election.[48]

Another black, Edward Long, ran for the city council in 1972 and was also defeated.[49] The city adopted its new charter the following year. The Department of Justice denied preclearance of the new charter provisions shortly before the November 1974 election. It concluded: "Our analysis shows that where, as in Thomson, there is increasing participation in the political process by the black community, the use of numbered posts, staggered terms and majority requirements have the potential for reducing the opportunity for minority voters to elect candidates of their choice."[50] The *McDuffie Progress* carried a front-page story headlined "Federal Unit Slashes New Thomson Charter."[51]

Prior to the 1974 city elections, the longtime incumbent mayor made a surprise announcement that he would not seek reelection. Three men qualified for the mayor's position – E. Wilson Hawes, a local white businessman; William M. Wheeler, the white county attorney; and Luther Wilson, a black assistant school principal.[52] After the objection by the Department of Justice to the majority-vote provision, the two white candidates for mayor began to have second thoughts. Fearing that they would split the white vote and that Wilson would be elected by a plurality, Hawes and Wheeler entered into a "gentleman's agreement" to conduct a minielection prior to the primary to decide, in the words of Hawes, "which white man was to run."[53] Each white candidate was to appoint twelve men, and the group would take a vote to decide which white candidate would stay in the race.

Hawes and Wheeler made their appointments, and the group assembled at city hall on Tuesday, October 22, 1974, to cast their votes. They elected Wheeler. The following day, Hawes announced that he was quitting the race. By week's end, however, he had changed his mind, and on Friday he announced that he was still a candidate. Wheeler, unhappy with this turn of events, announced that he was withdrawing from the mayoral contest. "Somebody had to honor the gentlemen's agreement of Tuesday night," he explained, "and since Hawes didn't, I will."[54]

Wilson took the occasion to pump up his campaign and predicted that "all this confusion will increase my chances of winning." He claimed to "have support in the white community" and said that voters were "tired of this back-room politics."[55] But as the campaign got under way, whites

[48] Ibid.
[49] Jack D. Evans to Department of Justice, July 1, 1974.
[50] J. Stanley Pottinger to Jack D. Evans, September 3, 1974.
[51] Oct. 3, 1974.
[52] *Augusta Chronicle*, Oct. 24, 1974; *Atlanta Constitution*, Oct. 26, 1974.
[53] *Atlanta Constitution*, Oct. 26, 1974; *Augusta Chronicle*, Oct. 24, 1974.
[54] *Atlanta Constitution*, Oct. 26, 1974.
[55] Ibid.

circulated rumors that Wilson was a black militant. "I was anything but a militant," he scoffs. "I never made a militant speech. I've never been a member of a militant group. I avoided racial appeals. I had white campaign workers. I ran, not on a platform, but a philosophy of improvement of the entire community. I had white support at the beginning, but it began to wane after the scare tactics were used."[56] In the November primary Hawes won a landslide victory, beating Wilson with 72 percent of the vote.[57]

The city of Rome, which was about one-quarter black, adopted three vote-dilution mechanisms – numbered posts, staggered terms, and a majority-vote requirement – in 1966 but did not submit them for Section 5 review. In 1974, however, it submitted an annexation for preclearance, which led to the attorney general's discovery that the 1966 changes had never been submitted. At the request of the attorney general, the city submitted the provisions for majority vote, numbered posts, and staggered terms, and the attorney general objected, noting that "these electoral changes would deprive Negro voters of the opportunity to elect a candidate of their choice." The city then filed a declaratory judgment action in the Federal District Court for the District of Columbia seeking approval of the 1966 voting changes and arguing, among other things, that the Voting Rights Act was unconstitutional and that Section 5 had outlived its "usefulness." The court rejected the city's arguments and denied preclearance to all three provisions. It concluded that "the electoral changes from plurality-win to majority-win elections, numbered posts, and staggered terms, when combined with the presence of racial bloc voting and Rome's majority white population and at-large electoral system, would dilute Negro voting strength."[58]

In 1972, the city of Butler, which was 46 percent black, abandoned its plurality method of electing the mayor, which had been in effect since 1919, and adopted a majority-vote requirement.[59] It implemented the change without seeking preclearance and was eventually sued in 1986 by local black residents. When the change was finally submitted, the attorney general objected, concluding that "the city has not demonstrated that the adoption of a majority vote requirement for mayoral elections will not 'lead to a retrogression in the position of . . . minorities with respect to their effective exercise of the electoral franchise.'"[60] Rather than conducting elections for mayor under a plurality-vote system, the city refused to conduct *any* municipal elections for a period of nine years, until it was ordered to do so by the federal court of appeals in 1995.[61]

[56] Author's interview with Luther Wilson.
[57] *McDuffie Progress*, Nov. 7, 1974.
[58] *City of Rome v. United States*, 446 U.S. at 161, 173, 183.
[59] Ga. Laws 1919, p. 849; Ga. Laws 1972, p. 3884.
[60] James P. Turner to Alex Davis, June 25, 1993.
[61] *Chatman v. Spillers*, 44 F. 3d 923, 925 (11th Cir. 1995).

IV

Race continued to drive and distort legislative and congressional redistricting in Georgia during the 1970s, demonstrating once again the critical importance of Section 5 in the state's political process. After the new census, the state enacted a legislative apportionment plan to comply with one person, one vote. It submitted the plan for preclearance under Section 5, but the attorney general objected to it. He rejected the house plan because it contained a number of discriminatory features – including multimember districts, numbered posts, a majority-vote requirement, and changes in the structure of potential black-majority single-member districts.[62] The attorney general objected to the senate plan because of the potentially discriminatory way in which districts had been drawn in Fulton and Richmond Counties.[63]

Under the compulsion of Section 5, the state adopted a new plan in 1972 that met the objection to senate redistricting, increased the number of single-member house districts from 105 to 128, and reduced the number of multimember house districts from 49 to 32. The attorney general approved the plan for the Georgia senate, which used all single-member districts, two of which were majority-black, but again rejected the house redistricting. He concluded that the plan did not remove the objectionable combination of multimember districts, numbered posts, and the majority-vote requirement.[64]

The state refused to take any further steps to comply with Section 5 and, digging in its heels, argued that it now believed that Section 5 did not cover reapportionment. If it did, the state said, then the statute was unconstitutional. The U.S. attorney general brought suit to enjoin use of the objected-to plan, and the courts upheld the Section 5 objection. The Supreme Court ruled that its prior decisions "compell[ed]" the conclusion that the state's plan was subject to the statute.[65] The state, despite its protests, was required once again to reapportion in conformity with the racial fairness provisions of Section 5.

The general assembly adopted a new plan in 1974 that used fewer multimember districts. It provided for 180 house members elected from 154 districts, 24 of which were majority-black.[66] At the November elections, two blacks were elected to the senate, and nineteen blacks were elected to the house.[67]

---

[62] *Georgia v. United States*, 411 U.S. 526, 529–30 (1973).
[63] *United States v. Georgia*, 351 F. Supp. 444, 445 (N. D. Ga. 1972).
[64] *Georgia v. United States*, 411 U.S. at 530.
[65] Ibid., p. 531.
[66] Ga. Laws 1974, pp. 16, 1233.
[67] *National Roster of Black Elected Officials* (Washington, D.C.: Joint Center for Political Studies, 1975), 50–1.

Georgia's 1971 congressional reapportionment – the first such reapportionment subject to Section 5 review – showed the extraordinary lengths to which the legislature was prepared to go to exclude blacks from the congressional delegation. The state's two black senators, Leroy Johnson and Horace Ward, proposed a plan in which the fifth congressional district took in the city of Atlanta, increasing its black population from 34 percent to 45 percent. The plan was defeated in the senate by a vote of 43 to 9.[68]

The plan that was finally adopted discriminated in three distinct ways. First, unlike the plans proposed by black legislators, it divided the black population concentrated in the metropolitan Atlanta area into districts four, five, and six in order to insure that district five would be heavily majority-white.[69]

Second, it excluded from the fifth district the residences of two prominent blacks who were known to be potential candidates: Andrew Young, who had run in the previous fifth district election in 1970 against Fletcher Thompson, and Maynard Jackson, the popular vice-mayor of Atlanta. The homes of both Young and Jackson were placed in the sixth district, just outside the new fifth district line.[70] Although there is no residency requirement in congressional elections, nonresidence would have been an obvious political obstacle.

Third, in order to maximize the chances of white control, the residences of whites who were recognized as potential candidates were included in the fifth district bounds.[71]

Supporters of the state's plan frequently exploited the white resentment against Julian Bond, who was rumored to be a likely candidate if a majority-black district were drawn. Fletcher Thompson had used what a federal judge characterized as "racist campaign tactics" in his 1970 contest with Young, whom he accused of being in sympathy with violence committed by the Black Panthers.[72] Thompson resorted to similar tactics in 1971, when he warned voters of the dangers of creating a majority-black congressional district. The "worst thing" the Democrats could do, he said, would be to "create a district that would put Julian Bond in office."[73]

Supporters of Lester Maddox made similar racial appeals in opposing the creation of a majority-black fifth district. "Would you want Julian Bond as a congressman?" they asked rhetorically.[74] The *Atlanta Constitution* reported that "[r]umors that black Rep. Julian Bond of Atlanta planned to run for

---

[68] Georgia Senate Journal, 1971, extraordinary session, pp. 84–5; *Atlanta Constitution*, Sept. 30, 1971.

[69] *Busbee v. Smith*, Civ. No. 82-0665 (D. D. C.), deposition of Andrew Young, pp. 29–31; *Busbee v. Smith*, 549 F. Supp. 494, 500 (D. D. C. 1982).

[70] *Busbee v. Smith*, 549 F. Supp. at 500.

[71] Ibid.; *Atlanta Constitution*, Sept. 8, 1971; *Atlanta Constitution*, Sept. 9, 1971.

[72] *Pitts v. Busbee*, 395 F. Supp. 35, 40 (N. D. Ga. 1975); *Atlanta Constitution*, Oct. 22, 1970.

[73] *Atlanta Journal*, Sept. 9, 1971.

[74] *Atlanta Constitution*, Oct. 8, 1971.

Congress helped Sen. Frank Coggin of Hapeville in his efforts to keep the black ratio down."[75]

Rep. G. D. Adams of Atlanta made clear his intentions in proposing a district with a 38 percent black population. It was to ensure the election of "a white, moderate, Democratic Congressman," he said.[76]

The 1971 plan also contained majority-white districts that were bizarrely shaped, something of no apparent concern to most members of the legislature. One columnist said that the legislature had drawn districts that "hack up Atlanta worse than Vietnam is divided." The eighth district, he said, looked "just like Laos," because it "runs from a little below Jackson down through Macon to the Florida line." The district was shaped like a turkey neck, and in places was "as skinny as a flamingo's leg."[77]

The state submitted its plan for preclearance, and the attorney general objected to it. He said that he was unable to conclude "that these new boundaries [between the fifth and sixth districts] will not have a discriminatory racial effect on voting by minimizing or diluting black voting strength in the Atlanta area."[78] Under the duress of Section 5, the general assembly enacted a new plan in 1972, increasing the black percentage in the fifth district from 38 percent to 44 percent and including the residences of Young and Jackson. The plan was precleared.

Andrew Young, who had played the role of peacemaker during his days with SCLC and who was an adroit campaigner, was a candidate for the fifth district seat in the 1972 election. In the biracial afterglow of the civil rights movement, and with crossover support from 25 percent of metropolitan Atlanta's white voters, he became the first black elected to Congress from Georgia since Reconstruction.[79]

V

The mayoral contest in Atlanta the following year, however, showed how fragile racial harmony was, even in the state's capital city, which had proudly labeled itself "The City Too Busy To Hate." Eleven candidates entered the primary, including Maynard Jackson, who as vice-mayor of Atlanta had earned a reputation as a vigorous advocate for the minority community. The city was in transition from being majority-white to being majority-black, and Jackson was the front-runner with 46.6 percent of the vote. Coming in second was the incumbent, Sam Massell, who was regarded

---

[75] *Atlanta Constitution*, Oct. 10, 1971.

[76] *Atlanta Constitution*, October 22, 1970.

[77] *Atlanta Constitution*, Oct. 1, 1971.

[78] David L. Norman to Arthur K. Bolton, February 11, 1972; *Bacote v. Carter*, 343 F. Supp. 330, 331 (N. D. Ga. 1972).

[79] Bartlett C. Jones, *Flawed Triumphs: Andy Young at the United Nations* (Lanham, Md.: University Press of America, 1996), 3.

Leroy Johnson, Sam Massell, Charles Weltner, and Maynard Jackson (l. to r.) on the campaign trail for mayor of Atlanta in 1973. In the ensuing runoff between Massell and Jackson, Massell accused his opponent of being "a racist" and said that "one can almost see them singing and dancing in the streets in anticipation of a black takeover" (photo from *Atlanta Journal-Constitution*).

as a racial progressive and who had been elected in 1969 with strong black support.[80] The primary had been issue-oriented for the most part, but in the runoff Massell, concluding that his only chance for success lay in mobilizing the white vote, made open appeals to race. At a televised mews conference, the erstwhile racial moderate startled viewers by charging that "Maynard Jackson is a racist," and saying that every time Jackson acted as vice-mayor "he's stopped and said,'Let's see, I've got to do what's black.'"[81]

Hosea Williams of SCLC was also running for president of the city council, and Massell, stoking the fires of racial fear higher, warned that if Williams and Jackson were elected, blacks would take over the government. "One can almost see them singing and dancing in the streets in anticipation of a black takeover," he said. Massell's billboards urged voters to support him because "Atlanta's too young to die," meaning that a black administration would precipitate white flight and kill the city's progress. "Right or wrong," Massell said, "that's the feeling in the white community."[82]

Jackson chastised Massell for "wallowing in the slime of racism and innuendo" and went on to make history. He won the runoff with approximately 95 percent of the black vote and 25 percent of the white vote, and became the city's first black chief executive.[83]

[80] "Mayor: A Tale of Two Cities," *Newsweek*, October 15, 1973.
[81] *Atlanta Journal*, Oct. 10, 1973.
[82] *Atlanta Constitution*, October 8, 1973; *Atlanta Constitution*, October 10, 1973.
[83] *Atlanta Constitution*, October 30, 1973.

VI

Andrew Young won reelection in the fifth district in 1974 and 1976. But shortly after the 1976 election, he announced that he was resigning to accept the position of United States ambassador to the United Nations. A special election was called to fill the vacant seat, and twelve people announced their candidacies, including John Lewis and Wyche Fowler, the former president of the Atlanta City Council who had been defeated by Young in the preceding Democratic primary. Fowler led the voting in the special election with 40 percent of the vote; Lewis was second with 29 percent. In the runoff, Fowler swamped Lewis with 62 percent of the vote, and the fifth congressional district once again had a white member of Congress.[84]

---

[84] John Lewis, *Walking with the Wind: A Memoir of the Movement* (New York: Simon and Schuster, 1998), 423.

II

The 1975 Extension of the Voting Rights Act:
The Private Enforcement Campaign

Did they want to run *everything*? Didn't they want you in *any* position?

Edward Brown of Camilla, Georgia

I

In 1975, against a backdrop of continuing opposition to Section 5 and the adoption of new discriminatory voting practices, Congress once again considered legislation to extend and expand the coverage of the Voting Rights Act. Georgia had begun to submit more of its voting changes for preclearance (809 by 1974), but it was tied with Louisiana for the most Section 5 objections (37).[1] Black voter registration lagged behind white registration, and there were still relatively few black elected officials. Of the 236 members of the general assembly, only 21 were black. Less than 2 percent of the members of county governing boards were black. There were 530 municipalities in the state, but only two black mayors. Only the barest fraction of the state's judges, justices of the peace, probate judges, and clerks of court were black.[2]

Blacks were routinely excluded from working at the polls in many areas of the state. In Harris County, prior to 1972 no black ever served as a poll worker.[3] That year local blacks and a lawyer from the Department of Justice asked the judge of probate, Roy Moultrie, to appoint some blacks to work the elections.[4] As Moultrie tells the story, and referring to the Justice Department lawyer's Jewish surname, "I received a phone call from a man who identified

[1] S. Rep. No. 295, 94th Cong., 1st Sess. 17 (1975), reprinted in 1975 U.S. Code Cong. & Adm. News 783.
[2] *National Roster of Black Elected Officials* (Washington, D.C.: Joint Center for Political Studies, 1975), 49–55.
[3] *Brown v. Reames*, Civ. No. 75-80 (M. D. Ga.), trial record, pp. 115, 173; trial transcript, p. 205.
[4] Ibid., trial transcript, pp. 173, 205.

himself as Barry Weinstein of the Civil Rights Division of the Department of Justice to which I said, who else would Barry Weinstein work for. He laughed. He said I was a nice fellow."[5] Moultrie appointed six blacks, out of thirty-eight people, to serve at the polls for the 1972 election. Only one black was appointed to serve in 1974. None were appointed in 1975.[6]

The situation was similar in Putnam, Bleckley, and Screven Counties. In an opinion written in 1981, a federal judge noted that "[b]lacks have never been appointed as election officials in the rural precincts of Putnam County."[7] In Bleckley County, which was nearly one-quarter black, from 1978 to 1986 the superintendent of elections appointed 224 poll managers for some 17 elections, and not a single manager was black.[8] In 45-percent-black Screven County, despite requests from local black residents, the superintendent of elections had never appointed a black as the manager of a local polling place.[9]

Blacks were also excluded from leadership positions in the Democratic Party in many places in the state. By the mid-1970s, no black had ever served as an officer or member of the executive committee of the Democratic Party in Harris County. The chair of the party, who had held the office since 1948, said he did not plan to do anything to include blacks in party affairs. "I'm going to mind my own business," he explained, "and I want everybody to do that, too."[10] No black served on the executive committee of the Democratic Party in Putnam County until 1972.[11] In majority-black Burke County, the first black was appointed to the twenty-four-member Democratic Party executive committee in 1976 – more than thirty years after the white primary had been formally abolished.[12]

The white leadership of Georgia essentially boycotted the 1975 congressional hearings on extension of the Voting Rights Act. John Tunney, the chair of the Senate subcommittee, had written to Arthur Bolton requesting that he submit a written statement, to be made part of the record, setting out the state's position on the proposed amendments being considered by Congress. In a terse and chilly response, Bolton advised Tunney that "[a]s Attorney General for the State of Georgia in a number of litigated cases my position with respect to the law in this matter is well established, and I do not at this time have anything further to add in this matter."[13] In one of the recent cases

[5] Ibid., trial transcript, testimony of Roy Moultrie, p. 151.
[6] Ibid., trial transcript, pp. 116, 205.
[7] *Bailey v. Vining*, 514 F. Supp. 452, 455 (M. D. Ga. 1981).
[8] *Hall v. Holder*, 757 F. Supp. 1560, 1563 (M. D. Ga. 1991).
[9] *United States v. Screven County*, Georgia, Civ. No. 692-154 (S. D. Ga. Dec. 16, 1992).
[10] *Brown v. Reames*, trial record, pp. 183–84, 205; trial transcript, pp. 283–86.
[11] *Bailey v. Vining*, 514 F. Supp. at 455.
[12] *Lodge v. Buxton*, Civ. No. 176-55 (S. D. Ga. Sept. 29, 1978), slip op. at 10.
[13] Extension of the Voting Rights Act of 1965, Hearings before the Subcommittee on Constitutional Rights of the Committee on the Judiciary, United States Senate, Ninety-fourth

referred to by Bolton, the state had argued that the Voting Rights Act was unconstitutional.[14]

Andrew Young, the only black member of Georgia's congressional delegation, testified in 1975 in support of preclearance. He cautioned that "it would be extremely dangerous to all of the progress we have made thus far, if we did not keep that section [5] very active in the bill."[15] Congress concluded that progress under the act "has been modest and spotty in so far as the continuing and significance deficiencies yet existing in minority registration and political participation." The Senate report noted that "[t]his past experience [of evading Section 5] ought not be ignored in terms of assessing the future need for the Act." It was "imperative," the report said, that Section 5 protection apply to the redistricting that would take place after the 1980 census.[16]

Congress passed legislation in 1975 that made permanent the nationwide ban on tests for voting, extended Section 5 for an additional seven years, broadened the reach of the statute by including the 1972 presidential elections in the coverage formula, and extended coverage for the first time to language minorities. Congress concluded that language minorities had been the victims of pervasive discrimination in voting and extended Section 5 and other special protections, including bilingual elections, to American Indians, Asian Americans, Alaskan natives, and those of Spanish heritage.[17] As a result of the 1975 amendments, the states of Alaska, Arizona, and Texas and counties in California, Florida, Michigan, and South Dakota were added to the list of jurisdictions covered by Section 5.[18]

One of the reasons for the depressed level of minority officeholding was that many jurisdictions countered the increases in registration by adopting new voting laws and practices that made it more difficult for blacks to win. Another reason was the widespread use of at-large elections that had been adopted prior to passage of the Voting Rights Act and were therefore beyond the reach of Section 5. Where whites were in the majority and refused to vote for blacks in any significant numbers, even if all the age-eligible blacks were registered, and even if they all turned out on election day, and even if they all voted for a black candidate, their choice would invariably be defeated

Congress, First Session, on S. 407, S. 903, S. 1297, S. 1409, and S. 1443, April 8, 9, 10, 22, 29, 30, and May 1, 1975, Arthur Bolton to Sen. John Tunney.

[14] *Georgia v. United States*, 411 U.S. 526, 530 (1973).

[15] Extension of the Voting Rights Act, Hearings before the Subcommittee on Civil and Constitutional Rights of the Committee on the Judiciary, House of Representatives, Ninety-fourth Congress, First Session, on H.R. 939, H.R. 2148, H.R. 3247, and H.R. 3501, February 25, 26, and March 3, 4, 5, 6, 13, 14, 17, 20, 21, 24, 25, 1975, p. 63.

[16] 1975 U.S. Code Cong. & Adm. News 781, 783–84.

[17] 42 U.S.C. §1973aa-1(a).

[18] 28 C.F.R. §51, Appendix to Part 51 – Jurisdictions Covered under Section 4(b) of the Voting Rights Act, as Amended.

by the bloc-voting white majority. The majority-take-all aspect of at-large voting, undergirded by white bloc voting, effectively nullified in most areas of Georgia the gains in black voter registration that followed passage of the Voting Rights Act.

There was no easy way for black candidates to breach the barrier of severe racial bloc voting. Jim Crow had been invalidated as a formal matter, but blacks and whites still lived in separate, polarized communities. Churches, social groups, the country club, and business, professional, and civic organizations were largely segregated. Blacks had little or no access to the institutions in the white community in which friendships and political alliances were formed and nurtured. And the old antiblack prejudices and fears still flourished.

II

Edward Brown, an officer of the state NAACP and widely respected in the black community, ran unsuccessfully for the state house from Mitchell County in 1976 and for mayor of his hometown, Camilla, in 1979. In doing so, he experienced firsthand the practical difficulties that a black faced campaigning for public office in a rural southwest Georgia county.

Brown started off his 1976 campaign by going to the courthouse and asking the registrar to appoint some black deputy registrars. The reception he got was a bitter residue of the old hostility of many whites to black political aspirations. As Brown tells the story,

Ed Hilliard was the chair of the board of registrars. I didn't threaten him or anything, but when I told him what I wanted he put down his pipe, balled up his fist, and came around his desk like he was going after me. He was known for his temper, you know, especially towards black people. But I stood my ground. You had to have a strong will, because the attitude was so against you, and I said to him, "I've always respected my elders, but if you hit me I'll give you something your parents never gave you," and he calmed down some.[19]

Brown is a soft-spoken, genial man and has the natural politician's affinity for people, but he found that being black was "a tremendous handicap" in campaigning if the white community. "I tried it," he says, "but whites were reluctant to accept my campaign material. On one occasion a man tore up my card as I stood on his front doorstep."[20] Another elderly white man told

---

[19] Author's interview with Edward Brown, December 9, 1999.
[20] Extension of the Voting Rights Act, Hearings before the Subcommittee on Civil and Constitutional Rights of the Committee on the Judiciary, House of Representatives, Ninety-seventh Congress, First Session, on Extension of the Voting Rights Act, May 6, 7, 13, 19, 20, 27, 28, June 3, 5, 10, 12, 16, 17, 18, 23, 24, 25, and July 12, 1981, p. 742 (testimony of Edward Brown).

Brown, "You're trying to take over. I've seen the time in Mitchell County when people like you would just disappear."[21]

Whites didn't feel comfortable with him, Brown thinks, because he was active in the NAACP and encouraged black voter registration. "They just didn't know any better, but they felt if you were in civil rights you had to hate white people," he explains. "I would always tell them that I never went to bed at night hating anybody."[22] Prior to the election, someone burned Brown's car.

Brown recalls that on election day a deputy sheriff drove whites to the polls "but never carried one black." When Brown's wife went to vote and was marking her ballot, she overheard the deputy instructing a voter in the adjoining booth "not to vote for Edward Brown, 'he is a nigger.'"[23] Brown shrugged. "A lot of people get upset about things like that, the 'nigger' talk and the white attitude, but that was just the way it was." Brown says that he was not intimidated by the white hostility, but "I was bewildered by it in a sense. Did they want to run *everything*? Didn't they want you in *any* position?"[24]

In places like Camilla and Mitchell County, social and private contacts are crucial in the operation of the political process. Candidates run on their status in the community, and rarely on issues. William B. Withers was mayor of Moultrie for 30 years, but he never campaigned a single day. He explained that being Presbyterian, he felt it was unnecessary to campaign; his success at the polls was predestined.[25]

Roy Moultrie, the judge of probate of Harris County, said that his campaigns involved no issues and no platform. Instead, he ran on his "personality."[26] Willie James Brown ran for coroner of Harris County in 1972, but he felt he couldn't campaign in white neighborhoods because of an atmosphere of racial prejudice. He received invitations to speak to black groups, but never to white groups. White candidates, such as Judge Moultrie, depended upon friendships and personal contacts built up over the years. But since blacks were excluded from membership in white social and civic clubs in the county, Brown's opportunities to draw upon personal ties and connections in the white community were virtually nonexistent.

Federal Judge Anthony Alaimo, in a case challenging at-large elections in Burke County, underscored the problem blacks faced in running for

---

[21] Author's interview with Edward Brown, December 9, 1999.
[22] Ibid.
[23] Extension of the Voting Rights Act, Hearings before the Subcommittee on Civil and Constitutional Rights of the Committee on the Judiciary, House of Representatives, Ninety-seventh Congress, First Session, on Extension of the Voting Rights Act, p. 742 (testimony of Edward Brown).
[24] Author's interview with Edward Brown, December 9, 1999.
[25] *Cross v. Baxter*, Civ. No. 76-20 (M. D. Ga.), trial transcript, pp. 187–88.
[26] *Brown v. Reames*, trial transcript, p. 192.

office under an at-large system. "[T]he social reality," he wrote, "[is] that person-to-person relations necessary to effective campaigning in a rural county [are] virtually impossible on an inter-racial basis because of the deep-rooted discrimination by Whites against Blacks."[27] Or, as the court of appeals succinctly put it, "The vestiges of racism encompass the totality of life in Burke County."[28]

After repeated unsuccessful attempts to run for office under at-large systems, blacks, such as Edward Brown, turned to the courts for relief. "We had plenty of people to run in Mitchell County," says Brown. "Blacks had run for county commission, coroner, sheriff, and tax commissioner, but really they didn't have a chance of winning. We knew that. For blacks to have a chance we had to change the system."[29]

Oscar Davis of Milledgeville gave a similar reason for the decision by local blacks to sue Baldwin County over its use of at-large elections. "We've tried many, many times to get blacks elected and we've never been able to do it, even when most everyone turns out to vote," he said. "We finally made the decision that the only thing we could do was sue."[30]

III

Georgia's failure to comply fully with Section 5 and its use of at-large voting spawned a massive litigation campaign. It was led by the civil rights and minority communities, and despite preclearance and the burden-shifting provisions of the Voting Rights Act, as important as they were in individual cases, black voters again suffered the disadvantages and delays of litigation.

Fortson v. Dorsey, a case involving legislative redistricting in Georgia, had established the proposition that a voting practice could be held unconstitutional if it "designedly or otherwise ... operate[d] to minimize or cancel out the voting strength of racial or political elements of the voting population."[31] But it was not until 1973, in *White v. Regester*,[32] that the Supreme Court invalidated an at-large election plan under the Fourteenth Amendment on the grounds that it diluted minority voting strength.

White v. Regester was a challenge by blacks and Hispanics to multiseat legislative districts in Texas. The Court looked at a variety of factors, which it described as "the totality of circumstances" – such as a history of discrimination, depressed voter registration, cultural and language barriers,

---

[27] *Lodge v. Buxton*, 639 F. 2d 1358, 1379 (5th Cir. 1981).

[28] Ibid., p. 1381 and n. 46.

[29] Author's interview with Edward Brown, December 9, 1999.

[30] *Atlanta Constitution*, June 8, 1984.

[31] 379 U.S. 433, 439 (1965).

[32] 412 U.S. 755 (1973).

and the effect of the at-large system – in concluding that minorities "had less opportunity than did other residents in the district to participate in the political process and to elect legislators of their choice."[33] The Court also affirmed the trial court's finding that single-member districts were necessary "to bring the [minority] community into the full stream of political life of the county and State by encouraging their further registration, voting, and other political activities."[34] *White v. Regester* gave a huge boost to the voting rights enforcement campaign in Georgia.

Actions to enjoin the use of at-large elections were brought against county commissions in Twiggs County in 1972;[35] Fulton in 1974;[36] Harris, Thomas, and Walton in 1975;[37] Burke, Dougherty, McDuffie, Morgan, Peach, Putnam, Terrell, and Wilkes in 1976;[38] Coffee, McIntosh, and Sumter in 1977;[39] Richmond in 1978;[40] Bulloch, Calhoun, Dooly, Henry, and Mitchell in 1979;[41] and Clay, Early, and Miller in 1980.[42]

Wilkes was the only county sued under Section 5 that subsequently sought preclearance in the Federal District Court for the District of Columbia, and preclearance was denied. The court held that "[i]f the system of election from single-member districts had been retained, it is probable that black residents of Wilkes County would have and would expect to have in the future a much greater influence in the political process than under the at-large system."[43] Of the twenty-five counties that were sued, all eventually adopted

---

33 Ibid., p. 766.
34 Ibid., p. 769.
35 *Bond v. White*, 377 F. Supp. 514 (M. D. Ga. 1974).
36 *Pitts v. Busbee*, 395 F. Supp. 35 (N. D. Ga. 1975).
37 *Brown v. Reames*; *Thomasville Branch of NAACP v. Thomas County*, Civ. No. 75-34 (M. D. Ga.); *Howard v. Board of Commissioners of Walton County*, Civ. No. 75-67-ATH (M. D. Ga. July 29, 1976).
38 *Lodge v. Buxton*; *Criterion Club of Albany v. Board of Commissioners of Dougherty County, Ga.*, Civ. No. 76-63 (M. D. Ga.); *Bowdry v. Hawes*, Civ. No. 176-128 (S. D. Ga.); *Butler v. Underwood*, Civ. No. 76-53 (M. D. Ga. Aug. 31, 1976); *Berry v. Doles*, Civ. No. 76-139 (M. D. Ga.); *Bailey v. Vining*, Civ. No. 76-199 (M. D. Ga.); *Holloway v. Faust*, Civ. No. 76-28 (M. D. Ga.); *Avery v. Wilkes County Board of Commissioners*, Civ. No. 176-38 (S. D. Ga. Jan. 17, 1979).
39 *NAACP Branch of Coffee County v. Moore*, Civ. No. 577-25 (S. D. Ga.); *McIntosh County NAACP v. McIntosh County*, Civ. No. 277-70 (S. D. Ga.); *Wilkerson v. Ferguson*, Civ. No. 77-30 (M. D. Ga.).
40 *Hamilton v. Board of Commissioners of Richmond County*, Civil No. 178-226 (S. D. Ga.).
41 *Love v. Deal*, Civ. No. 679-37 (S. D. Ga.); *Jones v. Cowart*, Civ. No. 79-79 (M. D. Ga. June 11, 1980); *McKenzie v. Giles*, Civ. No. 79-43 (M. D. Ga.) and Civ. No. 86-95 (M. D. Ga. Sept. 29, 1986); *Head v. Henry Board of Commissioners*, Civ. No. 79-2063A (N. D. Ga. June 17, 1980); *Cochran v. Autry*, Civ. No. 79-59 (M. D. Ga.).
42 *Davenport v. Isler*, Civ. No. 80-42 (M. D. Ga. July 1, 1980); *Brown v. Scarborough*, Civ. No. 80-27 (M. D. Ga. 1980); *Thompson v. Mock*, Civ. No. 80-13 (M. D. Ga. June 27, 1980).
43 *Wilkes County, Ga. v. United States*, 450 F. Supp. 1171, 1177 (D. D. C. 1978).

single-member plans as a result of the litigation. Bacon and Newton Counties finally made Section 5 submissions after they were threatened with lawsuits, and both drew objections from the attorney general.[44]

Seminole County was sued by local voters in a one person, one vote lawsuit in April 1980, and the court ordered the county to redistrict.[45] At the next election, Donald Moore, a black schoolteacher, was elected to the county council from the town of Donalsonville.[46]

Many of the boards of education that had ignored Section 5 were also sued under the Voting Rights Act and were required to adopt district systems: Walton in 1975;[47] McDuffie and Putnam in 1976;[48] Coffee in 1977;[49] Bulloch, Dooly, Henry, and Mitchell in 1979;[50] and Miller and Pike in 1980.[51] Newton County, rather than face litigation, adopted the existing county commission lines for school board elections.[52]

Terrell County was also sued in 1976 for failing to submit its at-large voting system for the board of education for Section 5 review.[53] The county made a submission, and the attorney general objected to the at-large elections.[54] Rather than adopt district voting, the county returned to grand jury appointments. A desegregated grand jury subsequently appointed five new members to the board, two of whom were black.[55]

A number of cities in Georgia were also sued over their use of at-large elections: Albany, Dublin, and Macon in 1974;[56] Eatonton, Madison, Moultrie, Thomson, and Waynesboro in 1976;[57] Americus, Covington,

---

[44] Author's interview with Christopher Coates, April 6, 1990; Hearings before the Subcommittee on the Constitution of the Committee on the Judiciary, United States Senates, Ninety-seventh Congress, Second Session, on S. 53, S. 1761, S. 1975, S. 1992, and H.R. 3112, Bills to Amend the Voting Rights Act of 1965, January 27, 28, February 1, 2, 4, 11, 12, 25, and March 1, 1982, Volume 2, Appendix, p. 696; U.S. Department of Justice, "Complete Listing of Objections Pursuant to Section 5 of the Voting Rights Act of 1965" (Sept. 30, 1988).

[45] *Williams v. Timmons*, Civ. No. 80-26 (M. D. Ga. June 28, 1980).

[46] Laughlin McDonald, *Voting Rights in the South: Ten Years of Litigation Challenging Continuing Discrimination against Minorities* (New York: American Civil Liberties Union, 1982), 43.

[47] *Howard v. Board of Commissioners of Walton County.*

[48] *Bowdry v. Hawes* (Jan. 3, 1978); *Bailey v. Vining* (April, 22, 1982).

[49] *NAACP Branch of Coffee County v. Moore* (Feb. 28, 1978).

[50] *Love v. Deal* (May 27, 1980); *McKenzie v. Giles* (July 5, 1980); *McRae v. Board of Education of Henry County*, Civ. No. 79-2064A (N. D. Ga.); *Cochran v. Autry*, (May 21, 1984).

[51] *Thompson v. Mock* (Feb. 23, 1981); *Hughley v. Adams*, Civ. No. 80-20N (N. D. Ga. Sept. 22, 1983).

[52] McDonald, *Voting Rights in the South*, 42; Ga. Laws 1976, p. 3505.

[53] *Holloway v. Faust.*

[54] U.S. Department of Justice, "Complete Listing of Objections Pursuant to Section 5."

[55] McDonald, *Voting Rights in the South*, 47.

[56] *Paige v. Gray*, Civ. No. 74-50 (M. D. Ga.); *Sheffield v. Cochran*, Civ. No. 374-14 (S. D. Ga.); *Walton v. Thompson*, Civ. No. 74-77 (M. D. Ga.).

[57] *Bailey v. Vining; Butler v. Underwood; Cross v. Baxter; Bowdry v. Hawes; Sullivan v. DeLoach*, Civ. No. 176-238 (S. D. Ga.).

Darien, Dawson, and Douglas in 1977;[58] and Statesboro in 1979.[59] In all but one of the cases, new district systems of elections were ordered into effect by the courts or were adopted by the legislature as part of an agreed-upon settlement. The suit against the city of Macon was dismissed by the court in an unreported opinion,[60] but following the dismissal the legislature enacted a new, district plan for the city council.[61]

Most of the challenges to at-large elections under Section 2 and the Constitution were settled, but in those that went to trial the courts made detailed findings of past discrimination and its continuing effects. The court struck down at-large elections in Fulton County after concluding that there was "a history of undisputable, pervasive de jure racial segregation in Georgia and Fulton County" and that "the government has never become equally open to participation by black and white members of the community." No black had ever been elected to the county commission under the challenged plan. The county had refused for racial reasons to build public housing or to permit anyone else to do so. There were no black department heads. Racist campaign tactics had been used in recent elections, and virtually every suspect voting procedure was in effect, including majority-vote and numbered-post requirements. At-large elections in Fulton County, according to the court, "grossly minimize" the possibility of blacks' electing candidates of their choice.[62]

At-large elections were invalidated in Albany for similar reasons. The city functioned "in every respect...as a racially segregated community." Schools, voting, the library, the city auditorium, tennis courts, swimming pools, public housing, juries, municipal employment, taxicabs, theaters, and city busses were segregated. The Democratic Party was "in the hands of an all-white committee." The black community "has just never had the opportunity or been permitted to enter into the political process of electing city commissioners." The at-large system, the court found, was "winner take all" and was unconstitutional.[63]

In invalidating the at-large system in Putnam County, the court found that voting was racially polarized. Schools and juries had been segregated. Few blacks were employed by the city or county or had been appointed to local boards and commissions. The municipal housing authority was operated on a racially segregated basis. The swimming pool was white-only until

---

58 *Wilkerson v. Ferguson; Newton County Voters League v. The City of Covington, Georgia*, Civ. No. 77-1802A (M. D. Ga.); *McIntosh County Branch NAACP v. City of Darien, Ga.*, Civ. No. 277-71 (S. D. Ga.); *Holloway v. Raines*, Civ. No. 77-27 (M. D. Ga.); *NAACP Branch of Coffee County v. Moore*.

59 *Love v. Deal*.

60 *Walton v. Thompson* (Jan. 23, 1975).

61 Ga. Laws 1975, p. 2799.

62 *Pitts v. Busbee*, 395 F. Supp. at 40–1.

63 *Paige v. Gray*, 437 F. Supp. 137, 153–58 (M. D. Ga. 1977).

Willie Bailey, George Thompkins, and Walter Daniel (l. to r.), plaintiffs in a lawsuit
challenging at-large elections in Putnam County, on the stoop of Eatonton's Uncle
Remus Museum, May 1978 (photo by Patricia McDonald).

1969. Public funds had been used to pave the road to an all-white private
school, which opened following the desegregation of the public schools. The
golf course, operated on land owned by the county, was segregated. Voting
lists were maintained on a segregated basis. No blacks were appointed as
deputy registrars until after a lawsuit was filed in 1976, and there were
virtually no black election officials in the city and rural precincts. Blacks
were excluded from participating in the affairs of the Democratic Party.
Majority-vote and numbered-post requirements were in effect. Blacks had a
depressed socioeconomic status that hindered their ability to support candidates for public office. Despite the fact that blacks were 49 percent of the
population, no black had ever won a contested at-large election in the county
during the twentieth century. The court concluded that under the at-large

system, blacks "have not had equal access to the political processes in Putnam County."[64]

In Burke County the court found, among other things, that there was discrimination in employment, the provision of services, and appointments to boards and commissions. Schools and juries were segregated. Public funds were diverted to support a private school established to circumvent desegregation. Blacks had a depressed socioeconomic status. "Black suffrage was 'virtually non-existent'." Blacks were excluded from participating in the affairs of the Democratic Party. The evidence of racial bloc voting was "clear and overwhelming."[65]

The facts in the city of Albany case and the Fulton, Putnam, and Burke County cases were egregious, but they were fundamentally no different from those that existed in other counties in the state that had significant black populations and used at-large elections. All shared a common history of discrimination; minorities were a depressed socioeconomic group; there were few, if any, black elected officials; voting was racially polarized; housing, churches, and civic and social organizations were largely segregated; blacks had been excluded from participating in government at every level; it was prohibitively difficult for blacks to establish political coalitions with whites. Christopher Coates, the lawyer who had represented the plaintiffs in the Putnam County case, said that "every at-large system in the state where there was a geographically compact minority was vulnerable to a vote dilution challenge."[66] Many jurisdictions, acknowledging that fact, bowed to the inevitable and adopted district systems of elections.

IV

In 1980 the Supreme Court abruptly changed the standard for proving vote dilution and precipitated a major crisis in the campaign for equal voting rights. In *City of Mobile v. Bolden*,[67] it held that minority plaintiffs could not rely on the *effect* of a challenged voting practice but had to prove an *intent* to discriminate on the basis of race by public officials in order to make out a violation of the Constitution or of Section 2 of the Voting Rights Act. Moreover, Section 5 was scheduled to expire in 1982. The combination of the *Bolden* decision and the expiration of Section 5 meant that jurisdictions such as Georgia, with proven track records of discrimination, would be able to return to their old ways, and that minorities would be powerless to stop them unless they could prove that state officials had acted with a discriminatory purpose.

[64] *Bailey v. Vining*, 514 F. Supp. at 454–62.
[65] *Lodge v. Buxton*, 639 F. 2d at 1375–80.
[66] Author's interview with Christopher Coates, April 1983.
[67] 446 U.S. 55 (1980).

The immediate impact of *Mobile v. Bolden* was dramatic. Because of the plaintiff's onerous new burden of proof, litigation challenging discriminatory voting practices under the Constitution and Section 2 dried up. Some plaintiffs (both the Department of Justice and private parties) who had cases pending dropped then, and virtually no new cases were filed. Defendants became intransigent and refused to discuss settlement.[68] And some cases, even though the evidence showed pervasive discrimination in the political process, were dismissed by the courts for failure to prove discriminatory intent. One of those cases arose in Moultrie, Georgia.

John Cross and several other black residents sued the city of Moultrie in 1976 over its use of at-large elections and its failure to seek preclearance of its majority-vote requirement.[69] A three-judge court enjoined further use of the majority-vote requirement,[70] and the city submitted it to the attorney general. The attorney general objected to the change because "bloc voting along racial lines may exist" in Moultrie, and the majority-vote requirement "may have the effect of abridging minority voting rights."[71] But the objection did not end the attempts of the white leadership of the town to manipulate the electoral process in an effort to maintain their control.

At the next election in 1977, Frank Wilson, a black florist and one of the plaintiffs in the lawsuit, ran for a council seat against four whites. The white candidates split the white vote, and Wilson was elected with a plurality.[72]

The district court held a trial on the challenge to at-large elections and dismissed the complaint. It concluded that "the Constitution does not require that elections must be somehow arranged that black voters be assured that they can elect some candidate of their choice."[73]

Three of the five council seats – posts 2, 4, and 5 – were up for election in 1978, and the incumbents announced their candidacies. Blacks also qualified for posts 2 and 4, and a white man, Roscoe Cook, qualified for post 5. Shortly before the candidate deadline, another black, Cornelius Ponder, Jr., also qualified for post 5, leaving that seat contested by two whites and one black and raising the possibility that a black might once again be elected by receiving a plurality. Cook then withdrew, leaving each seat contested by a single white and imposing the functional equivalent of a majority-vote requirement. The white candidates won a sweep of seats, receiving almost identical percentages (72 to 74 percent) of the vote.[74]

---

[68] Frank R. Parker, "The Impact of *City of Mobile v. Bolden* and Strategies and Legal Arguments for Voting Rights Cases in Its Wake," in *The Right To Vote: A Rockefeller Foundation Report* (New York: Rockefeller Foundation, 1981), 111–12.

[69] *Cross v. Baxter*.

[70] *Cross v. Baxter*, 604 F. 2d 875, 878 n.1 (5th Cir. 1979).

[71] James P. Turner to Hoyt H. Whelchel, Jr., June 26, 1977.

[72] *Cross v. Baxter*, 604 F. 2d at 880 n.7, Pl. Ex. 4.

[73] *Cross v. Baxter*, Oct. 26, 1977, slip op. p. 18.

[74] Ibid., trial record, Vol. II, p. 296, Vol. III, p. 102; Pl. Ex. 4; *Moultrie Observer*, May 17, 1978.

The plaintiffs appealed the decision of the district court dismissing their complaint, and the court reversed. It held that there was "substantial evidence tending to show inequality of access," that plaintiffs "have demonstrated a history of pervasive discrimination and . . . have carried their burden of proving that past discrimination has present effects."[75] The case was sent back to the district court for another trial.

At the retrial, held on January 25, 1980, a major element of the city's case was that a black man, Wesley Ball, had been elected to the city council at the May 1979 election. Ball, who was retired, had formerly worked as a waiter at the Colquitt Hotel in Moultrie. He had a seventh-grade education, had never run for office, and had never been involved in any political campaign. His opponents were Frank Wilson, the black incumbent, and Roscoe Cook, the white candidate who had withdrawn from the 1978 election.[76]

Cook testified that whites had urged him to get out of the race so that a black would be sure to be elected and thus give the appearance of racial fairness to the at-large system and defeat the black plaintiffs' lawsuit. According to Cook, "most businessmen around . . . white businessmen" had supported Ball or Wilson because if they were defeated by a white, "the ward system would be more effective to come in" and the city might lose the lawsuit. "[T]hey wanted . . . a black post, and they didn't . . . want me on there for that reason . . . said, let them two have it out."[77]

Ball had been recruited to run by several prominent whites in Moultrie, including Mitchell Smith, the president of a local bank, Billy Fallin, the chair of the county commission, and Sherrod McCall, a member of the city council. Fallin had told him, "Wesley Ball run – I guarantee you one thing. [You]'ll get two votes – me and my wife. And I guarantee you another. [You]'ll get elected." Ball told others who urged him to run, "I really just don't know – I don't – I'm not a politician. I don't care nothing – anything about getting in politics."[78]

Ball shared Cook's view that he had been supported by whites as a way of defeating the voting rights lawsuit. "I believe that the whites really wanted to keep a black . . . on the Council because there was a court suit in progress. . . . I think that they wanted to make sure that . . . you couldn't say, 'Hey, you don't have any blacks there.' . . . [T]he whites want to keep the at-large system . . . [b]ut they want to make it look fair."[79]

After the election, which Ball won, someone put a sign on Cook's place of business: "Got Beat by a Black Man – Business for Sale – Leaving Town."[80]

---

75 *Cross v. Baxter*, 604 F. 2d at 881, 883.
76 McDonald, *Voting Rights in the South*, 92–3.
77 *Cross v. Baxter*, trial transcript, Vol. IV, p. 187 (testimony of Roscoe Cook).
78 Ibid., deposition of H. Wesley Ball, December 7, 1983, pp. 11–12.
79 Ibid., pp. 18–20.
80 McDonald, *Voting Rights in the South*, 93.

Ball predicted that "[o]nce I get out of office, unless we have a ward system, we won't have any blacks up there. The white majority will be able to name whoever comes up, unless they get someone like me, and I don't know if there's any old-timers like me left or not."[81]

Following the retrial, the district court again dismissed the complaint. The plaintiffs appealed, but this time the court of appeals affirmed. It held that the plaintiffs had failed to prove a requisite element of vote dilution – that the city council was "unresponsive" to the needs of blacks – and that "the evidence does not measure up to the *Mobile* standard for the maintenance of a voting dilution case."[82] The plaintiffs appealed once again, this time to the Supreme Court. But absent a significant change in the law, their prospects for a reversal and a system of elections that provided them an equal opportunity to elect candidates of their choice were distinctly slim.

[81] *Cross v. Baxter*, deposition of H. Wesley Ball, p. 37.
[82] *Cross v. Baxter*, 639 F. 2d 1383, 1384 (5th Cir. 1981) (and concurring opinion of Judge Henderson).

12

Redistricting in the 1980s

> Representative Joe Mack Wilson is a racist.
>
> Finding of Fact No. 17, U.S. District Court, 1982

I

When it extended Section 5 in 1975, Congress concluded that it was "imperative" that preclearance apply to the redistricting that would take place after the 1980 census. In view of the redistricting in Georgia, Congress's judgment was well founded and was fully vindicated.

The state's initial 1980 house and senate redistricting plans drew Section 5 objections.[1] The attorney general concluded that the state had unnecessarily fragmented concentrations of black population in several areas of the state – DeKalb, Richmond, and Dougherty Counties – which was retrogressive and could have "a significant detrimental impact on black voting strength."[2] The plan finally adopted in 1982 increased the number of majority-black house districts from twenty-four to thirty, and the number of majority-black senate districts from two to eight, setting the stage for increased black representation in both houses of the general assembly.[3]

A number of city- and county-level redistricting plans submitted after the 1980 census also drew Section 5 objections. The plan for the Dougherty County Commission was rejected because it reduced the black percentages in several districts while unnecessarily concentrating blacks in two others.[4]

---

[1] Department of Justice, Civil Rights Division, "Complete Listing of Objections Pursuant to Section 5 of the Voting Rights Act of 1965" (Sept. 30, 1988).

[2] William Bradford Reynolds to Michael Bowers, Feb. 11, 1982.

[3] Ga. Laws 1982, pp. 444, 452; Georgia Legislative Information Services, Georgia State Senate Districts as Reflected in SB 388, statistical sheet, Updated April 1984, and Georgia state house districts, Updated March 1986.

[4] William Bradford Reynolds to C. Nathan Davis, July 12, 1982.

The plan for the city of McDonough in Henry County was rejected for similar reasons. Although blacks were 37 percent of the city's population, the Department of Justice concluded that because of a combination of fragmenting and packing concentrations of black population, black voters "likely can elect a candidate of their choice to only one of six council seats."[5] Objections were entered for the same reasons to redistricting plans submitted by Bibb County (board of education), Sumter County (board of education), and the city of College Park.[6]

The plan for Thomas County was objected to after the attorney general indicated that it had been designed purposefully to discriminate against black voters. Blacks were 38 percent of the population of the county. County officials, however, instructed the demographer who drew the plan to limit the number of districts in which black voters could elect candidates of their choice to two – or only 25 percent of the total number of districts.[7] But the state saved its most blatant attempts to contain black voting strength for congressional redistricting.

II

When the state reapportioned its congressional districts after the 1980 census, it resorted to its old strategy of trying to minimize black voting strength in the Atlanta area. The 1980 figures showed that the state's ten congressional districts drawn in 1972, while severely malapportioned, were still majority-white with the exception of the fifth district. The fifth district contained a slight (50.33 percent) black population majority.

The new plan drawn in 1981 maintained white majorities in nine of the ten districts, and increased the black population in the fifth district to 57 percent. Although majority-black in both total and voting-age population, the district actually contained a 54 percent white majority among registered voters.[8]

As in the 1971 plan, some of the majority-white districts were far from compact or regular in shape. Ben Jessup, a white Democrat from Bleckley County, described the plan as "one of the most outlandish things I have seen since I've been in the legislature."[9] Press accounts criticized some of the districts as "based more on rhyme than on reason."[10] The eighth district, as one article pointed out, "extends from Greene and Taliaferro counties in upper middle Georgia all the way to the Okefenokee swamp on the Florida

[5] William Bradford Reynolds to S. T. Ellis, Nov. 22, 1982.

[6] William Bradford Reynolds to Arthur Griffith, Jr., Nov. 26, 1982; William Bradford Reynolds to Henry L. Crisp, Dec. 17, 1982; William Bradford Reynolds to George E. Glaze, Dec. 12, 1983.

[7] William Bradford Reynolds to R. Bruce Warner, Sept. 25, 1985.

[8] *Busbee v. Smith*, 549 F. Supp. 494, 499 (D. D. C. 1982).

[9] *Atlanta Constitution*, Sept. 18, 1981.

[10] *Gainsville Times*, Sept. 20, 1981.

line. This is Billy Lee Evans' district," the paper continued, "and how he can adequately represent such a diverse and spread-out district is beyond comprehension."[11]

Terrell Starr, a senator from south Fulton, described the district lines as "snaking across the map of Georgia." The plan "looks funny," he conceded, but he said it was "the best possible political solution."[12]

The state submitted its plan for preclearance and argued that the fifth district's configuration could not be discriminatory because it increased the black percentage over the 1972 plan. The attorney general did not agree and denied Section 5 approval.[13]

The state then filed a declaratory judgment action in the District Court for the District of Columbia arguing that under the retrogression standard of Section 5 it was entitled to have its congressional reapportionment plan precleared. The Supreme Court had previously held, in *Beer v. United States*,[14] that the purpose of Section 5 was to maintain the status quo in voting and that a plan that was either ameliorative or nonretrogressive could not violate the "effect" standard of the statute. The state, however, still had to prove that its plan was not the product of intentional discrimination against black voters.

Given Georgia's record of discrimination in voting, it would not have been surprising had the 1981 congressional redistricting process been influenced by race. What is surprising is how pervasive and overt that influence actually was.

Julian Bond, by then a state senator, introduced a bill at the beginning of the legislative session creating a fifth district that was 69 percent black. The chair of the senate reapportionment committee, Perry Hudson, immediately criticized the proposal, resurrecting the old and discredited arguments that had been used to oppose school and residential desegregation – that whites were opposed to it and would flee to the suburbs. Creating a majority-black district, Senator Hudson said, would cause "white flight" from Fulton County. It would "bring out resegregation in a fine county like Fulton and a fine city like Atlanta," and it would disrupt the "harmonious working relationship between the races."[15]

The Bond plan had the strong support of two members of the state senate – Thomas Allgood, the Democratic majority leader from Augusta, and Paul Coverdell, a Republican.[16] In response to the charge that a majority-black district would be a segregated, or ghetto, district, Allgood said: "If it is a ghetto, so be it. We did not create it. We merely recognize in this amendment

[11] Ibid.
[12] *Atlanta Constitution*, Sept. 17, 1981.
[13] *Busbee v. Smith*, 549 F. Supp. at 494, 510.
[14] 425 U.S. 130, 141 (1976).
[15] *Busbee v. Smith*, 549 F. Supp. at 507.
[16] Ibid., deposition of Thomas Allgood, pp. 15–16.

what exists there, and we give those people an opportunity, a mere opportunity. If they want to elect [a] black, let it be."[17] As a result of the support of senators such as Allgood and Coverdell, the final plan adopted by the senate contained a 69-percent-black fifth district.

The leadership of the house rejected the Bond plan for the fifth district. Joe Mack Wilson, a Democrat from Marietta, was chair of the house reapportionment committee and the person who, by all accounts, dominated the redistricting process in the lower chamber. And, as he was want to say, he "hated" blacks and Republicans.

Another member of the reapportionment committee was Dorothy Felton, a proper, civic-minded white Republican from the north Atlanta suburb of Sandy Springs. During a deposition, she recalled her dismay over her first meeting with committee chair Joe Mack Wilson.

"He said if there was anything he hated worse than blacks and he didn't use the word blacks, he said it was Republicans."

"What was the word he used?" asked one of the lawyers representing a group of blacks who had intervened in the case to oppose preclearance of the state's plan. Felton squirmed, visibly uncomfortable, and then said firmly, "I'd rather not say."

"I think you have to answer the question," the lawyer said.

"Do I have to?" she replied.

"Yes, I think we're entitled to an answer."

"Very well. The word he used was – 'Niggers.'"[18]

The answer so startled the state's attorney, a lawyer from Washington who had been specially hired to prosecute the preclearance action in the District of Columbia, that he immediately asked the court reporter to read it back. The court reporter carefully picked up the tape of her transcription and in a flat, emotionless monotone read:

Question: What was the word he used?

Answer: Niggers.[19]

At that moment, in the small conference room in the Richard B. Russell Building in downtown Atlanta where the deposition was being taken, the state effectively lost its Section 5 preclearance case.

Wilson's use of the "n-word" in his conversation with Felton was not a lapse or an aberration. "Nigger" was an active, working part of his vocabulary. Blacks were simply "niggers," and he regularly denigrated legislation that benefitted blacks as "nigger legislation." During the redistricting fight, he told his colleagues on numerous occasions: "I don't want to draw nigger districts."[20] Bettye Lowe, a house member, recalls that Wilson told her in

---

[17] Ibid., 549 F. Supp. at 507.
[18] Ibid., deposition of Dorothy Felton, p. 14, and author's deposition notes.
[19] Ibid.
[20] Ibid., 549 F. Supp. at 501.

no uncertain terms, "I'm not going to draw a honky Republican district and I'm not going to draw a nigger district if I can help it."[21]

Wilson's language may have been more extreme than most, but his racial views were not. "To call someone a racist in Georgia is not necessarily flaming that person," said Felton. "You might call someone a racist, but that isn't the height of an insult, I'm sorry to say, but that's true."[22]

The speaker of the house, Tom Murphy, was also opposed to the Bond plan. "I was concerned," he said later, "that...we were gerrymandering a district to create a black district where a black would certainly be elected."[23] According to the District of Columbia court, Murphy "refused to appoint black persons to the conference committee [to resolve the dispute between the house and senate] solely because they might support a plan which would allow black voters, in one district, an opportunity to elect a candidate of their choice."[24]

While members of the legislature expressed their concern over creating a majority-black district, no one expressed similar concerns over creating majority-white districts. Zell Miller, the lieutenant governor and president of the senate, was an outspoken advocate for creating a district composed of the white communities in the mountain counties in north Georgia. "[I]t's a group of people that have the same culture, the same language, the same mores, the same religion for 200 years," he said. "They've been isolated from the rest of the country. They think very much alike. They think differently from other people. They talk differently from other people. They are more deprived economically than any minority groups that you can name."[25] All of that may have been true, and it argued for including the mountain communities in one district, the ninth district, even if it turned out to be 95 percent white.[26] But no one explained why blacks in the metropolitan Atlanta area were any less of a community with a common culture, language, mores, religion, and history. Nor did they explain why a 95-percent-white district was apparently integrated while a 68-percent-black district was regarded as being "segregated."

The fact that the creation of a majority-black fifth district was being promoted by Julian Bond, the house's nemesis from the 1960s, also contributed to its defeat in the lower chamber. According to Rep. Vincent Wall, "[i]t was viewed[ed] primarily as an effort to put Julian Bond in the U.S. Congress and most of those members of the House were not going to have any part of doing that."[27]

---

[21] Ibid., deposition of Bettye Lowe, p. 36.
[22] Ibid., deposition of Dorothy Felton, p. 24.
[23] Ibid., 549 F.Supp. at 520.
[24] Ibid., at 510, 520.
[25] Ibid., at 499; deposition of Zell Miller, p. 74.
[26] Ibid., 549 F. Supp. at 498–99.
[27] Ibid., deposition of Vincent Wall, p. 33.

After the defeat of the Bond plan in the house, the fragile coalition supporting the plan in the senate broke down. Several senators approached Allgood and said, "I don't want to have to go home and explain why I was the leader in getting a black elected to the United States Congress." Allgood acknowledged that it would put a senator in a "controversial position in many areas of [Georgia]" to be perceived as having supported a black congressional district. He finally told his colleagues to vote "the way they wanted to, without any obligations to me or to my position," and "I knew at that point the House plan would pass."[28]

Based upon the racial statements of members of the legislature, as well as the absence of a legitimate nonracial reason for adoption of the plan, the conscious minimizing of black voting strength, and historical discrimination, the District of Columbia court concluded that the state's submission had a discriminatory purpose and violated Section 5. The court also held that the legislature had applied different standards depending on whether a community was black or white. Noting the inconsistent treatment of the mountain counties and metropolitan Atlanta, the court found that "the divergent utilization of the 'community of interest' standard is indicative of racially discriminatory intent."[29]

As for Joe Mack Wilson, the court made an express finding that "Representative Joe Mack Wilson is a racist."[30] The Supreme Court affirmed the decision on appeal.[31]

A chorus of protests immediately went up from various state officials and congressional candidates.

The decision was "ridiculous," said Congressman Charles Hatcher of the second district.

"A disgrace," said Richard Castellucis, a candidate for the seventh district seat.

"Pathetic," said Jim Wood, a candidate from the sixth district.

"A flagrant abuse of the Voting Rights Act," added seventh district candidate David Sellers.[32]

Wood even called for the impeachment of Aubrey Robinson, one of two black judges on the three-judge panel that had decided the case. Robinson showed "an obvious prejudice against the state of Georgia," he charged.[33]

Joe Mack Wilson, who had been flogged by the court for his racism, took the greatest umbrage. At a meeting of the all-white Rotary Club of Marietta, he said he was just the "fall guy" and complained bitterly that "in modern

[28] Ibid., deposition of Thomas Allgood, pp. 42–5.
[29] Ibid., 549 F. Supp. at 517.
[30] Ibid., at 500.
[31] *Busbee v. Smith*, 549 U.S. 1166 (1983).
[32] *Atlanta Constitution*, Aug. 3, 1982.
[33] Ibid.

times, if you don't condescend and give in to everything black people want, you're tagged a racist."[34]

Forced yet again by the Voting Rights Act to construct a racially fair plan, the general assembly in a special session enacted an apportionment for the fifth district with a black population exceeding 65 percent. The plan was approved by the court.

Wyche Fowler, given his record of service and the advantages of incumbency, was reelected from the fifth district in 1982 and again in 1984. In 1986, however, he ran for the U.S. Senate, and both Julian Bond and John Lewis entered the contest for the vacant congressional seat. Although they had been SNCC colleagues and extremely close friends during the heyday of the civil rights movement, their friendship did not survive the bitter rough-and-tumble of the congressional campaign. "We knew we were not on the same team anymore," explains Lewis. "Our friendship, as it had been, was over."[35]

Bond was the heavy favorite and won the primary with 47 percent of the vote. Lewis came in second in the field of twelve candidates, but in the ensuing runoff squeaked by with 52 percent of the vote. The margin of victory was supplied by white voters, who voted overwhelmingly for Lewis. Or perhaps some of them simply voted against Bond.[36]

[34] Ibid.
[35] John Lewis, *Walking with the Wind: A Memoir of the Movement* (New York: Simon and Schuster, 1998), 438.
[36] Ibid., p. 453.

13

1982: Voting Rights in the Balance

> The Voting Rights Act was passed to appease the surging mob in the street.
> There is no longer any justification for it at all.
>
> Freeman Leverett, former assistant attorney general of Georgia

Shortly after the decision in *City of Mobile v. Bolden*[1] imposing a discriminatory intent standard in voting cases, a small group of voting rights lawyers, civil rights activists, and congressional staffers met with Congressman Don Edwards of California at the Rayburn Office Building in Washington. Their purpose was to assess the damage done by the Supreme Court's recent opinion and discuss legislation to extend the preclearance provisions of Section 5 and amend Section 2 by restoring an effects, or discriminatory results, test for vote dilution cases. One of those at the meeting was Jim Blacksher, a respected voting rights lawyer from Birmingham, Alabama, who had argued the *Bolden* case for the minority plaintiffs in the Supreme Court. Since he had been closest to the fray, everyone turned instinctively to Blacksher and waited for what he might have to say. "Sorry about that," he said with a rueful grin.

Edwards was a seasoned legislator and a strong supporter of the earlier extensions of the Voting Rights Act. But he warned that many of his congressional colleagues felt that the South had been in the "penalty box" long enough and that Section 5 should be allowed to expire. As for amending Section 2, Congress had just defeated an attempt to include a results standard for violations of the Fair Housing Act. "Frankly," Edwards said, "the prospects for getting anything through this Congress don't look very good."

The case for extension of the Voting Rights Act, particularly in Georgia, was as strong as ever. Fifteen years after passage of the act, and despite

---

[1] 446 U.S. 55 (1980).

the significant gains in black registration,[2] there were still few black officeholders. And the overwhelming majority of those were elected from majority-black jurisdictions. In 1980, only twenty (3 percent) of the members of county governing bodies were black. Of this number, nineteen were elected from two majority-black counties or single-member districts. There were also two black coroners, one black tax commissioner, and one black clerk of court. All four were elected from two majority-black counties, Hancock and Calhoun. There were no blacks elected to statewide office.[3]

Among the principal reasons for the depressed level of minority officeholding were racial bloc voting, the prevalence of at-large elections, and the adoption of new voting laws and practices that made it more difficult for blacks to win. Compliance with Section 5 had gradually improved, but as of 1980 the state had still not submitted for Section 5 review some 361 acts of the general assembly, and an unknown number of local changes, affecting voting.[4] As for the submissions that it *did* make, the state had drawn the highest number of objections of any covered jurisdiction – 226 as of February 1981.[5]

Congress considered legislation to extend and amend the Voting Rights Act in 1981 and 1982. One of those who testified before the Senate was Freeman Leverett, a former assistant attorney general of Georgia. He proudly recalled that he had argued on behalf of Georgia in *South Carolina v. Katzenbach* that the Voting Rights Act was unconstitutional and renewed his attack on the act. Disparaging the civil rights movement, he said that the Voting Rights Act had been passed in 1965 "to appease the surging mob in the street," and that Section 5 should be repealed because "there is no longer any justification for it at all.[6]

The city attorney for Rome, Robert Brinson, expressed his "distaste" for Section 5 and argued that the statute should be allowed to expire. But

---

[2] According to the secretary of state, by 1980 the number of black registered voters in Georgia had increased to 467, 783, or 70 percent of the voting-age population. Laughlin McDonald, Michael B. Binford, and Ken Johnson, "Georgia" in Chandler Davidson and Bernard Grofman, eds., *Quiet Revolution in the South: The Impact of the Voting Rights Act 1965–1990* (Princeton, N.J.: Princeton University Press, 1994), 75.

[3] *National Roster of Black Elected Officials* (Washington: Joint Center for Political Studies, 1980), 86–7.

[4] *Review of State Acts from 1965–1980 Affecting Voting and Not Submitted to US Department of Justice in Five Southern States under the Voting Rights Act* (Atlanta: Southern Regional Council, 1980).

[5] U.S. Department of Justice, "Number of changes to which Objections Have Been Interposed By State and Year, 1965 – February 28, 1981."

[6] Voting Rights Act, Hearings before the Subcommittee on the Constitution of the Committee on the Judiciary, United States Senate, Ninety-seventh Congress, Second Session, on S. 53, S. 1761, S. 1975, S. 1992, and H.R. 3112, Bills to Amend the Voting Rights Act of 1965, January 27, 28, February 1, 2, 4, 11, 12, 25, and March 1, 1982, pp. 942, 950.

"[i]f §5 is to be extended," he continued, "it should apply nationally."[7] The "nationwide" argument had surface appeal, but it overlooked the fact that the act's "pocket trigger" already allowed Section 5 to be applied to any noncovered jurisdiction in which a court found a constitutional violation of voting rights.[8] Moreover, applying preclearance to every jurisdiction in the country, with no showing of the need to do so, would raise questions about the act's constitutionality. It would also flood the Department of Justice with submissions, render Section 5 essentially unmanageable, and divert the attention of the attorney general away from jurisdictions with proven histories of discrimination. Drew Days, the assistant attorney general for civil rights, said that "anybody proposing nationwide preclearance is either naive or cynical."[9]

Griffin Bell, a native of Americus who served as U.S. attorney general during the Carter administration, was also opposed to extending Section 5. According to one newspaper account, Bell groused that "[i]t's gotten down to a question of whether you can govern yourself. . . . I think you still need to protect the right to vote, but the preclearance argument is poppycock."[10] In dismissing Section 5 as "poppycock," or nonsense, General Bell displayed a remarkable indifference to the kind of changes the state had been enacting. They were an inventory of potentially discriminatory election practices, and included at-large elections; numbered posts, staggered terms, and majority-vote requirements; reducing the number of illiterate voters who could be assisted by a single elector from ten to five; vague and subjective qualifications for poll officials; abolition of polling places; increases in candidate filing fees; postponing elections; annexations; multimember districts; and dual registration for city and county elections.[11]

A number of witnesses testified about the efforts of Georgia and other states to circumvent the act and warned of the consequences of weakening federal oversight of southern election procedures.[12] One of the witnesses was

---

[7] Extension of the Voting Rights Act, Hearings before the Subcommittee on Civil and Constitutional Rights of the Committee on the Judiciary, House of Representatives, Ninety-seventh Congress, First Session, May 6, 7, 13, 19, 20, 27, 28, June 3, 5, 10, 12, 16, 17, 18, 23, 24, 25, and July 13, 1981, p. 208.

[8] 42 U.S.C. §1973a(c).

[9] Extension of the Voting Rights Act, Hearings before the Subcommittee on Civil and Constitutional Rights, p. 2122.

[10] *New York Times*, September 27, 1981.

[11] U.S. Department of Justice, "Number of Changes to which Objections Have Been Interposed."

[12] The witnesses from Georgia who testified in support of the amendments included Rev. Ralph Abernathy, Julian Bond, Brain Sherman, J. F. Smith, Herman Lodge, Laughlin McDonald, Edward Brown, Steve Suitts, Raymond H. Brown, Coretta Scott King, Geraldine Thompson, David Walbert, and Rev. Joseph Lowery. Extension of the Voting Rights Act, Hearings before the Subcommittee on Civil and Constitutional Rights, pp. 86, 231, 573, 590, 596, 1800, 1938, 2029, 2068.

C. Vann Woodward, the dean of southern historians. He said that in view of the aggravated history of black disfranchisement in the South,

it [is] reasonable . . . to warn that a weakening of that act, especially the preclearance clause, will open the door to a rush of measures to abridge, diminish, and dilute if not emasculate the power of the black vote in southern states. Previous testimony before your committee has shown how persistent and effective such efforts have been even with the preclearance law in effect. Remove that law and the permissiveness will likely become irresistible – in spite of promises to the contrary.[13]

Congress heeded Woodward's warning, and that of other witnesses supporting the 1982 amendments, and extended Section 5 for an additional twenty-five years, the longest extension in the act's history. In doing so, it took special note of the efforts in Georgia to circumvent minority voting rights, including non-compliance with Section 5 and the switch by counties from district to at-large elections. The Senate report concluded:

All too often, the background of rejected submissions – the failure to choose un-objectionable alternatives, the absence of an innocent explanation for the proposed change, the departure from past practice as minority voting strength reaches new levels, and, in some instances, direct indications of racial considerations – serves to underline the continuing need for Section 5.[14]

Congress also amended Section 2 to prohibit voting practices, regardless of their purpose, that "result" in discrimination.[15] A voting practice violates the results standard if it causes minority voters to have "less opportunity than other members of the electorate to participate in the political process and to elect representatives of their choice."[16] This language was taken verbatim from the Supreme Court's decision in *White v. Regester* invalidating legislative districts in Texas because they diluted black and Mexican American voting strength.[17] Although Congress has no power to overrule the Supreme Court's interpretation of the Constitution, it does have the authority to provide, as it did in the 1982 amendments, that proof of racial purpose is not a requirement for a violation of the statute.[18]

The legislative history provides that "a variety of factors, depending upon the kind of rule, practice, or procedure called into question" are relevant in determining a violation of Section 2.[19] Typical factors identified in the Senate report include the extent of any history of discrimination in the jurisdiction

---

[13] Ibid., p. 2001.
[14] S. Rep. No. 97-417, 97th Cong., 2d Sess. 10, 13 (1982), reprinted in 1982 U.S. Code Cong. & Adm. News 187, 190.
[15] 42 U.S.C. §1973.
[16] 42 U.S.C. §1973(b).
[17] 412 U.S. 755, 766 (1973).
[18] *Thornburg v. Gingles*, 478 U.S. 30, 43–4 and n.8 (1986).
[19] 1982 U.S. Code Cong. & Adm. News 206–7.

that touches the right of the members of a minority group to participate in the democratic process; the extent to which voting is racially polarized; the extent to which the jurisdiction uses devices that may enhance the opportunity for discrimination, such as majority-vote requirements and anti–single shot provisions; whether the members of the minority group bear the effects of discrimination in such areas as education, employment, and health that hinder their ability to participate effectively in the political process; whether political campaigns have been characterized by overt or subtle racial appeals; and the extent to which members of the minority group have been elected to public office in the jurisdiction.

Congress did not specify the remedies for a violation of Section 2. Instead, it provided that a court should grant relief depending on the nature of the violation that completely remedies the vote dilution and fully provides minorities an equal chance to elect candidates of their choice.[20] In the absence of special circumstances, courts are required to use single-member districts in court-ordered plans.[21] But jurisdictions are free to experiment and can use alternative methods of election, such as limited, cumulative, and preference voting.[22] Section 2 is permanent, applies nationwide, applies to old as well as new voting practices, and is enforced in traditional lawsuits filed in local jurisdictions.

Congress rejected the intent test when it amended Section 2 for a number of reasons, the most important of which was that whether or not public officials acted out of bias or intended to discriminate against a minority group was the "wrong question." The relevant inquiry, according to Congress, was whether minorities "have equal access to the process of electing their representatives." The intent requirement was also "unnecessarily divisive" because it required plaintiffs to allege and prove that local officials, or indeed all the members of a community, were racists. Finally, the intent requirement imposed an "inordinately difficult" burden of proof on minority plaintiffs.[23]

The official, contemporaneous record of the adoption of a voting practice is always the best evidence of legislative intent. However, in many cases the contemporaneous record is sparse, consisting of little more than an entry in the minutes of a meeting of a commission or school board that a motion was made and carried to adopt a particular practice, or brief notations in the journals of the house and senate marking passage of a bill. In some cases, where a law was enacted in the distant past, there may be no existing contemporaneous record at all, and the decision makers cannot be subpoenaed from the grave to testify about their motives. Requiring plaintiffs to prove

---

[20] Ibid., p. 208.
[21] *Chapman v. Meier*, 420 U.S. 1, 26–7 (1975).
[22] The literature on alternative voting systems is fairly extensive. See, e.g., David M. Farrell, *Comparing Electoral Systems* (New York: Prentice Hall, 1997).
[23] 1982 U.S. Code Cong. & Adm. News 214.

racial purpose would therefore, as a practical matter, insulate many voting practices, even those that had a demonstrably discriminatory impact, from meaningful judicial review.

As applied to more recent enactments, Congress pointed out a "fundamental defect" in the intent standard, "namely, the defendant's ability to offer a non-racial rationalization for a law which in fact purposely discriminates."[24] After-the-fact reconstructions of legislative purpose are invariably self-serving and are notoriously unreliable. Legislators, being human, can be expected to try to avoid embarrassment and blame by reinterpreting their past actions in an effort to make them appear more acceptable in a changed political or social climate. They may mask one bad motive with another by claiming that the true object of their discrimination was not a racial minority but some other group, such as poor, illiterate whites.[25] Or they may simply lie. As Paul Brest has noted, "the ease with which one can lie successfully" about prior motives casts serious doubt on the utility and fairness of after-the-fact testimony about legislative purpose.[26]

Some lawmakers may have had several reasons for acting and, in retrospect, may give one reason more or less weight than it deserves. Others, with the passage of time, may simply forget why they acted as they did. Still others may become conveniently amnesic about matters of race once litigation is filed. A startling example of that occurred in Harris County after a voting rights lawsuit was filed against the board of commissioners in 1975.

George Teel had lived in Harris County for most of his life and had served on the board of commissioners for thirty-four years. Despite the general assembly's assurances in 1960 that "there has been ingrained forever in the hearts and minds of all Georgians the custom of segregation,"[27] after Teel became a defendant in the voting rights case he could scarcely remember *anything* about segregation. As the following exchange between Teel and the plaintiffs' lawyer shows, when it came to matters of race, far from being ingrained, Teel's mind was actually a blank.

Q   Are you aware of the fact that schools were segregated on the basis of race at one time in this county?
A   I don't remember.
Q   You have no knowledge?
A   I can't recall.
Q   Are you aware of the fact that penal facilities were racially segregated at one time in this county?

[24] Ibid., p. 215.
[25] See, e.g., *Hunter v. Underwood*, 471 U.S. 222, 231–32 (1985).
[26] Paul Brest, "Palmer v. Thompson: An Approach to the Problem of Unconstitutional Legislative Motive," 1971 Sup. Ct. Rev. 95, 124.
[27] Ga. Laws 1960, p. 1190.

A I can't recall.

Q You have no knowledge of that?

A (Witness indicates negative.)

Q Do you know whether or not public accommodations in this county were ever segregated on the basis of race?

A I have no knowledge.

Q Have you run for office or been a member of the Democratic Party?

A Yeah, always, I've been a Democrat.

Q And you are aware of the fact, are you not, that prior to 1945 blacks were not allowed to participate in Democratic Party Primaries?

A I can't recall that.

Q You have no knowledge of that?

A No.[28]

After the deposition was finished, Teel's lawyer conferred with his client in private and, in an attempt to rehabilitate him, requested that the deposition be reopened. Back on the record, the lawyer got Teel to say that schools in the county had indeed been segregated at one time, but Teel still professed to have "no recollection as to when it was."[29]

A judicial decision whether a voting practice was adopted with a discriminatory purpose that depended upon after-the-fact testimony such as Teel's could hardly be reliable. Taking into account legislative amnesia and denial, as well as the other difficulties of divining motive, Judge John Minor Wisdom of the Fifth Circuit Court of Appeals sagely observed in an early voting case that to require proof of an unconstitutional legislative purpose was "to burden the plaintiffs with the necessity of finding the authoritative meaning of an oracle that is Delphic only to the court."[30]

One of the cases relied upon by Congress in rejecting the intent test was *Cross v. Baxter*, the challenge to at-large elections in Moultrie. According to the Senate report, the plaintiffs' case "was rejected, even though the evidence showed pervasive discrimination in the political process."[31] Following the 1982 amendment of Section 2, the Supreme Court vacated the decision and sent the case back to the district court for yet another trial under the new "results" standard.[32] This time the city of Moultrie capitulated and agreed to the adoption of district elections. But the price it exacted from the plaintiffs was a plan that packed nearly every black (91 percent) in the city into a two-member district. Rather than prolonging the litigation before J. Robert Elliott of Columbus, a district court judge who had

---

[28] *Brown v. Reames*, Civ. No. 75-80-COL (M. D. Ga.), deposition of George Teel, pp. 9–10, 22.

[29] Ibid., p. 36.

[30] *Nevett v. Sides*, 571 F. 2d 209, 238 (5th Cir. 1978).

[31] 1982 U.S. Code Cong. & Adm. News 39.

[32] *Cross v. Baxter*, 460 U.S. 1065 (1983).

dismissed their complaint on two prior occasions, plaintiffs agreed to the settlement.[33]

Two days after the amendment of Section 2, the Supreme Court affirmed the decision in *Rogers v. Lodge*[34] from Burke County, Georgia, and essentially reversed *City of Mobile*. While the Court continued to require proof of racial purpose for a constitutional violation, it said that such purpose could be inferred from circumstantial evidence and the discriminatory effect of a challenged voting practice.

The Supreme Court later simplified the test for minority vote dilution in *Thornburg v. Gingles* (1986).[35] It identified three factors as most probative of a Section 2 violation: whether the minority was geographically compact, or could constitute a majority in a single-member district; whether the minority was politically cohesive, or tended to vote as a bloc; and whether the majority voted as a bloc usually to defeat the candidates preferred by the minority. Proof of the other "totality of circumstances" factors was supportive of, but not essential to, a vote dilution claim. In a later case, *Johnson v. De Grandy*,[36] the Court stressed that the three *Gingles* factors were "necessary preconditions" and that the ultimate determination of vote dilution must be based on an analysis of "the totality of circumstances."

Thornburg v. Gingles brought both simplicity and predictability to challenges to at-large elections. By focusing primarily on demographics to determine geographic compactness, and on election returns to determine political cohesion and the significance of racial bloc voting, the Court placed vote dilution claims on an evidentiary footing similar to that of one person, one vote. It also blunted the criticism that the totality of circumstances analysis was an amorphous concept that was difficult to understand or apply. The amendment of Section 2 and the decisions in *Rogers v. Lodge* and *Thornburg v. Gingles* represented strong congressional and judicial commitments to equal voting rights, and they also accelerated the pace of litigation and the adoption of district elections in Georgia.

---

[33] *Cross v. Baxter*, Civ. No. 76-20 (M. D. Ga. July 24, 1984).
[34] 458 U.S. 613 (1982).
[35] 478 U.S. 30 (1986).
[36] 512 U.S. 997, 1011 (1994).

14

Continued Enforcement of the Voting Rights Act

> I wouldn't run if I were black in Bleckley County. You're going to put your hard
> earned time and shoe leather campaigning throughout this county... under
> these circumstances?
>
> U.S. District Judge Wilbur Owens

I

Following the 1982 amendments to the Voting Rights Act, minority plaintiffs sued twenty six additional counties and twenty six additional cities over their use of at-large elections. The counties were Baldwin in 1982;[1] Evans, Jefferson, Lowndes, and Tift in 1983;[2] Butts, Camden, Cook, Crawford, Dodge, Effingham, Macon, Screven, Spalding, Tattnall, and Taylor in 1984;[3] Charlton, Greene, Marion, Monroe, and Treutlen in 1985;[4]

---

[1] *Boddy v. Hall*, Civ. No. 82-406 (M. D. Ga.).

[2] *Concerned Citizens for Better Government for Evans County v. Deloach*, Civ. No. 483-343 (S. D. Ga.); *Tomlin v. Jefferson County Board of Commissioners*, Civ. No. 683-23 (S. D. Ga.); *United States v. Lowndes County*, Civ. No. 83-106 (M. D. Ga.); *Mims v. Tift County*, Civ. No. 83-9 (M. D. Ga.).

[3] *Brown v. Bailey*, Civ. No. 84-223 (M. D. Ga.); *Baker v. Gay*, Civ. No. 284-37 (S. D. Ga.); *Cook County VEP v. Walker*, Civ. No. 84-044 (M. D. Ga.); *Raines v. Hutto*, Civ. No. 84-321 (M. D. Ga.); *Dodge County VEP v. Tripp*, Civ. No. 384-051 (S. D. Ga.); *LOVE v. Conaway*, Civ. No. 484-39 (S. D. Ga.); *Macon County VEP v. Bentley*, Civ. No. 84-126 (M. D. Ga.); *Culver v. Krulic*, Civ. No. 484-139 (S. D. Ga.); *Reid v. Martin*, Civ. No. 84-60 (N. D. Ga.); *Carter v. Tootle*, Civ. No. 484-219 (S. D. Ga.); *Carter v. Jarrell*, Civ. No. 84-87 (M. D. Ga.).

[4] *Smith v. Carter*, Civ. No. 585-088 (S. D. Ga.); *Bacon v. Higdon*, Civ. No. 85-40 (M. D. Ga.); *Storey v. Marion County*, Civ. No. 85-175 (M. D. Ga.); *Simmons v. Monroe County Commission*, Civ. No. 85-125 (M. D. Ga.); *Smith v. Gillis*, Civ. No. 385-42 (S. D. Ga.). The case against Marion County was stayed and then dismissed pending action by the legislature. After the legislature failed to act, the case was refiled as *McBride v. Marion County Commission*, Civ. No. 99-CV-134 (M. D. Ga.), and settled by consent order on June 13, 2000.

Lamar in 1986;[5] Long and Wilcox in 1987;[6] and Hart in 1988.[7] The cities were Claxton, Decatur, Hagan, Milledgeville, Valdosta, and Wrightsville in 1983;[8] Camilla, Carrollton, Donalsonville, Griffin, Jackson, Newnan, Pelham, Rochelle, and Waycross in 1984;[9] Cochran and Soperton in 1985;[10] Butler, Cordele, Jesup, and Lyons in 1986;[11] and Augusta, Eastman, Ludowici, Lumber City, and Warrenton in 1987.[12] In all but one of the jurisdictions, new district systems were ordered into effect by the court or were adopted by the legislature pursuant to settlement agreements. The exception was Dodge County, where the evidence of racial bloc voting was inconclusive. The case against Dodge was voluntarily dismissed without prejudice by the plaintiffs.[13]

Successful actions to enjoin at-large elections, many of which had been adopted without preclearance, were also brought against a number of additional county school boards: Baldwin in 1982;[14] Wayne, Camden, Cook, Macon, Marion, Meriwether, Toombs, Screven, and Taylor in 1984;[15] and Treutlen, Charlton, and Greene in 1985.[16] Newton County,

[5] *Strickland v. Lamar County*, Civ. No. 86-167 (N. D. Ga.).

[6] *Glover v. Long County*, Georgia, Civ. No. 287-20 (S. D. Ga.); *Teague v. Wilcox County*, Georgia, Civ. No. 87-80 (M. D. Ga.).

[7] *Mayfield v. Crittendon*, Civ. No. 88-56 (M. D. Ga.).

[8] *Concerned Citizens for Better Government for Evans County v. Deloach*; *Thrower v. City of Decatur, Georgia*, Civ. No. 83-1855 (N. D. Ga.); *NAACP v. City of Milledgeville*, Civ. No. 83-145-01 (M. D. Ga.); *United States v. Lowndes County*, Civ. No. 83-106 (M. D. Ga.); *Wilson v. Powell*, Civ. No. 383-14 (S. D. Ga).

[9] *Brown v. City of Camilla*, Civ. No. 84-248 (M. D. Ga.); *Carrollton Branch NAACP v. Stallings*, Civ. No. 84-122-6 (N. D. Ga.); *Moore v. Shingler*, Civ. No. 84-71 (M. D. Ga.); *Reid v. Martin*; *Brown v. Bailey*; *Rush v. Norman*, Civ. No. 84-150 (N. D. Ga.); *McCoy v. Adams*, Civ. No. 84-240 (M. D. Ga.); *Dantley v. Sutton*, Civ. No. 84-165 (M. D. Ga.); *Ware County VEP v. Parks*, Civ. No. 584-070 (S. D. Ga.).

[10] *Hall v. Holder*, Civ. No. 85-242 (M. D. Ga.); *Smith v. Gillis*.

[11] *Chatman v. Spillers*, Civ. No. 86-91 (M. D. Ga.); *Dent v. Culpepper*, Civ. No. 86-173 (M. D. Ga.); *Freeze v. Jesup*, Civ. No. 286-128 (S. D. Ga.); *Maxwell v. Moore*, Civ. No. 686-024 (S. D. Ga.).

[12] *United States v. City of Augusta*, Civ. No. 187-004 (S. D. Ga.); *Woodard v. Mayor and City Council of the City of Lumber City, Georgia*, Civ. No. 387-027 (S. D. Ga.); *Brown v. McGriff*, Civ. No. 387-019 (S. D. Ga.); *Wallace v. City of Ludowici*, Civ. No. 287-147 (S. D. Ga.); *Warren County Branch NAACP v. Haywood*, Civ. No. 187-167 (S. D. Ga.).

[13] *Dodge County VEP v. Tripp* (Sept. 4, 1987).

[14] *Boddy v. Hall* (May 17, 1984).

[15] *Keebler v. Burch*, Civ. No. 284-26 (S. D. Ga. May 22, 1984); *Baker v. Gay* (Oct. 7, 1985); *Cook County VEP v. Walker* (July 11, 1985); *Macon County VEP v. Bentley* (April 14, 1988); *Marion County VEP v. Hicks*, Civ. No. 84-117-N (N. D. Ga. Sept. 28, 1984); *Meriwether County Voter Education Project v. Hicks*, Civ. No. 84-117-N (N. D. Ga. Sept. 28, 1984); *Toombs County Branch of the NAACP v. Culpepper*, Civ. No. 684-21 (S. D. Ga. Dec. 12, 1986); *Culver v. Krulic* (Nov. 6, 1984); *Carter v. Taylor County Board of Education*, Civ. No. 84-81-COL (M. D. Ga. Feb. 28 1986).

[16] *Smith v. Gillis* (Apr. 14, 1986); *Smith v. Carter* (Mar. 31, 1986); *Bacon v. Higdon* (Jan. 10, 1986).

rather than face litigation, adopted the existing county commission lines for school board elections.[17]

Aside from the strengthened provisions of the Voting Rights Act, a major factor contributing to the willingness of jurisdictions to settle the lawsuits brought against them was the fact that if they lost in court they would have to pay the costs and attorneys' fees of the prevailing plaintiffs. Burke County not only had to pay its own lawyers, but also had to pay the plaintiffs' attorneys more than a quarter-million dollars.[18] The chances and costs of losing were strong incentives for jurisdictions to abandon their at-large systems. As R. C. Barnes, Jr., the administrator of Decatur County, put it, "there's really no sense in fighting something there's no way you can win. It's an injustice to the taxpayers."[19] According to a survey of probate judges conducted by the *Atlanta Constitution*, "the threat of costly lawsuits is prompting more and more local officials to adopt district elections."[20]

Minority plaintiffs also challenged three of Georgia's unique, and discriminatory, political institutions under the provisions of the Voting Rights Act: the sole commissioner form of county government, the grand jury method of appointing members of local school boards, and a self-perpetuating city board of education.

II

Georgia is the only state in the union that authorizes counties to use a sole commissioner form of government.[21] Under the sole commissioner system, all the legislative and executive powers of county government – including levying taxes, hiring and firing county employees, filling vacancies in office, supervising the county police, auditing county accounts, building roads and bridges, and controlling county property – are combined in a single officer elected at-large in a countywide election.[22] The sole commissioner system is the ultimate form of majority-take-all election. Whatever the theoretical good-government rationales for the system – that it is cost-effective, efficient, and so on – it has operated, like so many institutions in Georgia, to exclude blacks from effective participation in the political process. There is no record of any black ever being elected to office under a sole commissioner scheme.

---

[17] Laughlin McDonald, *Voting Rights in the South: Ten Years of Litigation Challenging Continuing Discrimination against Minorities* (New York: American Civil Liberties Union, 1982), 42: Ga. Laws, p. 3505.

[18] *Lodge v. Rogers*, Civ. No. 176-55 (S. D. Ga. March 23, 1983).

[19] *Florida Times-Union*, August 12, 1984.

[20] *Atlanta Constitution*, August 26, 1984.

[21] 1987 Census of Governments, Vol. 1, No. 2: *Government Organization: Popularly Elected Officials* [GC87(1)-2] (1990).

[22] Ga. Code Ann. §36-5-22.1.

Carroll County, which used the sole commissioner system, was sued under Section 2 in 1984. The district court dismissed the complaint, but the court of appeals reversed. It found that numerous factors showing vote dilution had been established, and that there was evidence tending to show that the sole commissioner system had been enacted with a discriminatory purpose.

The county had adopted the sole commissioner system in 1951.[23] Prior to that time it had had a three-member commission elected at-large. One of the sponsors of the sole commissioner bill was Rep. Willis Smith of Carroll County. He had first introduced a sole commissioner bill in the general assembly in 1947, and he had also been a sponsor in that same year of a bill designed to maintain the white primary by allowing the Democratic Party to conduct elections entirely without state supervision. According to Willis, "Georgia is in trouble with the Negroes unless this bill is passed. This is white man's country and we must keep it that way."[24] The court of appeals concluded that the statement in 1947 "was evidence of an intent to discriminate against black voters in any voting legislation before the General Assembly during that session, and that a finder of fact might well infer that such intent continued until 1951 when the bill was re-introduced under the same sponsorship."[25] After the case was sent back to the district court for reconsideration, the county agreed to the adoption of a plan expanding the size of the county government, with six members elected from districts and a chair elected at-large.[26]

Following the decision in the Carroll County case, lawsuits were brought against three other sole commissioner counties – Telfair, Webster, and Wheeler. All three settled the litigation on the basis of an increase in the size of the county government and elections from districts.[27] The general assembly also abolished sole commissioner systems in Cherokee County in 1989;[28] Dade, Heard, and Franklin Counties in 1991;[29] and Catoosa and Murray Counties in 1992.[30]

Another challenge was brought to the sole commissioner form of government in Bleckley County. Wilbur Owens, the federal district court judge, dismissed the complaint because he felt the plaintiffs had not carried their burden of proof, but he acknowledged that blacks had virtually no chance of winning under the existing system. "I wouldn't run if I were black in

---

[23] Ga. Laws 1951, p. 3310.

[24] *Carrollton Branch of NAACP v. Stallings*, 829 F. 2d 1547, 1551 (11th Cir. 1987).

[25] Ibid., p. 1552.

[26] *Carrollton Branch of NAACP v. Stallings* (Sept. 17, 1988).

[27] *Clark v. Telfair County*, Civ. No. 287-25 (S. D. Ga. Oct. 26, 1988); *Nealy v. Webster County*, Civ. No. 88-203 (M. D. Ga. March 16, 1990); *Howard v. Commissioner of Wheeler County*, Civ. No. 390-057 (S. D. Ga. Jan. 13, 1993).

[28] Ga. Laws 1989, p. 4295.

[29] Ga. Laws 1991, pp. 3893, 3976, 4681.

[30] Ga. Laws 1992, pp. 4501, 4649.

[Bleckley] County," he said from the bench at the end of the trial. "You're going to put your hard earned time and shoe leather campaigning throughout this county . . . under these circumstances?"[31] The plaintiffs were in complete agreement. "It'd be a waste of money" for a black to run for office in Bleckley County, said plaintiff David Walker. "If you know the trend and you know that you're going to lose, there's no sense in trying," added Rev. Wilson C. Roberson, another of the plaintiffs. A black "hasn't got a chance."[32]

The court of appeals reversed, concluding that "the evidence conclusively establishes a pattern of racially polarized voting" and that "the totality of the circumstances found in Bleckley County clearly reveal a situation where the electoral power of Bleckley County blacks has been abridged 'on account of race or color.'"[33] The court found, among other things, that Bleckley County "had enforced racial segregation in all aspects of local government"; it had "fought desegregation in all aspects of public life"; it "had deprived blacks of the opportunity to participate in public life and government, even prohibiting blacks from registering to vote and from voting"; "blacks are unable to sponsor candidates for Bleckley County's sole commissioner office because such candidacies are futile"; and "a substantial number of Bleckley County's voters were highly susceptible to racist, segregationist appeals . . . [and] voted accordingly."[34]

The county appealed to the Supreme Court, which, brushing aside the overwhelming evidence of vote dilution and elevating formalism and theory over fact and experience, held in a 5-4 decision that the size of an elected body could not be challenged under Section 2.[35] Three of the justices in the majority (Rehnquist, O'Connor, and Kennedy) said that it was impossible to establish an objective benchmark or standard for increasing the size of an elected body.[36] None of the counties that abolished their sole commissioner systems, however, had any difficulty in establishing new sizes for their county governments. The other two justices who made up the majority (Scalia and Thomas) said that the size of a governing body was not a voting "practice" within the meaning of Section 2.[37]

As the Bleckley County case was proceeding through the courts, a similar suit was filed against the sole commissioner system in Pulaski County.[38] It was dismissed after the Supreme Court ruled that Section 2 could not be used to challenge the size of an elected body.

---

[31] *Hall v. Holder*, 955 F. 2d 1563, 1571 (11th Cir. 1992).
[32] Ibid., record Vol. 4, p. 332; Vol. 3, pp. 104, 110.
[33] *Hall v. Holder*, 955 F. 2d at 1573–74.
[34] Ibid., pp. 1566, 1572–73.
[35] *Holder v. Hall*, 512 U.S. 874 (1994).
[36] Ibid., p. 885 (opinion of Justice Kennedy); Ibid., p. 890 (Justice O'Connor concurring in part and concurring in the judgment).
[37] Ibid., p. 892 (Justice Thomas concurring in the judgment).
[38] *Sutton v. Anderson*, Civ. No. 89-58-1 (M. D. Ga.).

Fewer than a dozen counties in Georgia still use the sole commissioner form of government.[39] And in none of them has a black ever been elected commissioner.

III

Georgia's grand jury method of choosing school board members, adopted in 1872, was also challenged under the Voting Rights Act. The state Constitution allowed counties to abolish the grand jury method of school board selection by a vote of a majority of the voters of the county.[40] Over the years the overwhelming majority of counties had opted for elected boards, some of them no doubt spurred to action by the desegregation of their grand juries. By the mid-1980s, only 27 of the state's 159 county school districts still retained the grand jury appointment system.[41]

The first challenge to the grand jury system was brought in 1983 in Johnson County, and the board agreed to adopt a system of district elections.[42] Senator Culver Kidd of Milledgeville called for statewide legislation to abolish the grand jury appointment system. "The courts are going to demand it," he said. "So why not go ahead and get rid of that headache and save the taxpayers a lot of money."[43]

A second challenge was brought against Ben Hill, a sparsely populated county on the state's eastern coastal plain, halfway between Albany and Waycross and not far from the spot where Jefferson Davis, president of the Confederacy, was captured by Union troops on May 10, 1865. Although blacks were 30 percent of the population in Ben Hill County, the grand jury had never appointed a black to serve on the board of education. Black residents of the county, assisted by the ACLU's Voting Rights Project, filed suit in 1988 alleging that the grand jury had systematically excluded them from service on the board of education, and that the 1872 grand jury law had been enacted with a racially discriminatory purpose.[44] The plaintiffs asked the court to invalidate the grand jury appointment system in Ben Hill and the other counties in the state that still used it.

The complaint alleged that the grand jury scheme violated the Constitution and Section 2. The two sides agreed, however, to try the discriminatory purpose claim first, since if the plaintiffs prevailed on it the more time-consuming inquiry into the effect of the system in each county would have been minimized or avoided. Shortly after the complaint was filed, the

[39] *Holder v. Hall*, 512 U.S. at 877.
[40] Article VIII, Section 5, para. 4.
[41] Georgia Department of Education, Georgia Public Schools, Georgia School Board Members and System Superintendents, Methods of Selection, 1987–88 (November 1988), 4, 12.
[42] *Wilson v. Powell* (Oct. 2, 1984).
[43] *Atlanta Journal*, Dec. 30, 1984.
[44] *Vereen v. Ben Hill County*, 743 F. Supp. 864 (M. D. Ga. 1988).

grand jury in Ben Hill County, breaking with its 166-year-old tradition of white-only appointments, at last put a black, James Wilcox, on the board of education.

The contemporaneous record of the adoption of the grand jury selection statute (summarized in Chapter 2) made out a strong case that the legislature in 1872 had been motivated by a desire to exclude blacks from service on school boards. And four respected southern historians – Peyton McCrary, Dan Carter, Emory M. Thomas, and Edward J. Larson – agreed. According to McCrary, one of the witnesses for the plaintiffs, race may not have the been the only motive for the legislature's adoption of the grand jury appointment system, but "that was the clearest motive of which I found evidence. . . . It is the most important motive."[45] Carter, another plaintiffs' witness, said that "the evidence supports the belief that the grand jury system was adopted in order to either minimize or totally eliminate black representation on the school boards."[46]

Thomas, who testified on behalf of the defendants, said that "race was a factor" in the decision to adopt the grand jury appointment statute, although he believed that other factors were present as well and was not prepared to say which of them was "dominant." Since the chances of blacks serving on juries were slim, giving the grand jury the power to make appointments "further removed education from any chance of black participation, certainly in a supervisory capacity," – a result that, according to Thomas, the legislature "intended."[47]

Larson, another witness for the defendants, generally shared Thomas's views. Based upon "the general activities of that particular legislature, of the timing, of the general context of the situation," he said, the legislature "certainly assumed that they were also consolidating white dominance. I don't think they would have adopted this bill unless they thought that it would also do that."[48]

Another historian who testified for the defendants, Harvey Jackson, gave testimony that was completely contradictory. He said both that race was "not a factor" in the adoption of the grand jury law and that "you can say that race was a factor . . . [i]n the passage of the school bill."[49] Jackson's testimony contributed very little, if anything, to the racial purpose inquiry.

The district court essentially ignored the testimony of the historians and ruled that the 1872 statute had not been enacted with a discriminatory purpose. The plaintiffs, in the court's view, had not presented "specific," or direct, evidence of racial purpose. While the plaintiffs had shown the

---

[45] Ibid., declaration of Dr. Peyton McCrary, Pl. Ex. 63, p. 106.
[46] Ibid., deposition of Dan T. Carter, July 24, 1989, p. 33.
[47] Ibid., deposition of Emory M. Thomas, July 25, 1989, pp. 8, 10–12, 55.
[48] Ibid., deposition of Edward J. Larson, July 25, 1989, pp. 25, 27, 102.
[49] Ibid., deposition of Harvey Hardaway Jackson III, August 3, 1989, pp. 2, 32.

"discriminatory propensities and practices of the 1872" legislature, they failed to show that the statute "was specifically designed to carry out the discriminatory intentions" of the legislature.[50] Apparently, nothing less than overtly racist statements from legislators could meet the court's exacting standard of proof. But as Carter pointed out, during the Reconstruction period, with the continuing fear of federal intervention,

the fact that there is an absence of an explicit racial reference to me is exactly what I would have expected, and I would be stunned as an historian if such an explicit purpose were stated in January of 1872.[51]

The opinion of the district court was soon overtaken by events. The general assembly, at the request of local officials, enacted a statute in 1990 abolishing the grand jury appointment system in Ben Hill County and adopting a seven-member board of education elected from single-member districts.[52] And at its 1991 session the legislature took the step that had been urged by Senator Kidd. It passed a statute abolishing the grand jury appointment system statewide and requiring that all county boards of education be elected.[53]

The passage of the local and statewide laws rendered the Ben Hill lawsuit moot. The district court, upon motion of the plaintiffs, "reluctantly" dismissed the complaint and vacated its opinion, bringing the litigation and the racially exclusive era of grand jury appointments to a close.[54]

IV

For many years the school board in the city of Thomaston was appointed by an institution that was, if anything, even more elite and racially exclusive than the grand jury. Under a unique self-perpetuating scheme, the board appointed its own members. Terms of office were staggered, and each year the members selected a new person to replace the member whose term was expiring.

Education was traditionally provided to whites in Thomaston by the R. E. Lee Institute, a private school incorporated in 1906 for the exclusive benefit of "white pupils and patrons." The institute eventually fell upon hard financial times, and in 1915 the general assembly created a public school system from the R. E. Lee Institute. The trustees of the institute, who were all white, were named as the new members of the public school board, and the self-perpetuating method of membership selection was installed.[55]

---

[50] *Vereen v. Ben Hill County*, 743 F. Supp. at 868–89.
[51] Ibid., deposition of Dan T. Carter, p. 36.
[52] Ga. Laws 1990, p. 4435.
[53] Ga. Laws 1991, p. 2032.
[54] Order of March 10, 1993, slip op., p. 1.
[55] *Searcy v. Williams*, 656 F. 2d 1003, 1005 (5th Cir. 1981).

For a period of sixty-one years the board never appointed a black to serve on the school board. It also operated a segregated school system until 1970, when it was forced to comply with the *Brown* decision. Even when it desegregated, it kept many of the traditions of the all-white school, including the name R. E. Lee Institute.

Not only was the school board racially exclusive, but its membership was dominated by a handful of prominent local families. The Hightower family, owners of a textile mill, placed six members on the board, the Adams family five, and the Hinson, Varner, and Thurston families placed two each.[56]

George Searcy and several other blacks in Thomaston, with the assistance of the ACLU's Voting Rights Project, filed suit alleging that the method of selecting the school board had been adopted and was being used to discriminate against blacks. In response to the suit, the school board finally appointed a black, Rev. Willis Williams, to the board and adopted a policy that it would not discriminate in filling future vacancies.

Rather than accepting the defendants' representations that they would no longer discriminate, the court of appeals invalidated the selection scheme itself. Citing the isolation of the board from "public pressure," it held there was "no assurance that the pattern of past discrimination is forever broken."[57] Following the decision, the general assembly enacted a statute in 1983 providing for appointments to the school board by the mayor and city council and requiring "that all segments of the community which it serves are adequately and properly represented on said board without discrimination as to any segment."[58]

[56] Ibid., p. 1006 n.1.
[57] Ibid., p. 1010 and n.9.
[58] Ga. Laws 1983, p. 3506.

15

The Demise of Georgia's Nineteenth-Century Voter Registration System: Taking Stock of the Impact of the Voting Rights Act

> The Voting Rights Act has brought about the most revolutionary change in Georgia since the Civil War. You're having a whole new distribution of power.
>
> Linda Meggers, state demographer

I

The fraud and intimidation that had been used to blunt black voter registration subsided in Georgia in the years following passage of the Voting Rights Act. But they were replaced for a time with what Ed Brown, the last active director of VEP, described as "an adversarial relationship."[1] Local officials often refused to designate additional registration sites in the black community or canceled previously authorized neighborhood registration drives.

Some of these restrictive practices were challenged in state and federal courts, but with mixed results. In 1980, blacks were successful in securing an injunction under Section 5 against the implementation of a new policy prohibiting neighborhood registration drives in DeKalb County, where only 24 percent of the black eligible voters were registered, as compared to 81 percent of eligible whites.[2] Blacks failed in their state court efforts to have additional registration sites designated in the black areas of Muscogee County, where 60 percent of whites but only 48 percent of blacks were registered. In a show of disregard for the depressed levels of minority registration, the state supreme court said that there were already enough registration sites in the county. And throwing in some state law legal obfuscation for good measure, the court said that the challenge should be dismissed for the additional reason that it was brought as an

---

[1] Author's interview with Ed Brown, April 25, 1990.
[2] *NAACP, DeKalb County Chapter v. Georgia*, 494 F. Supp. 668 (N. D. Ga. 1980).

action for a declaratory judgment; it should have been brought as one for mandamus.[3]

In another case, *VEP v. Cleland*,[4] a federal court dismissed a statewide challenge to Georgia's registration system when the state agreed in the stipulation of dismissal that it would "encourage" registrars to appoint black deputy registrars and establish additional registration sites. While *VEP v. Cleland* did not succeed in restructuring the state's system of voter registration, VEP's director said that it precipitated a change in the relationship between state officials and voter registration groups. "Since 1984," Ed Brown said, "there has been more cooperation. I think Max Cleland [secretary of state] was hurt by the suit and realized the adversarial relationship was self-defeating. It's not ideal now, but at least we talk. It's definitely better."[5]

As evidence of the thaw in relations, state and local officials entered into consent decrees in two subsequent cases facilitating access to voter registration by minority and poor citizens. In *Project VOTE! v. Ledbetter*,[6] the state consented to allowing registration at food stamp distribution centers, and in *Spalding County VEP v. Cowart*,[7] to establishing registration sites in the black community in Spalding County.

The National Voter Registration Act (NVRA) enacted in 1993 in large measure superseded Georgia's nineteenth-century voter registration system. Congress noted that restrictive registration procedures had been introduced in the United States during the late nineteenth century in order to keep certain groups from voting – "in the North, the wave of immigrants pouring into the industrial cities; in the South, blacks and the rural poor." The Voting Rights Act had eliminated the more obvious impediments to registration, such as literacy and other tests for voting. The "unfinished business" of registration reform, according to Congress, was to reduce the remaining obstacles to a minimum while maintaining the integrity of the electoral process.[8]

The NVRA required states to permit registration by mail, at motor vehicle driver's licensing offices, and at all offices in the state that provide public assistance and service to persons with disabilities.[9] The new federal law effectively relegated to history the once traumatic trip to the courthouse to register to vote. Perhaps nothing was more emblematic of the progress in black registration in Georgia than the decision by VEP in 1992,

---

[3] *Fourth Street Baptist Church of Columbus, Georgia v. Board of Registrars*, 253 Ga. 368 (320 SE2d 543) (1984).

[4] No. C84-1181A (N. D. Ga. Feb. 19, 1987).

[5] Author's interview with Ed Brown, April 25, 1990.

[6] No. C86-1946A (N. D. Ga. Sept. 12, 1986).

[7] No. 3-84-CV-79 (N. D. Ga. June 3, 1985).

[8] H. Rep. No. 103-9, 103rd Cong., 1st Sess. 2-3 (1993), reprinted in 1993 U.S. Code Cong. & Adm. News 106–7.

[9] 42 U.S.C. §1973gg.

shortly before passage of the NVRA, to shut down its voter registration program.[10]

II

Of the 115 counties in Georgia that had 10 percent or more black population and used at-large elections prior to 1965, 85 had switched to district voting by 1990. Nine of the counties that retained at-large voting had sole commissioner forms of government, which the Supreme Court had held are not subject to challenge under the results standard of Section 2. Of the 29 cities that had 10,000 or more people, 10 percent or more black population, and used at-large elections, 28 had switched to district voting by 1990.[11]

With the removal of barriers to registration and the gradual abolition of at-large elections, there was a significant increase in black officeholding at the local level in the state. The number of black county commissioners rose from twenty in 1980 to ninety-seven in 1990. During the same period, the number of black municipal officeholders increased from 146 to 246.[12] The increases occurred, predictably, in the cities and counties that had abandoned at-large voting. Those that had retained at-large systems showed only minimal gains in black representation.[13]

The increase in black representation hardly represented proportionality in a state where blacks were 27 percent of the population, but it was in excess of 100 percent, indicating that a fundamental change was taking place. Linda Meggers, the director of the state's reapportionment office, with some allowance for hyperbole, described the advent of district voting as "the most revolutionary change in Georgia since the Civil War. You're having a whole new distribution of power."[14]

III

A black was finally elected to a statewide office in Georgia in 1985 – Robert Benham to the court of appeals. Benham's election was the result of a special combination of factors. Judicial elections in Georgia are unique in that they are subject to considerable control by the bar and by the political leadership of the state. Candidates are frequently "preselected" through appointment

---

[10] Author's interview with Ed Brown, March, 2000.

[11] Laughlin McDonald, Michael B. Binford, and Ken Johnson, "Georgia" in Chandler Davidson and Bernard Grofman, eds., *Quiet Revolution in the South: The Impact of the Voting Rights Act 1965–1990* (Princeton, N.J.: Princeton University Press, 1994), 79.

[12] *Black Elected Officials: A National Roster* (Washington, D.C.: Joint Center for Political and Economic Studies, 1990), 13.

[13] McDonald, Binford, and Johnson, "Georgia," 80–1.

[14] *Atlanta Constitution*, August 26, 1984.

by the governor to vacant positions upon the recommendation of a judicial nominating committee dominated by the bar. The chosen candidate then runs in the ensuing election with all the advantages of incumbency. Judicial elections are also nonpartisan, low-key, low-interest contests in which the voters, if they vote for judicial candidates at all, tend to ratify the choices that have previously been made.[15] Benham, following this pattern of pre-selection, was appointed by the governor to the court of appeals in 1984. He ran for election in August of that year and won with 58.5 percent of the vote.[16]

Benham received special political treatment in other ways. According to Tyrone Brooks, chair of the Georgia legislative black caucus,

the governor felt they could sell Benham in the white community, with the support of the bar and the Democratic leadership, because nobody knew he was black. The plan was to get out the vote in the black community in the traditional way, but to ignore race in the white community. Benham's picture could appear only on brochures distributed in the black community and there could be no endorsements of Benham by Maynard Jackson, Julian Bond, Jesse Jackson, or anybody in the civil rights community.[17]

Ironically, the result of this consciously racial campaign was that Benham's election revealed relatively little racial polarization. Benham was elected to the state supreme court in 1990 using a similar campaign strategy. But his election was unusual in that he faced three white opponents; most incumbent supreme court justices have little or no opposition.

In 1990, Clarence Cooper became the second black to win statewide judicial office by following the same path as Benham. He was first appointed to the court of appeals and then ran for office to succeed himself.

The old patterns of racial bloc voting still persisted, however, particularly in nonjudicial elections. Allan Lichtman analyzed more than 260 black–white contests in 67 counties in Georgia from 1970 to 1990 and found "high levels of white bloc voting as white voters usually voted overwhelmingly against black candidates and for their white competitors."[18] Average black cohesion was 83 percent. The average level of white crossover voting for black candidates was just 12 percent.

An analysis of elections by Steven Cole also showed the existence of strong and pervasive polarized voting throughout the state. The study analyzed at-large county, legislative, and judicial contests from 1980 to 1989 in counties with substantial black populations and in which there had been a serious

[15] Philip L. DuBose, "The Significance of Voting Cues in State Supreme Court Elections," 13 Law and Society Review 757-79 (1979).

[16] *Carrollton Branch of NAACP v. Stallings*, 829 F. 2d 1547, 1558–59 (11th Cir. 1987).

[17] Author's interview with Tyrone Brooks, March 5, 1990.

[18] *Johnson v. Miller*, CV 194-008 (S. D. Ga.); Allan J. Lichtman, "Report on Issues Relating to Georgia Congressional Districts," May 26, 1994.

black candidate (defined as one who received at least half of the black vote). Fifty-one elections from twenty counties were included in the study. The analysis showed that a majority of whites voted for the white candidate, and a majority of blacks voted for the black candidate. On average, only 14 percent of whites crossed over and voted for a black candidate.[19]

Andrew Young's subsequent campaigns for elective office in Georgia after he left Congress were further evidence of the continuing reality of racially polarized voting, even for a highly gifted black candidate. In 1981, after being elected to Congress for three terms, after serving as U.S. ambassador to the United Nations, and after raising more money than in any previous campaign, Young got only 8.9 percent of the white vote in his successful runoff election against a white opponent for mayor of majority-black Atlanta.[20] In 1990, Young ran for governor of Georgia and got 28.8 percent of the total vote in the primary. In the required runoff election, he increased his share to 38.1 percent, but fell far short of the majority he needed. An analysis of the county returns showed strong evidence of racially polarized voting in both of Young's elections, indicating that he received less than 25 percent of the white vote.[21]

IV

The redistribution of political power in Georgia, far from being voluntary, was the direct result of the enforcement of the Voting Rights Act. And almost the entire burden of the enforcement litigation was borne by the civil rights community. The plaintiffs in each case were local black residents and voters. Many of them, such as Edward Brown in Mitchell County, Herman Lodge in Burke County, Willie Bailey in Putnam County, Lucious Holloway in Terrell County, and Rev. George Neely in Webster County, to name only a few of the many, had been active in the civil rights movement. They may not have stood in front of the Washington Monument in the glare of a national spotlight and thrilled the crowd with a passionate appeal for justice and human rights, and they certainly never achieved the celebrity status of other leaders of the civil rights movement. But they put themselves in harm's way and showed great courage and fortitude in waging the fight for equal rights. And they had an enormous impact on the course of events in Georgia.

The lawyers who represented the minority plaintiffs were mainly from the local and civil rights bars. The ACLU's Voting Rights Project in Atlanta

---

[19] *Brooks v. Georgia State Board of Election*, No. CV 288-146 (S. D. Ga. 1989), Steven P. Cole, polarized voting analysis.

[20] *Busbee v. Smith*, Civ. No. 82-0665 (D. D. C.), Pl. Ex. 25, p. 9, deposition of Andrew Young.

[21] Michael Binford, "Andrew Young and the 1990 Governor's Contest in Georgia," paper presented at the Voter Education Project Workshop, From Protest to Politics, Clark-Atlanta University, 1990.

provided representation to the plaintiffs in fifty-one of the cases brought from 1974 to 1990 challenging at-large elections for counties and cities. Georgia Indigent Legal Services (GILS) provided representation in five, VEP in four, the Southern Poverty Law Center (SPLC) in three, the NAACP Legal Defense Fund (LDF) in two, the NAACP in one, and the Center for Constitutional Rights (CCR) in one. In five of the cases, two or more of the organizations shared representation of the plaintiffs. Twenty-one of the lawsuits were brought by civil rights lawyers in private practice with no formal organizational affiliation. Only three of the cases were brought by the U.S. Department of Justice.[22]

V

As part of the mechanism for enforcing Section 5, Congress made failure to comply with the Voting Rights Act a crime punishable by fine and imprisonment.[23] Despite the pervasive, widespread noncompliance with Section 5 by Georgia's white elected officials, none has ever been prosecuted for failure to comply with the act. Ironically, the only prosecutions in the state involving Section 5 have been of black officials – the mayor and members of the city council of Greenville, Georgia – growing out of their attempt to *comply* with the preclearance law.

In the May 1987 election for mayor of Greenville, the incumbent, John Carter, narrowly beat a challenger, James Bray. Bray contested the election, alleging errors in the tabulation of absentee ballots, and after a hearing a judge of the superior court of Meriwether County set the election aside.[24] The court directed that a special election be held within forty days. Since the order contained a new voting practice within the meaning of Section 5, the mayor and council, upon the advice of the city attorney, submitted it to the U.S. attorney general for preclearance.[25] Under Section 5, the attorney general has sixty days within which to act upon a submission, a period of time that extended *beyond* the time set by the superior court for holding the election.

The day before the scheduled election, the mayor and council were advised by the attorney general that the submission had not yet been acted upon. City officials, again upon the advice of the city attorney, notified the superior court that the submission had not been precleared and that they were therefore

---

[22] See American Civil Liberties Union, "Table of Cases Challenging At-Large County Elections in Georgia, 1974–1990"; "Table of Cases Challenging At-Large City Elections in Georgia, 1974–1990."

[23] 42 U.S.C. §1973j(a).

[24] *Bray v. Carter*, Civ. No. 87-V-179 (Sup. Ct. Meriwether Cty. Sept. 21, 1988).

[25] An order of a state court by definition reflects state "policy choices" and is therefore subject to preclearance. *Gresham v. Harris*, 695 F. Supp. 1179 (N. D. Ga.), aff'd sub nom. *Poole v. Gresham*, 495 U.S. 954 (1990).

canceling the election. The courts have consistently held that unprecleared voting changes are "unenforceable."[26]

Bray then moved the superior court to hold the mayor and four council members in contempt for failing to hold the election, and the court did so.[27] In an extraordinarily punitive decision, the court fined each city official $500 and ordered them to pay Bray's attorney's fees in the amount of $5,250 – all out of their personal, as opposed to the city's, funds. The court also sentenced the mayor and council members to twenty days in the county detention center. They could avoid doing time only if they paid the fines and attorney's fees by a date set by the court.

The defendants removed the state case to federal court under a law that permits removal where a defendant is acting under compulsion or authority of federal law[28] – in this instance the Voting Rights Act. The defendants' lawyer issued a statement saying that "[l]ocal officials have regularly failed to comply with the preclearance requirements of the Voting Rights Act and none that I know of has ever been fined or sentenced to jail. This is surely the first time in the history of the Act that someone has actually been held in contempt merely because they were trying to comply with the law."[29]

The federal court issued an order staying the contempt convictions entered by the state court and directed the mayor and council to set a new date for the election, submit it for preclearance, and take all steps necessary to insure that the election was held.[30] As part of an agreement between the parties, the city agreed to pay Bray's attorney's fees and the court costs. The defendants complied with the order; the election was held on January 4, 1989; and Bray was elected the new mayor. All the conditions of its order having been met, the federal court dismissed the state court contempt action with prejudice.[31]

The mayor and city council could probably have avoided their conflict with the state court by holding the special election in violation of Section 5, hoping that the attorney general would subsequently approve the change. But such a course would have exposed them to a suit over their failure to comply with the preclearance requirement, as well as to the risk of having to conduct another election in the event of an objection. Given the choices that confronted them, the mayor and council can hardly be faulted for electing to comply with federal law.

[26] *Clark v. Roemer*, 500 U.S. 646, 652 (1991).
[27] *Bray v. The City of Greenville*, 88-V-374 (Sup. Ct. Meriwether Cty. Nov. 23, 1988).
[28] 28 U.S.C. §1443(2).
[29] Statement of Laughlin McDonald, December 1, 1988.
[30] *Bray v. The City of Greenville*, Civ. No. 3:88-cv-127-GET (N. D. Ga. Dec. 6, 1988).
[31] Ibid., order of Apr. 26, 1989.

16

Recreating the Past: The Challenge to the Majority-Vote Requirement

> Race was a dominant factor in the thinking and decision-making of the white members of the General Assembly during my service there and I do not think that the statewide majority vote requirement would have been passed had these members not been convinced of the racially discriminatory potential of the runoff system.
>
> U.S. Representative James Mackay

I

A broad coalition of Georgia's black leadership, led by Tyrone Brooks and with the assistance of the ACLU's Voting Rights Project, filed a lawsuit in 1990 challenging the statewide majority-vote requirement enacted by the general assembly in 1964. They claimed that the law had an adverse impact on black candidates and voters, and that it had been adopted with a discriminatory purpose. After all, Denmark Groover, the bill's chief sponsor in the house, had openly urged his colleagues to vote for the measure as a way of thwarting the "bloc vote" and countering the efforts of the federal government to increase the registration of Negro voters.[1] (For a fuller discussion of the circumstances surrounding passage of the majority-vote requirement, see Chapter 6.)

When the challenges to the grand jury method of appointing school boards were brought in the 1980s, all the members of the general assembly that had enacted the statute in 1872 were dead and unavailable to testify. But some of those who had been in the legislature when it enacted the majority-vote requirement in 1964 were still alive when the challenge to the law was filed in 1990, and thus were available to testify about their and their colleagues reasons for voting as they did. The plaintiffs, however, moved to exclude such testimony at trial on the grounds that the best evidence of legislative purpose

---

[1] *Atlanta Constitution*, March 1, 1963.

Tyrone Brooks, president of the Georgia Association of Black Elected Officials, chair of the Legislative Black Caucus, and a leading plaintiff in statewide voting rights litigation (courtesy of the Southern Regional Council).

was the contemporaneous record compiled in 1964, and that after-the-fact reconstructions of selected members of the legislature would be inherently unreliable and self-serving.

The trial judge denied the plaintiffs' motion, but he agreed that "[i]t's not very trustworthy for somebody coming along 25 years later to be able to say that ain't what happened. This is what happened." He assured the plaintiffs, "I'm not going to let Governor Sanders or anybody else come in and attempt to reconstruct what occurred 25 years ago."[2] But that is exactly what he did let happen. He not only allowed the former legislators to testify and reconstruct the past, but he, and the court of appeals, relied heavily, and selectively, on their testimony in ruling that the majority-vote requirement had not been enacted with a discriminatory purpose.

II

In rejecting the *Brooks* plaintiffs' claim of purposeful discrimination, the court of appeals concluded that "discrimination was not a substantial or

---

[2] *Brooks v. Miller*, Civ. No. 1: 90-CV-1001-RCF (N. D. Ga.), transcript of proceedings before the Honorable Richard C. Freeman, July 12, 1990, Vol. 4, pp. 46, 53.

motivating factor behind enactment of the majority vote provision." In doing so, it placed special reliance on the testimony – given more than two decades after the events in question had transpired – of former governor Carl Sanders; George T. Smith, the former speaker of the house; Melba Williams, who was a member of the Election Laws Study Committee; and Eugene Patterson, a former editor of the *Atlanta Constitution*.[3]

One of the remarkable things about the legislators called as witnesses by the state was that while they were very sure that *they* had not acted to discriminate against blacks when they passed the majority-vote bill in 1964, they were hard pressed to remember much more. Their testimony was a mixture of denial, evasion, amnesia, and self-rehabilitation that fully supports the admonition of Congress that after-the-fact reconstructions of legislative intent are inherently unreliable and are entitled to little, if any, weight.

Carl Sanders said he had no recollection of the circumstances surrounding passage of the majority-vote bill in the house in 1963, nor could he remember any of the legislative debates involving adoption of the majority-vote requirement in 1964. He did not know the reasons members of the general assembly voted for the bill.[4]

George T. Smith said he could not remember any discussions he may have had about the majority-vote requirement. He did not know the reasons other members of the general assembly supported Groover's majority-vote bill.[5]

Melba Williams was not appointed to the ELSC until *after* the decision to propose adoption of a majority-vote requirement had already been made. She admitted that "[a]fter I got on the committee, there was never any discussion [about] ... the majority-vote."[6] Her denial that race was a factor in adoption of the majority-vote requirement was not, therefore, particularly helpful or relevant.

Patterson's testimony was noteworthy because it was totally contradictory. He had covered the legislature's deliberations in 1964 and said at trial that in his opinion "discrimination" was not the reason the majority-vote requirement was included in the new code. However, on cross-examination he admitted that he had previously given a totally different account to Steven Lawson, a professor of history at the University of North Carolina–Greensboro who was preparing an expert report for use at trial. At that time, far from denying the existence of a racial motive for including

---

[3] *Brooks v. Miller*, 158 F. 3d 1230, 1236, 1241 (11th Cir. 1998).

[4] Ibid., Pl. Ex. 304, pp. 52, 60–1, deposition of Carl Sanders.

[5] Ibid., Pl. Ex. 305, pp. 15–16.

[6] Ibid., transcript of Proceedings before the Honorable Richard C. Freeman, July 12, 1990, Vol. 5, pp. 127, 135.

the majority vote requirement in the 1964 code, Patterson, whose comments were tape recorded, had been

sure that's why the legislature passed the law. As I said in the beginning, racial motivations were everything in the politics of that period. And so the county segregationists probably saw this as some means to diminish the influence of blacks.[7]

In trying to reconcile his contradictory statements, Patterson complained that he had been "blind-sided" by Lawson. It seems highly unlikely, however, that Patterson could have been taken advantage of or somehow been tricked in an interview into saying things he did not mean. After all, he was a veteran journalist who must have conducted hundreds, if not thousands, of interviews himself.[8]

Milton Carlton, another witness for the state, who was Sanders's floor leader in the senate in 1963 and 1964 and a member of the ELSC in 1964, said that he had no memory of Groover's advocacy of the majority-vote provision in the house. He did not remember that Groover had appeared before the senate rules committee in 1963 to promote passage of his majority-vote bill.[9]

The state's witnesses claimed that they could not remember whether race was a factor in the passage of measures that were plainly designed to shore up racial segregation, or they denied that their votes in favor of the bills were based upon race. Carlton didn't recall that race was a factor in the debate surrounding implementation of the majority-vote requirement for the 1964 Fulton County Superior Court race involving Don Hollowell. It was "something I know nothing about," he said.[10] Carlton "didn't remember" that the general assembly had passed legislation authorizing tuition grants to private schools, or that the general assembly had passed a law guaranteeing freedom from compulsory education.[11]

Carlton could not, in fact, recall a *single* occasion during the entire time he had served in the legislature when race was ever discussed in connection with the passage of a piece of legislation. When pressed on whether the general assembly had ever discussed race, Carlton said, "I have no recollection of any such. . . . No; I don't remember any such discussion."[12] During one of the most racially charged times in Georgia politics – in the midst of the demise of the county unit system, the desegregation of schools, reapportionment of the general assembly, passage of the modern civil rights acts, and increased

[7] Ibid., Joint Ex. 1, p. 25; trial transcript, pp. 247, 447, 464.
[8] Ibid., trial transcript, p. 446.
[9] Ibid., transcript of proceeding before the Honorable Richard C. Freeman, July 13, 1990, Vol. 5, p. 23.
[10] Ibid., p. 59.
[11] Ibid., p. 64.
[12] Ibid., pp. 57–8.

black political participation – Carlton could not remember *any* statements, bills introduced, votes, or actions taken by the general assembly that were motivated by a desire to discriminate against blacks.

George T. Smith testified that he didn't know why he had voted for the bill authorizing the governor to close the public schools. He couldn't recall the purpose of the tuition grant bill, which he had also supported. He had also voted for a bill providing for freedom from compulsory association in education. He acknowledged that the purpose of the bill was "probably" to thwart desegregation of schools, but insisted that "I voted for it not knowing what the purpose behind it was."[13]

Carl Sanders also denied that there were racial motives behind bills that were obviously designed to maintain racial segregation, including bills that he had sponsored. He denied, for example, that the purpose of the tuition grant bill, which he had sponsored in 1961, was to avoid the effect of the *Brown* school desegregation decision. He denied that his support of repeal of the state's compulsory education law in 1961 was related in any way to race. His explanation of his support for repeal – "to not make it compulsory" – was entirely tautological.[14]

The court acknowledged Groover's racial motivation, but held that the majority-vote requirement was the work of the Sanders administration and that Groover was essentially a bystander who had no control or influence over the legislative process. Groover, however, was by all accounts one of the shrewdest and most effective members of the general assembly. Sanders himself acknowledged that Groover was "absolutely" an effective, competent member of the house at the time that the majority-vote bill was considered and enacted.[15]

Sanders's view of Groover was shared by George T. Smith, who said that Groover "was an effective advocate for and against legislation."[16] The anti–facsimile ballot measure passed the senate by a vote of 28 to 18,[17] but it was defeated in the house in large measure because of the opposition of Groover.

Groover also opposed the provision in the ELSC proposal creating a state election board with subpoena power. According to Groover, "the state does not need a 'super board' with the power to supersede local officials on the basis of an affidavit which could be given for political purposes."[18] In response to Groover's opposition, "Administration leaders indicated...that they and Mr. Groover will come to amicable terms."[19] George Busbee, Sanders's

[13] Ibid., pp. 87, 97, 101.
[14] Ibid., pp. 203–5.
[15] Ibid., Pl. Ex. 304, p. 54, deposition of Carl E. Sanders.
[16] Ibid., Pl. Ex. 305, p. 11, deposition of George T. Smith.
[17] *Macon Telegraph*, May 27, 1964.
[18] *Atlanta Journal*, June 5, 1964; *Atlanta Constitution*, June 4, 1964.
[19] *Atlanta Journal*, June 5, 1964.

assistant floor leader in the house and an eventual governor himself, "worked out the changes from the Senate version with Rep. Denmark Groover of Bibb."[20]

Groover's importance and influence in the general assembly is documented in other ways. In 1964, the Sanders administration pushed for amendment of the state constitution to provide for home rule for cities and counties. Many rural legislators opposed the amendment because they wanted to retain their prerogatives under the existing legislative local bill system. Groover, however, sided with the administration and was given credit by the "Sanders men . . . for turning the tide on county home rule."[21] Groover was appointed that same year to the critical conference committee that was to design the new constitution for the state.[22]

The independence and importance of the house, which was still under the influence of rural segregationists such as Groover, was evident in numerous other ways. For example, the house rejected the senate's exclusion of county commissions from the coverage of the majority vote requirement, and it rejected the senate's liberalized test for voter registration. The house, led by Groover and the rural segregationists, had the final "cut" on the new election law. The inclusion of the majority-vote requirement was unmistakably their handiwork.

As for the Sanders administration, its head was, of course, a Georgia politician. Sanders could never have been elected to statewide office had he not supported measures designed to curb black political power.

In his first term in the Georgia house in 1955, Sanders supported a number of overtly racial measures, including a bill authorizing the governor to close the public schools in order to avoid integration; the resolution condemning the *Brown* decision as "null, void, and of no effect"; a bill sponsored by Groover requiring segregation in common carriers; a bill authorizing the state police to enforce segregation laws in any county or municipality; and a bill allowing public parks to be sold to private parties rather than be integrated.[23]

When he became president pro tem of the senate in 1959, Sanders sponsored bills to allow the governor to close public schools and universities and to rewrite the admissions policies of the University of Georgia.[24] He sponsored other anti-integration bills in 1960, including one elevating the crime of barratry from a misdemeanor to a felony.[25] In 1961, he sponsored

---

[20] *Atlanta Constitution*, June 9, 1964; *Macon News*, June, 1964.

[21] *Macon Telegraph*, May 30, 1964.

[22] *Macon Telegraph*, June 11, 1964.

[23] *Brooks v. Miller*, Pl. Ex. 304, pp. 16–19, 21–32, deposition of Carl E. Sanders; transcript of proceedings before the Honorable Richard C. Freeman, July 12, 1990, Vol. 4, p. 199; Georgia House Journal 1956, pp. 565–66, 782–93, 656, 1366–67.

[24] Georgia Senate Journal 1959, pp. 65–7.

[25] Ga. Laws 1960, pp. 1135–37; Georgia Senate Journal 1960, p. 731.

the bill to provide tuition grants to students who attended private schools
and voted to repeal compulsory education laws.[26] He supported continued
use of the literacy test for voting in 1964 as well as an anti–facsimile ballot
provision designed "to discourage bloc voting."[27] In 1964, when Congress
was considering passage of a public accommodations law, Sanders testified
against the bill on the grounds that it would violate private property and
state's rights.[28] The following year he wrote to President Johnson declaring
his strong opposition to the Voting Right Act.

Sanders has described himself, without apology, as a "moderate segregationist." As he explained it, "In my case 'moderate' means that I am a
segregationist but I am not a damned fool."[29] Sanders justified his support
of segregation and anti–civil rights measures because "that was the tenor of
the times, and at that time . . . my desire was to try to move on into a position
of leadership to lead this state."[30] The fact that Sanders acted in light of "the
tenor of the times" and to advance his political career does not make his actions, or those of any other politician who supported segregation, any less
discriminatory. Sanders's support of the majority-vote requirement, despite
his after-the-fact denial that he intended to dilute the black vote, is entirely
consistent with his support of other measures designed to maintain white
control and to contain black political power.

It is also implausible that elected officials in 1964 were unaware of the
operation of a majority-vote requirement or were oblivious to its racial implications. George T. Smith admitted that in a majority-white jurisdiction
where voting was racially polarized, a majority-vote requirement would
make it tougher for blacks to get elected to office. He also conceded, "I'm
sure everybody [in the general assembly] thought that or realized that."[31]
Milton Carlton also agreed that members of the general assembly at that time
understood that a majority-vote requirement would tend to disadvantage minority candidates in white jurisdictions where there was racially polarized
voting.[32]

While the court of appeals credited the testimony of the legislators
who said that they had not supported the majority-vote requirement in
an effort to discriminate against blacks, it ignored entirely the testimony

---

[26] *Brooks v. Miller*, Pl. Ex. 102; transcript of proceedings before the Honorable Richard C.
Freeman, July 12, 1990, Vol. 4, p. 202.

[27] *Atlanta Constitution*, May 15, 1964.

[28] Frank Daniel, ed., *Addresses and Public Papers of Carl Edward Sanders, 1963–1967* (Atlanta:
B. W. Fortson, 1968), 81–8; *Atlanta Times*, July 29, 1964.

[29] *Brooks v. Miller*, Pl. Ex. 300, p. 17, report of Stephen Lawson; transcript of cross-examination
of Eugene C. Patterson, May 15, 1996, p. 11.

[30] Ibid., Pl, Ex. 304, pp. 22–3, deposition of Carl E. Sanders.

[31] Ibid., transcript of proceedings before the Honorable Richard C. Freeman, July 13, 1990,
Vol. 5, p. 93.

[32] Ibid., p. 35.

of those called by the *Brooks* plaintiffs who said that the law *had* been enacted with a discriminatory purpose. Senator Leroy Johnson, for example, testified:

There is no question in my mind that Denmark Groover's 1963 bill was a direct precedent for the statewide majority vote requirement adopted as part of the election code in 1964.[33]

Johnson stressed that

many white members of the General Assembly favored adoption of a statewide majority vote requirement as a method of diluting minority voting strength. . . . The General Assembly would not have passed a statewide majority vote requirement, either as a house bill in 1963 or as part of the 1964 election code, unless the more conservative members were convinced that the runoff system would help maintain white control over local and state government.[34]

James Mackay, a member of the house in 1963 and later a member of the U.S. Congress, agreed that the majority-vote provision was passed with a discriminatory purpose:

Race was a dominant factor in the thinking and decision-making of the white members of the General Assembly during my service there and I do not think that the statewide majority vote requirement would have been passed had these members not been convinced of the racially discriminatory potential of the runoff system.[35]

The court of appeals also ignored the testimony of two historians that the majority-vote requirement was enacted with a discriminatory purpose. Morgan Kousser said that "[e]very factor that should be considered in a voting rights intent case points, in this instance, to the same conclusion, and every factor counts heavily against the alternative hypotheses." He concluded that "the majority vote requirement was adopted with a racially discriminatory intent."[36] Steven Lawson, based on his independent research, reached the same conclusion:

Having reviewed the succession of historical events starting in 1957 that culminated in enactment of the majority vote requirement for all elections in 1964, it is the author's professional opinion that race played an integral part in determining the legislative outcome.[37]

---

33 Ibid., Pl. Exs. 306, p. 6; 307, pp. 649, 668–69.
34 Ibid., Pl. Ex. 306, pp. 7–8.
35 Ibid., Pl. Ex. 308, pp. 3–4.
36 Ibid., Pl. Ex. 102, p. 27, 32. In *Colorblind Injustice: Minority Voting Rights and the Undoing of the Second Reconstruction* (Chapel Hill: University of North Carolina Press, 1999), Kousser reiterated the view that "[t]he majority-vote requirement was passed in Georgia in 1963–64 to preserve the rule of the white majority against the growing 'bloc vote'" (242).
37 *Brooks v. Miller*, Pl. Ex. 300, p. 60.

The genius of our federal court system is that it resolves disputes and not, as the *Brooks* litigation attests, that its judgments about history and legislative motive are always reliable.

III

The parties in *Brooks* conducted a survey of elections in Georgia and were able to quantify the actual impact of the majority-vote provision. From 1970 to 1995 there were 278 black–white runoffs, or election sequences in which black and white candidates were in both the primary or general election and the runoff. Of these 278, the majority-vote requirement changed the result in 85 (31 percent). Of the eighty-five, fifty-six (66 percent) were sequences in which blacks won the initial election but lost the runoff (W-L), and twenty-nine (34 percent) were sequences in which blacks came in second in the initial election but won the runoff (L-W). The net loss to blacks caused by the majority-vote requirement was thus twenty-seven nominations or elections to office.[38]

Not surprisingly, the majority-vote requirement had the greatest impact in majority-white jurisdictions. Of the sixty black–white runoff sequences in majority-white jurisdictions in which the majority-vote requirement affected the outcome, blacks lost forty-five (75 percent) of the runoffs.[39]

Under Section 2, the standard for a violation is whether or not a challenged practice causes members of a minority group to "have less opportunity than other members of the electorate to participate in the political process and to elect representatives of their choice."[40] The use of a majority-vote requirement that denied nomination or election to twenty-seven plurality-winning blacks arguably met the "less opportunity" standard. The court of appeals, however, imposed a higher burden of proof and held that the *Brooks* plaintiffs had failed to establish a violation of Section 2 because the system of elections did not "eviscerate" the ability of minority voters to elect their candidates of choice.[41]

The court also said that, in any event, Section 2 could not be used to challenge a majority-vote law because there was no "adequate remedy" for a violation – that is, because there was no acceptable alternative to a majority-vote requirement. The court reasoned that a plurality system could theoretically result "in a candidate's winning with 1% of the vote," which "would seriously undermine the legitimacy of the government."[42]

Most elections in Georgia prior to 1964, however – not to mention most elections in the United States – were conducted under a plurality system, and

[38] Ibid., 158 F. 3d at 1235.
[39] Ibid., trial transcript, pp. 287, 361, testimony of Steven Cole; Pl. Ex. 301, Table A.
[40] 42 U.S.C. §1973(b).
[41] *Brooks v. Miller*, 158 F. 3d at 1241.
[42] Ibid., p. 1240.

no one could seriously contend that for that reason they undermined the legitimacy of the government. Moreover, the notion that a candidate could actually be elected with 1 percent of the vote is based more on fancy than on fact. There would have to be a *minimum* of 101 candidates in a contest for any person to win with just 1 percent of the vote. Such elections don't exist in Georgia.

In addition, in the event of a Section 2 violation the state would be given the first opportunity to fashion a remedy.[43] While a pure plurality system could be one such remedy, the state would be free to adopt a substantial plurality rule. It is simply untrue that there is no alternative to the majority-vote rule that would not undermine the legitimacy of the government.

Congress clearly intended for Section 2 to reach majority-vote provisions. The Senate report not only identified "majority vote requirements" as a factor probative of minority vote dilution, but listed "at-large elections, majority vote requirements and districting plans" as among the practices directly subject to challenge under the statute.[44] The Supreme Court has also denied preclearance to majority-vote requirements under Section 5 of the act because of their potential for diluting minority voting strength.[45] And the attorney general has routinely objected to majority-vote requirements in administrative submissions under Section 5.[46] The court of appeals, however, ignored the intent of Congress, the decisions of the Court, and the practice of the attorney general in ruling that Section 2 did not apply to majority-vote requirements.

The court of appeals has further demonstrated its hostility to the Voting Rights Act by carving out another major exception to Section 2 involving the method of electing state court judges. The Supreme Court has held that Section 2 applies to judicial elections, on the unassailable theory that "if a State decides to elect its trial judges... those elections must be conducted in compliance with the Voting Rights Act."[47] But the eleventh circuit has ruled that the state's interest in maintaining its judicial selection system trumps the racial fairness provisions of Section 2. According to the court, "we would be compelled to rule against all plaintiffs who bring Section 2 cases involving judicial elections."[48] Despite the direct conflict with its prior opinions, the

---

43 *Voinovich v. Quilter*, 507 U.S. 146, 156 (1992).

44 S. Rep. No. 417, 97th Cong., 2d Sess., 29–30 (1982), reprinted in 1982 U.S. Code Cong. & Adm. News 206–7.

45 *City of Port Arthur v. United States*, 459 U.S. 159, 167 (1982); *City of Rome v. United States*, 446 U.S. 156, 184 (1980).

46 U.S. Commission on Civil Rights, *The Voting Rights Act: Unfulfilled Goals* (Washington, D.C.: Government Printing Office, 1981), 69.

47 *Houston Lawyers' Assoc. v. Texas Attorney General*, 501 U.S. 419, 426 (1991). See also *Chisom v. Roemer*, 501 U.S. 380, 404 (1991) ("state judicial elections are included within the ambit of §2 as amended").

48 *Davis v. Chiles*, 139 F. 3d 1414, 1423 n.19 (11th Cir. 1998).

Supreme Court, without explanation, refused to review the decision of the appellate court.[49]

IV

The state also defended the 1964 law by claiming that a majority-vote requirement was used "throughout the United States" and that without such a rule, fringe groups and "stalking horse" candidates could manipulate the electoral process by splitting the vote and allowing entrenched, corrupt incumbents who lacked majority support to stay in office. Moreover, the state said, the black plaintiffs were simply seeking "proportional representation" and "black maximization."[50]

Roy Barnes, a member of the house who was later elected governor, said that a majority-vote requirement was "essential" and that "there is nothing more American than to have a majority vote requirement." A majority-vote rule would also prevent the election of "extremist" or "nut" candidates, he said.[51] The only person whom he would identify as an extremist or a nut who had been elected in Georgia, however, was former governor Lester Maddox. Had a plurality-vote rule been in effect in 1966 when Maddox was elected governor by the general assembly, Callaway, the front-runner, would have won the general election and the governorship. It was precisely because of a majority-vote requirement that a candidate whom Barnes regarded as being an extremist or a nut was elected.

The state and Barnes were, of course, wrong in suggesting that majority vote was the norm in the United States. Georgia is one of only ten states, nine of them in the South, that have adopted statewide majority-vote requirements. Most elections in the United States are conducted under a plurality-vote system.[52]

In any case, in 1994 as the *Brooks* lawsuit was making its way through the courts, the legislature brushed aside the good-government arguments it had advanced in support of the majority-vote requirement and repealed the provision in favor of a 45 percent plurality-vote rule for general elections, except those for certain constitutional offices.[53] Four years

---

[49] *Davis v. Bush*, 526 U.S. 1003 (1999).
[50] *Brooks v. Miller*, No. 96-9284 (U.S. S. Ct.), brief of appellees, pp. 33–4.
[51] *Brooks v. Miller*, trial transcript, May 15, 1996, pp. 380–81, 399.
[52] *Runoff Elections and the Voting Rights Act of 1965, as Amended* (Washington, D.C.: Congressional Research Service, 1984), 2; National Municipal League, "Compilation of the 48 Direct Primary States" (1957); Douglas J. Amy, *Behind the Ballot Box* (Westport, Conn.: Praeger, 2000), 21 ("[t]he most prevalent system for legislative elections in the United States is the winner-take-all system – or in more formal parlance, the 'single-member district plurality system'"). See also *Timmons v. Twin Cities Area New Party*, 520 U.S. 351, 362 (1997) (describing plurality vote as one of the "features of our political system").
[53] Ga. Laws 1994, p. 279.

later, the legislature abolished the majority-vote requirement in general elections for the state's constitutional offices as well.[54] Self-interest and partisan politics lay at the heart of the general assembly's reassessment of the majority-vote law.

The catalyst for repeal of the majority-vote law was the defeat of Wyche Fowler, the incumbent white Democrat, by a Republican, Paul Coverdell, in the 1992 general election for the U.S. Senate. In a three-way contest, Fowler won a plurality of the votes but was defeated in the ensuing runoff by his Republican opponent. Responding to Fowler's loss, the Democratic-controlled legislature jettisoned the majority-vote requirement in an attempt to improve the chances of Democrats in future general elections. According to Tyrone Brooks, "it was a done deal on the part of the Democratic leadership in the house and the senate, and it passed and it was signed into law."[55]

Thomas Chambless, a house Democrat, explained that it was the majority-vote requirement itself, not the plurality rule as some had previously claimed, that allowed so-called fringe candidates to manipulate the electoral process by forcing runoffs. The people of Georgia were poorly served, he said, "by having a run-off election... because of the existence of some fringe or very small party candidate such as occurred in 1992."[56] If any real principle emerges from the state's adoption and subsequent rejection of the majority-vote requirement, it is that the party or faction in power can generally be counted on to adopt rules for elections that it thinks will promote its own interests.

The majority-vote law was superseded by other events as well, events that Groover and his supporters could not have foreseen. Since its passage in 1964, the impact of the majority-vote requirement in all elections had been substantially diminished by the transformation of the state's election procedures brought about by the Voting Rights Act. By the time the majority-vote lawsuit was finally ruled on by the court of appeals in 1998,[57] most of Georgia's counties with significant black populations had adopted districting plans. Of the nineteen counties which retained at-large voting for their county commissions, sixteen had very small black populations – Banks (3.5%), Brantley (5.4%), Echols (11.3%), Fannin (.03%), Floyd (13.7%), Forsyth (.03%), Gilmer (2.8%), Glascock (12.6%), Habersham (5.6%), Jackson (9.7%), Oconee (7.5%), Paulding (4.0%), Rabun (.4%), Rockdale (8.1%), Stephens (12%), and White (2.8%). The large white majorities in these counties would, as a practical matter, control the outcome of elections no matter

54 Ga. Laws 1998, p. 825.

55 *Brooks v. Miller*, trial transcript, p. 372; Pl. Ex. 313, p. 147 (*Georgia v. Reno*, Civ. No. 90-2065 [D. D. C.], trial testimony, Charles Allen Thomas, Jr.); Pl. Ex. 322, p. 1180 (*Georgia v. Reno*, trial testimony, Robert Irvin).

56 Ibid., Pl. Ex. 320, p. 1115 (*Georgia v. Reno*, trial testimony, Thomas, Chambless).

57 Ibid., 158 F. 3d at 1243.

what system was used for tallying votes. Two of the at-large counties were majority-black, Baker (51.5%) and Hancock (79.4%).[58] The majority-vote requirement was actually an advantage to black candidates and voters in these counties.

In the counties with district elections, the majority-vote requirement was a wash for black candidates; it was a disadvantage in the majority-white districts but an advantage in the majority-black districts. The requirement remains a significant factor only in primary elections, and only in those for single-member offices at the county level, such as sheriff and clerk of court, and state-level offices.

[58] *Georgia County Government Yearbook* (Stone Mountain: Association County Commissioners of Georgia, 1995), 29–108; 1990 U.S. Census population figures, Georgia.

17

The White Backlash: Redistricting in the 1990s

Shaw v. Reno is the greatest threat to the Voting Rights Act since it was written in August 6, 1965. If it wasn't for the Voting Rights Act, it would still be primarily white men in blue suits in Congress.

U. S. Representative John Lewis

I

By 1991, the number of blacks in the Georgia state legislature had grown to thirty-four, almost all of whom were elected from majority-black districts created as a result of litigation and Section 5 of the Voting Rights Act.[1] And as their numbers increased, the members of the legislative black caucus became more influential and more vocal in their demands for greater racial parity in redistricting.

Georgia was awarded an additional seat in the U.S. House of Representatives after the 1990 census, increasing the size of its delegation to eleven members.[2] Only one of the existing districts, the fifth, was majority-black, and it was also the only district represented by an African-American.[3]

When the general assembly took up redistricting in 1991, members of the black caucus urged their colleagues to increase the number of majority-black congressional districts. Tyrone Brooks, one of the leaders of the caucus, pointed out that while blacks were 27 percent of the population of the state, they were a majority in only 10 percent of the districts. He and other caucus members argued that because of racial bloc voting and the history of past discrimination, three majority-minority districts were needed to provide blacks with electoral opportunities roughly in keeping with the black

---

[1] *Black Elected Officials, A National Roster* (Washington, D.C.: Joint Center for Political and Economic Studies, 1991), xxii.
[2] *Miller v. Johnson*, 515 U.S. 900, 906 (1995).
[3] "Congressional Districts of the 103rd Congress," C.Q. Weekly Report, Vol. 51, 3473–87.

percentage of the state's population. A plan showing that it was possible to create three majority-black districts had been prepared for the caucus by the ACLU's Voting Rights Project. Known as the "Max Black" plan, a label that would later be used to discredit it, the plan had been endorsed by the NAACP, the Georgia Association of Black Elected Officials, and SCLC.[4]

The white leadership was prepared to make some concessions to the demands of the black caucus. Since passage of the Voting Rights Act, every one of the state's initial redistricting plans had been rejected by the Department of Justice, which finally convinced the legislature that it had to comply with Section 5. The state was also determined to avoid a repeat of the public censure and embarrassment it had suffered in 1982 at the hands of the federal court in the District of Columbia, which had labelled the chair of the house redistricting committee a "racist" and accused other white leaders in the general assembly of applying a racial double standard. And in view of the increase in size of the delegation, creating an additional majority-black district would be relatively painless politically, because it could be done without jeopardizing the seat of any incumbent.

Before the redistricting process began, both houses adopted guidelines that included avoiding "diluting minority voting strength and . . . comply[ing] with Sections 2 and 5 of the Voting Rights Act." They also agreed to increase the number of majority-black congressional districts from one to two. Bob Hanner, chair of the house reapportionment committee, explained that "we started off this process saying that we were going to meet the mandates of the Justice Department, and the one person/one vote, and not have the purpose of effectively diluting minority strength. And that was a positive thing the committee wanted to do."[5]

After a series of public hearings and work sessions held by the redistricting committees, the general assembly went into special session in August 1991 and adopted a new congressional plan. It contained two majority-minority districts – the fifth, with a 57.8 percent black voting-age population (BVAP), and the eleventh, with a 56.6 percent BVAP. A third district, the second, had a 35.4 percent BVAP.[6]

The state submitted the plan for preclearance, but the attorney general objected to it. The legislative leadership, he concluded, was "predisposed to limit black voting potential to two black majority districts" and had not made a good faith attempt to "recognize the black voting potential of the large concentration of minorities in southwest Georgia" in the area of the second district. He also found that the state had provided only pretextual

[4] *Johnson v. Miller*, Civ. No. 194–008 (S. D. Ga.), trial transcript, Vol. 4, pp. 86, 228, 230, 233.
[5] *Miller v. Johnson*, 515 U.S. at 906; *Johnson v. Miller*, trial transcript, Vol. 2, pp. 37–8, 69, 123; Vol. 3, p. 220.
[6] *Miller v. Johnson*, 515 U.S. at 906; *Johnson v. Miller*, 864 F. Supp. 1354, 1363 n.5 (S. D. Ga. 1994).

reasons for failing to include the minority population of Baldwin County in the eleventh district.[7]

After the objection, the senate passed a plan containing three majority-black districts and increased the black VAP in the eleventh district from 56.6 percent to 58.7 percent. Under the senate plan, the eleventh district included concentrations of black population in southern Dekalb County, Augusta, and Savannah.[8] The house, however, rejected the senate plan.

The second plan enacted by the legislature contained two majority-black districts, the fifth and the eleventh. In response to the attorney general's objections, it slightly increased the black percentage in the eleventh district and boosted the black VAP in the second district to 45 percent. The plan was submitted for preclearance, but once again the attorney general objected. The state remained "predisposed to limit black voting potential to two black majority voting age population districts," he said, and "alternatives including one adopted by the Senate included a large number of black voters from Screven, Effingham and Chatham Counties in the 11th Congressional District."[9]

The state decided not to seek judicial preclearance of its plan from the district court for the District of Columbia. Mark Cohen, the state's chief legal advisor during redistricting, felt that the state's chances of winning judicial approval "were very much harmed by the *Busbee* [1982 congressional] case, that we were in a similar situation because of the Senate's action" in adopting a plan containing three majority-black districts. Rep. Hanner agreed that the plan passed by the senate would cause the court to reject the state's first and second plans.[10]

The state enacted a third plan, and this time it contained three majority-black districts, the fifth (57.5 percent BVAP), the eleventh (60.4 percent BVAP), and the second (52.3 percent BVAP). The plan was precleared on April 2, 1992.[11]

II

From the point of view of racial minorities, the 1992 congressional redistricting was the most successful in the nation's history. Not only were two new majority-black congressional districts created in Georgia, but twelve additional majority-minority districts were drawn in other southern states.[12]

---

[7] *Miller v. Johnson*, 515 U.S. at 906–07; Joint Appendix, pp. 99, 105–7.

[8] Ibid., 515 U.S. at 906–7.

[9] Ibid., p. 907; Joint Appendix, pp. 17–8, 54, 120, 124–26; *Johnson v. Miller*, 864 F. Supp. at 1364 n.5 and 1365.

[10] *Johnson v. Miller*, 864 F. Supp. at 1366 n.11; trial transcript, Vol. 3, pp. 246, 262; Vol. 5, p. 6.

[11] Ibid., 864 F. Supp. at 1366–67.

[12] Bureau of the Census, U.S. Department of Commerce, "Number of Congressional Districts with Black or Hispanic Majorities Doubles Census Bureau Says," *U.S. Department of Commerce News*, Mar. 24, 1993, p. 2.

As a result of the 1992 elections, seventeen blacks were elected to Congress from the eleven states of the old Confederacy, compared to five who had been elected at the preceding elections, and all were elected from majority-minority districts.[13]

Social scientists and the courts have frequently commented on the "tipping phenomenon," a form of racial backlash that occurs when whites perceive that there has been "too much" integration and flee a neighborhood or take their children out of the public schools.[14] The 1992 elections were undoubtedly a tipping event for many whites who believed that their districts had become too black. The disaffected whites did not move, but instead asked the courts to redraw the districts so that whites would again be in the majority and have the ability to exercise their traditional privilege of electing members of Congress.

The first of the so-called wrongful districting cases was *Shaw v. Reno*, decided by the Supreme Court in 1993.[15] It opened a floodgate of challenges by disgruntled whites to majority-minority districts.

The plaintiffs in *Shaw* claimed that North Carolina's congressional redistricting plan was unconstitutional simply because it created two majority-black districts. Alternatively, they argued that the plan was unconstitutional because the two majority-black districts were highly irregular in shape.[16] The district court dismissed the complaint, holding that the creation of majority-black districts was not in itself unconstitutional and that the plaintiffs had failed to allege or prove that the plan diluted white voting strength.[17] Nor could they. While blacks were 20 percent of the voting-age population, they were a majority in only 16.7 percent of the state's congressional districts. On appeal, the Supreme Court reversed. In a 5-4 decision, it held that plaintiffs who alleged that districts were so "bizarre" or "irrational" in shape as to be "unexplainable on grounds other than race" stated a claim under the equal protection clause of the Fourteenth Amendment, and sent the case back for a trial.[18]

Shaw was a significant break with the Court's prior decisions, and it created a number of special rules facilitating challenges by white voters to

---

[13] 1990 U.S. Census, Population and Housing Profile, Congressional Districts of the 103rd Congress, C.Q Weekly Report, Vol. 51, 3473–87.

[14] See, e.g., A. Leon Higginbotham, Jr., et al., "Shaw v. Reno: A Mirage of Good Intentions with Devastating Racial Consequences," 62 Fordham L. Rev. 1593, 1632 n.194 (1994); Richard H. Pildes, "The Politics of Race," 108 Harvard L. Rev. 1359, 1382 (1995) ("[a]s the Black population reaches a critical mass, White voters begin to see Black participation as a credible threat; in reaction, White voters band together and develop more conservative preferences").

[15] 509 U.S. 630 (1993).

[16] *Shaw v. Barr*, 808 F. Supp. 461, 467, 470 (E. D. N. C. 1992).

[17] Ibid., pp. 470–73.

[18] *Shaw v. Reno*, 509 U.S. at 643, 658.

majority-minority districts. One of them was a new cause of action based solely on a district's shape.[19]

Majority-white districts that were highly irregular-looking had been drawn since time immemorial to protect white incumbents. The old eighth district in Louisiana, for example, described by one court as "certainly bizarre" in shape, was drawn to ensure the reelection of a white congressman, Gillis Long.[20] District 6 in Texas, created in the 1960s and known as "Tiger" Teague's district after the white congressman of the same name, spanned an ungainly rural and urban corridor running all the way from Dallas to Houston.[21]

Georgia had also drawn majority-white congressional districts in the 1970s and 1980s that were described derisively in the press and by legislators themselves as "outlandash," looking like "a flamingo's leg," and "based more on rhyme than on reason." None of these districts, despite the occasion they presented for media and political drollery, had ever been thought subject to challenge, because the Supreme Court had ruled that there was no federal constitutional requirement that a district be "attractive" or "compact."[22] Strangely shaped districts were politics as usual, nothing more than the expected efforts of incumbents to ensure their reelection.

In *Shaw*, the Court also relaxed the requirement, to the point of dispensing with it entirely, that white plaintiffs prove they have been personally injured by a challenged redistricting plan. In its prior decisions, the Court had laid down an absolute requirement that a potential plaintiff show a "concrete and particularized" injury in order to have "standing" to bring a case to federal court.[23] Otherwise, the courts would be reduced to settling disputes between mere "bystanders" who had no real interest in the outcome of litigation.[24]

But in *Shaw*, the plaintiffs did not claim that the redistricting plan "diluted" white voting strength. The Court nonetheless found that the plaintiffs had standing because they alleged that their right to participate in a "color-blind" electoral process had been violated. The injury was in being "stereotyped" or "stigmatized" by a racial classification.[25] In prior cases involving black plaintiffs, however, the Court had held that a similar abstract or stigmatic injury was *not* sufficient to confer standing.

In *Allen v. Wright*,[26] for example, black parents had challenged the practice of the Internal Revenue Service of granting tax-exempt status to

[19] Ibid., p. 680 (Justice Souter dissenting).
[20] *Hays v. Louisiana*, 862 F. Supp. 119, 122 (W. D. La. 1994).
[21] *Vera v. Richards*, 861 F. Supp. 1304, 1334 (S. D. Tex. 1994).
[22] *Gaffney v. Cummings*, 412 U.S. 735, 752 n.18 (1973).
[23] *Lujan v. Defenders of Wildlife*, 504 U.S. 555, 560 (1992).
[24] *Allen v. Wright*, 468 U.S. 737, 756 (1984).
[25] *Shaw v. Reno*, 509 U.S. at 641, 643.
[26] 468 U.S. 737 (1984).

discriminatory white private schools on the grounds that it perpetuated segregation and a dual school system. The Court, however, dismissed the complaint on the grounds that the plaintiffs themselves had suffered no concrete or personal injury, and that "stigmatic injury, or denigration" suffered when the government discriminates on the basis of race was insufficient harm to confer standing.[27] The Court in *Shaw* did not explain why the imposition of an alleged racial stigma was an injury to whites but not to blacks.

Shaw also eliminated the requirement that white plaintiffs prove as part of their constitutional claim that the state *intended* to discriminate against them in enacting a challenged redistricting plan. The plaintiffs did not claim that the state's plan was enacted for the purpose of diluting white voting strength. Indeed, the legislature's admitted purpose in creating majority-black districts was the entirely nondiscriminatory one of complying with the Voting Rights Act. The Court reasoned, however, that a racial classification was apparent or "express" where a majority-black district had a "bizarre" shape, and that accordingly "[n]o inquiry into legislative purpose is necessary."[28] That is a standard markedly different from the one applied by the Court in voting and other civil rights cases brought by blacks.

In *City of Mobile v. Bolden*,[29] in dismissing a constitutional challenge by black voters to municipal at-large elections, the Court stressed that "only if there is purposeful discrimination can there be a violation of the Equal Protection Clause." Even proof that black voting strength in the city had been diluted was, according to the Court, "most assuredly insufficient to prove an unconstitutionally discriminatory purpose."[30] Again, the Court failed to explain why dispensing with proof of legislative purpose was appropriate for white, but not for black, voters, or why a racial classification was "express" from a district's shape but not from the operation of a voting system that systematically diluted minority voting strength.

The *Shaw* decision – with its new cause of action based on district shape and its special rules involving standing and proof of purpose – transformed the Fourteenth Amendment in the area of voting rights from a law designed to remedy discrimination against racial minorities[31] to one that could be used to challenge majority-minority districts. Predictably, a lawsuit, *Johnson v. Miller*,[32] was filed soon after *Shaw* claiming that Georgia's congressional plan was unconstitutional.

[27] Ibid., pp. 754–55.
[28] *Shaw v. Reno*, 509 U.S. at 641–42, 635, 655.
[29] 446 U.S. 55, 66 (1980).
[30] Ibid., p. 73.
[31] See *The Slaughter-House Cases*, 83 U.S. (16 Wall) 36, 81 (1873) (the Fourteenth Amendment was adopted to remedy "discrimination against the negroes as a class, or on account of their race").
[32] Civ. No. 194-008 (S. D. Ga.).

III

One of the plaintiffs in the Georgia congressional challenge was George DeLoach, a white man who had been defeated in the 1992 Democratic primary for the eleventh district seat by Cynthia McKinney, an African-American and former member of the state house. DeLoach had moved to the tenth district by the time the complaint was filed, and under Supreme Court precedent lacked standing, as a nonresident, to complain about how the eleventh district had been drawn.[33] The district court, without explanation, refused to dismiss him from the litigation.[34] The United States and a group of black and white residents of the eleventh district, led by Lucious Abrams, a farmer from Burke County, and represented by the ACLU's Voting Rights Project, intervened to defend the challenged plan.

DeLoach and the other plaintiffs claimed that the eleventh district was "segregated" because it was majority-black.[35] They asked the court to redraw it as a majority-white district, not to remedy any injury they had received but so that DeLoach, in their words, could "run again without the outcome being predetermined on the basis of race."[36] Frank Parker, a veteran civil rights lawyer, has described the *Shaw-Miller* plaintiffs "not as injured parties, but as spoilers, intent on eliminating the new majority-black districts as a matter of principle."[37] Although the eleventh district was not as irregular in shape as the district in North Carolina challenged in *Shaw v. Reno*, the district court, in a 2-1 opinion, found it to be unconstitutional. It held that the "contours of the Eleventh District... are so dramatically irregular as to permit no other conclusion than that they were manipulated along racial lines."[38]

The court was especially critical of the Max Black plan and the role that the black caucus and the ACLU had played in redistricting. There was "a direct link," the court said, between the "plan formulated by the ACLU and the preclearance requirements imposed by DOJ." The influence of the ACLU on the U.S. attorney general was "an embarrassment." "The State's leaders were understandably nonplused," the court continued, at the control exercised by the black caucus and the ACLU over the state's redistricting efforts: "The ACLU was exuberant. Georgia officials and citizens were mystified."[39]

One may argue whether members of the black caucus were in fact among the state's "leaders," but one cannot deny, as the district court implicitly

---

33 See *United States v. Hayes*, 515 U.S. 737, 739 (1995).
34 *Johnson v. Miller*, order of Dec. 13, 1995.
35 *Johnson v. Miller*, complaint for declaratory and injunctive relief.
36 *Miller v. Johnson*, brief for appellees, p. 29 n. 28.
37 Frank R. Parker, "The Constitutionality of Racial Redistricting: A Critique of *Shaw v. Reno*," 3 D. Col. L. Rev. 1, 9 (1995).
38 *Johnson v. Miller*, 864 F. Supp. at 1378.
39 Ibid., p. 1368.

Cynthia McKinney, the representative from the majority-black eleventh congressional district that was declared unconstitutional by a federal court in Augusta on September 12, 1994 (photo by Ellen Spears).

does, that they were "Georgia officials and citizens." For certainly *they* were not nonplussed or mystified by the role that they and the ACLU had played in redistricting, or by the state's adoption of a plan creating three majority-black districts.

It should be obvious, moreover, that the attorney general has a positive duty to consult with minorities, and their representatives, on whether or not a submission should be precleared. They are, after all, the very group that the statute was designed to protect. It would be unrealistic in any event to expect a submitting jurisdiction to point out the ways in which its proposed voting changes violated Section 5. If it were inappropriate for the attorney general to confer with racial minorities in evaluating proposed voting changes, preclearance would in practice be a one-sided, largely meaningless affair.

While it invalidated the challenged congressional plan, the district court acknowledged the transcendent importance of race in the political life of the state and dispensed with any requirement that it be proved. "No one can deny," the court said, "that State and local governments of Georgia in the past utilized widespread, pervasive practices to segregate the races which had the effect of repressing Black citizens, individually and as a group."[40]

The state, the minority intervenors, and the United States appealed the decision of the district court, but the Supreme Court affirmed in another 5-4 decision. It did not find that the eleventh district was bizarrely shaped, but it held that the state had "subordinated" its traditional redistricting principles to race without having a compelling reason for doing so. The Court criticized the plan for splitting counties and municipalities and for joining black neighborhoods by the use of narrow, sparsely populated "land bridges." And according to the Court, compliance with the attorney general's Section 5 objection was not a compelling state interest justifying adoption of the plan, because the Department of Justice had adopted a policy of maximizing the number of majority-black districts that "was not required by the Voting Rights Act under a correct reading of the statute."[41]

One of the extraordinary things about the opinion of the majority of the Supreme Court was that it did not mention, much less discuss, the social and historical conditions in the state, including the history of discrimination and the persistence of racial bloc voting. Instead, it indulged the purest fiction of a color-blind political process that, in its view, majority-black districts offended. No decision involving minority voting rights that ignores the evidence of discrimination and racial bloc voting can claim to have been reliably decided.

Justice Ginsburg, in a dissenting opinion, remedied the omissions of the majority. She recited much of the history of discrimination in voting in Georgia and concluded that the eleventh district merely recognized a minority community defined by actual shared interests. "[S]tate legislatures," she wrote, "may recognize communities that have a particular racial or ethnic makeup, even in the absence of any compulsion to do so, in order to account for interests common to or shared by the persons grouped together."[42]

Justice Ginsburg also concluded that the state had not subordinated its traditional redistricting principles to race. The eleventh district split eight counties, but that was "about the state average in divided counties."[43] Splitting counties was not if any case a violation of the state's traditional redistricting principles. That was apparent from the configuration of the sixth district, in which *all* the counties were split. Democratic house speaker Tom Murphy would not allow any plan to be drawn that put the county in which he lived, Harrelson County, in the sixth district. The reason that his county had to be excluded was that the sixth district was represented by a Republican, Newt Gingrich, whom Murphy loathed. "Congressman Gingrich and I never got

[40] Ibid., statement of judicial notice.
[41] *Miller v. Johnson*, 515 U.S. at 908, 921.
[42] Ibid., p. 935.
[43] Ibid., p. 941.

along," Murphy said. "We didn't talk. We didn't like each other and I just wanted out of his district."[44] According to the state's demographer, the consequence of accommodating Murphy's anti-Gingrich bias was that "all the counties got split in the Sixth."[45]

As for land bridges, many of them had been created to accommodate members of the legislature, and not for reasons of race. The eleventh district was drawn in an irregular manner near the eastern border of DeKalb County at the request of an incumbent senator so that the majority-white precinct in which his son lived could be included in the district. The district was drawn as a narrow corridor through Effingham County at the request of a white state representative. It was drawn in Savannah by "the narrowest means possible" at the request of another white legislator. The district was trimmed to exclude a black community in Garden City because a state representative wanted to keep the city intact inside the neighboring first district. The eleventh district was not, as Justice Ginsburg concluded, "an outlier district shaped without reference to familiar districting techniques."[46]

The Supreme Court sent the Georgia case back to the district court for the adoption of a new plan. On remand, the district court allowed the plaintiffs to amend their complaint in order to challenge the majority-black second district, which the court then held was unconstitutional for the same reasons that it had found the eleventh district to be unconstitutional.[47] The court gave the legislature an opportunity to enact a remedial plan.

Governor Zell Miller issued a call for the legislature to convene in special session on August 14, 1995, to adopt a new plan. But after several weeks of wrangling and uncertainty over how to apply the Court's decision, the legislature adjourned without adopting a congressional plan. Peg Blitch, the chair of the senate reapportionment committee, lamented that "[w]e have heard from five different attorneys and we have received five different interpretations." She confessed that "[n]obody knows what they're doing."[48]

After the legislature failed to redistrict the congressional delegation, the district court issued its own plan on December 13, 1995. And it delivered its strongest, most emotionally laden condemnation of the role that the Department of Justice had played in the state's redistricting. "The positions taken by the Department of Justice...are, in my view, no red herring," one of the members of the three-judge court said from the bench. "They go to the center of the reason for this litigation. Not a herring at

---

[44] *Johnson v. Miller*, trial transcript, Vol. 2, p. 77.

[45] Ibid., Vol. 3, p. 729.

[46] *Miller v. Johnson*, 515 U.S. at 943.

[47] *Johnson v. Miller*, 922 F. Supp. 1552, 1553 (S. D. Ga. 1995).

[48] *Atlanta Journal and Constitution*, August 2, 1995.

all, but a Mackerel that is dead on the beach shining and stinking in the moonlight."[49]

The court's plan, a complete remapping of the state, contained only one majority-black district. The court relocated the eleventh district to "the Northeast Atlanta corridor," where it would have an "urban/suburban flavor."[50] Not a single county in the old eleventh was included in the new eleventh.

The court reduced the black VAP in the eleventh district from 60 percent to 11 percent, and in the second district from 52 percent to 35 percent. The court did hold, however, that a majority-black district in the metropolitan area of Atlanta was required by Section 2. Because of racial bloc voting, a district containing "the percentage of black registered voters as close to fifty-five percent as possible was necessary . . . to avoid dilution of the Fifth District minorities' rights."[51]

One of the principal justifications given by the district court for relocating the eleventh district to the northeast Atlanta corridor was that the new district followed a progression of counties, from metropolitan Atlanta to the South Carolina line, that "have Interstate Eighty-Five as a very real connecting cable."[52] Ironically, it was the configuration of the twelfth congressional district in North Carolina along the very same interstate that had drawn the sharpest criticism of the district and prompted the Supreme Court to conclude that it was subject to constitutional challenge. In *Shaw*, the Court described the twelfth district as being "unusually shaped," "bizarre," and "irrational on its face" because for much of its length it closely followed "the I-85 corridor."[53] Constructing a district along a major highway can, therefore, be evidence of "bizarreness" and "irrationality" or "a very real connecting cable" depending entirely on the redistricting outcome one favors.

The sweeping changes made by the district court in the state's congressional plan predictably drew criticism that the court, two of whose members were Democratic appointees, had acted out of partisan bias. Republican congressman John Linder groused that "[i]t appears that the two Democratic judges tried to draw a map for white Democrats. What [Georgia house speaker] Tom Murphy couldn't get done on the floor of the Legislature he got the judges to do for him."[54] The chair of the Georgia Democratic Party gloated that "[t]he changes that were made favored us in virtually every

---

[49] *Johnson v. Miller*, transcript of hearing, pp. 109–10, Dec. 13, 1995, comments of Judge Bowen.
[50] *Johnson v. Miller*, 922 F. Supp. at 1566, 1563–64.
[51] Ibid., pp. 1568, 1570–71 (Appendices A and B to the opinion of the district court).
[52] Ibid., p. 1564.
[53] 509 U.S. at 635, 644, 658.
[54] *Atlanta Journal and Constitution*, Dec. 14, 1995.

district."[55] Press accounts commented that the plan had been drawn in a way "that benefits white Democrats."[56]

Despite the advantages Democrats believed they had gained under the new court-ordered plan, only three Democrats were elected to Congress when the plan was implemented in 1996. John Lewis, the Democratic incumbent, was elected from the majority-black fifth district. Cynthia McKinney and Sanford Bishop, the black Democratic incumbents from the old eleventh and second districts, had been drawn into newly configured majority-white districts, the fourth and second respectively, but were able to win reelection.

Under the court-ordered plan, which was based on the 1990 census, the new second district was 39.2 percent black, and the new fourth district was 36.6 percent black.[57] The 2000 census, however, showed that the second district was 40.9 percent black, while the fourth district, based on total population, was in fact majority-black (50.6 percent). The voting-age population in the district was 45.9 percent black.[58]

Georgia had appealed the decision of the district court invalidating the eleventh district. But it refused to appeal the court's redistricting order. The Abrams intervenors and the United States filed notices of appeal, and the state switched sides and joined the white plaintiffs in defending the court-ordered plan.

No doubt believing that the Supreme Court would not require it to draw more than one majority-black district, the state, under white Democratic control, did a remarkable about-face and reinvented the facts surrounding the first redistricting plan that it had adopted in 1991, containing two majority-black districts. In its brief in the Supreme Court in the first case involving the eleventh district, the state had argued that the 1991 plan was a reasonable expression of state policy and that race was not the predominant factor in redistricting:

It is undisputed that the General Assembly as a whole found the initial [1991 congressional redistricting] plan enacted to be reasonable. It was not perceived as a 'racial gerrymander.'... *There is, in fact, no evidence that any legislator or reapportionment staffer ever believed the initial plan to be offensive as a racial gerrymander.*[59]

The state had repeatedly stressed "the undisputed consensus of all of the legislators involved – both white and black, Republican and Democrat – that the first plan was reasonable."[60]

55 *Washington Post*, Dec. 15, 1995.
56 *Atlanta Journal*, Dec. 20, 1995.
57 *Johnson v. Miller*, 922 F. Supp. at 1571.
58 William Cooper, "Georgia Congressional Districts, Federal Court Districts Based on Census 2000 Population Results," August 2, 2001.
59 *Miller v. Johnson*, No. 94–631, brief of appellants Miller, p. 49, emphasis in original.
60 Ibid., p. 18.

But in the case involving the new court-ordered plan, the state took an entirely different view of things. To the extent that the legislature had initially drawn a plan containing two majority-black districts, the state now argued, there was "uncontradicted evidence that that was the product of the perceived need to do so in order to satisfy the DOJ's demands." The 1991 plan, formerly described as "reasonable" and supported by "the undisputed consensus of all of the legislators," was now dismissed as the tainted product of "the illegal excesses of the DOJ."[61]

The Supreme Court, in yet another 5-4 vote, upheld the district court's remedial plan. The state's decision in 1991 to create two majority-black districts was not entitled to deference, according to the Court, because it was the result of "pressure" and "[i]nterference" by the Attorney General and was made "in the shadow of the Justice Department's max-black goal." But as the four dissenters pointed out, the Department of Justice's direct involvement "took place *after adoption* of the 1991 Plan."[62]

In reaching its decision, the majority of the Court cited the election of McKinney and Bishop as evidence of a "general willingness" of whites to vote for black candidates.[63] But despite the white votes they received, the voting in McKinney's and Bishop's elections was still racially polarized.

In the Democratic primary, McKinney got only 13 percent of the white vote. She won the nomination because she got most of the black vote, and whites mainly stayed home or voted in the Republican primary. White turnout was extremely low – only 11 percent of registered voters compared to 31 percent for blacks. As a consequence, the electorate in the Democratic primary was majority-black.[64]

In the general election, running in a heavily Democratic district, McKinney increased her percentage of the white vote, but voting was still along racial lines. Most blacks again voted for McKinney, while approximately 70 percent of whites voted for her white Republican opponent.[65]

The voting in the new second district was similarly polarized. In the general election, Bishop got most of the black vote, but approximately 61 percent of whites voted for his white opponent.[66] The Court's conclusion to the contrary notwithstanding, in the Bishop and McKinney elections most whites were generally *not* willing to vote for a black candidate.

McKinney has credited her victory to the fact that she was initially elected in a majority-black district (the old Eleventh) and thus had an opportunity

---

[61] *Abrams v. Johnson*, No. 95-1425, brief of appellees Miller, pp. 10, 25.
[62] *Abrams v. Johnson*, 521 U.S. 74, 106 (1977) (Justice Breyer dissenting), emphasis in original.
[63] Ibid., p. 92.
[64] Allan J. Lichtman, "Table 1, Ecological Regression Estimates: Black versus White Elections 1996 U.S. House Elections, State of Georgia, Bloc Voting"; "Table 3, Ecological Regression Estimates: Black v. White Elections, 1996 U.S. House Elections, State of Georgia, Turnout" (copy on file with author).
[65] Ibid.
[66] Ibid.

to establish a track record of service to constituents of both races and to ameliorate white fears over being represented by a black.[67] Nonincumbent blacks, by contrast, who ran in majority-white congressional districts in 1996 in Arkansas, Mississippi, and Texas all lost.[68]

The power of incumbency is substantial and is generally regarded as the single best indicator of outcome.[69] Not only do incumbents have franking privileges, they generally have greater name recognition, support from their colleagues, and better access to campaign contributions than their challengers. Nationwide, more than 90 percent of incumbent house members who sought reelection in 1996 won, including all eleven incumbents from Georgia.[70] And incumbency aside, the fact that the new fourth district in reality had a majority-black population was undoubtedly a major factor in McKinney's reelection.

The recent elections may be a sign of a gradual change in voter attitudes. If so, they will underscore the value of highly integrated majority-minority districts to voters of all races in helping to ameliorate the affliction of racial bloc voting. But given the persistence of voting patterns over time in the South, it is surely premature to claim that the electorate is suddenly colorblind and that racial bloc voting no longer exists.[71]

IV

The state also adopted new legislative redistricting in 1991 and for the first time used all single-member districts for both houses. The attorney general

---

[67] Cynthia A. McKinney, "A Product of the Voting Rights Act," *Washington Post*, Nov. 26, 1996, p. A15 ("my victory says more about the power of incumbency than anything else").

[68] David A. Bositis, "The Future of Majority-Minority Districts and Black and Hispanic Legislative Representation," in David A. Bositis, ed., *Redistricting and Minority Representation* (Lanham, Md.: University Press of America, 1998), 38–9. Vincent Tolliver was defeated in Arkansas's fourth district (6 percent black VAP), Kevin Antoine was defeated in Mississippi's fourth district (37 percent black VAP), and Teresa Doggett was defeated in Texas's tenth district (10 percent black VAP). Ibid.

[69] Ibid., p. 16. See also Gary King and A. Gelman, "Systematic Consequences of Incumbency Advantage in U.S. House Elections," 35 Am. J. Pol. Sci. 110, 112–16 (1991) (estimating the incumbency advantage over the last decade to be between six and twelve percentage points); Gary C. Jacobson, "The 1994 House Elections in Perspective," 111 Pol. Sci. Q. 203, 213–14 (1996) (concluding, on the basis of the 1994 elections, that the incumbency advantage was ten percentage points).

[70] *Washington Post*, Nov. 23, 1996; *New York Times*, Nov. 23, 1996.

[71] See Bositis, "The Future of Majority-Minority Districts," 15 ("[d]espite the noteworthy election of four black U.S. representatives in majority-white districts in 1996, there is little reason to believe that any significant barrier has been breached or that electoral politics in the United States have become de-racialized to any significant degree"); Richard H. Pildes, "The Politics of Race," 108 Harv. L. Rev. 1359, 1361 (1995) (describing the color-blind model of politics in the South as "among the great myths currently distorting public discussion").

precleared the change to districts but objected to certain features of the house and senate plans. He concluded that the legislature had fragmented concentrations of black population in a number of areas of the state in order to minimize the number of majority-black districts and to ensure the reelection of white incumbents at the expense of black voters.[72]

The state enacted a second plan, but it too drew an objection, and for basically the same reasons that the first plan had been rejected. The plan continued to "minimize overall black voting strength" in the state in an effort to protect incumbent legislators.[73]

The general assembly enacted a third plan in 1992, which was precleared. It created thirteen majority-black senate districts, an increase of five over the 1980 plan, and forty-one majority-black house districts, an increase of eleven over the 1980 plan. As in the past, black electoral success was confined almost exclusively to the majority-minority districts. Of the forty blacks elected to the house and senate under the 1992 plan, all but one was elected from a majority-black district. The lone exception was Keith Heard from house district 89 (42 percent black) in Clarke County, the home of the University of Georgia. Whites, on the other hand, not only won all but one of the majority-white districts, but also won fourteen (26 percent) of the majority-black districts.[74]

The ink had scarcely dried on the first decision in the congressional case when the lawyers for the plaintiffs publicly announced that they intended to take the state to court over its legislative redistricting as well. They claimed that seventeen house and five senate districts had been "racially gerrymandered."[75]

During its special session in 1995, the legislature was unable to redistrict the congressional delegation, but it did redistrict the house and senate. Using the threat of litigation as an occasion, or an excuse, it reduced the black percentages in thirteen districts.

Robert Holmes, a longtime member of the house and a political science professor at Atlanta University, has described redistricting as "a struggle for political survival" in which "everyone seeks to maximize his or her own position." Reducing the black population in the house and senate districts was an example of that struggle, he says, and was designed primarily to protect white incumbents, some of whom were among the leadership in the general assembly. According to Holmes, the "real agenda" of the house

---

72 John R. Dunne to Mark H. Cohen, Jan. 21, 1992.
73 John R. Dunne to Mark H. Cohen, Mar. 20, 1992.
74 Members of the Georgia General Assembly, Senate and House of Representatives, Second Session of 1993–94 Term (1994); *Johnson v. Miller*, Civ. No. 194-008 (S. D. Ga.), trial transcript, Vol. 4, p. 237; Stipulations Nos. 61–63; Joint Ex. 11.
75 Robert A. Holmes, "Reapportionment Strategies in the 1990s: The Case of Georgia," in Bernard Grofman, ed., *Race and Redistricting in the 1990s* (New York: Agathon Press, 1998), 212.

leadership was not concern that its plan might be challenged in court, but protection of "white Democratic committee chairs, the Majority Leader, and a few other close allies of [house] Speaker Murphy."[76]

In the senate, the black percentages in two majority-black districts represented by whites were reduced from 62 percent to 43 percent and from 59 percent to 42 percent. In the house, the black percentages were reduced in eleven majority-black districts. In district 141, represented by white majority leader Larry Walker, the black percentage was dropped from 59 percent to 26 percent. In district 159, represented by white committee chair Bob Hanner, the black percentage was lowered from 62 percent to 43 percent. In district 178, represented by another white committee chair, Henry Reaves, the black percentage was reduced from 63 percent to 27 percent. The black percentages were also reduced to voting-age minorities in two districts with black incumbents, districts 31 (Carl Von Epps) and 173 (E. C. Tillman).[77]

The total losses in majority-black districts were two in the senate and eight in the house. The state submitted the new plan for preclearance, confident that this reduction in minority voting strength would be approved by the Department of Justice in light of the recent congressional redistricting decisions.

The plaintiffs in the congressional case, despite the fact that a new plan had been adopted and submitted for preclearance, filed suit challenging the 1992 legislative plan. They now claimed that twelve of the state's senate districts and twentysix of its house districts were unconstitutional.[78] The attorney general initially objected to the special session plan but withdrew the objection on October 15, 1996.

Five months later, after court-ordered mediation, the parties settled the lawsuit. They agreed upon a plan that reduced the number of majority-black senate districts from eleven to ten compared to the 1995 special session plan, and the number of majority-black house districts from thirtythree to thirty.

From the point of view of black voters and the black caucus, the settlement was an exercise in damage control based on the likelihood that the court would have abolished even more of the majority-black districts. And though the total number of majority-black districts was reduced, the number of black caucus members at the beginning of the 1998 legislative term stood at forty-four, an increase of four compared to 1993.[79] Most of the formerly majority-black districts that had been converted into majority-white districts had elected whites in the first place. And in those that elected blacks, the incumbents, such as Von Epps, were able to hold onto their seats.

[76] Holmes, "Reapportionment Strategics," 207, 214.

[77] Ibid., p. 218.

[78] *Johnson v. Miller*, Civ. No. 196-040 (S. D. Ga.).

[79] Joint Center for Political and Economic Studies, "Number of Black Elected Officials in the United States, by State and Office, January 1998" ⟨www.jointctr.org⟩.

V

The origins of the Supreme Court's new redistricting decisions can be traced to changes in the composition of the Court in the 1980s and early 1990s. A new majority emerged that was generally hostile to civil rights and increasingly receptive to "reverse discrimination" claims by whites that they had been unfairly treated in employment, school admissions, and the awarding of government contracts. In a series of cases, the Court invalidated teacher layoff provisions in an affirmative action agreement,[80] declared unconstitutional a municipal set-aside for minority contractors,[81] and held that "all racial classifications, imposed by whatever federal, state, or local governmental actor" were constitutionally suspect.[82]

In striking down majority-black districts in Georgia and North Carolina, the majority of the Court drew heavily upon its affirmative action cases, indicating that majority-minority districts were simply another form of race-based preference.[83] Whether or not one thinks the affirmative action cases were rightly decided, their application to redistricting ignores the fundamental distinction between the race-conscious allocation of scarce employment or contractual opportunities and the far different task of reconciling the claims of political, ethnic, racial, and other groups in the redistricting process. Providing minorities with an effective political voice involves equal, not preferential, treatment.[84]

The other premises upon which the Court's recent redistricting decisions rest are also deeply flawed. In the Court's view, creating nonwhite-majority districts is a form of "segregation" that harms individuals and society.[85] Individuals are harmed because of "the offensive and demeaning assumption that voters of a particular race, because of their race, 'think alike, share the same political interests, and will prefer the same candidates at the polls.'" Society is allegedly harmed because "'[r]acial gerrymandering ... may balkanize us into competing racial factions.'"[86] Beguiling as these appeals to race neutrality may be, they are not supported by experience or the facts.

The majority-minority districts in Georgia created after the 1990 census, far from being segregated, were the most racially integrated districts in the state. They contained an average of 43 percent nonblack voters. No one familiar with Jim Crow could ever confuse, as a majority of the Court

---

[80] *Wygant v. Jackson Board of Education*, 476 U.S. 267, 284 (1986).

[81] *City of Richmond v. J. A. Croson Co.*, 488 U.S. 469, 494 (1989).

[82] *Adarand Constructors, Inc. v. Pena*, 515 U.S. 200, 227 (1995).

[83] *Miller v. Johnson*, 515 U.S. at 904 (citing *City of Richmond v. J. A. Croson Co.*, 488 U.S. at 494; *Adarand Constructors, Inc. v. Pena*, 515 U.S. at 224; and *Wygant v. Jackson Board of Education*, 476 U.S. at 274).

[84] See *Shaw v. Reno*, 509 U.S. at 675 ("efforts to remedy minority vote dilution are wholly unlike what typically has been labeled 'affirmative action'") (Justice White, dissenting).

[85] Ibid., p. 641.

[86] *Miller v. Johnson*, 515 U.S. at 912.

does, Georgia's highly integrated 1992 districts with racial segregation under which blacks were not allowed to vote or run for office. As Justice Stevens has put it, plans containing majority-minority districts are a form of "racial integration."[87]

Moreover, the notion that majority-black districts are "segregated," and that the only integrated districts are those in which whites are in the majority, is precisely the sort of race-based concept that the Supreme Court says it deplores. A constitutional doctrine that can tolerate only what is majority-white in redistricting is a perversion of the concept of equal treatment embodied in the Fourteenth Amendment.

The Court also erred in thinking that race is merely an "assumption" or a "stereotype." Race is admittedly not a scientific fact or a genetic condition, but it is a social and political reality.

Open appeals to race of the sort that had characterized the Jackson–Massell election in the 1970s and congressional redistricting in the 1980s had fallen out of favor by the 1990s. But some mainstream white politicians were still willing to interject race into a campaign, either subtly or overtly, when they thought it was to their advantage to do so.

In the 1992 Democratic primary for state labor commissioner, the David Poythress for Labor Commissioner Campaign made sure that voters knew that Poythress's opponent, Al Scott, was black. The campaign ran ads containing a prominent picture of Scott and accusing him of exploiting women and supporting nude dancing. Scott was a former state senator and had been appointed by Governor Zell Miller a year earlier to fill the unexpired term of labor commissioner. Running as the incumbent, he received a plurality in the primary, but in the ensuing runoff against Poythress he lost with 43 percent of the vote. Scott failed in his bid to become the first black in the modern era to be elected to a nonjudicial statewide office through a combination of the state's majority-vote requirement and racial campaign ads that, as noted in the press, "coyly highlight that Mr. Scott is black and Mr. Poythress is white."[88]

Mitch Skandalakis, the chair of the Fulton County Commission, resorted to even clumsier racial tactics in 1994 in an effort to help a political ally who was challenging a black incumbent member of the commission, Gordon Joyner. Skandalakis paid for a campaign flier that contained a crudely distorted picture of the light-skinned Joyner. His face was darkened, his lips were thickened, and an Afro hairdo was painted on his head.[89]

---

[87] Ibid., p. 932 (Justice Stevens dissenting).

[88] *Atlanta Journal and Constitution*, July 16, August 10, August 12, 1992; *Wheeler County Eagle*, August 5, 1992; *Brooks v. Miller*, Civ. No. 1:90-CV-1001-RCF (N. D. Ga.), Pl. Ex. 302 (runoff election sequences).

[89] *Atlanta Journal and Constitution*, Oct. 21, 1998; Oct. 30, 1998; June 21, 2000.

Skandalakis ran for lieutenant governor in 1998, and in another effort to appeal to white prejudice linked his opponent, Mark Taylor, with Atlanta's black mayor, Bill Campbell. In one advertisement, Skandalakis labeled Campbell an "incompetent boob" and, adopting the scare tactics of Sam Massell when he attempted to discredit Maynard Jackson in their 1973 mayoral contest, said that he would "kick Atlanta's ass and bring it in line before the city of Atlanta kills the state." A second political advertisement accused Taylor of favoring removal of the Confederate flag emblem from the state flag and showed him embracing Campbell. Whether or not the racial appeals backfired, Skandalakis was defeated by Taylor in the general election.[90]

Some whites were clearly unhappy about being drawn into majority-minority districts, but there is no evidence that such districts have been an independent cause of racial division, or have created it where it did not exist before. There is also no evidence that majority-minority districts have increased social or other kinds of harm. In 1982, opponents of the amendment of Section 2 claimed that the creation of majority-minority districts would "deepen the tensions, fragmentation and outright resentment among racial groups," "pit race against race," "foster polarization," and "compel the worst tendencies toward race-based allegiances and divisions."[91] Congress considered these claims and rejected them because there was no evidence to support them. It concluded that the amendment would not "be a divisive factor in local communities by emphasizing the role of racial politics." It found there was "an extensive, reliable and reassuring track record of court decisions using the very standard which the Committee bill would codify."[92]

None of the modern redistricting cases, moreover, indicates that any of the theoretical harms suggested by the majority of the Supreme Court have in fact come to pass. In the Georgia cases, the witnesses at trial testified without contradiction that the challenged plan had not increased racial tension, caused segregation, imposed a racial stigma, deprived anyone of representation, caused harm, or guaranteed blacks congressional seats.[93] In the face of such evidence, the district court concluded that "the plaintiffs suffered no

---

[90] *Atlanta Journal and Constitution*, June 21, 2000.

[91] Hearings before the Subcommittee on the Constitution of the Committee on the Judiciary, United States Senate, Ninety-seventh Congress, Second Session, on S. 53, S. 1761, S. 1975, S. 1992. and H.R. 3112, Bills to Amend the Voting Rights Act of 1965, January 27, 28, February 1, 2, 4, 11, 12, 25, and March 1, 1982, p. 662, statement of John H. Bunzel; p. 745, statement of Michael Levin; p. 1238, statement of Donald L. Horowitz; p. 1449, letter from William Van Alstyne.

[92] S. Rep. No. 417, 97th Cong., 2d Sess., 31–2 (1982), reprinted in 1982 U.S. Code Cong. & Adm. News 209.

[93] *Johnson v. Miller*, trans. Vol. 3, p. 268; Vol. 4, pp. 194, 106, 239, 240, 242; Vol. 6, pp. 36, 38, 45, 47, 56, 58, 117, 120.

individual harm; the 1992 congressional redistricting plans had no adverse consequences for white voters."[94]

Even if the creation of majority-minority districts *had* generated significant racial tension and polarization, that would not be a principled basis for maintaining the districts as majority-white. There is no question that allowing blacks to register and vote in places like Terrell, Sumter, and Webster Counties was deeply traumatizing for many whites and exacerbated racial tension. But that would not justify excluding blacks from the franchise, any more than white opposition to school desegregation would justify maintaining segregated schools. As Justice Frankfurter noted in one of the Supreme Court's school desegregation cases, "resistance to law cannot be made a legal reason for its suspension without loosening the fabric of our society."[95]

Perhaps the most troubling aspect of the Supreme Court's recent redistricting decisions is their double standard, depending on whether a district is majority-black or majority-white. A number of oddly shaped majority-white congressional districts were drawn during the 1990s. The *Congressional Quarterly* has described district 4 in Tennessee (96 percent white) as "a long, sprawling district, extending nearly 300 miles ... from east to west it touches four States – Mississippi, Alabama, Kentucky, and Virginia." The eleventh district in Virginia (81 percent white) has "a shape that vaguely recalls the human digestive tract." District 9 in Washington (85 percent white) has a "'Main Street' [which] is a sixty-mile stretch of Interstate 5." District 13 in Ohio (94 percent white) "centers around two distinct sets of communities... [t]he Ohio Turnpike is all that connects the two." District 3 in Massachusetts (94 percent white), dubbed the "Ivy League" district, "stretches from the town of Princeton in central Massachusetts to Dartmouth on the southeastern coast."[96] (The schools by those names, however, are located in other states.) No court has ever held or suggested that any of these oddly shaped majority-white districts were constitutionally suspect.

A racial double standard was starkly evident in a challenge brought after *Shaw* to congressional redistricting in Texas. The plaintiffs challenged twentyfour of the state's thirty congressional districts, eighteen of which were majority-white. The district court invalidated just three districts – the only two that were majority-black and one that was majority-Hispanic. The court admitted that the other districts were irregular or bizarre in shape – "[t]o call these districts 'configured' in any sense that implies order would be a misnomer" – but said that they were constitutional because they were "disfigured less to favor or disadvantage one race or ethnic group than to

94 *Johnson v. Miller*, 864 F. 2d at 1370.
95 *Cooper v. Aaron*, 358 U.S. 1, 22 (1958) (Justice Frankfurter concurring).
96 Phil Duncan, ed., *Congressional Quarterly's Politics in America* (Washington, D.C.: Congressional Quarterly Press, 1994), 103rd Congress, 724, 1210, 1418, 1602, 1635.

promote the re-election of incumbents."[97] Thus, the oddly shaped majority-white districts designed to keep white incumbents in office were tolerable as "political" gerrymanders, while the oddly shaped majority-black districts designed to permit the election of minority candidates were intolerable as "racial" gerrymanders.

On appeal, the Supreme Court affirmed. According to Justice Kennedy, "[d]istricts not drawn for impermissible [racial] reasons or according to impermissible criteria may take any shape, even a bizarre one."[98] The Court had stressed in *Shaw* that "reapportionment is one area in which appearances do matter."[99] In light of the Texas case, one can conclude that appearances do indeed matter, but only if the districts are majority-black or majority-Hispanic.

Prior to the 1990s, the Supreme Court frequently noted that one of the essential purposes of redistricting was to "reconcile the competing claims of political, religious, ethnic, racial, occupational, and socioeconomic groups."[100] For that and other reasons, "legislators necessarily make judgments about the probability that the members of certain identifiable groups, whether racial, ethnic, economic, or religious, will vote in the same way."[101] As Justice White has observed, "lawmakers are quite aware that the districts they create will have a white or black majority; and with each new district comes the unavoidable choice as to the racial composition of the district."[102] According to Justice Brennan, "[i]t would be naive to suppose that racial considerations do not enter into apportionment decisions."[103] Linda Meggers, Georgia's chief demographer, who has drawn hundreds of redistricting plans at the federal, state, and local levels over the past two decades, has acknowledged that race is always a consideration in redistricting. "[I have] never drawn a redistricting plan...that didn't take race into account," she says. "[I]f taking race into account were unlawful...there is not a redistricting plan in the State of Georgia that would be valid."[104]

Voting districts have regularly been drawn to accommodate the interests of white racial or ethnic groups, such as Irish Catholics in San Francisco, Italian-Americans in South Philadelphia, Polish-Americans in Chicago, and Anglo-Saxons in north Georgia.[105] In light of *Shaw* and *Miller*, black and

97 *Vera v. Richards*, 861 F. Supp. at 1309 and n.4, 1343–44.
98 *Bush v. Vera*, 517 U.S. 952, 999 (1996) (Justice Kennedy concurring).
99 *Shaw v. Reno*, 509 U.S. at 647.
100 *Davis v. Bandemer*, 478 U.S. 109, 147 (1986) (Justice O'Connor concurring).
101 *City of Mobile v. Bolden*, 465 U.S. at 87 (Justice Stevens concurring).
102 *Beer v. United States*, 425 U.S. 130, 144 (1976) (Justice White dissenting).
103 *United Jewish Organizations of Williamsburg, Inc. v. Carey*, 430 U.S. 144, 176 n. 4 (1977) (Justice Brennan concurring).
104 *Johnson v. Miller*, trial transcript, Vol. 2, p. 265.
105 *Miller v. Johnson*, 515 U.S. at 945 (Justice Ginsburg dissenting); *Busbee v. Smith*, 549 F. Supp. 494, 502 (D. D. C. 1982) (in the state's 1980 congressional plan, "keeping the cohesive [majority white] mountain counties together was crucial").

brown minorities are now the only groups that are targeted for special disadvantages in redistricting. White groups of all descriptions – political, religious, occupational, socioeconomic – may pursue a common political agenda
in the redistricting process and seek the construction of districts in which their
members are in the majority. Only the comparable efforts of nonwhites are
subject to the exacting and debilitating standards of strict scrutiny. Such a
result cannot be reconciled with the purpose of the Fourteenth Amendment,
which was to confer equal rights upon racial minorities.[106]

From a purely practical standpoint, the standards announced by the Court
in *Shaw* and *Miller* are contradictory and unmanageable. A legislature may
properly "be aware of racial demographics," the Court said, but it may not
allow race to "predominate" in the redistricting process. A state "is free
to recognize communities that have a particular racial makeup, provided
its action is directed toward some common thread of relevant interests."[107]
Redistricting may be performed "with consciousness of race." Indeed, it
would be "irresponsible" for a state to disregard the racial fairness provisions of the Voting Rights Act. A state may therefore "create a majority-
minority district without awaiting judicial findings" if it has a strong basis
in evidence for avoiding a Voting Rights Act violation.[108] The majority itself has acknowledged that it "may be difficult" to make and apply such
distinctions.[109]

The four justices who dissented in the *Shaw* cases have said that the Court's
new standards are "unworkable," lack "a definable constitutional core," and
"rende[r] redistricting perilous work for state legislatures."[110] Exhibit A for
that proposition is the *Shaw* litigation itself.

The issue of the constitutionality of North Carolina's congressional redistricting was before the Supreme Court four times within the decade:
an 1993, when it reversed the trial court for dismissing the plaintiffs'
complaint; in 1996, when it reversed the trial court again for upholding
the challenged plan;[111] in 1999, when it reversed the trial court a third
time for summarily invalidating the remedial plan drawn by the legislature in 1997, in which the challenged twelfth district was only 47 percent black;[112] and in 2001, when it reversed the trial court for a fourth
time after concluding that the state's remedial plan was constitutional

---

[106] *Shaw v. Reno*, 509 U.S. at 679 (Justice Stevens dissenting).
[107] *Miller v. Johnson*, 515 U.S. at 916, 920.
[108] *Bush v. Vera*, 517 U.S. at 958, 993, 994.
[109] *Miller v. Johnson*, 515 U.S. at 916.
[110] *Abrams v. Johnson*, 521 U.S. at 116 (Justice Breyer dissenting); Bush v. Vera, 517 U.S. at 1074
       ("[t]he Court has been unable to provide workable standards") (Justice Souter dissenting);
       at 1005 (Justice Stevens dissenting); *Miller v. Johnson*, 515 U.S. at 949 (Justice Ginsburg
       dissenting).
[111] *Shaw v. Hunt*, 517 U.S. 899 (1996).
[112] *Hunt v. Cromartie*, 526 U.S. 541 (1999).

because it had been drawn predominantly for reasons of politics, not race.[113]

In redrawing the twelfth district in 1997, the legislature had relied to some extent upon race, but it also included Democratic voting precincts in the district in order to maintain the existing partisan balance in the state's congressional delegation. The Democratic "performance" precincts correlated highly with race, since blacks were predominantly Democratic, but that was not enough to call the constitutionality of the district into question.

The Supreme Court's latest decision in the North Carolina case indicates that legislators may safely draw majority-manority districts when the motivation for doing so is primarily political. But the Court did not significantly alter its inherently confusing and contradictory redistricting jurisprudence. The decision may mean nothing more than that Justice O'Connor, who broke ranks and joined the four members of the Court who had dissented in most of the earlier cases, simply wasn't offended by the shape of the new twelfth district. In any event, the Court handed down its decision only weeks after the release of the new decennial census, and, baring a miracle, the whole protracted process of legislative enactment and legal challenge will start all over again in North Carolina, no doubt to the continuing dismay and confusion of the voters of the state.

VI

Elections under the 1990s congressional plans may have been a triumph for minorities, but they were a disaster for the Democratic Party. In 1994, Republicans captured a twenty-five-seat majority in the House and a six-seat majority in the Senate.[114] And in looking for a scapegoat, some Democrats pointed a finger at the new majority-minority districts.

One commentator writing for *The New Yorker* made the extravagant, and ahistoric, claim that the creation of majority-black districts triggered the "collapse of the Democratic Party in the South." And more than that, it "had an even larger impact" on the national Democratic Party by providing the Republican Party "with the power to dominate national politics and dictate national policy."[115]

Claude Sitton, a former correspondent for the *New York Times*, was of a similar view. After the 1994 election, he wrote an angry letter to the national ACLU director, Ira Glasser, complaining about the organization's Voting Rights Project. "Your regional legal counsel," Sitton said with dripping

---

[113] *Hunt v. Cromartie*, 532 U.S. 234 (2001).

[114] David A. Bositis, *African-Americans and the 1994 Midterms: What Happened?* (Washington, D.C.: Joint Center for Political and Economic Studies, 1994), 14.

[115] Michael Kelly in *The New Yorker*, Nov. 20, 1995.

sarcasm, "spends his time creating and maintaining racially segregated congressional districts. The Republicans think he's a lovely fellow."[116]

The U.S. Senate, of course, is elected statewide. Drawing majority-black
congressional districts could not have been the cause of Democratic losses
in the upper chamber. As for the House, most accounts place the actual political "cost" to Democrats of creating majority-minority districts – that is,
of concentrating predominantly Democratic black voters in fewer districts –
at only between one and thirteen seats.[117] Democrats, however, lost a total
of fifty-four House seats in 1994, twentyfour of which were in states where
there were no majority-minority districts.[118] Eighteen of the lost House seats
were in states with small or negligible (0.3 percent to 6.6 percent) black populations.[119] Racial redistricting, by definition, could not have been a major
factor in any of these states. The party's loss of control of the House cannot
be laid at the door of majority-black congressional districts. The real causes
for the decline in fortune of the Democratic Party must be found elsewhere.

The Solid South, which could always be counted on to vote Democratic,
began to crumble long before the 1990s round of redistricting. Republicans
made significant inroads on Democratic control of southern House seats
following the presidential elections involving high-profile Republican candidates in 1952 (Eisenhower), 1964 (Goldwater), and 1972 (Nixon). The
Nixon landslide in 1972 marked the first time since Reconstruction that all
eleven southern states had sent at least one Republican to Congress. Following Ronald Reagan's reelection in 1984, Republicans increased their control
of southern house seats to 37 percent. By the time of the 1994 elections, the
Solid South had long since ceased to exist.[120]

Many things contributed to the demise of the Solid South, including
migration patterns, generational turnover, changes in ideology, and the

---

[116] Claude Sitton to Ira Glasser, December 18, 1995 (copy on file with author).

[117] Bositis, *What Happened?*, 17 ("the creation of majority-minority districts *per se* cost the
Democrats comparatively few seats in the south, say 10 (of 125)," half in 1992 and half
in 1994); David Ian Lublin, "Racial Redistricting and the New Republican Majority: A
Critique of the NAACP Legal Defense Fund Report on the 1994 Congressional Elections"
(unpublished paper, 1995), 19 ("Democrats lost around thirteen seats in 1994 due to racial
redistricting") (copy on file with the author); NAACP Legal Defense and Educational Fund,
"The Effect of Section 2 of the Voting Rights Act on the 1994 Congressional Elections"
(November 30, 1994), 2 (the construction of majority-minority districts cost "with certainty
only one Democratic seat in North Carolina") (copy on file with the author).

[118] NAACP Legal Defense Fund, "The Effect of Section 2," 2.

[119] Bositis, *What Happened?*, 36.

[120] Charles S. Bullock III, "Creeping Realignment in the South," in Robert H. Swansbrough and
David M. Brodsky, eds., *The South's New Politics: Realignment and Dealignment* (Columbia:
University of South Carolina Press, 1988), 220; Harold W. Stanley and David S. Castle,
"Partisan Changes in the South: Making Sense of Scholarly Dissonance," in ibid., 238
("Republican victories, particularly at the presidential level, mark the death of the solidly
Democratic South").

always-predictable white backlash. Lyndon Johnson foresaw the defection of conservative whites from the Democratic party in 1963 when he urged the Kennedy administration to push for a strong civil rights act. It was the just and moral thing to do, he said, but "[i]t might cost us the South."[121]

The slow bleeding of whites from the Democratic Party reached hemorrhage proportions in 1994. The Democratic share of the vote in congressional elections in Georgia in 1990 was 61.3 percent. In 1994 it dropped to 45.5 percent.[122] The Democrats' problem in the midterm election was not majority-black districts, but the abandonment of the party by white voters.

The Democratic Party was also plagued by defections. Four Democrats were elected to Congress from Georgia in 1994: three black – Lewis, McKinney, and Bishop – and one white, Nathan Deal. But Deal soon defected to the Republican Party. That same year, Michael Bowers, the state's longtime Democratic attorney general, left the party and was reelected as a Republican. These defections were symptomatic of a significant shift in partisan alignment in the state and cannot be explained simply in terms of congressional redistricting.

Remarkably, a few black Democrats joined in the criticism of majority-minority districts. One of them was John Lewis, a hero of Bloody Sunday and the representative from the majority-black fifth congressional district in Georgia.

Lewis was quoted in *USA Today* as saying that the creation of majority-minority districts "looks too much like South Africa. It seems like we're creating little black townships. You shouldn't just put people together because they are the same color."[123] Those were, of course, nearly verbatim the words of the strongest opponents of the 1982 amendment and extension of the Voting Rights Act. Senator Orin Hatch, for example, had said that the adoption of a results standard for Section 2 would lead to the creation of "political ghettos for minorities."[124]

Lewis was not alone. Several other members of the congressional black caucus, including Louis Stokes, Alan Wheat, Mike Espy, and Craig Washington, made similar charges in an amicus brief they filed in the Supreme Court in a redistricting case from Ohio. The brief, which was written by the Democratic Party, argued that the Voting Rights Act was not intended to lead to "political segregation" in which minority voters controlled a few districts but lacked "influence" in the rest. It warned against creating a political

[121] Vaughn Davis Bornet, *The Presidency of Lyndon B. Johnson* (Lawrence: University Press of Kansas, 1983), 97.

[122] David A. Bositis, *Redistricting and Representation: The Creation of Majority-Minority Districts and the Evolving Party System in the South* (Washington, D.C.: Joint Center for Political and Economic Studies, 1995), 54 (citing exit poll data from Mitofsky International).

[123] "Districts create black 'enclaves,'" *USA Today*, May 11, 1992, p. 11A.

[124] S. rep. No. 417 , 97th Cong., 20 Sess. 103 (1992), reprinted in 1982 U.S. Code Cong. & Adm. News 276.

system that "could resemble an American version of apartheid."[125] This was the precise rhetoric that the Court had used in destroying majority-black districts in Georgia and North Carolina.

Despite the views expressed in the party's brief, majority-black districts bear no principled resemblance to apartheid. Apartheid is the exclusion of one race from the government and the domination of that race by another.[126] Majority-minority districts merely provide minorities with the same opportunities as whites to elect candidates of their choice. The attempt to equate the two not only trivializes apartheid, but misapprehends the purpose of remedial redistricting, which is to include minorities in the mainstream of political life, not to exclude them.

After the opinion in *Shaw v. Reno*, the congressional black caucus, some of whose members' districts were suddenly put at risk, denounced the decision and said that it cast "a chilling pall across the face of electoral politics." As for creating majority-minority districts, the caucus was of the view that it "is a clear and warranted practice."[127] John Lewis, who must have understood that his election had been made possible in the first place by a majority-black district, said that *Shaw v. Reno* was "the greatest threat to the Voting Rights Act since it was written in August 6, 1965. If it wasn't for the Voting Rights Act, it would still be primarily white men in blue suits in Congress."[128]

The argument in the party's brief that majority-black districts diminished the influence of black voters ignored the fundamental purpose of Section 2, which is to give minority voters an equal opportunity to *elect* candidates of their choice.[129] It was also patronizing, since it implied that minorities would be better served by officials effectively chosen by white voters and whose election blacks could only influence. And it was more than a little dishonest. If political influence were all that it was said to be, whites would surely attempt to maximize their influence by creating as many districts as possible in which they were in the minority. Most whites, and certainly the *Shaw* and *Miller* plaintiffs, would laugh at such an idea.

VII

Judge John Minor Wisdom, in a case involving school desegregation in Jefferson County, Alabama, drew the distinction between a "color blind"

---

[125] *Voinovich v. Quilter*, No. 91–1618, brief amici curiae on behalf of Congressman Louis Stokes et al., pp. 21–2.

[126] See John Dugard, *Human Rights and the South African Legal Order* (Princeton, N.J.: Princeton University Press, 1978), 6, 103 (under apartheid, minorities "enjoy no representation in the central" government and "there is a clear denial of full political rights on account of their race").

[127] Congressional black caucus, news release, June 29, 1993.

[128] Laughlin McDonald, "Voting Rights and the Court: Drawing the Lines," *Southern Changes*, Fall 1993, 1, 5 (Southern Regional Council).

[129] 42 U.S.C. §1973(b).

Constitution that, in his words, prohibits "a classification that denies a benefit or imposes a burden" and a Constitution that must be "color conscious to prevent discrimination being perpetuated and to undo the effects of past discrimination."[130] Wisdom's words apply with equal force to redistricting.

States may legitimately consider race in redistricting for a variety of reasons – to overcome the affects of prior and continuing discrimination, to comply with the Fourteenth Amendment and the Voting Rights Act, or simply to recognize communities that have a particular racial or ethnic makeup and take account of their common, shared interests. Only when the consideration of race causes harm, such as the denial or abridgment of the right to vote or to participate equally in the electoral process, should there be a warrant, and a duty, for federal judicial intrusion.

The Supreme Court should reconsider its unfortunate and misguided *Shaw* line of cases. They have created subjective and unworkable standards. Legislators no longer know the extent to which race can or should be taken into account in drawing district lines, the result of which has been to draw the federal courts increasingly, and unnecessarily, into the redistricting process. The Court has created rules that give political preferences to whites and shackle racial minorities with special disadvantages in redistricting. That this should be done in the name of the Fourteenth Amendment is one of the great ironies of the Court's modern redistricting jurisprudence.

The nation as a whole has a substantial interest in the racial diversity that majority-minority districts have produced. White elected officials can fairly represent racial minorities, but our history shows that they frequently have not, and that some have been the architects of virulent forms of racial discrimination and political suppression. Racial diversity in legislative bodies ensures that minorities will in fact be represented and that their views will be heard. It ensures that a variety of backgrounds and experience is brought to legislative decision making and problem solving. It promotes innovation and the likelihood that the concerns of all Americans are identified.

Racial diversity and pluralism also help to create trust and mutual respect. They ensure the legitimacy of representative bodies by giving them, and the electoral process as a whole, the appearance of fairness. In the words of James Madison, diversity is proof that government is for all Americans, "[n]ot the rich more than the poor; not the learned more than the ignorant; not the haughty heirs of distinguished names, more than the humble sons of obscure and unpropitious fortune ... [but] the great body of the people of the United States."[131] And not one race more than another.

---

130 *United States v. Jefferson County Board of Education*, 372 F. 2d 836, 877 (5th Cir. 1966).

131 *The Federalist* No. 57 (James Madison), quoted with approval in *Wesberry v. Sanders*, 376 U.S. 1, 18 (1964).

18

Keysville, Georgia – A Voting Rights Crucible

> You have to love the hell out of people.... We had to prove to whites that we
> were not going to have power and leave them out.
>
> Mayor Emma Gresham of Keysville, Georgia

Black political participation was always about dignity and respect, and
about repudiating the myths of Reconstruction that blacks were incapable
of voting and holding elected office. But it was also about such intensely
practical matters as bringing running water, paved streets, and fire protection to the long-neglected black community. Nowhere was that more evident
than in the small town of Keysville in rural Burke County, which became a
modern-day crucible for the opposing forces in the struggle for equal voting
rights.

Keysville was chartered in 1890 and for many years was a bustling agri-
cultural center. It had a post office, a school, several general stores, a lumber
mill, two factories (chair and glass), and a half-dozen churches. The Augusta
and West Florida railroad ran through town, and its steam engines regularly
stopped at a tower just south of Brier Creek to take on water for the run
to Blyth and Augusta. Local boosters confidently predicted that one day
Keysville would become "a great metropolis." The town was "taking on
new life," they said, "and is bound to spring further forward in the race of
prosperity." Money invested in Keysville was "sure to bring large returns in
a few years."[1]

But Keysville did not prosper. Over the years, farming and commerce
declined, and as people moved away looking for jobs elsewhere the life of
the town slowly ebbed. The railroad stopped running, and the water tower
was torn down. Most of the stores, the lumber mill, and the chair and glass
factories were abandoned and left to decay. In 1933, as the country was
sinking deeper into the Great Depression, the town held its last elections for

---

[1] *True Citizen*, July 12, 1890; *True Citizen*, Oct. 18, 1890.

the mayor and town council. After that, for reasons no one can fully explain, the municipal life of the town died altogether.

Fifty years later, there were only 300 people still living in Keysville, 80 percent of whom were black. The better-off lived in small frame houses or cheap mobile homes, the rest in dilapidated shacks. Since there was no municipal government, there was no central water system. A few families had wells, but most of them were contaminated by coliform bacteria. Those without wells borrowed from a neighbor, hauled water in buckets from nearby Brier Creek, or caught rainwater in large barrels set under the gutters of their homes. Sewerage was primitive or nonexistent. Most of the streets were unpaved, unmarked, and unlighted.[2]

Keysville reached a turning point in 1985, when a mobile home in the black community went up in flames. Neighbors called the nearest fire station – some twenty-five miles away in Waynesboro – but it did not respond. Nollie Mae Morris, a local black resident, said "that's when we realized that Keysville ought to have fire protection and some of the other public services that people elsewhere take for granted."[3]

The black community, organized under the banner of the Keysville Concerned Citizens, took on the task of revitalizing municipal government. But they were met with fierce resistance from local whites.

White opposition to black political participation was nothing new in Keysville. When the town was first chartered in 1890, municipal boundaries were defined as "extend[ing] one-half mile in every direction from the school house now located in said town of Keysville."[4] According to a local press account, in their enthusiasm for preparing for the economic boom that they thought was certain to come to Keysville, the founding fathers failed to "circumscribe" the town limits and took in the so-called black belt.[5] The inclusion of black residents had a decisive impact on the town's first election.

As the local paper described it, "[t]here was an opposition ticket in the field, and early in the morning before the regular ticket had left its little bed, the opposition had aroused old cuff and like dum [sic] driven cattle had induced him to exercise the rights of freedom." As a result of the black vote, the new town council was split between the regular and opposition tickets. The regulars, however, refused to serve, and a second election was held to fill the vacant seats. This time, two "negro preachers" were elected, a turn of events that reportedly "greatly annoyed" the "better

---

2 "The Revival of Keysville," *Civil Liberties*, Fall 1987; "Reaffirmation or Requiem for the Voting Rights Act?," ACLU monograph, May 1995, pp. 17–18; *Dallas Morning News*, Jan. 29, 1989.
3 "The Revival of Keysville."
4 Ga. Laws 1890–91, Vol. 2, p. 657.
5 *True Citizen*, March 7, 1991.

element of the white voters." The paper predicted "trouble ahead."[6] And there was.

The Red Shirts, a paramilitary arm of the regulars, sent both black council members a notice "emphatically advising their speedy resignation." Being prudent men, they agreed, but on condition that all council members resign and that a new election be held to fill the vacant seats. It is unclear how the immediate issue of elections was resolved, but the eventual disfranchisement of blacks in Georgia ensured that as long as whites in Keysville wished to have municipal government, they would control it.

In modern-day Keysville, however, circumstances had changed. The Voting Rights Act had abrogated the post-Reconstruction disfranchisement system, and a majority of the town's residents were black. In the event elections were held, it would be likely that some or most of the elected officials would be black. From the white perspective, that was an eventuality that was to be avoided at all costs.

Resurrecting the old shibboleths from the nineteenth century, local whites claimed that blacks were irresponsible and incapable of governing, and that they were motivated by a desire for power and revenge against whites. Geneva Marshall, who owned a nursing home in Keysville, said that "black people in this town can't even keep bread in their homes, much less keep up any obligations to the city."[7] James Pole, Jr., another white resident, said that blacks were "racists" and that their efforts to restore local government was "reverse discrimination. They're trying to do to us what they say we did to them back in the 60s."[8]

Whites also feared that if the town were revitalized, a black-dominated government would tax them to pay for services that whites already had. "I have a well," said Poole. "Seems if they want something bad enough, they can get it. They got cars and TVs. If they want water and sewerage, then let them pay for it." The suggestion that the small, impoverished black community of Keysville – where unemployment ran as high as 40 percent and where the per capita income was less than a third of the national average – could purchase modern water and sewer systems on its own was hardly realistic.[9]

Emma Gresham, a retired schoolteacher and a leading force in Concerned Citizens, tried to reassure the white community that it had nothing to fear from new elections. "We have no anger in our hearts towards our white brothers and sisters," she told a gathering at a local church. "All we want is a government elected by the people, black and white, that can help bring this town back to life and do something about the water and the sewerage

[6] Ibid.
[7] "The Revival of Keysville."
[8] *Atlanta Constitution*, Oct. 19, 1988; *True Citizen*, March 1, 1989.
[9] *Dallas Morning News*, Jan. 29, 1989.

and the other problems. If we all come together, we can make it work."[10] As for the charge that blacks were looking for power, Gresham says they were simply looking for "a better life. I had never even thought about what we were doing in terms of trying to get power."[11] Despite Gresham's assurances, whites remained skeptical and fearful.

Aside from the white attitude, the proponents of municipal government in Keysville faced other obstacles. One of them was determining the boundaries of the town. The old log schoolhouse, formerly the center of town, had been blown down by a tornado in the late 1890s. A local pig farmer had salvaged the logs and carried them away to build a home, and no physical trace of the school remained.[12]

One black resident of the town, however, was sure that he knew where the schoolhouse had stood. He was George Key, the ninety-four-year-old great-great-grandson of Josh Key, the white slave owner for whom Keysville was named. He took a group of local residents and visitors on a tour of Keysville and, leading them to a grove of oak trees on a rise overlooking the Methodist cemetery, pointed with his walking stick and exclaimed in a loud voice, "Before God, here is where the school house stood. Why would I tell you a lie?"[13]

Several deeds and plats in the county court house made reference to the old school property, but they put it in different locations. Although George's Key's recollection was unwavering, as a legal matter the exact location of the schoolhouse, and thus the boundaries of the town, remained unsettled.[14] Concerned Citizens knew, of course, that Keysville had in fact existed, and they determined to approximate its boundaries as best they could.

There were also other problems. State law provided that municipal elections must be conducted by elected officials appointed by the local governing body.[15] Since there was no governing body in Keysville to make appointments, there was no way for an election to be held in strict conformity with state law. In seeking a way out of this dilemma, and upon the advice of Jeff Lanier, an assistant state attorney general, blacks organized a town meeting to which all residents were invited. The meeting voted to hold an election and appointed two elections superintendents, one black and one white. January 6, 1986, was set as the date for the election.[16]

Candidates duly qualified for mayor and the five council positions; all were black and all were unopposed. Since there was no need to hold an election, the

---

[10] Ibid.
[11] "The Burden of Power," *Time*, August 7, 1989.
[12] *Richmond Times*, June 26, 1988.
[13] "The Revival of Keysville."
[14] *Richmond Times Dispatch*, June 26, 1988.
[15] O.C.G.A. §21-3-8(3).
[16] *Gresham v. Harris*, 695 F. Supp. 1179, 695 (N. D. Ga. 1988).

county probate judge administered the oath of office to the black candidates. On the same day, however, James Poole and several other whites filed a suit in state court arguing that the election had not been held in accordance with state law and that the boundaries of the town were unknown. The state court agreed and granted an injunction prohibiting the blacks from taking office and from conducting any more elections that were not in strict compliance with state law.[17]

Concerned Citizens took another tack. This time they asked their representative in the legislature, Emory Bargeron, to introduce legislation activating the town. Whites, for their part, asked Bargeron to get the legislature to draw boundaries that would exclude them from the town limits. But Bargeron refused to get involved in the controversy. "I don't have any intention to introduce anything," he said. "Nobody ever asked me to go to a meeting about Keysville until they got everybody mad with each other. When it's resolved, then I will do what I can."[18]

Concerned Citizens turned next to the governor and asked him to fill the vacant mayor and council positions, as he is authorized to do by the state constitution.[19] He refused, claiming that the boundaries of the town were too uncertain to allow him to make appointments. As an alternative, he suggested that the legislature enact a law requiring county officials to conduct special elections to fill vacancies in municipal offices.[20]

The legislature, under the urging of the legislative black caucus, passed such a law in 1987 and authorized the board of registrars for the county to prepare a list of voters for the election.[21] After being advised by the attorney general that the new statute was mandatory, Burke County officials prepared a map designating the town's boundaries, and issued a call for an election in Keysville to be held on January 4, 1988. Preston Lewis, the county attorney, acknowledged that setting the town boundaries had been "a problem" but said "we now believe that the boundaries have been reasonably determined, and the election can go forward."[22]

The new election procedures were precleared by the Department of Justice, but, before an election could be held, Poole and the other white plaintiffs went again to the state court and got another injunction against the pending election. According to the state court, the boundaries of Keysville "were improperly determined" and were still essentially unknowable. And although the state court order plainly embodied a change in voting procedures – the

[17] Ibid.
[18] *Augusta Chronicle*, Jan. 7, 1989.
[19] Constitution of Georgia, Article V, Section 2, para. 7.
[20] *Gresham v. Harris*, 695 F. Supp. at 1181; *In Re: Contest of Election Results of the Keysville Municipal Elections Held January 4, 1988*, Civ. No. 88-V-21 (Sup. Ct. Burke Cty., May 23, 1988).
[21] Ga. Laws 1987, p. 178.
[22] *Poole v. Gresham*, No. 89-1564, motion to affirm, p. 7.

canceling of an election – the court nevertheless concluded that the change was not subject to preclearance under Section 5 of the Voting Rights Act.[23]

Emma Gresham and other members of Concerned Citizens, with the assistance of the ACLU's Voting Rights Project and the Christic Institute South, promptly filed a suit of their own in federal court arguing that the state court order canceling the election could not be implemented absent Section 5 preclearance. Judge Owen Forrester granted an immediate hearing and on December 31, 1987, issued an injunction allowing the January election to go forward.[24] "Either Keysville never existed," he said, "or you do the best you can."[25]

White opposition, however, remained unabated. On the day of the election, several whites filed an action with the county board of registrars challenging the eligibility of forty-one voters on the grounds that the boundaries of the town had not been determined and the residency of the voters could not be established. The board of registrars dismissed the challenge, and there was no appeal.[26]

There were two slates of candidates in the election, one supported by Concerned Citizens and the other by those who opposed the restoration of municipal government. Candidates on the two slates got almost identical vote totals, indicating that the voting was sharply polarized. Emma Gresham was elected mayor, outdistancing her white opponent by ten votes. Blacks were elected to four of the council positions, while James Poole, who had been endorsed by Concerned Citizens in an effort to include whites in the new government, was elected to the fifth council seat.[27]

After the election, whites challenged the results in state court, alleging once again that the boundaries of the town were indeterminable and that it was impossible to ascertain who was a qualified voter or candidate. The contest was denied, and the state court affirmed the results of the election based on the map and voters list prepared by the county registrar.[28] Shortly thereafter, the federal court issued a permanent injunction that the state court order "changed a previously precleared practice and therefore should also have been precleared."[29]

Whites in Keysville pressed on with their opposition to municipal government in Keysville. "We're in it for the duration," vowed their lawyer.[30] The white plaintiffs appealed the decision of the federal court to the U.S.

[23] *Poole v. Lodge*, Civ. No. 85-V-414 (Sup. Ct. Burke Cty., Dec. 31, 1987).

[24] *Gresham v. Harris*, 695 F. Supp. at 1181.

[25] *Atlanta Journal and Constitution*, Nov. 23, 1989.

[26] *In Re: Contest of Election Results of the Keysville Municipal Elections Held January 4, 1988*.

[27] Ibid.

[28] Ibid.

[29] *Gresham v. Harris*, 695 F. Supp. at 1184.

[30] *Dallas Morning News*, January 29, 1989.

Supreme Court and tried to block the enforcement of various ordinances enacted by the newly formed government by filing suits in state court.

The town council had adopted a license ordinance charging a small tax for conducting business in Keysville. Several months later, in response to a petition from landowners, the council agreed to annex several areas adjacent to the town. The Keysville Convalescent and Nursing Home filed suit seeking a declaration that it was not required to pay a license fee or tax because it was impossible to tell if the nursing center was inside or outside the boundaries of the town.[31] A second group of whites filed another suit seeking a declaration that the proposed annexation was null and void on similar grounds that the boundaries of the town were indeterminable.[32] The city removed both cases to federal court.[33]

On May 29, 1990, the Supreme Court affirmed the lower court decision, and on September 21, 1990, the federal court dismissed the state court tax ordinance and annexation challenges. With entry of these court orders, the dispute over municipal boundaries in Keysville was finally, irrevocably, over. And under the leadership of Emma Gresham and the town council, Keysville blossomed.

The town started a junior city council program for young people and instituted programs to fight illiteracy and teen pregnancy. A small library was begun in the temporary town hall. The county built a fire station just outside of town, street lights were installed for the first time, and a new post office was established. Streets have been paved. There is a new city hall, a clinic, and a handsome playground and recreation center. And rising above it all is a gleaming new water tower, dedicated in 1993 and a symbol of the town's triumph over the dead hand of the past and the closed fist of more recent times.[34]

The changes that have come to Keysville in just a few short years are nothing short of remarkable. Perhaps more remarkable still is the extent to which relationships between the races have changed. Upton Cochran, who ran against Gresham for mayor in 1988, gradually began stopping by town hall "just to talk," says the mayor. When a vacancy came on the council, she urged him to run, which he did and won. "He is now one of my best working city council persons," she says proudly. She also recalls that when the pipes were being laid for the new water system, the owner of the Keysville Nursing Home wrote her a letter saying "we want to be a part of what you're doing.

---

[31] *Keysville Convalescent and Nursing Center, Inc. v. City of Keysville, Georgia*, Civ. No. 88-V-280 (Sup. Ct. Burke Cty. Ga.).

[32] *Poole v. City of Keysville, Georgia*, Civ. No. 88-V-293 (Sup. Ct. Burke Cty. Ga.).

[33] *Keysville Convalescent and Nursing Center, Inc. v. City of Keysville, Georgia*, Civ. No. 188-184 (S. D. Ga.); *Poole v. City of Keysville, Georgia*, Civ. No. 188-183 (S. D. Ga.).

[34] *Atlanta Constitution*, Oct. 19, 1988; "Reaffirmation or Requiem for the Voting Rights Act?"; *Dallas Morning News*, Jan. 29, 1989. The closed fist metaphor is John Minor Wisdom's. See *United States v. Jefferson County Board of Education*, 372 F. 2d 836, 854 (5th Cir. 1966).

Annex us to the city and we'll be your best customer." The town agreed, secured a supplementary grant, and extended the water pipes to the nursing home.[35]

The resurgence of Keysville had a great deal to do with the increased influence of the legislative black caucus, which shepherded through the general assembly the legislation requiring officials to conduct a town election. It also had a lot to do with the Voting Rights Act – which prohibited whites from blocking the efforts of blacks to participate in the governance of the community in which they lived – and those who helped to enforce it. But most important, it had to do with the indomitable spirit of local residents, such as Emma Gresham, Nollie Mae Morris, and George Key, who persevered against the odds and who refused to succumb to the racial fears and distrust that had for so long held the white community in thrall.

"You have to love the hell out of people," says Emma Gresham, as a way of explaining Keysville's success.

I think whites felt threatened, but I very much did not want to be guilty of some of the things they were guilty of. It takes close contact and a lot of communication to get across the message that you have nothing to fear from the next person. We had to prove to whites that we were not going to have power and leave them out. The burden was on us to include them. That approach has done more for race relations in this town than anything else.[36]

---

[35] "Reaffirmation or Requiem for the Voting Rights Act?".
[36] Ibid.; "The Burden of Power."

Index

Abrams, Lucious, 217
Adams, G. D., 150
Aderhold, O. C., 120
Aeloney, Zev, 113
affirmative action, application to redistricting, 227
Akerman, Amos T., 32
Akerman Law of 1870, 25, 30
Alaimo, Anthony, 111, 157
Alapaha, 143
Albany, 108, 114, 160, 161
Albany Movement, 108
Alexander, T. M., 71
All-Citizens Registration Committee, 49, 51
Allen, Ralph, 103–6, 113, 122
Allen v. Wright, 215
Allgood, Thomas, 169–70, 172
Alverson, Fred, 53
American Civil Liberties Union (ACLU), 187, 190, 195, 198, 212, 217–18, 233, 243
American Union, 25
Americus, 112–14, 116–18, 136, 160
An American Dilemma: The Negro Problem and Modern Democracy (Myrdal), 58
anti–facsimile ballot provision, 100–2
armed forces: desegregation of, 58–9; effort to maintain segregation in, 66
Arnall, Ellis, 50, 85, 140
Ashburn, 143
Athens, 143
Atlanta, 19, 25, 30, 38, 45, 62, 97–8
Atlanta Constitution, 25, 37, 88, 92, 184
Atlanta Journal, 15, 40, 42, 74
Atlanta Journal-Constitution, 74
Atlanta race riot of 1906, 41
Atlanta Voters Guild, 74
at-large elections: adopted after passage of the Voting Rights Act, 131–2, 141–2;

challenges to, 159–63, 182–4; impact on black officeholding, 193
Augusta, 24, 38, 45, 54, 62, 143, 183
Augusta Chronicle and Sentinel, 26, 28
Augusta Daily Constitutionalist, 20

Bacon County, 131, 160
Bagby, George, 87
Bailey, Willie, 162, 195
Baker County, 46, 118, 210
Baker v. Carr, 80, 83
Baldwin County, 23, 158, 182, 183
Balkcom, James, 115
Ball, Wesley, 165–6
Banks County, 209
Barfield, Ed, 88, 95
Bargeron, Emory, 242
Barnes, R. C., Jr., 184, 208
Barnes, Roy, 208
Barnesville, 63
Barnum, John, 113
Barnwell, A. S., 35
barratry statutes, 71, 76
Beer v. United States, 169
Bell, Charles, 116
Bell, Griffin, 176
Bell, Mary Kate, 116
Ben Hill County, 187
Benham, Robert, 193–4
Bibb County, 76, 78, 115, 143, 168
Big Johnny Reb, 96
Bishop, Sanford, 222–3, 235
Black Codes, 17–18
black elected officials: expelled from office in 1868, 3, 21–3; returned to office in 1870, 24; number during Reconstruction, 25; violence against, 1867–72, 35; number prior to passage of the Voting Rights Act, 10; number in 1975, 153; number in

1980, 175; number in 1990, 192; number
in 1991, 211; number in 1992, 225;
number in 1998, 226; *see also* at-large
elections
Black, Hugo, 126
Black Power, 122
black suffrage: denial of, 1–3, 15–18; grant
of male suffrage in 1868, 19; *see also*
disfranchising offenses
black voter registration: during
Reconstruction, 18; from 1920 to 1930,
45; in 1947, 49; in 1958, 75; in 1963, 94;
in 1968, 129–30; Talmadge challenges in
1946, 52; voter purges, 3, 56–7; use of
fraud and intimidation in preventing, 3,
9–10, 46–7, 52–4, 56; prior to passage of
the Voting Rights Act, 10; registration
campaigns, 75, 103; segregation in,
114–15
Blacksher, Jim, 174
Bleckley County, 53–4, 56, 118, 154, 185–96
Blitch, Peg, 220
bloc vote, 76–7, 84, 87, 92, 94, 95
Bloch, Charles J., 11–12
Bloody Sunday, 8, 235
Bolton, Arthur, 139–40, 154
Bond, Julian, 136–8, 149, 169, 172, 173
Bonner, James C., 82
Borders, William H., 60, 70
Bowers, Michael, 235
Bownes, Lillie Mae, 112
Branch, H. M., 33
Brantley County, 209
Bray, James, 196
Brinson, Robert, 175–6
Brooks, Tyrone, 194, 198, 209, 211
Brown, Ed, 191–2
Brown, Edward, 156–8, 195
Brown, H. "Rap," 122
Brown v. Board of Education, 59, 60; reaction
to, 65–7, 68, 70, 75, 127
Brown, Willie James, 143, 157
Brownell, Herbert, 68
Bryan, William Jennings, 37–8
Bulloch County, 132, 159
Bullock, Rufus B., 21, 29
Burgamy, Charles, 85
Burke County, 33, 57, 111, 159, 163, 184
Burke, Frank, 135
Busbee, George, 202–3
Butler, 143, 147, 183
Butts County, 63, 182

Cairo, 143
Caldwell, Johnnie, 91, 101
Calhoun County, 131, 159, 175
Callaway, Howard H., 9–10, 12, 114, 140,
208

Camden County, 118, 182, 183
Camilla, 23, 143, 156, 183; massacre of
1868, 23–4
Campbell, Bill, 229
Campbell, Tunis, 23, 30, 33–5
Cannon, W. T., 33
Carlton, Milton, 201–2, 204
Carmichael, James V., 81
Carmichael, Stokely, 122
Carroll County, 55, 185
Carrollton, 183
Carswell, Lewis, 53–4
Carter, Dan, 188–9
Carter, Jimmy, 65
Carter, John, 196
Castellucis, Richard, 172
Catoosa County, 185
Center for Constitutional Rights (CCR), 196
Chambless, Thomas, 209
Chappell, Fred, 113
Charlton County, 142, 182, 183
Chatfield, John, 106
Chatham County, 102, 131
Cherokee County, 185
Chickasawhatchee, 107
Christic Institute South, 243
Citizens Democratic Club of Georgia, 97
City of Mobile v. Bolden, 163–4, 174, 181,
216
City of Rome v. United States, 4
Civil Rights Act of 1957, 3, 69–72, 115, 123,
126
Civil Rights Act of 1960, 3, 123
Civil Rights Act of 1964, 3, 123, 139;
legislature's condemnation of, 99
civil rights enforcement, abandonment by
Congress and Supreme Court after
Reconstruction, 42–4
Civil War, 2, 17
Clarke County, 142, 225
Claxton, 183
Clay County, 131, 159
Clement, Rufus E., 10
Coates, Christopher, 163
Cobb County, 68
Cochran, 118, 143, 183
Cochran Journal, 54
Cochran, Upton, 244
Coffee County, 132, 159
Coggin, Frank, 150
Cohen, Mark, 213
Cole, Steven, 194
College Park, 168
color-blind Constitution, 236–7
Colquitt County, 46, 47, 65
Columbus, 95–6, 119
Columbus Daily Sun, 28
Committee of 121, 101

communism, 64, 70
Communist Party, 50, 69
Confederacy, 2, 16–17, 35, 214;
    disfranchisement of leaders of, 19
Confederate flag, 8, 68, 229
Congress of Racial Equality (CORE), 103,
    113, 129
congressional investigations, 1871–72, 29
congressional redistricting, 4, 6, 7; in the
    1960s, 89–90; in the 1970s, 148–50; in the
    1980s, 168–73; in the 1990s, 211–13;
    challenge by white voters to 1990s plan,
    216–24; 1995 court-ordered plan, 220–3;
    see also *Shaw v. Reno*
Constitution of Georgia: of 1777, 15; of
    1789, 15; of 1861, 17; of 1865, 17; of
    1868, 19, 31; of 1877, 35
Constitution of the United States, 2
constitutional convention: of 1865, 17; of
    1867, 19–20
Cook County, 132, 182, 183
Cook, Eugene, 68–9, 73, 97, 120
Cook, Roscoe, 164
Cooper, Clarence, 194
Cordele, 119, 183
county unit system, 3, 80–4; *see also*
    majority-vote requirement
Coverdell, Paul, 169–70, 209
Covington, 160
Craig, Calvin F., 97
Crawford County, 182
Crawfordville, 119, 143
Crisp, Charles F., 64, 120
Crisp County, 131
Crisp, Henry, 96
Cross, John, 46, 47, 53, 62, 135, 164
Cross v. Baxter, 180
Culpepper, Brooks, 87
Curtis, Robert, 143

Dade County, 185
Daniel, Walter, 52, 145
Daniels, Carolyn, 106–7, 110
Darien, 161
Davis, James C., 69
Davis, John, 12
Davis, Oscar, 158
Dawson, 104–6, 112, 161
Dawson News, 120–2
Days, Drew, 176
Deal, Nathan, 235
Decatur, 183
Declaration of Independence, 2, 49
DeKalb County, 89, 90, 167, 191,
    220
DeLoach, George, 217
Democratic Party, 1, 20–1, 54–5, 96, 115,
    154, 221; and 1990s congressional

elections, 233–4; impact of redistricting
    on, 233–6; defections from, 235
Dent, B. L., 10
Deveaux, John H., 45
discriminatory results test, 177–81; see also
    Voting Rights Act of 1965
Disfranchising Act of 1908, 40–1
disfranchising offenses, 2–3, 36
Dodge County, 182–3
Donalsonville, 142, 160, 183
Dooly County, 131, 159
Dougherty County, 33, 114–15, 159, 167
Douglas, 135, 161
Doyle, W. H., 37
Dred Scott v. Sandford, 16
Dublin, 160
durational residency requirements for voting,
    1, 3, 34
Dykes, James M., 53

Early County, 131, 159
East Dublin, 143
Eastman, 183
Eatonton, 55, 160
Echols County, 83, 209
Edenfield, Newell, 76, 120
Edwards, Claybon, 51
Edwards, Don, 174
Effingham County, 182, 220
eighteen-year-old voter law, 1, 49–50
Eisenhower, Dwight, 75
Elberton, 24
elected offices, abolition of, 3, 30–2
election code of 1964, 12
Election Laws Study Committee: of 1957,
    72–4; of 1961, 91 n.1; of 1963, 91–100,
    202–3
elections of 1868, 21, 23–4
elections of 1870, 26
elections of 1872, 33
elections of 1874, 34
electric chair, 62
Elliott, J. Robert, 50, 55, 180
Ervin, Sam, Jr., 140
Espy, Mike, 235
Evans County, 182

Fallin, Billy, 165
Fannin County, 209
federal examiners, 129
Felton, Dorothy, 170
Fifteenth Amendment, 1, 2, 14, 48, 114;
    ratification of, 24; attempts to circumvent,
    30; call for repeal, 71
Financing Schools (McCuiston), 58
Finch, George, 88

Flanagan, Robert, 74
Floyd County, 209
Flynt, John, 12
Folsom, John, 133
Forest, Nathan B., 21
Forman, James, 122
Forrester, E. L., 66
Forrester, Owen, 243
Forsyth County, 209
Fortson, Ben, 91, 95–8
Fortson, Warren, 113, 116
Fortson v. Dorsey, 4, 89, 90, 158
Fort Valley, 51
Fourteenth Amendment, 2, 48; refusal to
  ratify, 17–18; ratification of, 21, 24;
  efforts to circumvent, 30; interpretation by
  Supreme Court, 42, 44; call for repeal, 71;
  modern enforcement of, 59
Fowler, Wyche, 152, 173, 209
Frankfurter, Felix, 70, 230
Franklin County, 185
Franklin, John Hope, 22
fraud and intimidation, 3
Freedmen's Bureau, 23
freedom-from-compulsory-association law,
  76
Fulton County, 52, 81–3, 90, 159, 161; 1962
  senate elections, 86–9; use of plurality
  vote, 93
Fuqua, J. B., 62, 95, 98

Garden City, 220
Gate City Bar Association, 62
Geer, Peter Zack, 73, 82, 94
Geer, W. I., 85
George, Walter F., 81
Georgia Association of Black Elected
  Officials, 212
Georgia Bar Association, 11, 62, 76
Georgia Indigent Legal Services (GILS),
  196
Georgia League of Women Voters, 87
Georgia State Patrol, 117
Georgia Teachers Association, 30–1
Giles v. Harris, 43–4
Gilmer County, 209
Gingrich, Newt, 219
Glascock County, 209
Glasser, Ira, 233
good character and understanding test for
  voting, 3, 12, 41; 1949 revisions of,
  55–6; 1958 revisions of, 72–4; proposed
  repeal of, 94–8; reenactment of, in 1964,
  102; suspension of, in 1965, 124;
  nationwide suspension of, in 1970, 141;
  permanent nationwide ban on, in 1975,
  155; *see also* Election Laws Study
  Committee of 1963

grand jury appointment of school board
  members, 30–2, 132–4, 187–9, 198;
  refusal of segregated juries to appoint
  blacks, 134
grandfather clause, 1, 41
Gray v. Sanders, 4, 83, 90
Green, Raymond, 136
Greene County, 53, 118, 132, 182, 183
Greene, Joseph, 145
Greenville, 196
Gresham, Emma, 238, 240–1, 243–5
Griffin, 183
Griffin, J. R., 30
Griffin, Marvin, 66, 71, 81; 1962
  gubernatorial campaign, 84–5
Groover, Denmark, 12, 68, 92–4, 101, 138,
  198, 201–3
Gulliver, Hal, 94

Habersham County, 209
Hagan, 183
Hagan, Elliott, 12
Hamilton, E. D., 64
Hancock County, 131, 175, 210
Hanner, Bob, 212–13, 226
Hardwick, Thomas W., 40, 42
Harlan, John Marshall, 66
Harris County, 47, 134, 153, 154, 159,
  179
Harris County Journal, 54, 65
Harris, Nathaniel, 81
Harris, Don, 113
Harris, Roy, 51
Hart County, 183
Hartsfield, William B., 83
Hartwell, 143
Hasty, Fred, 86
Hatcher, Charles, 172
Hawes, E. Wilson, 146
Hayes, Clyde, 110
Hayes, Rutherford B., 43
Hayes-Tilden Compromise of 1877, 43
Heard County, 185
Heard, Keith, 225
Henderson, Jacob, 51
Henry County, 131, 159
Hicks, M. K., 50
Hill, Jesse, Jr., 117
Hillyer, H. L., 30
Hinesville, 143
Hogansville, 143
Holloway, Emma Kate, 110
Holloway, Lucious, 105, 195
Hollowell, Donald, 62, 85, 100, 102, 114,
  201
Holmes, Oliver Wendell, 44
Holmes, Robert, 225
Holt, Jack, 119

Homerville, 143
Hooks, George, 63
Horn, Ely, 96
Horn, Eugene, 85
Howell, Clark, 40
Hudson, Perry, 169
Humphrey, Hubert, 99
Hunter, Charlayne, 120

I-85 corridor, and redistricting, 221
insurrection, prosecution of civil rights
    workers for, 113
Interposition Resolution, 67

Jackson, 63, 183
Jackson County, 209
Jackson, Harvey, 188
Jackson, Maynard, 149, 150–2, 229
James, Agnew, 107
James, Odethia, 107
Jefferson County, 182
Jenkins County, 132
Jesup, 143, 183
Jesup, Ben, 168
Jim Crow, 5, 38–9, 58, 59, 66, 85, 78, 133,
    156, 227
Johnson, Andrew, 17
Johnson County, 115, 133, 187
Johnson, James, 17
Johnson, Leroy, 10, 42, 76, 86, 88–9, 95,
    100, 205
Johnson, Lyndon, 3, 8–9, 11, 117, 139, 235
Johnson v. De Grandy, 181
Johnson v. Miller, 216
Jones, C. R., 63
Jones County, 115
Jonesboro, 143
Jordan, Clarence, 63
Jordan, Florence, 64
Jordan, Vernon, 141
Joyner, Gordon, 228
judicial elections: in Fulton County in 1964,
    93, 100, 102; statewide, 193–4; challenge
    to method of, 207
jury selection, discrimination in, 17–18,
    31–2, 133–4

Kennedy, John, 97
Key, George, 241, 245
Key, Josh, 241
Key, V. O., Jr., 56, 81–2
Keysville, 7, 238–45
Keysville Concerned Citizens, 239, 240,
    242–3
Kidd, Culver, 187, 189
King, C. B., 114
King, Martin Luther, Jr., 75, 139
King, Primus, 49, 51, 54–5

Kingsland, Georgia, 118
Koinonia Farm, 63–4
Kousser, Morgan J., 93, 205
Ku Klux Klan, 21, 33, 54, 63–4, 97, 118

Laite, William, 86
Lakeland, 143
Lamar County, 63, 114, 183
Landrum, Phil, 12
language minorities, 155
Lanier, Jeff, 241
Larson, Edward J., 188
Lawson, Steven, 200–1, 205
Lee County, 107, 129
legislative redistricting, 3, 84; in the 1960s,
    86–90, 101; in the 1970s, 148; in the
    1980s, 167; in the 1990s, 224–6; challenge
    to, by white voters, 225–6
Leverett, Freeman, 91, 175
Lewis, John, 8, 116, 122, 152, 173, 211, 222,
    235–6
Lewis, John R., 28–9
Lewis, Preston, 242
Liberty County, 33–4
Lichtman, Allan, 194
Lincoln, Abraham, 13
Linder, John, 221
literacy tests for voting, 2–3, 9, 12, 41, 46,
    56; upholding the constitutionality of,
    43–4; proposed repeal of, 94–8;
    reenactment of, 102; suspension of, in
    1965, 124; nationwide suspension of, in
    1970, 141; permanent nationwide ban on,
    in 1975, 155; *see also* Election Laws Study
    Committee
Lodge, Herman, 111, 195
Lokey, Hamilton, 67
Long County, 142, 183
Long, Edward, 146
Long, Gillis, 215
Long, Oscar, 76
Louisville, 143
Lowe, Betty, 170
Lowe, Eddie G., 46
Lowndes County, 182
Ludowici, 183
Lumber City, 143, 183
lynching, 39, 47
Lyons, 183
Lyons, Judson, 45

MacIntyre, Dan, 100
Mackay, James, 12–13, 93, 205
Macon, 25, 33, 38, 45, 56, 160–1
Macon Bar Association, 77
Macon County, 182, 183
Macon Voters League, 56
Maddox, Lester, 85, 117, 139–40, 149

Madison, 143, 160
Mahone, Sammy, 116
majority-vote requirement, 12; adopted for
  state senate in 1962, 87; adopted statewide
  in 1964, 91–4, 98–102; adoption by cities,
  135, 143–4, 147; challenge to, 198–9;
  plaintiffs' claim of purposeful
  discrimination, 199–205; plaintiffs'
  discriminatory results claim, 206–7; repeal
  of, in 1994 and 1998, for general
  elections, 208–9
majority-white districts: oddly shaped, 150,
  168–9, 215, 230; and racial double
  standard, 230–2; drawn to accommodate
  white ethnic groups, 231
Mansfield, Mike, 99
Marion County, 132, 182, 183
Marshall, Burke, 115
Marshall, Geneva, 240
Massell, Sam, 150–1, 229
Matthews, Zeke, 105–6, 110
Mattox, H. W., 33–4
Max Black plan, 217, 212, 217
McCall, Sherrod, 165
McCrary, Peyton, 188
McCrimmon, G. R., 97
McCuiston, Fred, 58
McDonough, 168
McDuffie County, 44, 65, 114, 159
McDuffie Progress, 146
McGee, Collins, 116
McIntosh County, 23, 30, 34, 41, 159
McKinney, Billy, 62
McKinney, Cynthia, 217, 222–3, 235
McKinnon, Florrie, 108
McMillan, Garnett, 29
Meggers, Linda, 191, 193, 231
Meriwether County, 131, 183, 196
Milledgeville, 19, 28, 183
Milledgeville Federal Union, 31
Miller County, 73, 131, 159
Miller, Lawton, 115
Miller v. Johnson, 6
Miller, Zell, 171, 220, 228
minority-vote dilution, 4, 89–90, 158
miscegenation, 17–18, 61, 120
Mitchell County, 23, 118, 133–4, 156–7, 159
Monroe County, 182
Montezuma, 95
Moore, Donald, 160
Moore, Howard, 138
Morgan County, 142, 159
Morris, Nollie Mae, 239, 245
Moultrie, 114, 118, 135, 160, 164, 180
Moultrie Observer, 47, 64
Moultrie, Roy, 153, 157
Mount Mary Church, 107
Mount Olive Baptist Church, 105, 107, 110

Murphy, Tom, 171, 219–20
Murray County, 185
Muscogee County, 49, 191
Muscogee County Democratic Party, 95
Myrdall, Gunnar, 58

NAACP Legal Defense Fund (LDF), 196
Nashville, 143
Nation, 44
National Association for the Advancement
  of Colored People (NAACP), 69, 70, 74,
  103, 129, 156–7, 196, 212
National Voter Registration Act (NVRA),
  192–3
Neely, George W., 108–10, 121, 195
Neill Primary Act of 1917, 80; *see also*
  county unit system
New Deal administration, 58
New York Times, 122
New Yorker, The, 233
Newnan, 143, 183
Newton, 119
Newton County, 141, 160, 183
"nigger-hook," 111
Nineteenth Amendment, 1
Nixon landslide, 234
numbered-post requirement, 12, 99–100,
  102, 147

Ocilla, Georgia, 119
Oconee County, 209
one person, one vote principle, 4, 83, 89,
  101
O'Neal, Maston, 12
Owens, Wilbur, 182, 185–6

Pace, Stephen, Jr., 113–14
Page, Adell, 110
Palmetto, 144
Parker, Frank, 217
Pascall, Willie, 136
Patch, Penelope, 120–1, 122
Patterson, Eugene, 86–8, 92, 200–1
Paulding County, 87, 209
Peach County, 57, 114, 159
Pelham, 183
Perdue, John, 113
persons of color, definition of, 18, 60
Peters, James S., 73
Pettit, Ephriam, 145
Pickrick, The, 139
Pierce County, 57
Pike County, 142
Pilcher, J. L., 69
Plessy v. Ferguson, 66
plurality vote, 93; *see also* county unit system
political question doctrine, 80
poll officials, and exclusion of blacks, 153–4

poll tax, 1, 3, 20, 25–6, 30; payment of taxes due, 36–7, 39; upholding the constitutionality of, 43–4; abolition of, 49–51
Ponder, Cornelius, Jr., 164
Poole, James, Jr., 240, 242–3
Pope, John, 18, 31
Populist movement, 38
Porter, James, 25
Poythress, David, 228
President's Committee on Civil Rights of 1946, 59
Preston, Prince H., 72
private white clubs, conduct of elections by, 118
Project VOTE! v. Ledbetter, 192
property ownership requirement for voting, 2, 41
prosecution of black elected officials, for complying with the Voting Rights Act, 196–7
public accommodations law of 1870, 25
public schools: criminal penalties for teaching blacks how to read or write 20; segregation in, 18, 20, 32–3; and elections of 1871, 25–8; controlling the curriculum, 28–9; abolition of elected school boards, 30–2; financing of, 58, 65, 67; desegregation of, 59; repeal of compulsory attendance law, 75; authorizing school closures, 75
Pulaski County, 186
Putnam County, 52, 154, 159, 161–3
Putney, F. F., 30
Pye, Durwood T., 88, 100, 102

R. E. Lee Institute, 189
Rabun County, 209
race mixing, 40–1, 119–22
race mythology, 66–7
racial campaign appeals, 149; in 1957 Atlanta municipal election, 71; in 1962 gubernatorial election, 84–5; in elections for judge and solicitor, 85; in legislative contests, 86; in 1973 Atlanta mayoral election, 150–1; in 1974 Thompson mayoral election, 146–7; in 1992 state labor commissioner election, 228; in 1994 Fulton County commission election, 228
racial covenants, in deeds to real estate, 59
racially polarized voting, persistence of, 194–5
Racial Relocation Commission, 99
racial violence: in elections of 1868, 21–4; in elections of 1870, 26; in elections of 1872, 33; in elections of 1874, 34; in elections of 1892, 37; *see also* lynching

railroads and streetcars, segregation of, 38–9, 66
Randall, William, 56
Randolph County, 56
Randolph County Voters League, 57
Rau, William, 117
readmission into the union: first, 21; second, 24
Reaves, Henry, 226
Reconstruction Acts of 1867, 18
Reconstruction in Georgia: 1865–68, 17–21; 1869–70, 24
Red Shirts, 240
Reeb, James, 9
Reed, John C., 21
Reese, Augustus, 31
registration and purge law of 1949, 55
Republican Party, 19, 21, 45
Reynolds v. Sims, 89, 101
Richardson, Frederick, 135
Richardson, Willis J., 91
Richmond County, 159, 167
Roberson, Wilson C., 56, 186
Robinson, Aubrey, 172
Rochell, 63, 183
Rockdale County, 90, 209
Rodgers, Paul, Jr., 10, 50, 98
Rogers v. Lodge, 4, 181
Rogers, William H., 41
Rome, 147
Roosevelt, Franklin, 47
Rucker, Henry L., 45
Russell, Isaac, 30
Russell, Richard B., 11–12, 99
Rutherford, John, 32
Rutland, Guy, 86

Sanders, Carl, 11–12, 62, 82, 117, 120; 1962 gubernatorial campaign, 84–6; and 1962 senate redistricting, 86–8; defense of majority-vote law, 200, 202–4; support of measures designed to maintain segregation, 203–4
Sanders v. Gray, 83–4
Sandersville, 144
Sasser, 105, 107
Savannah, 24, 27, 33, 38, 54, 95, 213
Savannah Republican, 28
Schloth, William J., 98
school board, self-perpetuating, 189
Scott, Al, 228
Screven County, 129, 132, 154, 182, 183
Searcy, George, 190
Section 2 results standard, *see* Voting Rights Act of 1965
Section 5 preclearance, *see* Voting Rights Act of 1965

segregation, 38–9; in the 1950s and 1960s, 60–5; state laws providing for, 68
Segregation and You (Talmadge), 119
Sellers, David, 172
Selma, Alabama, 8–9
Seminole County, 142, 160
Shady Grove Baptist Church, 107, 121
Shaw v. Reno, 214–17, 221, 227; and preferential treatment for white voters, 214–16, 230; mistaken premises of, 227; unmanageable standards announced in, 232; congressional black caucus response to, 235–6
Shelton, Opie, 97
Sherman, William T., 32
Sherrod, Charles, 106, 108, 119
Shorter, Ben T., 57
Sibley Committee, 75–6
Simpson, Willie, 47
Sitton, Claude, 233
Skandalakis, Mitch, 228–9
Slaughter-House Cases, 42
slavery, 2, 15–17
Smith, George T., 200, 202, 204
Smith, Hoke, 40
Smith, James M., 29, 32
Smith, Mitchell, 165
Smith v. Allwright, 48
Smith, Willis, 55, 185
sole commissioner form of county government, 184–7, 193
Solid South, decline of, 234
Soperton, 183
South Carolina v. Katzenbach, 41, 126–7, 175
Southern Christian Leadership Conference (SCLC), 75, 97, 103, 116, 121, 129, 150–1, 212
Southern Politics in State and Nation, 81
Southern Poverty Law Center, 196
Southern Regional Council, 103
Southern Way of Life, 5, 65, 85
Spalding County, 54, 142, 182, 192
Spalding County VEP v. Cowart, 192
Starkey, Edward, 135
Starr, Terrell, 169
Statesboro, 161
States' Rights Councils, 66
states' rights doctrine, 11
States' Rights - The Law of the Land (Bloch), 11
Stephens, Alexander H., 16, 18
Stephens County, 209
Stephens, Robert, 12
Stevens, William, 33

Stokes, Louis, 235
Stone, D. L., 57
Student Nonviolent Coordinating Committee (SNCC), 103, 106, 113, 116–17, 119, 122–3, 129, 136
Summers, Jack, 71
Sumter County, 63–4, 65, 96, 112–14, 115–17, 120, 159, 168
Swift Manufacturing Company, 96–7
Sylvester, 144

Talbot County, 87, 95
Taliaferro County, 118
Talmadge, Eugene, 51, 52–4, 55, 81–2
Talmadge, Herman, 11–12, 54, 55, 66–7, 70, 119–20
Tattnall County, 131, 182
Taylor County, 142, 182, 183
Taylor, Mark, 229
Teague, "Tiger," 215
Teel, George, 179
Telfair County, 185
Terrell County, 9–10, 46, 103–7, 120–1, 123, 129, 159, 160
Terry, Alfred, 24–6, 32
Thirteenth Amendment, 13, 17
Thomas County, 159
Thomas, Emory, 188
Thomaston, 189
Thomasville, 144
Thompson, Fletcher, 140, 149
Thompson, M. E., 54–5
Thompson, Mildred, 32
Thomson, 114, 144, 160
Thornburg v. Gingles, 181
Tift County, 182
Tillman, E. C., 226
Tillman, Martha, 110–11
tipping phenomenon, 214
To Secure These Rights (President's Committee on Civil Rights), 59
Toombs County, 142, 183
Toombs, Robert, 35–6
Toombs v. Fortson, 84, 86
Trammell, L. N., 21
Trelease, Allen, 24
trespass-after-notice law, 76
Treutlen County, 142, 182, 183
Truman, Harry, 59
tuition grants, 67
Tunney, John, 154
Turner, Henry M., 20–1
Tuten, Russell, 12
Twenty-fourth Amendment, 1
Twenty-sixth Amendment, 1
Twiggs County, 142, 159
Twitty, Frank, 87

United Nations Charter, 58
United States Commission on Civil Rights, 59, 71, 129
United States Department of Justice, Civil Rights Section, 4, 58, 109, 115, 123, 196, 220
United States v. Cruikshank, 43
United States v. Reese, 43
University of Georgia, 225
Upson County, 95
USA Today, 235

Valdosta, 183
Vandiver, Ernest, 83
VEP v. Cleland, 192
Vinning, Milton, 145
Vinson, Carl, 68
Von Epps, Carl, 226
voter assistance, proposed prohibition of, 94–8
voter challenges and purges, 3, 52–3
Voter Education Project (VEP), 103, 129, 191–3, 196
voter registration: by race, 39; prohibition of campaigns for, 191; prohibition of additional sites for, 191; challenges to state procedures, 129, 191–92; *see also* National Voter Registration Act
Voting Rights Act of 1965, 3; state's opposition to, 8–14; basic provisions of, 124–8; 1970 extension of, 139–41; 1975 extension of, 153–5; 1982 amendments to, 3, 4, 174–8; Section 2 results standard, 124, 163, 177–81, 229, 235; Section 5 preclearance, 125–7; voting changes adopted after passage, 176; and at-large elections, 131–2, 141–2; and majority-vote requirements, 135; enforcement by Johnson administration, 137; enforcement by Nixon administration, 137; noncompliance with Section 5, 130, 132, 175; Section 5 objections, 153, 167–8, 175; private enforcement campaign, 195–6

Wadley, 144
Walden, A. T., 70
Walker, David, 186
Walker, Henry Lewis, 143
Walker, Larry, 226
Wall, Vincent, 171
Wallace, George, 23
Wallace, George C., 117
Walton County, 131, 159
Ward, Horace T., 10, 149

Ware County, 51, 70
Warren, Earl, 13, 70, 127
Warrenton, 183
Washington, Craig, 235
Watson, Tom, 37–40
Waycross, 183
Wayne County, 132, 183
Waynesboro, 144, 160, 239
Webb, Julian, 100
Webb, Paul, Jr., 100
Webster County, 7, 46, 83, 108–10, 121, 185
Weltner, Charles, 12
Wesberry v. Sanders, 4, 89, 90
West, J. H., 145
Westin, Willie, 106
Whatley, Andrew, Jr., 117
Wheat, Alan, 235
Wheeler County, 185
Wheeler, William M., 146
Whitaker, J. W., 9
White County, 209
white primary, 1, 3; origins of, 38; abolition of, 45, 48–9; response to abolition of, 52–5, 114
white supremacy, 5, 15–17, 37–41, 54, 82
White v. Regester, 158, 177
Whitfield County, 31
Wilcox County, 63, 142, 183
Wilcox, James, 188
Wilkes County, 35, 142, 159
Wilkinson County, 33
Williams, Hosea, 116, 151
Williams, John Henry, 47
Williams, Melba, 200
Williams, Sam, 102
Williams v. Mississippi, 43–4
Williams, Willis, 190
Williamson, Q. V., 10
Wilson, Frank, 164
Wilson, Joe Mack, 167, 170, 172–3
Wilson, Luther, 110, 146
Wisdom, John Minor, 180, 236
Withers, William B., 157
Wohlwender, Ed, Jr., 114
Wood, James, 77–8
Wood, Jim, 172
Woodall, Allen M., 96
Woodward, C. Vann, 177
World War I, 58
World War II, 58
Wrens, 144
Wrightsville, 183

Young, Andrew, 149–50, 152, 155, 195
Young, Samuel, 136